THE SMART GUIDE TO

Wine

BY PHILIP SELDON

The Smart Guide To Wine

Published by

Smart Guide Publications, Inc.
2517 Deer Chase Drive
Norman, OK 73071
www.smartguidepublications.com

For information, address: Smart Guide Publications, Inc. 2517 Deer Creek Drive, Norman, OK 73071

International Standard Book Number: 978-1-937636-34-0

Library of Congress Catalog Card Number:
11 12 13 14 15 10 9 8 7 6 5 4 3 2 1

Printed in the United States of America

Cover design: Lorna Llewellyn
Copy Editor: Ruth Strother
Back cover design: Joel Friedlander, Eric Gelb, Deon Seifert
Back cover copy: Eric Gelb, Deon Seifert
Illustrations: James Balkovek
Production: Zoë Lonergan
Indexer: Cory Emberson
V.P./Business Manager: Cathy Barker

ACKNOWLEDGMENTS

First, let me thank my parents for introducing me to wine at a tender young age in our religious ceremonies. While the wine wasn't very good, it was a start that got me intrigued. Then, when I was in my late teens as a member of the Amateur Astronomers Association in New York City, a fellow member and wine lover by the name of Richard Priest introduced me and a number of other members to the great wines of France. It was a revelation to taste such great wines.

Perhaps the greatest influence in my life of wine and gastronomy was Charles H. Baker, whom I would have loved to have met. In his 1946 two-volume work that I read in college titled "*A Gentleman's Companion*", alternatively titled "*Around The World With Knife, Fork And Spoon*", he regaled his readers with his travels to the great vineyards and temples of gastronomy. This inspired me to follow suit for a two-year stint in Europe following graduation from college. There I learned all about the great wines of France, Italy, Spain, Portugal, Germany, and Switzerland. Upon my return to New York City in 1971, I launched *Vintage Magazine*, America's first wine magazine, which I edited and published for seventeen years.

I wish to thank all the members of the wine industry who opened their wineries to me over the years and taught me everything I know about wine. Robert Mondavi was particularly helpful, as was Peter Sichel, famous for the German Liefbraumilch Blue Nun. Peter is now ninety, in excellent health, and going strong—he was a regular contributor to *Vintage Magazine.*

World-renowned graphic designer Herb Lubalin designed *Vintage* and was instrumental in its launch. Without him, there would have not been a magazine, nor my career in wine. I also wish to thank all the wine and food writers who made *Vintage* a success.

I wish to thank Lorna Llewellyn, who contributed to the design of the cover of the Smart Guide series cover and designed my "*Vintage Magazine Consumer Guide to Wine*", published by Doubleday in 1978. She is an extraordinary graphic designer now living in London. A big thank you to James Balkovek for his extraordinary illustrations for this book and to Zoë Lonagon, who did a superb job on the production of the book. And to Cory Emberson for her diligence in proofreading and indexing—a job well done.

Finally, a huge thank you to those faceless and anonymous workers who toil in the vineyards and wineries during the growing season and the harvest to make the wine we drink. Without them, we could not experience the joy we feel when we imbibe the fruit of the vine.

TABLE OF CONTENTS

PART ONE

Let's Toast Wine

CHAPTER 1

The Wonders of Wine

In This Chapter

- The benefits of wine knowledge
- What wine is
- Types of wine
- Quality categories

In this chapter you'll discover that wine is more than an ordinary beverage. But let's start with the most basic fact: Wine is the fermented juice of grapes (or other fruit, but in this book we'll deal only with grapes).

Grapes! Through a marriage of ancient tradition, modern technology, and our ever-widening (or is it shrinking?) global connectedness, these unassuming fruits can be turned into just about anything—ranging from a simple and enjoyable quaff to a complex and noble tribute to the winemaker's art. And what an art it is. From the get-go, wine was used by ancient cultures to seal business deals, for political treaties, and in performing religious rites. There was even a time before the discovery of purification systems and sanitary plumbing, when wine was more palatable for the masses than water. Sip on that for a minute!

Wine comes in many types and qualities, and in this chapter I'll provide an introduction to the awesome but thoroughly accessible world of wine.

The Road to Savvy Sipping

Imagine wine is just a thirst-quenching beverage with a little bit of a kick. Imagine one bottle is as about as good as any other, or maybe you might say one's a little flat, another a little sweet. Believe me, you'll have some good experiences, but it's doubtful any would be what you might call great.

To be sure, a glass of wine can augment the pleasure of a good meal. Wine enhances any social gathering. And there's nothing quite like a contemplative glass or two during a quiet evening at home.

Let's compare drinking wine with listening to a great piece of music. Sure, you can listen while you're dressing for work, paying your bills, or microwaving popcorn. But can these ever equal the joy of sitting back, attuning your mind, and savoring utterly transporting and intricate flavors and harmonies that separate style, composer, and interpreter?

Those of us who know wine—and that can include you!—know that a glass can reward us with many variations of style and taste. All you need to do to really get there is think about it along the same lines of the scenario above—sit back, attune your mind (and palate!), and savor. Add in a little knowledge (and you'll get plenty of it here), and that's all there is to it.

Heard it Through the Grapevine

You may know that every major orchestra has its own unique style: the bite of the strings, the color of the woodwinds, the sonority of the brass, the balance of all of these instruments and their good timing in harmony. Sometimes orchestra, conductor, and composition all come together in your listening presence, and you know you are in the middle of a very big experience. At the end you simply have to find release for all that accumulated feeling—joy, pathos, humor. A little polite applause simply won't do. You are up out of your seat crying, "Bravo! Bravo!" A great bottle of wine—when its myriad components work together in perfect harmony and balance—can give you exactly the same feeling.

Honing Your Palate

If you're serious about tasting wine and increasing your knowledge of wine, you've probably got a lot of questions. Perhaps one of the biggest ones is this: What distinguishes a mediocre wine from a great wine? Let me develop my music analogy:

Imagine you're hearing, say, Beethoven's Fifth Symphony played by a community symphony orchestra. The orchestra has rehearsed. Everyone's playing the right notes at the right time. Sure, the listening experience is pleasant. But if this is your very first exposure to Beethoven, you may wonder why so many generations have been so awed by the scowling, shaggy-haired maestro.

On the other hand, if you'd heard the same work played by one of the world's great orchestras, you would have experienced all those things that community orchestra couldn't deliver: subtlety, style, and flavor. Only a great conductor can reveal the most subtle nuances of orchestration, to draw on the talents of each musician.

Please indulge me as I milk this music analogy a little further. Here's an exercise you can do that may bring my point home:

1. Go through your CD collection. Anything: classical, jazz, rock, whatever.

2. Pick out a really superlative recording—one where all the elements add up to produce nothing less than what you would call the best. Then pick out another one that is so-so. Your choice.

3. After listening to both of them, get paper and pencil and make a list of all the things that make the superb recording stand out and all the things that the mediocre version lacks.

Chances are that with only a few slight modifications, you'll be able to apply this very list to tasting wine. Now that wasn't so intimidating, was it? And yet, so many of us avoid getting to know wine because we think it's beyond our capacity. It's not. If you approach it exactly as I suggest above, you're opening yourself up to a whole world of wonderful discovery.

Complexity Builds Confidence

Learning about wine isn't entirely easy, though. There's a lot more to it than, say, remembering which foods go with red wine and which with white (and even within that, there's a lot of room for experimentation and interpretation!). The first important thing you must do is to free yourself from the constraints of other people's decisions. We live in a fluid society where rigid ideas of how things should be done aren't acceptable anymore.

The Sommelier Says

Pay no attention to wine snobs. These are people who take more pleasure in being correct than they do in wine, itself. Your wine experiences are for your own pleasure, not to deal with the hang-ups of others.

Think of learning about wine as a tool of empowerment. Imagine some know-it-all insisting that red wine has no place with seafood. Imagine, now, you disagreeing heartily, knowing you can back up your own stance with vigor and confidence. You'll feel good on two counts: You'll have the pleasure that comes from the fullest appreciation of the qualities of a good wine. And you'll have defended your own taste, rather than having bowed meekly to some bully's passé assertion.

Wine Defined

Wine is fermented fruit juice. Fermentation is the conversion of sugar—in the case of wine, grape sugar—into alcohol when it reacts with added or natural yeast. (If we go too far, the process continues all the way to acetic acid, better known as vinegar, which is lovely on a salad, but not so nice in the glass.) Wine can be made from a number of fruits—from apples to pomegranates—but the scope of this book is limited to wine made from grapes. (Whew!)

Vino Vocab

Fermentation is a biochemical process that turns sugars into alcohol and carbon dioxide. It takes place inside one-celled fungi called yeasts.

The complexity of wine lies in the fact that good wine does not just appear naturally, although grapes will ferment into wine on their own and then turn into vinegar.

Three factors interact to determine the character of a wine: 1) the grape variety and how it's grown, 2) the climate and soil where it is grown, and 3) the vintner's (winemaker's) creative or commercial objective and winemaking skills.

The odds do not favor the winemaker. In an ideal world, a superior grape planted in a favorable environment automatically would produce a great wine. But in the real world of winemaking, it is surprisingly easy to turn a potentially great wine into an expensive bottle of mediocrity, if not some awful-tasting microbiological disaster.

The vintner has the dual role of scientist and artist. Europeans tend to favor the artistic element, while New World winemakers accent the scientific. This distinction may not be surprising in light of the fact that we live in a society where Microsoft is more of a household word than Michelangelo. It may also have to do with the fact that the growth of the American wine industry has coincided with the technological advances of the past 40 or so years.

Winemakers today have sophisticated technology that enables them to make good quality wine at the lowest price (a good thing to know when you feel like telling off snobbish acquaintances). Technology serves as the background for artistry, enabling winemakers to infuse their wines with the subtle differences in flavor and style that distinguish the products of one vintner from another, grapes and environment being the same.

Heard it Through the Grapevine

Research studies suggest drinking wine in moderation is good for your health. That does not mean that you should cancel your health insurance and buy more wine with the money you save! A glass or two of red wine each day will reduce both your cholesterol and your risk of heart disease, as the antioxidents called polyphenols, contained in the skin of red grapes, may help shore up the lining of blood vessels in the heart (particularly, the polyphenol resveratrol, which is thought to prevent blood vessel damage and reduce bad cholesterol). One or two glasses of any kind of wine a day will reduce the risk of heart attack from other causes. However, keep in mind that drinking any alcoholic beverage in excess can cause serious health problems.

What's My Wine?

An appreciation of harmony and subtlety is essential to the experience of fine wines. But it takes more than that to discriminate between a superb wine and one that simply is good. Or the good from the merely mediocre. We need to understand why some German Rieslings stand head-and-shoulders above those wines made from the same grape variety in California. Or how a Napa Valley Cabernet Sauvignon may run circles around a Cabernet grown in Long Island.

There is nothing inherently better or worse about European or New World wines. A number of factors are involved, and the quality of the end product depends on the interaction among them.

To help you understand what to expect from a particular wine, you first need to understand what kind of wine it is. So let's examine the basic types of wine: table wine, sparkling wines, fortified wines, and apéritif wines.

Red, White, and You!

If the term table wine evokes an image of a bottle or carafe sitting on a red-and-white checkered table cloth, you have the right idea! Table wines, simply, are reds, whites, and

Tasting Tip

Table wines range in alcohol content from 9 to 16 percent (by volume).

Wines with more than 16 percent alcohol (that is, fortified wines) are subject to higher taxation and are classified separately.

rosés produced to accompany a meal. Most of the wines we drink (and will discuss in this book) fall into this basic category.

Wineries are required to state alcohol content on the label. But this rule is a little lax: The stated amount may be off by as much as 1.5 percentage points! That is, a wine designated as 12 percent alcohol could fall anywhere between 10.5 and 13.5 percent.

Despite this legal laxity, some labels are very accurate. When you see a number like 11.2 percent or 12.6 percent, chances are the winemaker is giving you a more precise reading. I mean, would you make up a number like 11.2 percent?

Varietals Are the Spice of Life

Varietal wines are named for the primary grape used to make the wine. Some varietal wines use one grape exclusively, while others blend the dominant grape with other grape types. When more than one grape is used, the minimum percentage of the designated grape is regulated by law. There's considerable variety in the regulatory codes.

Here are a few examples:

- In California and Washington, the minimum percentage of the named grape is 75 percent.
- In Oregon, it's 90 percent (with the exception of Cabernet, which may be only 75 percent, like its northern and southern neighbors).
- In Australia and the countries of the European Union, the required content is 85 percent.

Drinking Stars

Sparkling wine is wine with bubbles—like soda, but not artificially carbonated. Sparkling wine was first perfected in Champagne in the early 1700s by the Benedictine monk and cellarmaster, Dom Perignon. Upon seeing the bubbles in his glass, the good brother eloquently captured the essence of his discovery with the words, "I am drinking stars!"

In the United States, the terms champagne (that's a lowercase 'c'!) and sparkling wine often are used interchangeably. Legally, winemakers in the U.S., Canada, and Australia are allowed to use the name champagne for their sparkling wines with one catch: the bubbles must be produced naturally during the fermentation process and not added through artificial carbonation. Within that requirement, the choice of grape varieties is up to the producer, and champagne can be made by several methods (not necessarily those used by the French).

In France, the home of the real (capital 'C') Champagne district (or appellation), the story is entirely different. Understandably, the proud French are not amused that others use the name of their fine and cherished creation for just any effervescent wine.

Vino Vocab

Appellation is a fancy English word (and a perfectly good French one) meaning name, title, or designation. In the world of wine, it's commonly applied geographically.

In France, only sparkling wines made from grapes—specifically, Chardonnay, Pinot Noir, and Pinot Meunier—grown in the Champagne region may bear the name Champagne (or anything resembling it). This rule is law, also, in all the member nations of the European Union.

Strong, But Sweet

Fortified wines are those whose alcohol content has been increased by the addition of brandy or neutral spirits. They usually range from 17–21 percent alcohol by volume. Ports, Sherries, Marsalas, and Madeiras all are fortified wines. In the U.S., many look on these as a matter of acquired taste.

Dessert wines almost always are fortified wines. Most, though not all, are quite sweet. They are best suited to drinking alone, after a meal, or paired with a dessert of equal sweetness or pungent cheeses. The terms fortified wines and dessert wines often are used interchangeably.

More Than Mixers

Technically, apéritif (appetizer) wines are white or red wines flavored with herbs and spices to give them a unique flavor (and often, a unique color). Vermouth falls into this category. Lillet is another example. Lillet is a lot more popular in Europe than in the U.S.

Heard it Through the Grapevine

The word apéritif seems to be a fancy way of saying appetizer, but originally it meant something very different—a purgative, literally something that opens you up. Traditionally, mixtures of bitter herbs did the job. Some milder concentrations of these happen to taste good and remain with us today in such popular forms as vermouth.

The Subtle Shades of Wine?

The three basic colors of wine are white, red, and pink (rosé). Within each color category, there are a countless gradations. Sometimes, these can provide clues to the wine's taste quality (such as lightness, fullness, clarity, brilliance) and age. More important, the appearance of the wine can reveal flaws that should place you on guard when you take that tasting sip.

Tasting Tip

Like people, wines look best in natural or incandescent lighting. Unless you're drinking your wine at the office party, avoid fluorescent lights because they give the wine a false color. Fluorescent light is missing parts of the spectrum, and it will distort the colors of red wines, giving them the brownish appearance of wines that have aged past their primes.

From Straw to Gold

To say a wine is white essentially means it lacks red pigment. If wine shops had swatch books for customers like paint emporiums, white wines would present a rich palette from pale straw, through light green-yellow, through yellow, to a deep golden color.

White wines attain their color (or lack of color, depending on your perspective) in one of two ways. Most frequently, they are made from white grapes. (Of course, white grapes actually are green or yellow or a combination of the two.)

White wine also can be made from the juice of red grapes! In fact, the red pigment resides only in the grape's skin, not in the juice. Therefore, when wine is fermented without the skins, the wine will remain white regardless of the grape variety.

White wine comes in a number of styles such as light-bodied and refreshing, soft and mild, full-bodied and fruit-forward, or oaked and complex. We will go into greater detail about wine styles and qualities later in this book.

Red and Rich

Red wine is easily identified by its deep red color. Without even making the association, you may have, at some time or another, used the name of the most famous red wine region—Burgundy—to describe the color of a scarf or sofa or dress or the upholstery of the car with the six-figure price tag. To many people, the very color of red wine denotes richness.

Heard it Through the Grapevine

In a decorator's swatch book, red wines would range in color from pale brick, through deep ruby, through purple, to inky-dark. In winemaker's language, the grapes they are made from are black grapes (although here I will continue to refer to them as red). During the fermentation process, the dark skins remain in contact with the colorless juice, and voilà!—red wine.

Tannic or Tart?

The skins of red grapes contain tannin, which is the key to the major taste distinction between red and white wines. The longer the juice is left in contact with the skins, the higher the tannin content.

If you're not used to the taste of a strong red wine, you may find yourself puckering up. You may have had a similar sensation the first time you tasted strong tea (which, like wine, contains tannic acid) or even lemonade (citric acid). Once you become used to the taste and sensation of tannin, you'll miss it when it's not there.

In wine language, tannins produce the firmness of a red wine. A wine with a high tannin content may taste bitter to even the most seasoned wine lover. This is one reason that red wines are matched carefully with a meal. A wine that tastes unpleasantly bitter on its own may be the perfect complement to a steak or roast beef dinner.

A Bit of Blush

The third shade (type) of wine is recognized by its pink color—and no, it is not made by mixing red and white wine together! Rosé wines are made from red grapes that are left in contact with the skins for only a few hours—just long enough to absorb a tinge of color and very little tannin.

The Sommelier Says

Blush wines are even lighter than rosé wines. There was a time when producers found that wines with the term "blush" on them sold better, but no more. Rosé has become an accepted (and much better understood!) wine choice for consumers, whose growing demand for it has even spanned beyond the traditional summer season for this often refreshing pink-hued quaff.

Light and Rosy

Because, more often than not, the skin contact in rosés is minimal, their tannin content is low. No puckering up. Like white wines, rosés are served chilled and go better with lighter foods. They make a refreshing summer drink and a good party beverage.

Quality Control

Wine comes in a range of quality; the wine industry and many authors differentiate between three categories—everyday, or jug wine; premium wine, with the premium category encompassing wines ranging from a low of $9 a bottle; and ultra-premium wines, which start at around $35 to $40 and go up to several hundred dollars a bottle.

The wine industry uses the term fine wine to denote, simply, wines that are bottled in glass and closed with a cork, although screwcaps have become far more accepted in the premium category—even in the ultra-premium category. Gone are the days when screwtops denoted cheap plonk, so don't write-off a bottle based solely on its closure. .

Good Ol' Wines

What does the term jug wine invoke? But back in the day when screwtops meant scary wine, mystery reds or whites were labeled with vague titles like "hearty Burgundy" or "Chablis," even though they were created from a mix of grapes far from the venerable Burgundy region. You remember them—they were the ones that many of our parents used to keep in the 'fridge in the garage indefinitely.

Actually, jug wines don't always come in jugs. Many now come in magnums (double-sized bottles) and, in a heartening growth of popularity, tetra packs (e.g., box wines). Over the years, they've gotten a lot of bad press. Jug wines are simple wines made for immediate consumption. They're not really bad—just ordinary. Like the community orchestra playing Beethoven, it's still Beethoven. Just don't look for a lot of complexity or finesse.

Tasting Tip

Good everyday wines can be tasty, pleasant, and refreshing. They offer vinous (grape-like) flavor, along with body, balance, and straightforward appeal.

Premium and Super-Premium

Premium wines have more character and finesse. They have texture and complexity. They evoke the flavors and aromas of the grape variety (or varieties) of the region of origin. Unlike jug wines, which have a short aftertaste, the taste of premium wines lingers on the palate, which adds another dimension to the wine tasting experience: Frequently new flavors appear in the aftertaste.

Premium wines span a price range from $9 to $35 per bottle, with a similar range in quality.

Nobility and Breeding

In the scheme of quality categories, noble wines are the best-of-the-best among fine wines. Simply to call them fine wines would be like calling Japan's prized Kobe beef steak or a Triple Crown-winning racehorse a nag.

The producers of noble wines spare no expense or effort in producing them, and the result is a wine of breathtaking beauty. Noble wines have distinctive characteristics that set them apart from all other libations. Breeding is a good word to describe them, and it's not meant for snob appeal.

These wines are like a performance on the cello by Rostropovich or a flawless operatic performance in Vienna with a once-in-a-lifetime dream cast. It's the nature of these rare wines to be complex, leading us to such assessments as, delicate, yet assertive. These wines are multifaceted, like diamonds. In the world of wine, noble wines are truly the greatest works of art.

Heard it Through the Grapevine

The unique qualities of noble wines are most apparent after prolonged aging. Just as with the world's greatest artists, their performance gains in stature as they mature. We may find our noble wines cloistered in climate-controlled cellars, developing their maximum potential as great works of art.

Vino Vocab

Estate bottling means no part of the winemaking operation is farmed out to someone who might be content to give less than an all-out effort.

Estate Bottling: Doing It All

An estate is a wine plantation where the grapes are grown, fermented, and ultimately, bottled. This all-in-one approach to winemaking is a good way to ensure quality. In the world of business, this is called vertical integration.

With estate bottling, there are no gaps in the chain of accountability. The winery controlling the vineyards is responsible for the whole deal, from the raw materials through the end product. Winemakers take pride in their operations and strive toward products that satisfy customer tastes. Most estate-bottled wines say so on the bottle, but not always. While in days gone by, the term estate bottling was used only on the finest of wines, today many inexpensive and sometimes inferior wines use the term estate bottled as they legally qualify.

Nothing But the Best

As noted before, wine is the midpoint between grape juice and vinegar. Noble wines like Chateau Lafite-Rothschild don't just happen by accident, and there's not much market for noble vinaigrette.

The more expensive wines are the product of superior grapes, technical expertise, artistic indulgence, and loving care. A lot of personal involvement goes into the process, along with skills, flair, and finesse (and some blood, sweat, and tears, too).

Harmony, symmetry, complexity, finesse, and elegance are some of the adjectives defining the unique character of a noble wine. Close your eyes and see what images those words invoke. Now you know why some wines cost so much.

Simple, but Satisfying

Barring some strange disaster, any winemaker can produce a decent jug wine. There's no need for split-second timing in harvesting, no subtle blending, no anxious nail-biting during fermentation. The result is simple and pleasant and virtually guaranteed.

Producing a wine that's merely competent is less labor-intensive, less chancy, and consequently less expensive than producing an extraordinary wine. They cost less to make; so they cost less to buy.

CHAPTER 2

Savvy Serving

In This Chapter

- How to open a bottle
- Choose the right wine glass
- Proper temperatures to serve wine
- Breathing and decanting
- Keeping an opened bottle

In this chapter you'll become acquainted with those strange gadgets, called corkscrews, and those crystalline bowls on stilts, called wineglasses. In addition to having its own accessories, serving wine also requires a bit of special knowledge.

Here, you'll learn the best temperatures for serving red and white wines, and you can join the debate over breathing versus non-breathing (that is, letting it stand before serving or pouring immediately). You'll learn that a decanter is more than a decorative item.

Finally, you'll find out how to keep an open bottle without having to use it as salad dressing. Opening and serving wine may not be as simple as pouring a Pepsi, but it is not the arcane task you might have thought.

Conquering the Cork

Wine bottles don't come with pop tops (well, there are a few, like Domaine La Boheme from southern France, who put a pop-top on their sparkling, but that's a rare exception, indeed!). And, yes, many these days do come with screw caps, far more acceptable these days than they were even a mere few years ago.

The Sommelier Says

Many people insist on bottles sealed with corks, disdaining screw caps. They believe the bottle closure is an indicator of quality. It isn't. You will easily find screw cap wines in the finest restaurants across the country. What they lack in that romantic "pop" sound, they make up for in freshness.

It's possible that part of the cork's elite image is due to the trouble it takes to open one. You figure with all the effort involved, there has to be something worthwhile inside. That's one good reason to increase your wine know-how. It increases the chances that the beverage inside this sealed bottle really will be worth opening.

There is one practical reason for the traditional association of corks with good wine: Corks used for noble wines are longer (two inches) and less porous than those used for many premium wines. There has been much debate over the notion of aging wines under screw cap, and with good reason as the technology is really only a few decades old. What appears to be the case is that wines under screwtop do age—just more slowly than those closed with cork. Why? High-quality cork is a natural product that allows a tiny amount of oxygen to seep into the bottle, thus, react with the wine over time. Screw cap bottles do let in some oxygen, but a much smaller amount than cork, hence slowing down the aging process dramatically.

Heard it Through the Grapevine

Screw caps aside, the reason for using a cork seal is not to make us wine lovers feel like klutzes fumbling with bottles. Cork has some very special properties. This lightweight wonder is made of millions of hollow cells, each separated by a strong, impermeable membrane. A cork can be compressed for insertion, and once in place, it will expand to create a tight fit. Most wine producers prefer a straight, untapered cork at least one and one-half inches long.

If you'd like to serve up some esoteric knowledge along with your wine, try this: Most corks used throughout the wine world come from Spain or Portugal, which provide close to 90 percent of the world's total supply. The tree used for cork is the cork oak, Quercus suber, which grows in warm climates. Cork trees can last up to 200 years, and it is their bark that is harvested—which can in turn be re-harvested every seven. Talk about renewable resources!

If a cork is extremely dry or even crumbles when you try to remove it, it is a sign that the wine has not been stored properly on its side to keep the cork moist. Most of the time, the wine still will be okay, but if it isn't you have a good reason to reject it in a restaurant. Sniff the cork to see if it smells like wine. If it smells of vinegar or mold (or anything else), you know the wine is spoiled.

First the Foil

Before you even get to the cork, you will need to deal with the foil (called the capsule). You can remove it any of three ways:

- Cut through it with a knife below the lip area at the top of the bottle.
- Slice through the foil around the neck and rip the whole thing off in one motion.
- Use the foil cutter on your wine-opening tool, which makes cutting the foil a breeze.

I prefer removing the foil entirely. That way you can see the length of the cork and the chateau name or trademark printed on it before you open the bottle. Sometimes the vintage date or even the brand may be different from what is on the label. In this case, go with the cork!

You Need a Good Gadget …

Removing a cork requires neither the brain of Albert Einstein nor the brawn of Arnold Schwarzenegger. It takes just a little practiced skill and an instrument of some sort.

For years, our choice in corkscrews was very limited. Today, there are a variety on the market. Some are great, some not so good. Select the corkscrew that best suits your own wine-opening style.

The most popular corkscrew is the waiter's corkscrew, which looks like a shiny, scaled-down Swiss Army Knife (without the red handle). The waiter's corkscrew has a helix-type worm (spiral screw) that works well because it grips the cork firmly, allowing for easy removal. Avoid the augur type, with its point set dead-center. With this, the cork is more likely to emerge in pieces.

Vino Vocab

A helix is what you'd get if you wound a wire several turns around a pencil and then stretched it out a bit. An auger is similar, but shaped more like a spiral staircase.

Waiter's corkscrew.

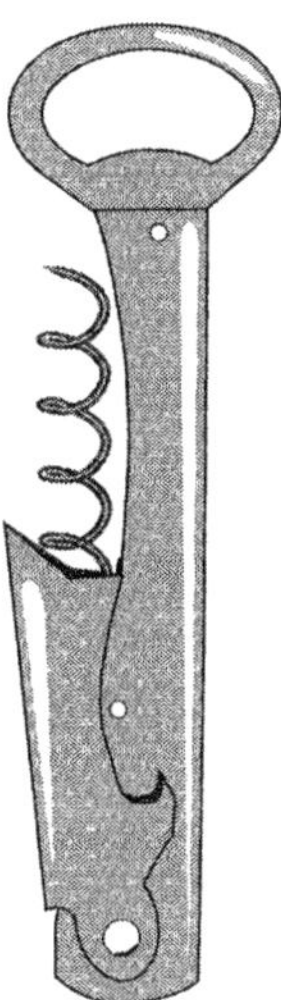

The waiter's corkscrew has a fold-out piece for a fulcrum and a knife for cutting the foil. It takes some practice to use it efficiently, but once you acquire the skill, you will appreciate its traditional simplicity. Here's how: You place the tip of the helix in the center of the cork, and screw into it. Then you place the little fulcrum arm on the lip of the bottle. Finally, you use the body of the instrument as a lever to pull the cork.

The "Ah-So" (pronged cork-puller) or pronged corkpullers (you can invent your own reason for this unusual name), or Pronged Cork-puller, is not a corkscrew at all, but a two-pronged device developed in Germany.

Ah-So corkpuller.

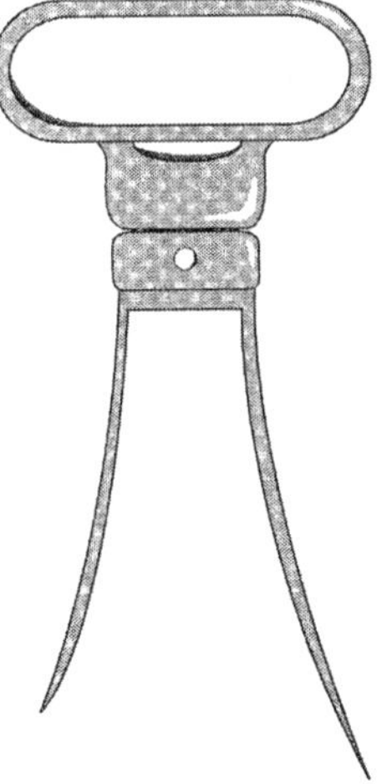

To use it, you insert one slender steel leg, the longer one, a little way alongside the cork. Then you insert the other prong along the other side. Then you use a rocking motion to get the prongs fully inserted around the cork. (Be very careful you don't push the cork into the bottle!) Finally, you remove the cork by twisting gently and pulling.

Tasting Tip

For all the trouble the Ah-So cork-puller can be, I recommend you get one. Here's why: Once your corkscrew has drilled a big hole through the cork, and the cork remains in the bottle, the Ah-So is your only hope.

I think the Ah-So is a difficult gadget. Not only does it demand a tender touch, but it does not work on all corks. When it does work, the Ah-So has two major advantages. The first is the reasonable ease and speed of operation. The second is that the cork is removed intact and can be reinserted easily.

The drawbacks are that the Ah-So requires much more skill than most corkscrews, and it's severely challenged by a dried-out cork. If the cork is at all loose, the Ah-So pushes it into the wine before it can be gripped. This is the nightmare of many wine novices (and non-novices). If the thought of it makes you sweat, try another device.

At first glance, the twin-lever and twin-screw corkscrews look like Rube Goldberg inventions. They are somewhat clumsy in size, but both are simple to use. Both gadgets rely on the principle of mechanical advantage to make removing the cork easier.

The twin-lever works by twisting the screw into the cork and then using another lever to pull it out. If the device is made well, it really will be effortless. To use the twin-lever corkscrew, follow these simple steps:

1. Place the instrument over the wine bottle.
2. Turn the handle attached to the screw to get the worm into the cork.
3. Turn the second handle attached to the cylinder. The cork glides out of the bottle.

Depending on the manufacturer, these devices can range from excellent to awful. Twin-levers come in either wood or metal. Look for a sharp point and a wide-helix worm.

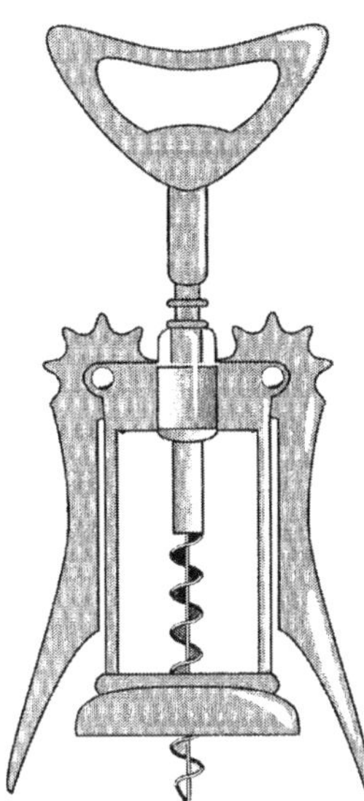

Twin-lever corkscrew.

But Not a Trendy One!

It was all the rage a decade or so ago—the device with a needle, which pumped air to force out the cork. It seemed to be a clever gadget, but in the end, it wasn't very smart. It should have disappeared. Instead, it seems to have proliferated, and now comes in electric versions, as well! Pick up any wine accessories catalog and I'm sure you'll see one.

This horrible instrument is all wrong for wine in nearly every respect. First, it pumps air into the wine, which can stir up the sediment, especially in an older wine. Second, the needle simply may push a loose cork in. Third, if a cork is no longer airtight, the air simply escapes and the cork stays put. The last drawback can be disastrous. In a case where the cork is tight and the bottle defective, the pressure can cause the bottle to shatter.

Another trendy wine gadget is the rechargeable electric wine opener, whose novelty lies as much in its gizmo-ness as it does in its ability to remove a cork without much physical effort. To use one, you simply set the device atop a wine bottle, press the button, and the helix inserts itself into the cork and retracts, pulling it out smoothly. The downside: You have to make sure it's fully charged at all times.

Simply the Best Corkscrew

The Screwpull is the patented name of a sculptural-looking item that minimizes finger pressure and offers great strength and durability for long-term use. This nifty piece of design comes with a long, powerful worm and a strong plastic design for the needed support. Its self-centering action removes corks with minimal effort.

Screwpull corkscrew.

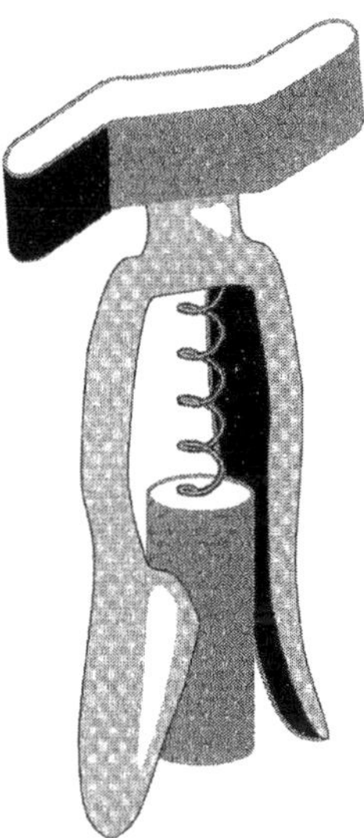

The Screwpull makes it easy for even the most inept to pull any cork like a pro, using the following steps:

1. Simply put the Screwpull over the bottle's top, centering the worm over the cork, and turn the handle on the top counterclockwise.
2. After the worm is in the cork, keep turning and the cork moves out of the bottle.
3. After the cork is out of the bottle, hold on to the cork and turn the handle counterclockwise some more—the cork will pop right off the worm.

The Sommelier Says

Unfortunately, the worm of the Screwpull can come out of its housing and present a serious hazard to children (and adults as well) as it is extremely sharp. Keep the Screwpull in a place safe from little ones.

The Screwpull also comes in a completely automatic lever version, which is my favorite (and several other companies manufacture a similar device under different names, like the Quicksilver). It makes pulling the cork a breeze in a two-step process. You place this gadget over the bottle and pull the lever—the screw goes in and the cork comes out in one simple operation. Then you pull the lever again and the cork slips off the screw. Really neat!

The Sommelier Says

I have experienced some crystal stemware that was so delicate it shattered even when I gave it a gentle bump. Serious wine service needs something a bit hardier.

Glass Act

Does it make a difference what kind of glass you drink your wine in? Indeed it does! Let me give you a few simple guidelines for choosing the right glass (once you've chosen the right wine, that is).

Crystal glasses are ideal but not necessary. Their beauty and clarity make the wine sparkle with a true radiance. However, ordinary glass vessels are fine and less likely to break in a dishwasher (and, if they do, you won't have to shell out as much to replace them).

You can find good, ordinary glass wine glasses for about \$50 to \$75 for a box of 8. Crystal wine glasses start at around \$100 to \$150 for a set of 8, and the sky is the limit—\$40 or \$50 a stem is not unusual, and the best sell for upwards of \$100.

The Sommelier Says

Beware of lead crystal. Research studies have determined that the lead in the glass leaches out into the wine in as short a period as a half hour. Wine, particularly Ports and other high alcohol wines, should not be stored in lead crystal decanters. Many crystal glass manufacturers are using other ingredients other than lead to harden their glass—look for crystal that does not use lead.

Red Wine; Not Green Glasses!

Colorful Art Deco glasses are not what you should choose for your wine. After all, the wine's color is a clue to its body, richness, and quality. You'll never be able to weed out wines with imperfections when viewing them through colored glass. Any glass that masks or changes the wine's true color certainly will not enhance your sensory experience.

Stick with the old rule of clear, colorless glasses. Not only do they give you a view into your wine, you won't get sick of them in a few years when you decide that it's blue you now love, not red (or gold, or green, or black, or rainbow!).

Shape and Stem

Some are fatter and rounder and some are elliptical. Is there really a reason, you ask? And why do they all have that long stem that makes breakage so easy, if not inevitable?

There is a reason that wine glasses have a long stem (and it's not to make glass makers rich as you keep replacing them). The stem is there to keep you from touching the bowl, which can result in a temperature change of the wine from the heat of your hand. It also keeps fingerprints off the bowl. Remember, enjoying wine is a pan-sensory experience. Do you really want to be looking at thumb whorls as you examine the deep, rich color of a tawny Port?

The Sommelier Says

The latest rage in glassware has been the stemless wine goblet. As I said above, there's a reason for the stem, and a very good one at that, and that is why I would not recommend stemless glasses for serving your premium and ultra-premium bottles. However, for sipping an everyday, inexpensive selection with some take-out or a simple supper, they're perfectly fine.

The capacity of the glass should be ample. This is hardly surprising when you consider that your nose is going to dive part-way in.

The actual shape of the glass is less important. But there is one rule to follow: The rim of the bowl should curve in slightly to help capture the aroma you generate by swirling.

Tasting Tip

Either the classic Bordeaux or Burgundy glass makes a fine all-purpose wine glass. One exception is Champagne, which needs its own glass (and even some recent proponents say that to get the full effect of a sparkling wine's aroma, a white wine glass is better than the traditional flute). Get these two types of glasses, and you'll be set!

An All-Purpose Vessel

If you don't want to splurge on five or six types of glasses, or you don't have the room to store them, you're in the company of most wine drinkers. The usual all-purpose glass is a round-stemmed glass with an 8- or 12-ounce capacity.

The Burgundy Bowl

The Burgundy glass is a large, round-stemmed wine glass with a large, curved bowl and a width approximately the same dimension as its height. It has a large opening, and is particularly suitable for capturing the exquisite perfume and bouquet of a fine Burgundy. A typical size will be 12 or 16 ounces (although many come 24 ounces or larger). Of course, it's good for any kind of wine and it is ideal for wine with very complex aromas.

The Burgundy glass.

The Oblong Bordeaux

The Bordeaux glass is quite different from the Burgundy glass in that its height is much greater than its width. Generally, it has a smaller opening than the Burgundy glass to capture the vinous quality of a fine Bordeaux. It is also a good choice if you can select only one wine glass.

The Bordeaux glass.

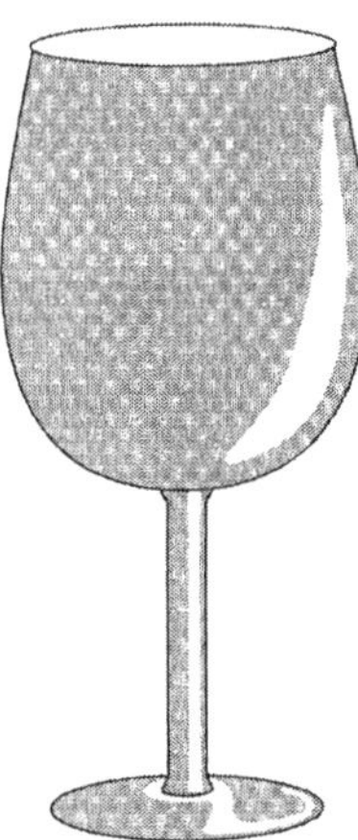

The Magic Flute

To fully appreciate the bubbles, pour your Champagne only into glasses with a high, narrow, tapering bowl—like the traditional Champagne flute. These come usually in a six- to eight-ounce size that can be filled to the top.

You mustn't swirl your Champagne (see Chapter 3, The Art of the Swirl, for more about swirling). Its forceful bubbles exude the wine's flavor, so you don't need to have a large space above the wine as with most other table wines.

Champagne flutes.

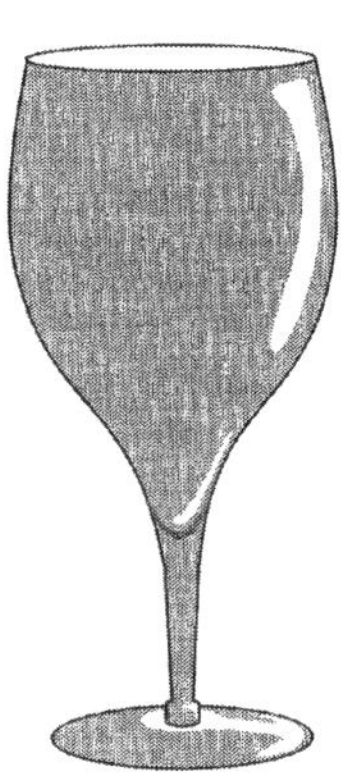

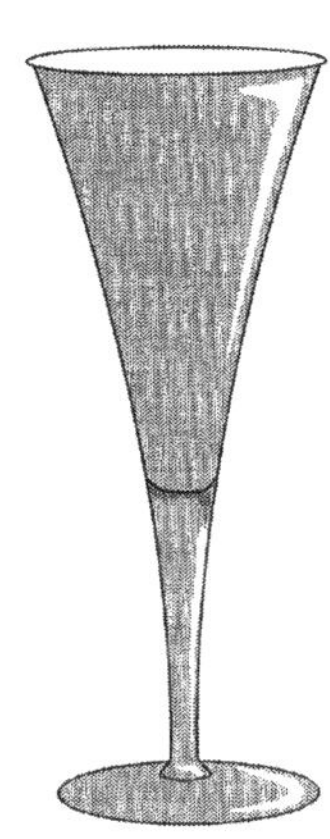

Hocks, Snifters, and Balloons

If you're a white wine enthusiast, you might want to try the tall, slender Hock glass, originally intended for Rhine wines. If your choice is red, a big Burgundy balloon glass can add some variety to your table, although some wine drinkers find it too unwieldy.

No doubt you've seen the oversized Cognac or Brandy snifters. Their large size enables devotees to capture the wine's essence, slowly funneling it to your nose. Snifters add an elegant touch to your table, and this is one case where bigger is definitely better. (A 16-ounce snifter is actually meant to hold no more than one or two ounces!) However, do be careful when sniffing the aroma—brandies have up to 60% alcohol, and therefore pack a punch on your unsuspecting nostrils. Approach brandies slowly and sniff from a few inches off the rim, as opposed to getting up close the way you would with a wine.

Heard it Through the Grapevine

There's a special Sherry glass, called a copita. It's a small glass with a narrow taper and a small opening. The Sherry glass is made to capture the wine's aroma, and it's also perfect for enjoying other cordials, or even high-quality spirits.

Keeping 'Em Clean

Regardless of whether you opt for the basics or set aside room for a wine connoisseur's collection of glassware, caring for wine glasses requires special attention. Not only do you want to avoid breaking any, but you want to keep your wines looking and tasting their very best, and therefore keeping your glasses odor and residue-free.

Wine glasses must be absolutely clean. This is especially true if they've been resting in the cabinet for a while and have picked up dust or musty off-odors. Always wash your glasses prior to use. Choose a good dishwashing detergent, and be sure to rinse them thoroughly several times to remove all detergent residue. You don't want to hear a guest saying, "This is a fine Burgundy with just a hint of anti-bacterial lemon."

The best way to be sure your glass is really clean is to exhale gently into the glass and then smell it. Any residual odors that remain will reveal themselves. You don't want these to spoil your experience after you pour the wine into the glass.

Tasting Tip

Don't be afraid to smell the glass when dining out. Even some of the best restaurants are notorious for stale glasses. You're paying enough for your wine; the least you deserve is a clean, unadulterated glass.

Practice Perfect

Well, you've practiced with your corkscrew and foil cutter. Now what? What's the best way to pour?

Believe it or not, there's no standard technique for pouring wine in your home, except to get the contents into the glass, and to fill the glass one-third to one-half full—wine glasses should never be filled to the top.

Hold the bottle any way you feel comfortable. If you feel insecure holding it from the bottom, no problem. Just be sure your fingers are far away from the lip.

Aim for the center of the glass and pour slowly, keeping alert for that invisible one-third to one-half full zone. When you've poured the right amount, give the bottle a slight twist as you raise it to avoid drips.

Heard it Through the Grapevine

Some restaurateurs insist their staff pour wine by holding the bottle at the bottom with the thumb in the indentation, or punt. This isn't always practical. First, not all bottles have indentations. And second, a heavy bottle could mean an embarrassing (and costly) accident. And especially since they shouldn't be doing that in a restaurant either (and no matter how cool you think it looks), do not try that at home!

Serving at Seventy

The rule of "room temperature" for serving red wines originated long before central heating. When you're talking about wine, room temperature means about 70 degrees. (Some wine devotees prefer 65 degrees.)

If you're taking your bottle from a controlled-environment wine storage area (mid to high 40s Fahrenheit for whites; mid to high 50s Fahrenheit for reds), chances are it's ready for serving as-is. If your home or apartment is overheated, or if you've just brought a bottle home on a hot day, don't be afraid to put your red wine in the fridge. A short layover there will bring it down to the 70 degree mark without damaging its contents.

Avoiding a Cold Chill

White wines taste best when served chilled, but too much cold can interfere with the aroma and flavor. Quite a few restaurants are guilty of over-refrigeration. This goes for rosé wines as well as whites. If the glass feels like a snow cone and you can't smell anything, let it stand a little while before drinking.

Tasting Tip

Did you leave that bottle of red too long in the cooler? Use your microwave on low power for 20-30 seconds. Repeat, if needed. (But make sure glass is microwave safe. And no lead crystal or wine bottle foil!)

To Stand or Not

How long should you wine stand before pouring? It's tempting to say, "Until you're ready to drink it, of course." However, there is some debate on this issue, and it's been going on for years. Read on....

Breathers vs. Non-Breathers

The debate over when to open the bottle rages between the breathers and non-breathers. The breathers insist that exposure to air makes the wine come to life because the aromas are unleashed. They may be right. First, certain flavor components in the wine may erupt with exposure to air. Second, some odors that block our perception of more delicate smells may dissipate with airing, allowing the more subtle odors to come through.

Vino Vocab

Breathing is the process of exposing wine to air (by opening the bottle) for a few minutes to a few hours before drinking it.

While it's true that breathing allows some off-odors to dissipate, the non-breathers maintain we can accomplish the same thing by swirling. Breathers also argue that standing time enhances the flavor of young (recently vinted) wines, although I'm not quite convinced.

I don't want to take sides here, though I admit I'm more of a non-breather. There are no hard-and-fast rules. Try it both ways and see which you like better. Perhaps you'll find your breathing time varies with the type of wine, the vintage, or even the particular bottle.

Tasting Tip

Wine, properly stored on its side, will collect sediment on the side of the bottle. So a few days before you serve, stand the bottle upright, allowing the sediment to fall to the bottom before you decant it.

If you opt for breathing, I suggest you open the wine bottle 15 to 20 minutes before serving. Then pour some into glasses a few minutes before you and your guests are seated. If breathing really brings improvements, they will be more likely to come along in good-sized wine glasses than in the bottle with its tiny opening.

Decanter de Rigeur?

Decanters can be beautiful, decorative objects, but are they necessary? Decanting does have a purpose, and that purpose is not just to impress your friends with your elegant taste in cut glass. Decanters are made for old wines, which collect sediment during the aging process.

Bottle-aging wines for 10 or more years (sometimes even less) can build up a deposit. When this sediment is mixed with the wine, the taste is bitter and unpleasant. In its mildest form, the sediment will mask the subtle nuances that have been developing over the years. The last thing you want is a bottle of very expensive sludge.

Not all aged wines have deposits. The ones that do were usually made with minimal filtering, so the flavors become more intricate and complex during aging. All the more reason to get rid of the sediment before drinking.

Incidentally, decanting also aerates (lets the wine breathe). While the decanters sold in wine shops and catalogs are sure to get compliments from your friends, you actually can use any vessel as a decanter. Just be sure it's absolutely clean and free from any off-aromas.

During decanting, you should have good, bright light illuminating the bottle's neck so you can see when the sediment is close to being poured. Once any sediment is near the neck, stop! If your decanter has a stopper, replace it until you are ready to serve the wine (unless, of course, you have found you fall into the breather camp—then leave it open-topped). Bring the bottle with you to the table. It's an impressive touch, and your guests will want to know the wine they are enjoying.

Aerating for Aroma

If you decide that you want to aerate your wine, there are several ways to do it. The traditional method is simply to open the wine an hour or so before you plan to drink it. Or you can decant it and leave the stopper off the decanter. Some wine drinkers like to aerate their wines in the glass, but if the wine needs several hours or more of aeration (some wines may benefit from prolonged aeration), this is not practicable. Depending on the circumstances, all methods have their benefits.

Will It Keep?

Theoretically, wine begins to deteriorate from oxidation immediately on opening, and even breathers will admit a bottle of wine is best consumed within a few hours. (Isn't that a great excuse to have more than one glass?) But if you're enjoying your wine by yourself, or the two of you really don't want half a bottle each, there are good ways to keep wine for several weeks without losing too much flavor.

Here's a general rule: The more ordinary the wine, the better it will keep. Jug wines and boxed wines, made with thoroughly modern techniques, have no microorganisms in the wine to culture and spoil. Finer wines are more of a risk.

Chill Out

Like any perishable food, wine will keep longer if it's chilled. However, unlike your cottage cheese or orange juice, wine does lose some of its flavor in cold storage, but in a decade of experiments, I have found that there is very little flavor deterioration even with fine wines if it is well-chilled in the refrigerator for as long as two to three weeks.

The best way to keep a wine after it is open is to cork the bottle and put it into a cold refrigerator. This will prevent the air that has been absorbed by the wine after it has been opened to oxidize the wine. It's the oxidation of the wine that impairs the flavor in most cases. Also, chilling the wine prevents the formation of vinegar, the natural by-product of wine.

Freeze Frame

Believe it or not, open bottles can be frozen for prolonged storage after it has been opened! In one experiment, I froze some of the finest grand cru Bordeaux and Burgundies after a really big winetasting of premier cru wines.

That was 18 years ago! And in my experience, this wine retained its character from the time it was frozen—the wine did not age a decade later. I still have a few bottles in the freezer and will let you know in a decade or so how long a wine can be kept frozen. Incidentally, the wine can be thawed out and re-frozen with little flavor impairment.

Under Pressure

There are systems that dispense wine by using CO2 (carbon dioxide gas) under pressure. I approve! In fact, you have even seen one or two in boutique wine shops and wine bars that dispense taste portions for sampling multiple wines.

Because the gadget is inserted into the bottle immediately after opening, there is less risk of oxidation. The wine will keep for several days. This is an excellent method of always having a bottle available for a glass or two without having to keep it in the refrigerator. Some of the units are highly attractive and make a fine addition to a bar or dining room.

Forget Gadgets!

There are gadgets that purport to preserve the wine by removing the air from the bottle or to prevent oxidation by squirting CO2 into the bottle after it has been opened. In my experiments, I have found these methods to be useless. Once the bottle is opened, the air has been absorbed by the wine and the damage has been done.

What will preserve the wine is not a vacuum or CO2 in the bottle, but a procedure that will prevent the absorbed oxygen from acting on the wine. As iron does not rust much in the winter, you can similarly impede the oxidation of the wine by keeping it chilled. Forget these gadgets! Simply refrigerate your wine for future drinking.

No Rebottling Necessary

Some wine experts advise that you pour the leftover wine into a smaller bottle. Or do this when first opening the wine. This also serves no useful purpose, as the wine already has absorbed air and will oxidize if not refrigerated. As I have said before, if you want to preserve a bottle after it has been opened, keep it in the refrigerator or freezer.

CHAPTER 3

Sensory Sipping

In This Chapter

- Become a good wine taster
- Evaluating wines
- Why vintage dating?

I'm sure this is what you've been waiting for—how to taste your wine. In this chapter you'll learn what to look for when you bring the glass to your lips, and why your nose is as (if not more!) important as your taste buds. You'll learn how to tell a great wine from one that merely is competent and what all those vintage dates really mean. Also, we'll cover the basics of matching wine with food to enhance your tasting experiences.

Here we're going to discuss a few things you can do when you savor your wine. It doesn't matter if you're tasting different wines to become familiar with them, or if you're enjoying a bottle you've just opened for dinner.

More Than a Beverage

Yes, it's wine, but it's more than just a beverage. It's something wonderful to behold, to smell, to taste, to swallow! So let's learn some preliminary techniques before we move to the next chapter. That's where we'll cover what's in the glass and how to spot different wine attributes.

The Art of the Swirl

Now that you've chosen an uncorking gadget and you're ready to try out your skills, it's time to get down to some basics of tasting. The first step in this venture is swirling. Before you actually get down to tasting wines, you should practice swirling just to become comfortable with the act.

Here is where the shape of the traditional wine glass makes a real difference. Swirling wine in your glass helps bring the aroma and flavors up to the surface, where they are trapped by the curved design of the glass.

For some new swirlers, though, the act of circulating wine in the glass can feel awkward at first, and even lead to some overly enthusiastic moves that lead to splashing. So let's practice: Fill a wine glass roughly one-third of the way with water. Slightly more is fine, but be sure it's no more than half-full. Keep the rim of the glass parallel to the floor, and use your wrist to make a subtle, circular motion. The trick is to keep the motion minimal and the glass straight rather than tilted.

One way to perfect this is to try it first with the glass still on the table. Place the glass on a broad, flat surface, like a table or countertop, press your fingers on the base of the glass, and gently push it in a circular, counter-clockwise motion. When you feel secure, try it at waist level. (Now you know why I suggested water.) When you graduate to the real thing, try it this way: Pale white wines first; deep red wines last—this way, you'll have the action perfected by the time you get into clothing or table-cloth staining territory.

Heard it Through the Grapevine

After you swirl the wine, you may notice rivulets of wine clinging to the side of the glass. These are called legs or tears and are a sign of a wine's body or alcohol. The fuller the body and higher the alcohol, the more slowly the legs drip down the inner sides of the glass. These occur because the different components of wine evaporate at different rates. Sometimes the legs are caused by glycerin in the wine as well. Legs are a clue that the wine is a superior wine, but as with most other things in wine, this is not always the case.

Light, Color, Wine!

Have you ever watched a wine-lover examining a fresh glass of wine? What can we learn from just looking?

For one thing, examining appearance will reveal obvious flaws. For examples:

- Brown color in either a white or red wine is a sign of over-oxidation.
- Cloudiness (not be confused with sediment) is a sign the wine is spoiled.

But let's not get too hung up on appearance. This custom of visual checking comes from the old days when wines often were neither clean nor clear because of poor winemaking techniques. Today, with improved techniques and quality standards, there's little chance of this.

The Sommelier Says

Check for clarity. Haziness usually is a sign of a biological instability or a bacterial or chemical taint, usually from faulty winemaking. Of course, tasting will reveal this for sure.

Remember what we said (Chapter 1, Tasting Tip) about illumination? It's important. Natural or incandescent lighting allows you to see how the wine really looks. Soft lighting is fine, especially if you're enjoying your wine as part of a romantic dinner. But avoid fluorescent lighting, especially when you are drinking red wines. To view a glass of wine of rich color and gem-like brilliance is a sublime experience.

Trust Your Nose

You've diligently practiced your swirling. You've mastered whites, rosés, and reds, and you're even keeping the tablecloth on the table clean. The question now is: What do you learn when you place your nose into a wine glass?

Wine is the only natural beverage that offers a complete and complex palette of aromas, fragrances (there is a difference between the two; I'll get to that in a moment), and flavors. Orange juice always smells like orange juice; milk, like milk.

Inhaling a fine wine is like the opening of an artist's retrospective at a metropolitan art museum. When you enter the gallery, you will be confronted with variety—canvasses, large and small; many colors, textures and designs. And yet, there is a unity of vision that informs you these all are works by Monet, or Picasso, or Chagall.

You might call wine a sensory art gallery. Or a sensory symphony. Or an elaborate ballet on the palate. The range of smells and fragrances is almost unlimited. Wines can be vinous, wine-like, and grapey; they can be like nesting Russian dolls, with layers upon layers upon… You get the picture.

The scent of a wine is referred to as its nose. Aroma is used to describe the scent of a young, undeveloped wine. For an older, more complex wine, the term we use is bouquet. This distinction is easy when you think of the image that goes with each word.

- When you think of aroma, you tend to think of a single item like coffee.
- A bouquet, in contrast, is an intricate arrangement whose fragrance results from the delicate interaction of its components.

Before I discuss what you want to smell, let me say a little about what your nose doesn't want to find. Some of these less pleasant odors are so powerful your nose won't even get near the rim of the glass before you know something's wrong. Others are more subtle, so it's even more important you know what they are to tell a good wine from a flawed one.

- Vinegar is an obvious one, indicating your wine bottle has been open too long or something has gone wrong in the winemaking.
- The smell of raisins or cooked or baked qualities are also indications that something is wrong, usually that the wine is too old. (Have you ever heard anyone describing a fine wine as "raisiny"?)

There are a number of faults that are signs of microbiological contamination. The most frequently encountered ones are:

- Sulfur dioxide (think of the smell of a just-struck match).
- Hydrogen sulfide (rotten eggs).
- Dekkara (the smell of rancid corn chips).
- Volatile acidity (vinegar).
- Ethyl acetate (nail polish remover).
- Mercaptins (range in smell from garlic and onion to skunk).
- Smells of decay (wilted lettuce, dead leaves, mucus, manure, vomit).
- Petrochemical smells (diesel fuel, Vaseline).
- Geraniums (from bacterial spoilage).
- Potassium sorbate. (Believe it or not, this one smells like bubble gum.)
- Corky (actually, the scent of a particular mold that grows on corks; wines with this flaw are said to be corked).

The nose of a wine can be nonexistent, weak, moderate, or intense. Closed refers to a nose that is weak because it has not had the chance to develop, or is simply very cold in temperature. The other taste components provide the clues to whether the nose is closed or simply weak. It takes some experience to interpret these clues, but it's not hard to pick up.

Wines that display an array of flavors both on the nose and on the palate, usually with subtle or supple undertones, are complex. When the various elements work in harmony, the wine is said to be balanced. When one element dominates all the rest, the wine is unbalanced. The balance is described in relative terms that resemble a ratings quiz. For starters, here are a few terms that experts use, grouped accordingly:

Superlative	Adequate	Inadequate
harmonious	good	poor
excellent	normal	acidic
perfect	average	unbalanced

Heard it Through the Grapevine

Most wines contain sulfur dioxide, a preservative. Sulfur dioxide is sort of a wine wonder drug (which works as an antibacterial, antioxidant) and anti-yeast agent (which keeps sweet wines from refermenting in the bottle).

Winemakers are required by law to put the words "Contains Sulfites" on the labels of all wines with sulfur dioxide that are sold for U.S. consumption to caution those rare persons who are hypersensitive to sulfites.

Good winemakers opt for the minimal levels of this additive, and any residual smell should dissipate with airing. Occasionally, wines get an overdose and airing the wine won't help. In this case (as with all of the flaws mentioned above) you're justified in returning the wine.

Many wine scents may seem strange at first:

- The scent of a fine Burgundy frequently resembles wild violets, tar, or truffles.
- An aged Bordeaux smells pleasantly roasted, like in pot roast.
- A Late Harvest Riesling smells nutty and honeyed.
- A young Riesling or a Muscat resembles pine oil.
- American labrusca varieties, referred to as foxy, have a pungent odor all their own.
- Some Rhone reds have an initial barnyardy earthiness.

Some wine smells require getting used to. Others require getting used to the fact that they're just plain unusual.

Tasting Tip

Besides intensity, you should examine the nose for structure and balance—the relationship among flavor, alcohol, and acidity. A young white wine, high in acid, can be refreshing. But an equally acidic red will be unpleasant, even flawed. Some wines are simple in their flavor. You might describe them as straightforward or one-dimensional.

Taste Will Tell

Now that your nose is out of your glass and you've uttered all your adjectives, it's time to take a sip.

- Take a sizable sip, filling your mouth with wine.
- Roll the wine over your tongue and palate to get the feel, or the body, of the wine.
- Savor and evaluate the wine.

Body is determined by the wine's alcohol, glycerin, and extract. Either it's light, moderate, or full, and may or may not be in balance with the flavor and other components. The body will appear firm when there's sufficient acidity, but it may be flabby when acidity is lacking.

Many other words may come to mind to describe what you experience as body. It may feel heavy from residual sugar. Or body can seem harsh, rough, coarse, silky, velvety, smooth, or creamy, depending on its structure. Trust your palate here.

The tannins in red wines frequently add a necessary and pleasing astringency to fine wines. This may not seem so pleasing at first pucker, but as your wine experience progresses, certain wines will begin to seem flat and dull without it.

Button Your Lip and Gurgle

Okay. You've swirled and sniffed and mouthed. Now it's time to gurgle. (The wine's still in your mouth, right?) Just purse your lips and draw air into your mouth, slightly gurgling the wine to vaporize it. The result is a whooshing sound that identifies experienced wine tasters. This isn't really bad manners, though I wouldn't suggest it for quiet, formal gatherings.

Gurgling the wine permits the full flavor of the wine, warmed by the mouth, to flow through the nasal canal to the olfactory bulb. In short, it's tasting and sniffing rolled into one. It does have a purpose (other than startling your guests). It enables you to experience fully every nuance of flavor.

It's really simple: Purse your lips as if you are going to whistle; then suck in the air over the wine.

The Sommelier Says

You can tell when a wine is beginning to pass the peak of maturity by its finish. There may be a hint of dead leaves, or a lack of vinous flavor, which is called dried out.

From Swirl to Finish

Continuity is the sign of a well-structured wine. There should be no conflict between what you taste and what you smell. The flavor in your mouth should confirm your initial olfactory impression.

After you swallow the wine, you usually will notice a lingering aftertaste, known as the finish. The finish may be described as long, short, lingering, fleeting, or nonexistent. Accompanying these temporal adjectives are complex, acidic, sharp, or dull. Often, the wine's finish will be a taste experience in itself, adding new dimensions and flavors. Professionals evaluate the finish in terms of the time (usually in seconds) that the flavor lingers.

Heard it Through the Grapevine

Scents, flavors, body, alcohol, acidity, and astringency provide the total impression of a wine, all of which make up its structure. Here are a few adjectives you may use when describing a wine's structure:

- Well-defined.
- Firm.
- Broad.
- Tightly-knit.
- Good backbone.
- One-dimensional.
- Multifaceted.

When all the elements of structure, flavor, and complexity attain a perfect harmony (this is really hard to describe) the result is breed or finesse. These are terms we use frequently to describe classic noble wines.

Vintages: Quality or Hype?

The structure of a high-quality wine often is related to its vintage (year it was produced). A famous wine property might produce one-dimensional wines in a poor vintage but glorious, multifaceted wines in a superb vintage. For that reason, it is important to know what vintage your wine comes from.

We've all seen it in the movies. One way to show that the hero or heroine is elegant and sophisticated, the party is chic, or the occasion momentous, is to have someone hold up a bottle announcing, "Lafite '61." (Or '45 or '72 or '59.)

The Sommelier Says

American consumers have been led to believe that a vintage date means quality, and that only inferior or inexpensive wines are not vintaged. In reality, having a vintage date on a bottle has little bearing on the quality of its contents. (However, knowing the vintage still is important with high-quality wines.)

A declaration of vintage on a label merely indicates when the grapes were harvested and when the wine was made.

- California law requires at least 95 percent of the grapes be picked that year.
- In France, the minimum generally is 80 percent, and in Germany, 75 percent.
- Each country or region establishes its own standards for determining vintage.

A vintage date declares when the wine was made, but not how or under what conditions. In short, if you're not familiar with the reputation of an individual producer or vintage, all the label reveals is the wine's age or freshness. Most wines—probably at least 80 percent—do not improve with cellaring (prolonged aging). They were meant to be enjoyed two to three years after the vintage date.

Tasting Tip

There are factors that make one vintage better or worse than another. The grapes, climate, and winemaker are all important and they're all interrelated. The one factor determining the quality of the finished product is ultimately the climate.

An ideal vintage means that certain weather conditions were met the entire year. The perfect winter has ample rainfall and enough cold (to let the vines have the grapes' equivalent of REM sleep). The spring is mild and free from frosts, rains, or other assaults. The mid-season begins cool and heats up slowly, without any environmental mood swings. The ripening period is neither too hot and arid nor too rainy and humid.

The gradual heat over the late mid-ripening period increases the grapes' natural sugars. Incremental warming with cool evenings lets them retain high acidity. The absence of rain in the mid- or late-season keeps the berries from becoming diluted, or swollen with water.

No matter how skilled or experienced, the vintner's role always includes some high-stakes gambling.

- For those with conservative leanings, when the vines are pruned in midwinter to control vine growth, they can be pruned to produce a small crop of guaranteed high-quality fruit.
- Growers (vineyardists) can bet that the vintage will bring warm (but not hot) and dry conditions so they'll get equal quality from a larger crop.

The better growers understand the unique capabilities of each grape variety they work with. If they hold out for both quantity and quality, unpredictable climate can cost them both. If they play it conservative and prune drastically for a small crop, a spell of bad weather can mean a complete wipeout.

Harvesting is always a crucial decision. Vineyardists are more likely to harvest too early rather than too late. Picking too late carries many risks: rains, hail, unwanted molds from high humidity, and loss of acidity. Sometimes an early-harvest decision is a wise one, based on experience. Sometimes it's just loss of nerve.

Heard it Through the Grapevine

One decisive factor in vintage quality is whether a vineyard, variety, or the whole crop is picked in a short time, or whether the process is staggered, based on the peak ripeness of the vineyard, row, or even a single vine.

For example, the vine's age makes a big difference. Young vines typically ripen early, producing a light (small) crop. Really old vines also produce light crops, but they take much longer to ripen. Average-age vines (7 to 25 years), not surprisingly, yield average-size crops.

All of this barely touches a few of the intricate mechanisms involved in coming up with a great vintage (or not). Even in so-called great vintages, producers can make a mistake or two, and the quality will be below par. It's worth your while to get to know high-quality producers and pay a little extra attention to the weather of your favorite wine regions to get a leg up on the quality found in your favorite bottles.

CHAPTER 4

The Vino Vault

In This Chapter

- Wine racks
- Wine vaults and furniture
- Temperature and wine-storage

They're not just for rich guys who live in castles. Consider your own needs for a wine cellar. Many enthusiasts consider home-cellaring an important part of serving and enjoying wine at home.

You really don't need a castle or monastery or a deep dark hillside cavern (although if you should have one, you'll no doubt be the envy of your wine-loving friends)—or even a basement (for all you apartment dwellers out there). All you really need is a place that's away from direct sunlight, free of vibration, and with temperatures that don't change quickly.

Wine racks or wine closets make your storage task easier to manage. A beautiful assemblage of wine racks or a fine-furniture wine closet has aesthetic value beyond its utility. This chapter introduces you to the best methods for keeping your wines in good condition.

Side by Side

Whether you need a wine rack depends on your cellaring needs. Remember, we store wine bottles on their sides to keep the cork from drying out. This makes it difficult to keep your wine on a shelf or on top of a cabinet, because they like to roll.

Vino Vocab

Cellaring means putting wine away for months or years. But you don't need an actual cellar to cellar your wines.

If you prefer to keep only a few cases or a few bottles on hand for occasional use, there's no need to invest in elaborate storage units or racks. Many people keep a few bottles of wine on hand just so they won't have to go running to the local wine shop at the penultimate moment.

You might begin that way, until one day you realize that wine bottles have taken over the bookcase and dresser. Then, if you find yourself sliding carefully from your bed to avoid a protruding wine bottle, you know it's time for a special storage unit.

Tasting Tip

If you're still in the stage of short-term storage, the cardboard boxes or wooden cases the wines come in will serve nicely. Just tilt them so that the wine is lying on its side. But beware: These are not made for stacking. If you try to stack them too high, the bottom row can collapse. (Do you really want a stream of deep crimson leading a path from your living room?)

Wine Racks; Wine Walls

Wine racks will hold your bottles in the perfect lying-down orientation. They come in a variety of sizes and structures and materials. There are inexpensive materials, like white pine, and expensive ones, like clear Lucite or polished brass. Some designer-decorated homes boast a custom wine wall, a built-in rack that can easily cost several thousand dollars. But no, you don't need to have one—as long as you're storing your wine properly, you will enjoy it just as much if its stored on an inexpensive rack as an über-pricey, tricked-out wine cellar.

The type of rack you choose will depend on your needs, taste, and budget. If you're thinking of going for glitter, remember this: Assuming you have located your collection away from bright light, heat, and vibration your wine rack rarely will be on public display.

Where to Find It

You can find wine racks in most department or houseware stores. In states where wine dealers may sell merchandise in addition to beverages, many offer their own fine selection. There also are several wine accessory catalog companies that sell wine racks, wine rack wall units, and wine storage furniture by mail-order. (Refer to Chapter 26 for more information.)

The Right Rack

Wine racks come in two basic configurations—the 12-bottle shelf and the much larger bookcase-style. Unless you're thinking of getting serious fast, and you've got a lot of extra space, the bookcase-style may be a bit much.

Many small racks are very well-designed and easily stacked without danger of toppling. They fit easily into closets, on bookshelves, or in other convenient nooks, and they allow you to add as needed. But however small your rack might be, make sure the bins are large enough to accommodate Burgundy and Champagne bottles!

Bookshelf-style wine racks come either with openings for single bottles or with square or diamond shaped ports that hold from six to a dozen bottles. You can find attractive models in fine furniture hardwoods, wrought iron, brass, chrome, or Lucite. The single-bottle models generally are more expensive. It's not necessary to splurge, but if you decide to pull out all the stops... well, why not?

The Monk's Cellar at Home

If you really want to go all out, there are completely self-contained, temperature-regulated wine cabinets. Your own private storage vault, the urban equivalent of a monk's cellar!

These storage vaults are available everywhere from specialty wine supply catalogues to big box stores like Costco, and come in a variety of styles, woods, and finishes. Prices range from several hundred dollars to several thousand. If you seek an impressive and attractive way to show off your wine collection, consider investing in one of these units.

Different models make use of different types of cooling units. Some use ordinary refrigerator units or air conditioners. These are unsuitable. You're better off using devices intended specifically for wine cooling. Vibration is a serious enemy because it can prematurely age your wine; so make sure the manufacturer guarantees the unit is vibration-free. And regular refrigeration units don't offer humidity control, and thus may well dry out a cork-sealed bottle's closure.

Another factor to consider is how to arrange your bottles. In some models, you have to remove the front bottles first to get to the others. You may find this a real nuisance. Or you may not.

The Sommelier Says

Companies that make self-contained wine storage range from reputable to fly-by-night. Some years ago, a leading mail-order wine storage company simply disappeared, along with hundreds of thousands of dollars of wine lovers' money. Beware. Always consider the age of the firm, its reputation, its warranty, and whether they have local service agents in case of trouble (because just like wine, nothing lasts forever!).

I recommend buying one of these more expensive units only from a local department store, a reputable furniture store, a decorator with a good reputation and high profile, or one of the mail-order companies mentioned in Chapter 26, but only if they have arrangements for on-site guarantee service. Buying from someone you trust guarantees that your wine cellar stays user-friendly.

The Three F's: Fifty-Five Fahrenheit

Some experts will tell you that a wine-storage temperature of 55 degrees is essential. It isn't. Relatively cool temperature uniformity is more important. Ideally, the temperature should not change by more than 10 Fahrenheit degrees, either direction, over the course of a week.

You can store your wines at temperatures up to 65 or even 70 degrees without damage. However, fine wines do not develop to their fullest potential if stored at too high a temperature. If your home has a root cellar, this might work well for storing your wine.

Keep It Steady

As I noted, many experts believe your cellar should be kept at a constant 55 degrees. By all means, strive for this! But if it's not practical for you, don't despair. As long as the changes in temperature are gradual and there are no extremes of heat and cold, your wines won't suffer. If your storage conditions vary from, say, 50 degrees in winter to a high of about 70 degrees in summer, you don't have to worry.

CHAPTER 5

Talking Wine Talk

In This Chapter

- Describe your taste sensations
- The role of oak in fine wine
- The complex flavors of wine
- Aroma, taste, and finish

Ever peek at a wine taster's notes? "Subtle yet assertive, with just a hint of violets and a trace of truffles." Oh yes, and maybe with "a touch of tar." Sounds pretty neat, doesn't it? Being able to say something that sounds like nonsense to most people while being taken for an expert.

No. The idea is not to confuse or bamboozle. It's to provide some order to our own recollections of our own impressions of the wines we experience. Of course, tasting is subjective. Indeed, you might read someone else's notes at a wine tasting and wonder if they had sampled the same wine.

Wine tasting and state funerals are the two areas where society accepts, even encourages, purple prose. In the case of wines, this is not unreasonable. Wines do have the scents of flowers, herbs, fruits, and a host of other evocative elements. We may describe them as robust or flabby, silky or coarse, with a fleeting or lingering finish.

As wine allows you to expand your sensory experiences and awareness, it must engage your vocabulary as well. You no longer will think "astringent" refers only to your mouthwash or facial cleanser.

Speaking the Language

You've noticed by now that some words seem to crop up repeatedly. Complex, for example. Or acidic. Or herbaceous. Just as English, French, Italian, and German (four languages that may appear on labels of fine wines) have their parts of speech, wine jargon has its categories for classification. The three adjectives, above, fit into the category of wine tasting.

The possibilities are vast, but not unlimited. Someday some over-enthusiastic wine writer might proclaim, "This wine has a triangular structure with a diminished-seventh harmony, an Olympic balance, and a nose reminiscent of wild mushrooms, rose hips, and comfrey, with just a soupçon of Dijon mustard. Oh, and a bracing but irresolute aftertaste." (Of course, only the writer will understand what this means!)

Yes, you can be creative. But where you can, stick with the terms you see in this book and in the wine magazines and newsletters. In general, it's better to use common terms than make up your own. Try to evoke comparisons with scents and flavors that you already know such as violets, mushrooms, chocolate, berries of all sorts, and the like. (Of course, it is perfectly acceptable to say that a wine tastes like a Bordeaux, a Cabernet Sauvignon, or Chardonnay, once you understand what the general traits of a grape, or a grape grown in a particular region, are.)

Oaky, Not from Muskogee

In wine jargon, the term oaky has nothing to do with the song by Merle Haggard or the novel by John Steinbeck. We say a wine is oaky if it exhibits oak flavors from being in contact with oak. Look for a woody or oaky scent and taste.

Tasting Tip

Like many things that bow to the whims of fashion, oak falls in and out of favor. These days, you may hear a bit about the ABC crew—"Anything but Chardonnay…" because the once-trendy oaky Chards from California that were very much in favor in the '80s and '90s have taken a bow to steel-fermented versions with just a kiss of oak, or none at all. Is one better than the other? Absolutely not. Remember, all this is subjective; there's no reason why you should not prefer a non-oaky wine).

How does wine come into contact with oak? Oak barrels. These (typically) 62-gallon containers may house the wine during both fermentation an aging. The most expensive wines reach maturity in brand-new barrels with full-power oakiness (barrels lose their oakiness with use, and these used or "seasoned" oak barrels may be used on wines for which a winemaker wants less oak influence, as well as a way to save a little money—oak barrels are very expensive!).

Contact with oak imparts special flavor and aroma to the wine. Oaking also acts as a catalyst for chemical changes in the wine, although most wine lovers would consider this secondary (or tertiary) to the distinctive quality of an oaked wine.

The Sommelier Says

Some lesser wines are made by immersing oak chips or shavings in the maturing liquid or even with the addition of liquid oak essence (illegal in some places; legal in others). The best wines, however, are allowed to sleep happily in those wonderful oak casks.

The term barrel-fermented refers to those white wines that went into barrels (usually oak) as grape juice and emerged as wine. The term barrel-aged refers to wine put in barrels after fermentation. Because they are fermented with their skins, red wines are fermented in stainless steel containers or large wooden vats and then aged in small oak barrels after the skins have been removed from the liquid. Some fruity wines (red or white) are not aged in oak at all in order to maintain a fresher, more fruit-forward quality.

Vino Vocab

The Brix scale is named for Alfred F. Brix, a nineteenth-century German wine chemist, who developed this method of determining sugar content through measuring specific gravity.

Brix

Brix refers to a measure of potential alcohol, based on the sugar content of the grape. The more sugar, the higher the potential level of alcohol. Frequently you will see this term on the back labels of wines (California in particular) and in the wine literature.

Recipe for a Fine Wine

Actually, we're not adding any ingredients here. It's just that we may detect a vanilla flavor with our oaked wines. And this is not a trick of our imagination. New oak barrels contain vanillin, the organic substance that gives vanilla beans their flavor. American oak most notably imparts this flavor to a wine. Wines aged in these barrels take on vanilla flavor as part of their oaky charm. As an ice cream flavor, vanilla may be simple; in a wine, it adds complexity and smoothness.

Heard it Through the Grapevine

Butter gets its characteristic taste from diacetyl compounds, which are a by-product of the malolactic fermentation (see Chapter 8, Fermentation: Take Two). Some winemakers make a point of putting their wines through a malolactic fermentation to impart this taste to their wines.

Terms of the Taste and Trade

Our wine vocabulary has very few terms unique to it. Instead, it features dozens of everyday words in special senses. If you've looked through wine magazines or newsletters, you will have seen these, perhaps puzzled over them.

Here are a few of the most useful terms, enough to let you get the sense of almost anything you might read about wine.

Bouquet

Bouquet is the smell of a wine after it has lost its grapey fragrances (something like losing baby fat). A genuine bouquet may develop only after years of aging and continue as the wine matures in the bottle. The result is a complexity of flavor nuances that did not previously exist. It's very much like smelling a floral arrangement of many different flowers.

Backbone

Our backbones are built of vertebrae, which anchor the most important parts of our skeleton. A wine's backbone also is the structure on which its character is built: the wine's alcohol, acids, and tannins.

What do you think of when you hear that a person has backbone? Quiet strength. And a wine with a firm backbone is well structured and provides a pleasing mouthfeel. However, a wine that lacks acidity, tannins, or flavor has the undesirable character of flabbiness.

Finish

As we noted earlier, finish is the aftertaste left in your mouth once you have swallowed the wine. The quality of the wine determines the finish. Simple wines have a short finish—or no finish at all. Premium wines generally have a finish that lingers on the palate for several seconds or more and mirrors the taste of the wine. With noble wines, the finish can linger and linger on the palate, as it takes you through a kaleidoscope of flavors. It's this kind of sensory experience that makes wine appreciation so fascinating.

Aged

An aged wine is one that has had a chance to mature in the bottle for a number of years to acquire complex scents and flavors different from what it displayed in its youth. A wine aged to maturity is said to be at its peak. And a wine that has become tired or lost its flavors from being aged too long is said to be over-the-hill. (Just as with people.)

Bottle-Sick

After a wine is bottled, it suffers from the shock of the process. For some period of time, it may be deficient in aroma and taste. When this occurs, the wine is described as being bottle-sick, or having gone through bottle shock. Usually recovers after a few months.

Cru Classé

We find this term frequently on French wine bottles and in the wine literature. Cru Classé refers to the classification system in which French wines are defined specifically under French wine law. (I will discuss this at some length in Chapters 10–13.)

Elegance

Like people, some wines show elegance and others do not. It's like being well dressed and perfectly coiffeurred. An elegant wine is one that provides a sense of grace, harmony, delicate balance, and beauty. It is a characteristic that is found only in the finest of wines.

Éleveur

You will find the French term Éleveur (or its equivalent in other languages) on some wine labels. This refers to a wine company that buys finished wines and cares for them in its barrel aging and refining procedures. Often, this firm will be a wine distributor or shipper.

Négociant

You may see the term Négociant on some French wine labels. It refers to the wine broker or shipper responsible for the wine. Some négociants buy bottled wines from the wine producers and others buy finished wine and produce blends under their own name. A number of these firms have acquired a reputation for fine wines; their names are worth looking for.

Extract

Extract refers to the non-sugar solids in a wine that are frequently dissolved in alcohol. A wine with a lot of extract will feel fuller on the palate.

Goût de Terroir

No, goût de Terroir has nothing to do with Ivan the Terrible! Think "territory." This term is a little hard to define, but translates into the flavor that comes from the specific vineyard or wine area, embracing soil, microclimate, drainage, and other territorial characteristics.

Herbaceous

You will find the term herbaceous appears frequently in wine-tasting notes. It refers to an aroma and flavor evocative of herbs that are frequently found in wines made from Cabernet Sauvignon, Sauvignon Blanc, or Pinot Noir. Sometimes this is desirable, and sometimes not.

Legs

No, not referring Marlene Dietrich or Charlize Theron! The legs of a wine are the tears, or streams of wine that cling to the glass after a wine is swirled. It is a result of different evaporation rates of alcohol and other liquids, such as glycerin, in the wine. Usually it's a sign of a wine with body and quality and something wine lovers look for. Besides being a sign of a good wine, these are pretty to look at as they develop, stream down the side of the glass, and then disappear.

Maître de Chai

A wine cellar in France is called a Chai; so the cellarmaster is the Maître de Chai. He is responsible for tending the maturing casks of wine. Frequently, he may be the winemaker, too. This is the position of highest importance in a French winery.

Tasting Tip

Never become intimidated by someone's use of unfamiliar terminology. It's okay to ask for clarification. Anyone who is more interested in communicating knowledge than in putting someone down will be happy to explain.

Mis en Bouteilles Sur Lie

The term Mis en Bouteilles sur lie indicates wines that were bottled off the lees, directly from the barrel, without racking. That is, the wine was removed from the solid mater (the post-fermentation spent yeast cells, or lees) without undergoing aeration during fermentation (racking).

Wine bottled this way retains a fresh, lively, zany quality, often with a slight effervescence (prickly sensation) due to carbon dioxide absorbed during fermentation that did not have the time to dissipate before being bottled.

Middle-Body

You will find the term middle-body in wine writers' tasting notes, frequently published in wine magazines and newsletters. This refers to that part of the taste sensation that you experience after the initial taste impact on your palate. Middle-body provides the core of the taste on which you usually base your assessments. The first taste, or entry, and the last, finish, will harmonize with the middle-body in a well-structured wine.

Round

Round is a wine-tasting term that describes the smooth, gentle feel of a wine with a particular alcohol/acid balance that smoothes the sharpness of the acidity and makes a wine feel round in the mouth rather than sharp-cornered.

Unresolved

Unresolved or unbalanced is a negative term you might apply to an impression that the wine has not yet harmonized its various components to create a smooth or balanced whole, a result of aging.

Charm

Like people, a wine can display charm. Wines that have a lovely scent and taste and are generous with their attributes frequently are characterized as having charm. This characteristic transcends quality categories, and is frequently found in young and fruity wines like those from Beaujolais or Provence.

Off-Dry

A wine that contains a slight amount of residual sugar—from one-half to two percent—is said to be off-dry. When the residual sugar is low, it tempers the acidity of the wine and gives the impression of a wine that is softer and easier to drink. At the higher end, the wine is slightly but pleasingly sweet.

Blind Tasting

No, you need not use a blindfold! The term refers to the important practice of hiding the identity of the wine from the wine taster so that the impression will not be influenced by the label. All you need to do is conceal the bottles in rumpled brown bags when you do a tasting (see Chapter 30, What's a Winetasting?).

Heard it Through the Grapevine

Blind tasting is fun at home, but it is de rigueur when judging at wine competitions worldwide. It's human nature: Wine judges don't want to award a low score to some famous vintage lest it be a reflection on their tasting ability.

Some experienced professional tasters in the wine trade point out that they do not need to taste blind when they have confidence in their palates. Frequently, famous wines are flawed or not up to snuff in a particular vintage, and it's up to these professionals to determine this so that they do not reach the marketplace. Tasting "blind" protects the integrity of the wine judge.

On a non-professional level, though, blind-tasting is a great method for learning. Without preconceived notions about a grape, a winemaker, or a region, you're experiencing the wine from a fresh, objective approach, weighing all its attributes (or lack-thereof!) without influence.

PART TWO

Wine Doesn't Grow on Trees

CHAPTER 6

Tune Up Your Taste Buds

In This Chapter

- New and marvelous flavors not found anywhere else
- Why wine tastes good
- Taste and aftertaste
- Finesse and breed
- Wine-with-food basics

Wine is just grape juice and alcohol, right? Wrong! Grape juice is made up of simple flavors that stay simple, regardless what you add. It's the process of fermentation makes wine a multi-dimensional product, intriguing and intricate. That's why I wrote this chapter, to help you train your own taste buds to these wine wonders.

Many of the scents and flavors created by the transformation of grape juice into wine cannot be found anywhere else in nature. Wine writers try to describe wines by evoking comparison with various berries, bell peppers, leather (think fine leather glove), chocolate, and so forth.

These descriptions are far from exact. The flavors they seek to characterize are unique to wine. Describing a wine is kind of like telling a friend what a banana tastes like. Your friend just will have to eat a banana to know.

Scent and Sensibility

Very often, what we call taste really is our perception of a scent or scents that enter the olfactory canal through the mouth. In fact, we experience most flavors through our sense of smell. Think how food tastes when you have a cold. With a stuffed-up nose, there's not much difference between your favorite cookie and the cardboard box it came in.

That's why I advised you (Chapter 2, Glass Act) to allow enough room in your wine glass to stick your nose halfway in while drinking. Scientists have identified more than 300 chemical components in wine, and they believe at least 200 are odor-producing.

We detect smells through a complex of nerve endings called the olfactory bulb, which is located in the upper part of the nose. This little bulb is a very acute sensor. Sometimes only a few molecules of a substance are enough. These nerve endings become particularly sharp when we inhale, which is why we sniff to experience wine's full flavor.

Although there are some excellent theories, scientists have yet to tell us what mechanism allows us to discriminate among this vast catalogue of aromas we sense. We do know we can detect certain weak scents despite the presence of a dominating one, or that certain substances can mask the smell of others. And we know the olfactory sense may become used to a scent after it's experienced. After a short time, it may lose its impact.

Premium and noble wines contain numerous aromatic and flavor compounds. Many of these compounds will not be present in jug or ordinary wines. These contribute to the wine's character by providing its aroma, or bouquet—an aromatic or perfumed scent. These finest wines contain myriad delicate nuances of flavor, making them comparable to fine works of art or music.

Coaching Your Tastebuds

You've known since grade school that taste resides in the tongue. Our tongues can detect four specific basic tastes: sweet, salt, bitter, and sour (and some even profess to being able to detect a fifth flavor known as umami in Japan, or, for lack of a better English language descriptor, savoriness). In recent years, the notion that specific parts of the tongue detect the particular tastes has been debunked by science, in favor of the notion that all areas of the tongue can detect the four (or five) basic flavors.

The taste buds themselves are contained within the papillae, those tiny cell-like structures that seem to pave our tongues. Sensations pass through the pores of these sensitive little cells and travel via nerve endings to the cortex of the brain. Not surprisingly, these nerves end very close to where the smelling nerves end. It's not difficult to see how the two processes of taste and smell are intertwined.

Two things govern the way our senses work when confronted with taste and aroma. The first, of course, is the character of the taste and scent. The second is our individual ability to perceive the taste and scent.

In wine circles, we have debated for years whether tasters are made or born. I believe the answer is something of both. Some people do smell and taste more acutely than others. For the most part, though, tasters are made.

It's like learning to appreciate any art. If you're not familiar with modern art and you see a Picasso for the first time, you may wonder why the eyes are in such a weird place or why those funny lines go through somebody's cheekbone. You may miss the subtleties of color and form entirely. But once you learn what to look for in a painting—how to really see what is on the canvas—it's like having a new pair of eyes (although maybe not eyes quite like Picasso's version).

You've probably noticed that your abilities to taste or smell aren't always the same. The most obvious blocker to full flavor is having a cold or active allergy. Mood and mental state are two other factors. If you're even mildly fatigued, familiar objects like your briefcase or gym bag can feel a lot heavier. Images start swimming across the page or computer screen. It's the same with taste and smell, although you may not be as aware of it.

Have you ever felt a bit blue and said, "Food doesn't taste the same anymore."? It's not just a figure of speech. Your taste buds are just feeling like the rest of you. Even the stress of breaking bread with people you don't like can diminish your food pleasure.

On the bright side, the whole idea of tasting wine is going to put you into a good mood. That will rouse your taste buds to peak condition, and surely, you will enjoy the company of your tasting partners.

Heard it Through the Grapevine

Taste is an individual thing. If you read the tasting notes of three wine experts, you may think they've sampled different bottles. So just because someone waves a glass at you, saying, "Ah! The outdoors! This wine tastes of fresh leaves and wild flowers!" doesn't mean you're a philistine because you don't taste a single daisy.

So let's do it! First, I want you to clear your mind of ideas, beliefs and expectations. This tasting business is an individual experience, though it's not an exercise in free association. Those flavor adjectives wine lovers use don't emerge only from the imagination. The comments of an experienced taster actually can help you discover more of your own tasting capacity.

Tasting Tip

Fresh leaves and wild flowers often are associated with wine. So are raspberries, ripe cherries, cinnamon, sage, and roses. When the flavor is less distinct, you might just say it tastes fruity. It's a positive quality, although not particularly well defined.

A good wine is characterized by continuity. Your taste buds confirm what your nose has promised, and you experience a lingering aftertaste when you swallow. The aftertaste or finish may be fleeting, barely perceptible, or it may evoke a whole new vocabulary of adjectives.

Most often, the aftertaste will add new perceptions of taste that didn't seem to be there when the wine was still in your mouth. Below are some qualities you can seek when savoring a wine.

Body

The body is the fullness (or lack of) that you feel when you roll the wine over your tongue and palate. Body is the product of the wine's alcohol, glycerin, and extract. It may be light, moderate, or full. It may or may not be in balance with the flavor and other constituents.

Viscosity

No, we are not talking about motor oil. A wine characterized by viscosity is thicker, fuller, and has a heavier body than the average wine. The term to use for a full-bodied wine high in alcohol and glycerin, and with more flavor than acidity is said to be fat. A wine with viscosity frequently will display legs, formed by wine clinging to the side of the glass.

Acidity

Acidity refers to the non-volatile acids in wine, which are principally tartaric, malic, and citric. These acids provide the wine with a sense of freshness and (we hope) balance.

Sufficient acidity gives a wine firm body, while lack of acidity may make it feel flabby. (And no, despite what you'd like to believe, drinking acidic wines will not tone up flabby thighs and abdomens.)

Balance

Balance refers to the proportion of the various elements of a wine in relation to one another. For example, acid against sweetness; fruit flavors against wood; and tannins and alcohol against acid and flavor.

When all the components are working together, like the colors and fabrics in a decorated home, the wine is balanced. Harmonious is the adjective of choice. When wines are unbalanced, they may be acetic, cloying, flat or flabby, or even awkward. Ever wonder why negative descriptions always outweigh the good ones? I think it's because many wine writers compare wines with their ideas of utter perfection, noting what they lack while neglecting what they afford. Too bad for them!

Backbone

We defined this in Chapter 5 (Terms of the Taste and Trade). The backbone is the structural framework of a wine provided by the alcohol, acids, and tannins. A wine with good backbone leaves a positive impression on the taste buds and olfactory sense.

Mouthfeel

The mouthfeel of the wine is its texture. Don't confuse this with body, which is the wine's weight or viscosity. Never neglect to savor it fully, rolling the wine over your mouth. And if the tasting environment permits, don't forget your gurgling. The texture and feel of the wine in the mouth is part of the beauty that makes wine so exciting.

Overall, the adjectives used to describe mouthfeel are tactile (the same ones we use to describe textures): silky, velvety, rough, coarse, or smooth. The one exception to this rule is the pucker of tannic red wines. The puckering quality may seem strange at first, but as your wine tasting experience progresses, certain wines will seem flat or dull without it.

Harmony

Harmony refers to the interplay of the wine's constituents. Harmony means smooth, flowing, and compatible. When everything is in sync, the result is a balanced wine.

Finesse and Breed

Finesse and breed are two descriptors that speak for themselves, like Cary Grant or George Clooney emerging from your wine cellar. (If you can't think of contemporary stars who measure up, don't worry about it. Hollywood has changed.)

Heard it Through the Grapevine

Wines with breed and finesse are the loveliest, most harmonious, most refined wines. The classics. These are the wines that age gracefully and wondrously. We don't find these qualities in mid-premium or lesser wines.

Wines with breed and finesse are those rare noble wines in which all elements of structure, flavor, and complexity combine to a peak of almost indescribable perfection. For these noble beauties, fermentation merely is the beginning of a long life, culminating in an artwork of the highest standard.

It's hard to speak of finesse and breed without throwing in at least a touch of romanticism. Technically, finesse is the quality of elegance that separates a fine wine from one that simply is good.

Breed goes up even higher. Breed is the term we use to describe wines that achieve classical proportions. It's star quality at its utmost. The quality is usually elusive to describe, but you'll know it the moment you experience it. Noble wines such as Chateau Lafite-Rothschild, Chateau d'Yquem, or the legendary Burgundy, Romanée-Conti, have finesse and breed from decades upon decades of growing grapes on the best lands with exceptional winemakers at the helm.

Making a Perfect Match

Now that we know what to look for in a wine, the next step is to know how to match wine with food. The following is a first look. For a more complete discussion, see Chapter 32.

Say it with Rosés

When it comes to matching with food, sometimes it seems like everyone has a forceful opinion on which wines go best with particular foods and dishes. When it comes to rosé, you might hear some say that it's merely a summer wine, meant for simple suppers or snacks. Don't listen.

While it's true that the grape skin contact in making rosés is minimal, there is a range of styles and, therefore, a fairly good range of foods they can go with. And while they don't have the tannic quality that makes red wines heavier and harder to match with foods (and sometimes harder to drink on their own), some—like rosados from Spain, rosatos from

Italy, or even certain rosés from California-—get a little extra time muddling around on the skins and thus have a little more tannic grip allowing them to hang in there with lighter meats, like pork and even the dark meat of chicken. They also work as a pretty good flavor equalizer on the Thanksgiving table with roast turkey and the like. And, of course, rosés are also great for barbecues and outdoor parties. Do rosé wines go with everything? Certainly not and, with the exception of a few rare and oddball aged versions, they tend toward the simple.

Tasting Tip

Rosés are often light wines in taste as well as in color. Even those that hang around on their skins for a day or so are in all likelihood going to be thoroughly overpowered by steaks and roasts. They may not be the best match for very sweet or salted tidbits, or anything too assertive in taste. Think of the foods you tend to enjoy in warmer weather, and chances are, you'll be able to come up with some good matches for a light-style rosé.

Lighter-style dry rosés, like those made iconic in Provence and other parts of southern France, are a great match with the same dishes you usually pair up with light white wines. Things like fish or shellfish, or vegetarian favorites, go well with rosés. A good dry rosé, like a French Tavel, goes beautifully with ham, white meat, and poultry dishes.

Delicate to Dominant Whites

Contrary to popular assumption, white wines actually are a varied lot. They range from pale and delicate young wines (in danger of being overpowered if your chef salad has too much Roquefort dressing) to tawny grandes dames (grands hommes?) that can give any red a run for its vintage.

Traditional, But Tricky Reds

Let me come right out and say it: The best way to impress people with your wine expertise is the tried-and-true method of showing them how well you can choose the perfect red wine for dinner. With their tannic influence on the taste buds, red wines can be tricky critters. The finest red wine without a proper pairing can make your cheeks hollow in seconds.

Heard it Through the Grapevine

Light young reds, like Beaujolais Nouveau (serve this one slightly chilled), are a good choice with the same type of foods you'd usually pair with white wine. This is a handy thing to know if you have a guest with an allergy to white wines. (White wines contain more sulfites than reds.) And some guests simply may prefer reds.

Reds that are high in tannins are perfect with high-protein foods like beef or cheese. A well-chosen red wine is a superb complement to a cheese platter (equally well-chosen). In general, you'll want to avoid sweet or excessively salty foods, which tend to make tannic wines taste even more tannic. Remember, most red wines are best served slightly cooler than room temperature.

CHAPTER 7

Grape Vine Diversity

In This Chapter

- White grape varieties
- Red grape varieties

Botanists have identified more than 8,000 varieties of grape. But don't panic! Only a select number of these are on display at your local wine shop. You don't need to learn thousands of varieties, but the number used for fine wines still is large. Knowing the characteristics of these will reward you next time you shop.

In this chapter, we will list white first, then red—for no particular reason.

The Most Popular White Grape Varieties

Most (but not all) white wines are made from white grapes. There are hundreds of white grape varieties that are made into wine, but only a handful are seen on wine labels as varietal wines. Here are some of the most popular.

Vino Vocab

Vitis is the genus of vine fruit; vinifera is the species of wine grape with which 99% of winemakers concern themselves; thus, vitis vinifera is the grape variety—e.g., Chardonnay, Merlot, Sauvignon Blanc, etc., and are grown throughout the world's wine regions.

Chardonnay

Chardonnay remains the most popular varietal among white wine grapes. It is known as the king of white grape varieties. Power and finesse are two qualities of this white vinifera, which yields the world's finest white wines.

In northern France, Chardonnay is responsible for Champagne, and especially those called blanc de blancs, which are made entirely from white grapes. Some people call Chardonnay the Champagne grape. This is correct on two levels: Chardonnay is the primary grape variety in the finest Champagnes. Both Chardonnay and Champagne are names that evoke images of high quality.

In California, the styles of Chardonnay vary widely. Some made from ripe grapes are fermented and aged in French or American oak barrels to yield round, rich wines—flavorful, powerful, and oily in texture. Others approximate this style, but to a lesser degree. More and more these days, the popularity of non-oaked versions of the grape are catching on for their ability to capture the direct fruitiness of the Chardonnay in a crisp style. Most California Chardonnays are fuller in body and higher in alcohol than their French cousins.

Heard it Through the Grapevine

Many wine grape varieties became famous by turning up in the right place. Some wines are named for their places of origin, Corton-Charlemagne in Burgundy, for example, that became popular in their own right for exquisite Chardonnay. They do not always appear on wine bottles named as varietal wines.

It's impossible to discuss Chardonnay without mentioning oak. Most Chardonnay receives a restful yet invigorating treatment in an oak bath. The best Chardonnays get their spa treatment inside the traditional French oak barrel, which imparts spiciness, among other aromas and flavors. Some producers, however, also prefer the vanilla notes that are more prevalent in American oak. Less expensive wines have to be content with soaking oak chips or even with the addition of liquid essence of oak.

The flavors imparted by oak have a vanilla, smoky, spicy, or nutty character. That's easy to associate—they're all woodsy qualities. The Chardonnay flavors and scents are rich and fruity. You can name any fruit you like, from apples to mangoes, and chances are you'll taste at least a hint of it in a cool glass of Chardonnay.

Tasting Tip

Chardonnay grows successfully in many different countries, but it's practically synonymous with the celebrated white wines from France's Côte d'Or region of Burgundy. There, we associate it with such legendary names as Montrachet, Meursault, and Corton-Charlemagne. If these still sound like the sites of ancient battles, don't worry. Soon they'll become more familiar to you.

Pinot Grigio (Pinot Gris)

Pinot Grigio, or Pinot Gris, is a white vinifera, related to the Pinot Noir. It used to be known as the Tokay d'Alsace in Alsace, but European Union wine laws struck the term from our wine vernacular in order to avoid confusion with the famed Hungarian regional wine, Tokaji. In Germany, Pinot Grigio is known as Rulander, and found in good quantities in Pfalz and Baden.

Heard it Through the Grapevine

The skin of Pinot Grigio is strikingly dark for a white variety, and some of its wines are unusually deep in color. They're medium- to full-bodied, somewhat neutral in flavor and low in acidity when well made.

Picked before fully ripe, these grapes can be high in acidity and undistinguished. Often dismissed as without distinction, some Pinot Grigios from Italy, especially from the northern Alto Adige region, have become wildly popular. Pinot Grigio wines are inexpensive and, when well made, easy to drink.

Northeastern Italy is the most characteristic locale for this grape. It's also grown in the U.S., mainly in Oregon, with great success, and has also become more popular in California.

Sauvignon Blanc

Sauvignon Blanc is an adaptive white vinifera. It's a fairly productive grape that ripens in mid-season. Harvested at full maturity, it offers wines with a characteristic herbaceous, sometimes peppery aroma. Picked early, the grape is intensely grassy (and yes, that can be a compliment, though not always). Left to hang a little longer, and it can take on exciting tropical notes.

In France, Sauvignon Blanc is the important grape of the Loire Valley wines from Sancerre to Pouilly-Fumé, and makes pleasant table wines in the Entre-Deux-Mers region of Bordeaux as well. The grape also provides backbone and flavor to the luscious, sweet wines of Sauternes, Barsac, and Monbazillac.

White Graves and Pessac-Leognan wines of Bordeaux are primarily Sauvignon Blanc, too. They range in style from dry to semi-sweet and are usually mediocre quality, although some are of exceptional quality. As the Bordeaulais learn to make better white wines, you will see more and more good wines from this region.

Sauvignon Blanc is higher in acidity than Chardonnay. Some wine lovers savor its crispness; others prefer Chardonnay. Sauvignon Blanc wines are light- to medium-bodied and generally dry. The European varieties are largely unoaked. The California versions usually are oaked. Maybe Californians just like to experiment. California Sauvignon Blancs range from dry to slightly sweet. "Fumé Blanc" is a popular varietal label.

You would also do well to take note of the grassy, gooseberry-like Sauvignon Blancs that have nearly defined New Zealand as a New World wine region, especially those of Marlborough. The Valparaiso region of Chile, too, is sticking its flag in the ground for a region of quality for Sauvignon Blanc.

The Sommelier Says

The noble grape is the Johannisberg Riesling, but vast quantities of simple jug wines from South Africa and Australia are designated Rieslings, although they bear little resemblance to the fine wines of the Rhine.

Riesling

If Chardonnay is the king of white grape varieties, Riesling is its queen. Riesling is a white vinifera variety that gained its ranking among noble grapes through the great Riesling wines of Germany. Unfortunately, the name has suffered a lot of misuse on wine labels.

Riesling does thrive in a few places outside of Germany, notably Alsace in northeastern France (near Germany), Washington state, the Finger Lakes district of New York, and the Eden and Clare Valleys of Australia. Quality varies, so be sure to use caution here as well.

Riesling wines have long been treated with equal amounts of slap and tickle from the wine press, but recent international efforts by new quality groups like the International Riesling

Foundation, which formed in 2009 to promote Riesling as a noble variety, have helped to bring about a whole new era of Riesling enthusiasm. They often are good values as well, and I urge you to try them.

Rieslings refuse to be oaked. (An oaked Riesling would taste awful!) They're lighter in body than Chardonnay, but light can be refreshing quite satisfying to the palate. Overall, Rieslings are high in acidity, low to medium in alcohol content, and have a fruity or flowery taste and scent that is distinctive, and ranges from dry and crisp to honey-sweet.

German Rieslings come in a variety of styles, all with their own levels of dryness, aromas, and flavors. If you're looking for a top-quality dessert wine, a fine German late-harvest Riesling is the perfect choice.

Gewürztraminer

Gewürztraminer (guh-VERTZ-tra-MEE-ner) wines are a lot easier to drink than pronounce. The grape is a clonal selection of the once widely planted traminer white vinifera. Its name means, literally, "spicy grape from Traminer."

Gewürztraminer wines have a distinctive appearance and taste. The wines are deep gold in color, with the spicy aroma ginger, and often with alluring notes of roses and lychee fruit. They're exotic and intriguing. The scent is spicy, floral, and fruity, but the flavor surprisingly dry.

Heard it Through the Grapevine

The Gewürztraminer grape tends to be high sugar, low acid. The result is a soft wine with a high alcohol content. However, Gewürztraminer wines also have high extract (essentially, the solid matter of the wine left after you boil off the water and alcohol), which counteracts the feeling of softness. In short, the high extract adds substance and verve and keeps the wine from being flabby.

The most distinctive examples of Gewürztraminer come from Alsace. U.S. styles tend to be lighter and sweeter than their Alsatian counterparts, but dry Gewürztraminers now are produced in California and Oregon, too.

Chenin Blanc

Chenin Blanc is a fruity wine ranging from bone dry to slightly, or even very sweet. The best sweet versions come from the Côteaux du Layon and Vouvray in France, and can rise to legendary quality. Wines of the highest quality have high acidity and an unusual oily texture, age to a beautiful deep gold color, and can last for 50 years or more! The aroma typically is reminiscent of fresh peaches and pears; when harvested early, it's slightly grassy and herbaceous.

This noble white grape originally hails from the Loire Valley in France, where it is used both for still wine and vin mousseux (sparkling wines). It's also popular in California, Australia, South Africa, and South America.

Müller-Thurgau

Müller-Thurgau is Germany's most often planted white vinifera, although its ancestry is uncertain. It may be a cross between Riesling and Sylvaner or between two clones of Riesling. It ripens earlier than the Rieslings, which gives it an edge in cool climates. The wine is fragrant, soft, and round and may lack character. It is also grown in Alto Adige in northeastern Italy.

Muscat

The Muscat family includes Muscat Blanc, Muscadelle, and Muscat of Alexandria. All are white grape varieties with a unique, easily recognizable aroma—pungent, musky, piney, and spicy. The Muscat Blanc offers the best potential for winemakers, although all varieties have been made into table, sparkling, and fortified wines. Muscat is used for Italy's sparkling Asti, where it is known as Moscato d'Asti, and tastes just like the ripe grape itself.

The Sommelier Says

Do not confuse the Muscat family with Muscatel, a cheap fortified wine usually consumed for its high alcohol content. Most of the Muscats you'll find in your wine shop bear little resemblance to this nefarious brew. Muscat wines are low in acidity and have a perfumed, floral aroma ranging from spicy to evergreen, and an inherent bitterness often countered by sweetness. Some newbie wine drinkers also confuse Muscat with Muscadet, the dry, acidic, stony wines made from the grape Melon de Bourgogne of the Loire Valley that go oh-so well with oysters—definitely not the same grape!

The Muscat character ranges from subtle to overpowering, depending on growing conditions and winemaking. The styles range from dry to very sweet. Alsatian Muscat is a light, dry, pleasant wine, and California produces some appealing semisweet table wines.

Pinot Blanc

Pinot Blanc, the white variant of the noble Pinot Noir, is grown in many regions. Its main production is in Burgundy, Alsace, Italy, Germany, Austria, and California. In Germany, it's Weissburgunder (White Burgundy), and in Italy it goes by Pinot Bianco.

The better versions present a spicy fruit, hard, high acid, almost tart profile that demands some cellaring. In California, it is used by many wineries as a sparkling wine blender. As an early ripener and very shy bearer, the grape has lost out in competition with Chardonnay.

Semillon

Semillon is the blending partner of Sauvignon Blanc in the sweet wines from Sauternes. Grown throughout the wine world, it is always the bridesmaid, its main role is as a blender.

Semillon is relatively low in acid and has appealing but subtle aromas. It can have the scent of lanolin or smell mildly herbaceous when young. It yields Sauternes-like wines in South Africa and pleasant, dry wines in South American countries. The Australian versions range from dry to semisweet. In California, the wines are finished sweet and are blended into generics.

Trebbiano

Trebbiano is a white vinifera that's grown widely in Central Italy. It ripens late, is very productive, and derives its importance from its blending role in making Soave, Orvieto, and other popular Italian white wines. In France it is called Ugni Blanc or St.-Emilion, and it's favored for Cognac production. Characteristics are high acidity, low sugar, light body, and neutral aromas.

Viognier

Native to the Rhône Valley of France, the Viognier grape is a shy bearer, which limits its production. The wines are marked by a spicy, floral aroma, similar to melons, apricots, and peaches. It is medium- to full-bodied with low acidity. Viognier grapes recently have interested California winemakers, especially in the Central Coast, and has proved to make lovely, spicy, full-bodied whites in Virginia, as well as oddball regions like Texas as well.

The Most Popular Reds

As with white wines, there are a large number red wine grape varieties. Similarly, only a handful appear on wine labels as varietal names. The following section will introduce you to the most popular red grape varieties.

Cabernet Sauvignon

Cabernet Sauvignon is the red counterpart to the royal Chardonnay. It's the reigning monarch of the red vinifera. Ideally, Cabernet Sauvignon wines offer great depth of flavor and intensity of color, and develop finesse and breed with bottle aging.

Heard it Through the Grapevine

The red, royal Cabernet Sauvignon grows well in many wine regions, yielding wines that range from outstanding to mediocre in quality. (After all, it takes more than just a grape for success.). In France, this distinguished grape takes the credit for the grand reputation of Bordeaux red wines. It's the prime element in many of the finest bottlings.

In northern Italy, this grape yields a reasonable facsimile of Bordeaux. Cabernet also grows in many eastern European countries, where it is made into pleasant, light-style wines.

Indeed, Cabernet is one émigré that thrives in the California sunshine. Some of its California bottlings actually are on par with Bordeaux, with a few even attaining noble quality. Other California Cabernets run the entire quality gamut. New World wine regions, particularly Chile, Argentina, and Australia produce Cabernet in vast quantities.

Tasting Tip

Wines are at their best and longest-lived when made with close to 100 percent Cabernet grapes. However, this versatile vinifera blends well with other wines. A few of its favored companions are Cabernet Franc, Merlot, Malbec, and Petit Verdot in Bordeaux; Merlot and sometimes Zinfandel in California; and Shiraz in Australia.

Cabernet Sauvignon wines are high in tannin and medium- to full-bodied. Their distinctive varietal character is a spicy, bell pepper, and blackberry aroma and flavor with high astringency. Deeply colored wines made from very ripe grapes are often minty and cedary, with a black currant or cassis character.

Merlot

Merlot is a French variety of red vinifera that's grown in many wine regions. It is an early-ripening, medium-colored red grape. As a varietal, it makes wines that are soft and subtle, yet substantial. (Say that very fast while swooshing the wine in your mouth!) The finest Merlots possess great depth, complexity, and longevity.

Merlot has a distinctive, herbaceous aroma quite different from the bell pepper quality of the Cabernet. It is softer in tannins and usually lower in acidity, producing a rounder, fatter, and earlier maturing wine.

The very qualities that make Merlot less powerful than Cabernet Sauvignon make it more palatable for some wine drinkers. Don't be intimidated by wine snobs. Merlot is easier to drink by itself and it goes well with lighter foods.

Heard it Through the Grapevine

In the Médoc and other regions of Bordeaux, Merlot is used as an elegant and mellowing component in Cabernet Sauvignon. In the St.-Emilion and Pomerol regions of Bordeaux, Merlot is the star, usually making up 60-80 percent of the blend, and producing complex, velvety, and sometimes frightfully expensive wines. In California, Italy, Chile, and elsewhere, an increasing number of wineries now produce varietal Merlots, but it is used primarily as a blending agent with the more powerful Cabernet. In Hollywood terms, Merlot is the best supporting actor, while Cabernet Sauvignon remains the big draw.

Pinot Noir

Pinot Noir is one of the noblest of all wine grapes. It is grown throughout the wine world, but success varies because of its thin-skinned sensitivity to soil, climate, and the clonal variant of the vine. This is one temperamental vinifera!

Tasting Tip

In France, Pinot Noir is the principal red grape of the Côte d'Or region of Burgundy, where it produces some of the world's most celebrated and costly wines. It is also used as the base of many a fine Champagne, and it's admired for body and elegance.

Pinot Noir grows best in well-drained chalky or clay soils and cool climates. Happily ensconced in clay, it produces wines that often go on to a long aging process, replete with complex fragrances resembling violets, cherries, roses, truffles, or other intricate scents. Under less ideal conditions, its wines have a distinctive grapiness, which still is appealing. Under poor conditions, it produces coarse, undistinguished wines, frequently thin and acidic, and unworthy of varietal bottling. (I said it was temperamental!)

Until fairly recently, winemakers believed that Pinot Noir would remain a true French patriot, giving its best only under the tricolor banner. However, the advent of the film "Sideways" seemed to tip the scales, and now Pinot is in incredibly high demand among the masses. Wineries in the U.S. (California, Oregon, and Washington in particular), Australia, South Africa, and Italy have shown that with the proper selection of the vine's clones, exacting care in the vineyards, and appropriate winemaking techniques, the variety can be grown to rival its French counterparts.

In Switzerland, Pinot Noir is grown in Valais and produces a wine called Dole, which is full-bodied and rich, with some aging potential. In Germany, it is known as Spätburgunder or Rotclevner and yields light-bodied reds that have been gaining in popularity.

In northern Italy, Pinot Noir is known as Pinot Nero, and produces wines with verve and aging potential. In Hungary, Romania, and South America, it yields medium- to full-bodied wines, simple and direct for jug wine consumption.

Zinfandel

Zinfandel is a red vinifera that is grown commercially only in California (an interesting sort of status). It's related to a Croatian grape, and boasts no French heritage whatsoever; so it's exempt from the unfair comparisons many fine California wines have to endure.

Heard it Through the Grapevine

Although not as finicky as Pinot Noir, Zinfandel is sensitive to climate and location. It tends to raisin in hot climates and overproduce in others. (Quantity and quality go in inverse proportion.) The wines range from thin, jug wine quality to wines intensely rich in flavor, heavy-bodied with tannins and extract. The typical character is berrylike—blackberry or raspberry—with a hint of spiciness. Styles vary from light and young to heavy, syrupy, and late-harvest. The current trend favors heady wines that are warm, tannic, and rich in flavor, which call out for some cellaring.

Even more popular than a full-bodied red Zinfandel in today's market is the blush wine known as White Zinfandel. Skin contact for these Zinfandels is minimal. (In contrast, Zinfandel reds exhibit the richest, deepest colors.)

Syrah/Shiraz

Syrah traces its origin to the days of the Roman and Greek Empires. And while its initial origins have made for much debate in the wine world, its true ancestral home is the northern part of the Rhône Valley, where it is used to make the full-bodied, deeply-colored, powerful, long-lived wines from the Côte Rôtie, Chateauneuf-du-Pape, and Hermitage regions.

In Australia, where it's known as the Shiraz grape, it yields potent wines that often are blended with Cabernet. In California, the Central Coast produces full-bodied, fruity, spicy versions, and it is occasionally used to blend with Pinot Noir to create a more fruit-forward style of the wine.

Syrah's firm and full-bodied wines have aromas and flavors that suggest roasted peppers (á la Cabernet Sauvignon), smoked meat, tar, and even burnt rubber. (Did I tell you that some wine scents are just plain strange?) Some of the Australian varieties are softer and more berrylike than the archetype Syrah.

Nebbiolo

Nebbiolo is the pride of Italy's Piedmont region. This pride is well-earned! This high-acid red vinifera is sensitive to subtle changes in climate and soil and grows well in few places. It reaches its peak in the rich, aged wines of Barolo, Barbaresco, and Gattinara (in some districts it is known as Spanna).

Most Piedmont versions share a deep color and full body. They have a distinctive fragrance of violets, truffles, or earthiness, sometimes with a hint of tar. Some are herbaceous, and the young wines have a fruity aroma.

Sangiovese

Sangiovese is the principal grape variety used to make Chianti and several other red wines from Tuscany. A small-berry variant called Brunello is used in Brunello di Montalcino wines.

The wines have moderate to high acidity and are moderately tannic. They can be light- to full-bodied, depending on the exact location of origin and the winemaking style. The aromas and flavors are fruity, particularly cherry, with a subtle hint of violets. Sometimes they have a slight nuttiness, and even piney notes. Basically, their style is direct and simple, but Chianti Riservas and Brunello di Montalcino can be complex and age-worthy.

Tempranillo

Tempranillo is a Spanish vinifera. Its wines have medium acidity and moderate alcohol. The grape itself has a deep color, but this is often masked by long American oak aging and blending with lighter varieties like Grenache as in many traditional Rioja wines. However, new, young producers are bucking the system of both blending and aging, releasing younger, fresher verions, and even opting for the spiciness of French oak instead of the traditional American.

Aglianico

Indigenous to southern Italy, the Aglianico is a grape used to make Taurasi and other powerful red wines that can demand cellaring.

Barbera

Barbera is grown primarily in Italy and California. In many Italian districts it is bottled as a varietal identified by a place name (for example, Barbera d'Asti). Depending on the growing conditions and the location, the Italian versions range from pleasantly fruity to slightly rich and tart in flavor.

In California, the plantings are primarily in warm to hot regions, with the resulting wines fruity and soft. They usually are intended for blending into jug wines, but every now and then a robust, rough, rich wine emerges. The current trend is to age the wine in new oak to increase the tannin level and enhance crispness.

Gamay

Gamay reaches its peak in the Beaujolais district of France, at the southernmost tip of Burgundy. Traditionally, Gamay has been banned in most of Burgundy by a royal edict from centuries ago, but it thrives in Beaujolais where it produces light to medium-bodied, delightfully fruity wines with a slightly herbaceous and minerally character as Beaujolais-Village and, especially, Cru Beaujolais. Beaujolais Nouveau style yields a fresh, fruity wine with strawberry or raspberry flavors is unaged and released on the third Thursday of November as a celebration of the good harvest, and it is meant to be consumed within months of its release. Check out the wine shops in late fall; you're guaranteed to see signs announcing the arrival of Beaujolais Nouveau!

Grenache

Grenache is Spanish by heritage, but most often identified with France's Rhône Valley, where it yields full-bodied rosés and fruity reds ranging from simple Côtes-du-Rhône to magnificent Châteauneuf-du-Pape. In Spain, it is known as Garnacha, and is one of several varieties blended to make Rioja. In neighboring Navarra, it is used for bright-hued rosé wines, as well as varietal reds.

Tasting Tip

The Grenache grape has a distinctive orange color and a fruity, strawberry flavor that makes it ideal for rosés and blending. A prime example is Tavel, a rosé produced in the southern portion of the Rhône Valley. At its best, it is full-bodied, assertive, dry, and bronze-colored.

Grenache is used as a blending variety in Châteauneuf-du-Pape, Gigondas, and Côtes du Rhône, the well-known reds of the Rhône. It also produces some full-bodied, fruity reds and stylish rosés in the Languedoc and Provence regions. It thrives in hot climates, and is found in many wine regions throughout the world, where it is blended into generic reds and rosés.

CHAPTER 8

Hot Off the Vine

In This Chapter

- How wine is made
- How winemakers adjust the taste
- Wine flaws you can spot

Unless you plan to read wine magazines or advanced books on wine, you really don't need to know how wine is made. But aren't you just a bit curious?

Do you imagine vineyard folk taking off their shoes, hiking up their pant legs or skirts, and climbing into a vat of grapes? If so, you'll be disappointed. Winemaking today is like any other modern manufacturing process—with clean environments and rigorous quality control.

Let's review: The three factors that interact to determine the character of a wine are 1) the grape variety and how it is grown, 2) the climate and soil in which it is grown, and 3) the vintner's (winemaker's) intent and expertise in making the wine.

In this chapter, you'll see the tricky relationship between the grape, the climate, and soil. And you'll learn a little of the humans who must deal with these.

Grapes Rule!

Each grape variety has its own exacting requirements. Once these are met, the trick lies in picking the grapes when they have developed the target level of sugar, acidity, and flavor for the type of wine being made.

As grapes head toward maturity, these three components undergo rapid change. In warm wine-growing regions, a big concern is the changing sugar/acidity ratio. The vintner wants good sugar without losing the necessary acidity. In the coolest winegrowing regions, the growers concern themselves with achieving the desired sugar and flavor ripeness. Too often, grapes grown in cool climates will ripen with inadequate sugar levels. Fortunately, this can be corrected. You'll see.

Grapes signal their ripeness by changes in composition, with sugar levels increasing and acidity falling when the grape is ready. A few varieties, such as Gewürztraminer and Sauvignon Blanc, are flavor-mature within a narrow range of sugar development. When picked too late or too early, the grapes lack their distinctive character. This can occur within a matter of hours, so the winemaker has to be very attentive!

Heard it Through the Grapevine

Even within the same vineyard, grapes may vary in maturity for many reasons. Differences in the direction of the slope in relation to the sun, soil type, depth, fertility, and water penetration are some factors. That's why vintners test their grapes in every part of the vineyard.

Winemakers use an instrument called a refractometer. With this handy gadget, the vintner walks through the vineyard and measures ripeness (degrees Brix); the sugar content of the grapes on the vine. Today's sugar is tomorrow's alcohol. The sugar is expressed in terms of degrees Brix, which may range from 17 to 25 degrees Brix for an average still wine (it's higher in dessert wines, like icewine or Sauternes), depending on desired outcome.

The grape cluster (bunch) consists of three parts, each of which contributes to the quality of the wine.

- Stems make up 2 to 6 percent of the cluster's weight. These are rich in wood tannins, but they also can leave the wines with a bitter flavor. For most wines, the stems are removed prior to fermentation, but they may be left in some wines to augment the tannins, adding complexity to the flavor.
- Skin represents about 5 to 16 percent of the grape's weight. When mature, the skin is covered with a bloom of wild yeasts that sometimes is used for fermentation. The skin and the layers just below it contain most of the aroma and flavor constituents of the grape. They also contain the grape tannins. In this case, there's a distinction between tannins: The ones found in the skin tend to be softer and less bitter than the ones in the stems and pits. Grape tannins are the essential element of red wines intended for aging.

- Pulp, which contains the juice in a fibrous membrane, makes most of the grape's weight. The juice consists of the ever-changing proportions of water, sugar, and acid. Within the pulp, the membrane responds to the changing needs of the juice. It gets filled or depleted as the grape vine responds to its environment.

The Sommelier Says

The sugar in the grape can drop drastically if it is needed to support the vine. It may end up being diluted if the vine receives too much moisture. This is where soil and climatic conditions are critical.

The pulp also contains a number of complex fruit acids that undergo chemical changes—along with glycerins, proteins, and other elements that may or may not be desired by the winemaker. In the end, the pulp presents the winemaker with a serious concern. All of it must be removed to get only clear, clean wine.

Thanks to advances in technology, grapes can be harvested and transported to the winery with a minimum of damage. Hand-picking still is practiced by the very best producers. Generally, giant machines resembling praying mantises work night and day in the vineyards to harvest grapes at their peak. (Not a bad idea for a sci-fi flick, actually; they really do look like giant insects!)

The machines sometimes work in tandem with portable crushers. The juice, crushed in the vineyard, is sent to the winery protected by an atmosphere of carbon dioxide to prevent premature fermentation and oxidation. Whichever way the grapes are harvested, the trick is to transport them to the winery as quickly as possible. Those quirky wine-bearers begin to deteriorate as soon as they leave the vine.

Artist, Scientist, Winemaker

The winemakers set to work as soon as they have the grapes in their hands. When the grapes are picked, they go into a crusher/de-stemmer, where the stems are removed. In the case of a white wine, the harvest goes directly into a wine press where the juice is extracted and the skins separated.

Heard it Through the Grapevine

Yeast enzymes react with the sugar, producing alcohol and carbon dioxide. The process may also yield minute quantities of certain organic compounds that may or may not be pleasing. That's why many modern vintners don't like to leave anything to chance.

Heard it Through the Grapevine

Modern winemaking techniques have engendered ways to soften the harsh tannins of red wine during the fermentation process. One method is performing malolactic fermentation—the process of changing harsher, lactic acid to softer, malic acid—entirely in new, French oak barrels, so that the wine isn't as overtly affected by the new wood (e.g., the leaching of more harsh tannic structure).

The vintners pump the juice into a tank or vat. There it ferments on its own wild yeasts. Or more likely, the winemaker will inoculate it with a selected yeast strain. That's because each yeast has particular characteristics of fermentation and flavors it leaves behind.

Prior to fermentation, the liquid in the vats is called must. After fermentation, the transformed juice has become wine. The winemaker stores the product in either casks or tanks. The last steps are clarification (to get rid of any residual particles or other matter), stabilization, and bottling. (Winemakers wish it were all that simple!)

Stems and Skins

The juice of most grapes is white, which is why we can make white wine even from red grapes. Red wine gets its color from the pigmentation of the skins during contact with the skins.

With most white wines, the must is separated from the skins immediately after crushing. However, the skins can add bitterness (not necessarily a bad thing!) or tannins to a white wine. Depending on the type of wine being made, the winemaker may allow some skin contact prior to fermentation.

For red wines, the skins remain with the juice and go with it into the fermentation vessel. During the fermentation process, both color and tannins are leached from the skins. Sometimes the winemaker will allow the stems to remain with the must. Some may even add a quantity of stems to the wine. This enhances the firmness and complexity of certain red wines.

Rosé wines remain with their skins just long enough to pick up the required tint. Then they're vinified in much the same way as white wines.

Heard it Through the Grapevine

The popularization of this in Bordeaux, however, has driven the price of barrels into the stratosphere. For producers who can't afford such finery for their ferments, other techniques such as micro-oxygenation—-a technique created in 1990 in which the harsh tannins of red wine are softened by injecting carefully controlled "micro" amounts of oxygen into the fermenting juice. The attribute is that this technique is a way of speeding up the natural aging process that occurs in (expensive!) barrels, as well as downplaying, if not getting rid of entirely, green, stemmy characteristics that can make a red wine seem harsh on the palate.

Fermentation: Take One

During fermentation, winemakers perform both as scientists and creative artists. (Actually, in the case of jug wines, the vintners basically are hands-off manufacturers.) But for distinctive, high-quality wines, they work rather like film directors, molding their characters and shooting their scenes until they have a full-scale artistic work. (Unfortunately, they don't get to re-take the bad scenes, which often make it to market.)

Tasting Tip

Dark-skinned grapes are used to make full-bodied Champagnes and the still (no bubbles) white table wines called Blanc de Noirs. The vintner can moderate the color by separating the must from the skins at first blush.

The skillful winemaker directs the wine, molds its structure, flavors, nuances, and character to correspond to some personal vision (or, it must be acknowledged, the vision of the desired consumer). The result: a vinous work of art. Maybe. The process of fermentation can be as fickle as a movie audience.

The vintner's greatest concern is a healthy fermentation. Certain yeasts are good for wine, while others can turn a wine straight into vinegar or leave it with some very unpleasant aromas and flavors. The idea is to create a vigorous population of the appropriate yeast before some alien yeast can take over.

Bordeaux vintners harvest some of their grapes early to develop a starter vat. Once that early fermentation is underway, they add the actual full harvest.

Heard it Through the Grapevine

Alcoholic fermentation is the reaction between yeast and sugar that creates alcohol and carbon dioxide. It's a complex chemical reaction involving numerous stages. In its simplest form, the chemical equation looks like this:

$C_6H_{12}O_6$	=	$2C_2H_5OH$	+	$2CO_2$	+	HEAT
natural		ethyl		carbon		
grape		alcohol		dioxide		
sugar		(ethanol)		(a gas)		

Tasting Tip

When ingredients are labeled in percentages, it's usually by weight. One exception is ethanol (the kind of alcohol in fermented beverages), which always is denoted by volume.

Once started, fermentation continues slowly, but soon picks up speed. As the yeast cells multiply, fermentation proceeds, usually until all the sugar is transformed into alcohol or until the vintner deliberately calls a halt. For most table wines, this means something between 11 and 14 percent alcohol by volume (or abv). Should the alcohol level reach 15 or 16 percent, fermentation will stop in any case. Few yeasts can survive in a high-alcohol environment.

The traditional fermentation vessel is a wooden vat or cement-lined tank. More and more common these days with modern vintners, however, use a temperature-controlled stainless steel tank. Stainless steel, of course, adds no flavor, and these tanks are easy to clean. Also, it's easy to equip these with cooling coils and a thermostatic temperature-controlled refrigeration unit to control the temperature of fermentation (and thus, the final product).

Climate Control

Fermentation temperature is an essential consideration. Each grape variety or strain of yeast reacts differently to various temperatures, affording a whole universe of winemaking possibilities. The winemaker's ability to control temperature to produce individual flavors, nuances of character, and harmony of structure is like having a magic wand. And the magic spell becomes the vintner's unique signature.

Temperature control seems to be a simple thing. It's not. Fermentations, you see, produce heat as a by-product of transforming sugar into alcohol. Too much heat can be a real problem. For example, higher temperatures cause fermentation to proceed at an irregular rate, often too rapidly. This can oxidize or break down certain flavor compounds, resulting in a baked flavor, or it can spur the growth of undesirable organisms.

Heard it Through the Grapevine

The rate and length of fermentation have a great influence on the fruity fragrance, or complexity, of a wine. At cooler temperatures, fermentation proceeds slowly, frequently over weeks. With white wines, this leisurely process retains the aromatic flavors of the grape and provides flowery, pleasing wines. It even enhances the flavor of wines made from the lesser grape varieties. In fact, cold fermentation has been responsible for the vast improvement in most American jug wines.

The range of fermentation temperatures for most white wines is between 45 and 55 degrees F. Reds generally ferment in the 55–75 degree range. The character of many red wines is determined by the rate of fermentation at specific stages of the process. This is regulated under the winemaker's meticulous control.

Since reds are fermented with both their skins and seeds, the mass of solids, called the cap, rises to the surface. To extract maximum flavors and tannins, as well as to allow for the release of heat, the cap must be broken from time to time. Winemakers do this in a number of ways:

- Pumping the must up over the cap
- Punching the cap down several times a day
- Adding a false top to force the cap into the must

During the growing season, the winemaker—however skilled and experienced—is a gambler. During the fermentation process, science replaces chance. In contemporary winemaking, winemakers act on knowledge, rather than on gut.

The vintner monitors the fermentation frequently by checking the sugar, alcohol, acid, and balance—both through tasting and laboratory analysis. Tasting is critical; no matter how advanced and elaborate the machinery, there's nothing that equals the knowledge and discrimination of human taste buds.

Many winemakers taste each of their wines at least once a day during crucial periods. That way, they can make any needed adjustments or corrections. Where needed, they can alter the process, applying new techniques to their quest for a balanced wine.

Microbes: Good, Bad, and Noble

Yeasts are minuscule, one-celled organisms (fungi, actually) that are entirely responsible for the fermentation process. They reproduce by growing buds that break off when they get large.

Without yeasts, we'd have grape juice instead of wine (and breakfast cereal instead of beer and whiskey). Yeasts produce enzymes that convert sugars into ethanol (the kind of alcohol in wine) and carbon dioxide. When their work is complete, voilà! Vino!

Yeasts, generally, are friendly microbes (as are most bacteria). In fact, without microbes, life as we know it couldn't exist. Microbes are natures little chemical factories that perform countless specialized tasks in the chain of life and death on this planet.

Certain microorganisms, which may come along with the grape itself or be present in the wine casks, can survive both the fermentation process with its development of alcohol. (Some bacteria even survive at the bottom on the seas where hot sulfuric acid is vented from the earth.) Two bacteria we are concerned about here are Acetobacter xylinium and Lactobacillus.

Acetobacter xylinium always is present in small amounts in fermenting wines. It produces small, though acceptable, levels of acetic acid (vinegar). This reacts with the alcohol to make ethyl acetate, which smells a little like nail polish remover. But as long as these exist in very small quantities, these compounds actually add to the complexity of a wine.

Now add a little oxygen, and these bacteria become a real threat. Acetobacter xylinium thrives on fermented wine, and in the presence of oxygen, quickly turns the wine into vinegar by converting its alcohol into acetic acid. Winemakers have to stay on their toes to prevent air and Acetobacter from becoming an evil wrestling tag team determined to ruin their product.

The Sommelier Says

Certain bacteria can cause the wine to undergo a second (or malolactic) fermentation. This can be good or bad, depending on the type of wine being made (see Fermentation: Take Two). In many cases, vintners must be on the lookout for this microbial actor.

Lactobacillus is the most common variety of lactic acid bacteria, and it's essentially harmless. During fermentation, it produces by-products that add to the complexity of the wine. But occasionally, Lactobacilli run out of control, producing the peculiarly pungent and offensive odor of geraniums that can be corrected only by stripping the wine of all its flavors.

Not Too Sweet!

Many styles of wine require that some of the grape's natural sugar remain unfermented. Among these are the low alcohol, sweet, late harvest wines for which Germany is renowned. So sometimes, vintners must arrest the action of yeast once the desired level of alcohol or sweetness is achieved.

One way to accomplish this is by chilling the fermenting must and removing the yeast cells by filtering. In the case of fortified sweet wines, the winemaker adds alcohol to the fermenting wine. This extra alcohol kills the yeast, and fermentation stops.

Many styles of white wines retain a slight sweetness, usually around 2 percent. Chilling will not always give the winemaker enough control over the balance needed for these wines. A modern technique is to ferment the wine completely. Then the vintner adds a small amount of the grape juice, which has been set aside to sweeten the wine. The sweetness of the resulting wine can be adjusted with great precision, and makes it easy for the winemaker to stabilize the wine to prevent it from refermenting in the bottle.

This technique is known as sweet reserve or sweet must. It's widely used in the U.S. and Germany, where fine, well-balanced, fragrant, slightly sweet table wines can be a favored commodity.

Fermentation: Take Two

Sometimes it's desirable to put wine through a second fermentation, using bacteria, rather than yeast. Malolactic fermentation transforms the wine's malic acid, which tastes hard and biting, into the softer, less acid-tasting lactic acid. The transformation takes place with only a slight decrease in the actual measured acidity of the wine.

This second fermentation also produces certain by-products that may or may not be desirable for a particular kind of wine. It's up to the winemaker to decide whether to encourage or prevent malolactic fermentation.

With most whites, this process is decidedly undesirable. It reduces the wine's sense of crisp freshness. One notable exception is Chardonnay. When Chardonnay undergoes a malolactic fermentation, it produces diacetyl compounds, the major flavor components of butter. As a result, the wine develops a buttery complexity, which marries well with the flavors of the Chardonnay grape.

For noble reds like Cabernet Sauvignon and Pinot Noir, the malolactic fermentation is favored to soften the acid taste. It also enhances the wine by adding considerable complexity, flavor nuances, and suppleness.

Heard it Through the Grapevine

Some wines may undergo a spontaneous second fermentation when temperatures warm up in the spring after the harvest. Winemakers can choose to let this happen naturally by leaving the wine in barrels or tanks that will warm with the weather. Or they can induce it by introducing a malolactic strain of bacteria.

The vintner must take scrupulous care that malolactic fermentation is complete before bottling. Red wines cannot be preserved the same ways many simpler wines can. These reds are particularly susceptible to problems that can develop later in the bottle. A malolactic fermentation that continues after the wine is bottled causes the wine to become fizzy, with stinky flavors that will not dissipate after the wine is poured. Baaaaad bottle!

Racking

The fermentation is done, and it's time to clarify the wine. Vintners use gravity in a process we call racking. This traditional method is still the best one for fine wines.

To rack, the winemaker puts the wine into small casks to allow the suspended solids to settle. Then the clear wine or juice is pumped or siphoned from the lees (sediment—old yeast, grape skins and solids, and potassium bitartrate) and into a clean, fresh tank or cask.

The racking schedule is frequent within the first year, often five times or more. It requires considerable labor and includes cleaning the previous casks. It's sort of like those hourly feeding schedules for newborns. A lot of loving care goes into making a noble wine!

The Sommelier Says

Frequent rackings aerate the wine, ridding it of natural by-products of winemaking such as foul-smelling hydrogen sulfide that can impair its healthy development. But racking must be done with extreme caution. Excessive contact with air, and you're left with a cask of noble vinegar!

Wine Ailments You Can Taste in the Glass: A Closer Look

Winemaking is fraught with potential disaster, either from the microbes that float in the air looking for wine to ruin or from less-than-perfect care in the winery. Here are some of the wine ailments that can affect the wine you buy. When you spot these, return wine to the store where you bought it or reject such wine served in a restaurant.

Pediococcus

This is a peculiarly pungent strain of bacterium. It gives your wine the ripe smell of sweaty socks. Under no circumstances should your wine have the aroma of your gym bag or any of its contents!

Sulfur Compounds

One natural by-product that must be removed from wine is hydrogen sulfide. This gives off the smell of rotten eggs. Hydrogen sulfide occurs naturally during yeast fermentation (more or less, depending on the strain of yeast) and usually is dissipated early in the clarifying process. If not, you'll know it immediately.

Vintners use sulfur dioxide, a pungent gas, as a preservative. Used properly, it's very effective and leaves nothing behind to interfere with your pleasure. But too heavy a dose of this can. If your wine smells or tastes like a newly struck match, you've got a bad bottle.

Mercaptan

If hydrogen sulfide is left in the cask or tank during fermentation, it rapidly combines with the alcohol to form ethyl mercaptan. Mercaptan is the most odorous of all chemicals, similar to the stuff they put in natural gas to alert you to leaks.

Its odors range from onions to children's clay to garlic to skunk! Once it has completely bound with the alcohol, there is no getting it out. Careful winemakers make sure that all the hydrogen sulfide has been aired out of the wine. Still, the mercaptan odors do occur—a mark of sloppy winemaking.

Dekkara

Dekkara is a bacteria that creates the aroma and taste of rancid corn chips. If you don't see a pile of stale Fritos on the table, chances are your wine's been infected.

Corkiness

Corked wines have the scent of a mold that likes to grow on wine corks. (I can't say I blame the mold for its choice of habitat, but it's not something that enhances the wine's appeal.) This makes your wine smell and taste moldy—kind of like old, wet cardboard or newspapers that got caught in a flood in your basement. Yuck. Even the most costly wines may succumb to this blight.

Old-World Charm

The traditional Old-World winery may lack modern equipment, such as stainless steel fermentation tanks, filtration, centrifuge, and sterile bottling. All these are important innovations, essential to modern viniculture (winemaking).

Some of the world's finest wines still are produced the old-fashioned way. The trend over the last decade, especially in California, South America, parts of Spain, and increasingly even in Bordeaux and elsewhere, is to invest in modern equipment to avoid the pitfalls of the traditional winery. Still, the trend these days among many young-gun winemakers is finding the happy medium between both worlds—using more back-to-basics techniques combined with modern controls to keep good juice from going bad.

Heard it Through the Grapevine

When white wine is made by the traditional method, the grapes, either white or red, are crushed and destemmed and pumped directly into the wine press. The wine is pressed quickly to prevent it from picking up color or tannins from the skins. Following pressing, the wine may settle or be pumped directly into fermentation tanks.

Some wines are aged in oak following fermentation; some are not. Most wines are clarified (solid particles removed) with egg white. Following clarification, the wine may be pumped into a "cold room" or into refrigeration tanks to precipitate any tartrate crystals. This allows for removal of these tiny little crystals that can cause cloudiness in a wine before the wine enters the bottle. However, some traditional wineries leave out this step, which explains why some wines' bottles may have these crystals in the bottle and on the cork.

Traditionally, red wine grapes pass through a crusher/destemmer and are pumped into wooden or concrete vats (cuves). There, the wine ferments with its skins, pulp, pits, and (sometimes) stems. Following fermentation, the free-run juice is removed for the best wine. (The wine that flows freely, without heavy pressure from the wine press, is called free-run juice.) It is the cleanest and usually most distinctive wine.

Red wines are aged in small oak barrels or in larger upright casks. The aged wine is clarified by fining, usually with egg white. After clarification, the wine is bottled. Occasionally, bottling is still done by hand, although rarely in the U.S.

Once the first fermentation is complete, the wine is drawn off the lees (solids in the bottom of the barrel) and placed in tanks or large casks. This allows the remaining solids suspended in the wine to settle.

For wines fermented on their skins, the remaining juicy pulp is pressed, leaving behind a cake-like mass of solids called pomace. This wine is called press wine. It varies from light press to heavy press depending on the pressure exerted.

Often, each press batch is handled and aged separately. Later on, it may be combined with another wine in some proportion. Or not.

Tasting Tip

Frequently, the wine is separated into different vats as the pressing proceeds. The heavier the press, the darker the color, the fuller and coarser the flavor, and the more bitter and tannic the wine will be.

High-Tech

The modern winery uses advanced technology that make for better control of the winemaking process. These actually give the winemaker more artistic control over the winemaking process, resulting in a product closer to the vintner's vision.

White wine grapes are brought to the winery in gondolas or special tank trucks blanketed with inert carbon dioxide or nitrogen gases to prevent oxidation. Machines may do the harvesting and field crushing. The grapes are crushed in a special horizontal press—gently, to avoid harsh tannins.

Prior to fermentation, the winemaker may use a centrifuge (see The Centrifuge, below) to remove solid matter from the juice. Or, perhaps, after fermentation. Or both. As you remember, these wines will be cold-fermented to preserve their freshness and fruitiness. Some may be aged in wooden casks, large or small.

If the fermented wine has not been centrifuged, it will be filtered. Then it will be cold-stabilized to precipitate and remove those little tartrate crystals. Finally, the vintner bottles the wine on a sterile line to prevent air and other contaminants from entering the bottle.

The modern vintner pumps red wine's crushed grapes into concrete or stainless steel fermentation vats. Ordinary, or everyday, wines may be heated first to extract color and flavor rapidly without tannin. Next the wine is aged in small or large wooden casks. The desired quality of the wine determines the type of cask: new oak for most super-premium or noble wines; used oak or redwood for lesser wines; or even oak chips, staves, or no wood for everyday wines.

The Centrifuge

Some vintners call the centrifuge, "God's gift to the winemaker." Those who have one swear by it. Most of those who do not, swear at their bad luck. But there are a few odd ones who believe centrifuges strip their wine of its flavor.

The centrifuge is a little like a giant Cuisinart. This nifty device has a vast and varied usefulness in the winemaking process. How's it work? It whirls the wine at high speed, using centrifugal forces to separate heavier components from lighter ones. Unwanted items like yeast cells, pulp, dirt, and dust are discarded, leaving behind a clear, clean liquid.

Heard it Through the Grapevine

Many winemakers find that the centrifuged juice ferments more easily and produces a cleaner wine than batches not so cleaned. That's why they use the centrifuge to clean white wine must before fermentation. Both white and simple reds may be centrifuged instead of racking or filtering.

Wines with certain off-flavors may receive a heavy centrifuging. (Sounds like a punishment, doesn't it?) This can strip them of all character, but salvage an otherwise unusable wine. For jug wines, subtle character isn't a consideration. The centrifuge is widely used to clean jug-quality wines prior to bottling.

Chaptalization

Chaptalization is the addition of beet or cane sugar to the fermenting wine. This type of "cheating" compensates for the insufficiently ripe grapes from a cool vintage. It increases both body and alcohol level, enabling the wine to meet quality standards.

There are legal standards, national and regional, that limit the amount of sugar vintners may add. (Few winemakers, of course, would choose to go sky-high on sweetness.) Chaptalization is permitted in France, Germany, and most other European countries (Italy is one exception) in certain, designated regions where ripening can be an issue. And it's allowed in the winemaking states of the U.S., except for California (where it isn't needed anyway).

Vino Vocab

No, chaptalization was not named for some Chaptal region in France! It was named after Jean-Antoine Chaptal, the French Minister of Agriculture who invented the process.

When used to increase the alcohol level of a wine by a small amount, say one percent, and applied carefully, the process is virtually undetectable to even the most discerning wine expert. The amount of sugar needed is meticulously computed. No guessing!

Some purists decry the process, claiming it affects the quality of the wine. But I'd bet they've drunk chaptalized wine themselves, blissfully ignorant. Only when the process is ineptly applied or used to excess is the character of the wine adversely affected.

With excess chaptalization (although within legal limits), wine can become alcohol-unbalanced, tasting hot and harsh. Also, such wines will taste thin, or diluted in flavor or character. However, this is unusual. The vast majority of winemakers value their product and reputation too highly to abuse their technology.

PART THREE

Bottle of Red; Bottle of White

CHAPTER 9

C'est Magnifique

In This Chapter

- Understanding French wine laws
- Regions of origin
- Are French wines better?

Before Louis XIV, before Joan of Arc, before Charlemagne, even France was a wine country. When the seafaring Greeks founded Marseilles, France's oldest city (around 600 B.C.E.) they brought wine. When Julius Caesar took over in 49 B.C.E., Romans diffused knowledge of wine throughout Gaul. And France has been a big-time wine producer ever since.

Wine was most important to the ancient world. Until modern times, very little water was safe to drink. And people had to drink something, right?

Those ancient wines had little in common with those we enjoy today. But after centuries of practice, the French have made winemaking into an art. French wine knowledge became their gift to the whole world. In this chapter, we'll explore France and its venerable winemaking culture.

Regulations and More Regulations

The French seem to regulate everything: their language, distribution of safety matches, even names new parents may choose for their children! In the case of wine, though, this is a good thing.

French wine laws ensure that what's printed on the label is clear, correct, and informative. Taken individually, these wine regulations are simple and logical. But when they appear in one place—as on a wine label, they can be intimidating. Especially, in the case of France's very finest wines. So I'd like to give you some essential background knowledge.

What Are Appellations?

The French system of identifying and regulating wine regions is known as the Appellation d'Origine Contrôlée (AOC or AC), translated simply as "regulated place name." Most French wines are named for places, not grapes.

Here's where things get messy. Each wine district has its own organization for enforcing the Appellation Contrôlée regulations that are specific to that region. These controlling bodies determine and implement criteria that may vary from place to place. These systems guarantee minimum quality levels. They also provide classification schemes that denominate the various quality levels.

French culture is very conscious of hierarchical standing. This is true particularly in the case of French wines. Under French laws, a wine can aspire to one of four status levels. One of these must appear on the label:

- Appellation d'Origine Contrôlée (or AOC). The highest tier. Most labels give the actual place name in place of "d'Origine." For example: Appellation Bordeaux Contrôlée indicates a wine from the Bordeaux region. These wines range from mid-premium to noble in quality.
- Vins Délimités de Qualité Supérieure (VDQS), the second highest level, translates as "demarcated wine of superior quality." These wines range from average to to premium in quality.
- Vins de Pays means, literally, "country wine." On the label, you'll see this written with a place name. But this place will encompass a much larger area than the places named in the two higher grades. These wines resemble the jug and magnum wines you might find from California, Chile, or Italy—simple-premium wines.
- Finally, we have Vins de Table, or ordinary table wine. These wines are not allowed to list a region, vintage, or a grape on their labels. Wines of this quality rarely come into the United States. In France, these are sold in plastic bottles. At best, they are jug quality, sometimes not even.

VDQS wines, despite the "superior quality" designation, are relatively ordinary, though some display extra flavor and distinction. You will see some of these in your wine shop. However, the most French wines consumed in the U.S. are AOC wines. And when we select from this top level, we find it's broken down into its own hierarchy of quality. (Just when you thought you understood it all!)

Heard it Through the Grapevine

Until recently, few of the wines from the two lower classifications were sold in the U.S. Now, however, wines labeled "Vins de Pays D'Oc" (or some other region) have become far more widely distributed as some wine regions now make fine varietal and blended wines, above their traditional quality level. Oftentimes, a Vins de Pays wine you might find here in the U.S. will be the product of a creative, forward-thinking winemaker who, for example, wishes to use a grape varietal not designated with the AOC region.

This is an example of the continuing progress made in French winemaking. Many French winemakers provide good value and pleasing, flavorful wines at this level.

Many French wines are named for the places they come from in France

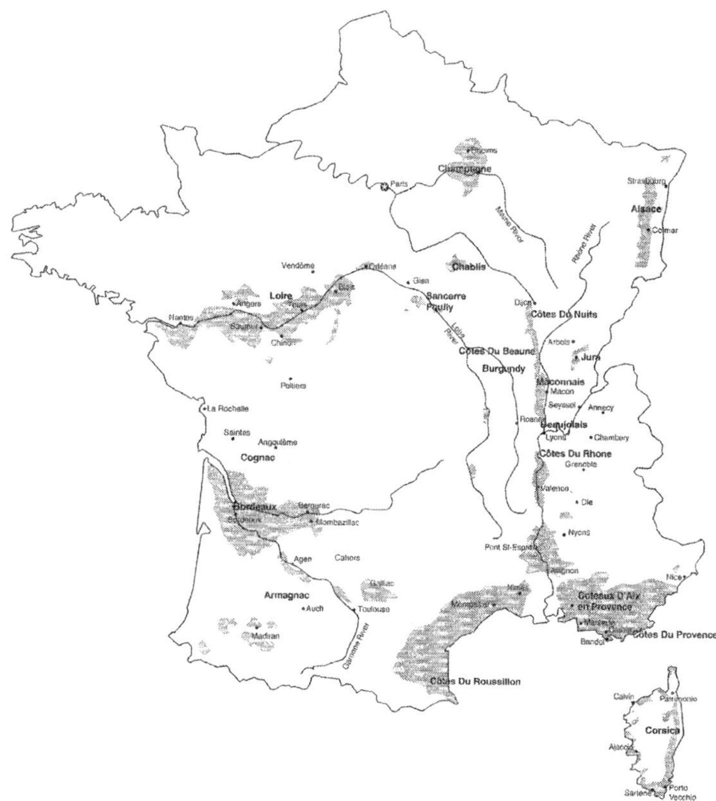

At the bottom of the AOC ladder we have a category that refers only to the broadest regions whose wines meet certain standards. Moving upwards, the designations get tighter in geography and higher in quality. At the very top, some of the greatest vineyards have their own appellation.

You can think of these classifications as concentric circles, with the smallest denoting the best. Let's begin with the largest circle and work inward (and upwards):

- An entire region, say Bordeaux or Burgundy, average to premium quality. The label will designate, simply, Bordeaux, Bordeaux Supérieur, or other.
- A district within a region, such as Haut-Médoc or Côte de Beaune. Somewhat higher in quality, but still ranging from average to premium, with a few better wines. Within this tier may be sub-districts that produce somewhat better wine, e.g., Côte de Beaune Villages, Beaujolais Villages.
- A village or commune within a district; Pauillac or Meursault, for example. These wines may be considerably better than those of the previous appellation, depending on the producer. When wines are blended from several vineyards within the commune or district, they are known as Regional or Village wines, depending on the custom of the locality. These wines range from mid- to super-premium quality and noble.
- A single vineyard, such as Le Montrachet. In Burgundy and (rarely) other districts, a wine of extraordinary distinction and fame is honored with its own appellation. These wines are designated as a Grand Cru and are the equivalent of a First Growth (Premier Cru Classé) of Bordeaux.

Tasting Tip

Within a village or commune appellation, some wines can be much better than others. (You really need to know the château or vineyard names.) In Bordeaux, a number of the commune wines are classified as growths or Cru Classé, which are immediate indicators of, respectively, higher or highest quality. Some of these wines are equal to those designated by vineyard.

There's more to French wine regulation than appellations. Much more. For instance, the government stipulates the quantity of grapes that can be produced in any hectare (about 2.5

acres) in each AOC district. And there are several specific quality regulations as well, such as the designation of crus (growths). As the wines go up the quality tier, these regulations grow more stringent.

In many AOC regions, the wine actually has to pass a government tasting test in order to get its AOC designation for that vintage. Sometimes a vineyard making wine from a higher classification will allow some of its wine to be labeled under a broader designation. For instance, wine from younger plantings may be declassified and sold under a second label or in bulk to a négociant or éleveur (see Chapter 5, Terms of the Taste and Trade) to be used in their blends.

Heard it Through the Grapevine

French labeling requires little more than the correct appellation. To assess the quality of wine by its appellation alone, you'll need to do some homework. In general, the more specific the appellation, the costlier the contents. But cost, alone, does not assure quality.

But do look for the word "Cru" on the label. Within certain appellations, wines classified into Crus have legal standing. The Cru designation can assure you the quality of the wine is quite high.

Yes, the French wine label looks fairly simple. And what you've learned so far can help you shop for quality or value. Up to a point. You still need some more specific knowledge of French wines to know better what's in that bottle.

Does Français Mean Supérieur?

Before the 1960s, wine lovers considered French wines de rigueur. Simply, they were the only wines one drank! With those legendary vineyards and all, everybody knew the best wines came from France. End of story.

California wine? Oh, yeah—before the 60s, jugs of plonk (cheap wine) with the name of a huge producer on them! Italian wine? Cheap bottles of thin and acidic Chiantis where you threw away the wine to use the bottle as a candle-holder. Spain? Well, Franco did his own damage that the country only seems to be just recovering from. And South Africa? Unless you lived there, most of us hadn't sampled a single one before the early 1990s.

But change is something that happens, like it or not—and in the case of wine, there is much to like. Think about the '60s—things happened, like Kennedy, the Beatles, Woodstock—and new attitudes toward wine gurgled to the surface. Politics aside, scientific winemaking with modern equipment put many countries on the wine map. The U.S. and Italy, for instance, began to produce wines that rivaled the best French vintages. And bear in mind, the lesser French wines never were much better than those from other countries.

Tasting Tip

So why buy French wines? For one thing, France offers a very wide variety among its very best wines, far and beyond the famed Bordeaux and Burgundy. For another, many of these wines are unique, found nowhere else. Finally, when you go shopping for fine wines, France offers many excellent bargains, from the Loire Valley to Languedoc, and all applaud-worthy appellations in between.

As you gain confidence in your skills as a wine enthusiast, you'll do your own taste comparisons. You'll answer for yourself whether French wines really are the best of their kind. Never forget, the most important opinion is your own.

CHAPTER 10

Bordeaux – Le Roi de Vin

In This Chapter

- The appellations and communes of Bordeaux
- The Médoc
- St. Emilion and Pomerol
- Sauternes
- Bordeaux values
- When to drink Bordeaux

The Bordeaux wine region is named for the Atlantic seacoast city (With a population of about 213,000, it is the ninth largest city in Ma Mere) in southwestern France. The Bordeaux winegrowing districts lie on slopes near the seacoast, through the valleys of the Garonne and Dordogne rivers, and along the Gironde estuary these rivers flow into. It is by far the largest and most prolific producer of famous and high-quality wines. Bordeaux, itself, is a major commercial port. Many top wine brokers and shippers maintain their offices along the port's Quai de Chartrons.

In this chapter, we'll tour this renowned wine region. Bordeaux is the stuff of legends—home to such famous names as Château Lafite-Rothschild, Château Latour, and Châteaux Margaux. Not all the region's exports are in this rarefied category (fortunately for most of us). Bordeaux winemakers are known also for many high-quality, enjoyable, and affordable wines.

With its appellations, communes (jurisdictions) and crus (growths), it's easy to get a bit lost in Bordeaux. This chapter will unravel the mysteries of the region we call "the King of Wine."

We'll cover the inner appellations and vineyards that make up Bordeaux, and the different wines, grapes (they're not all Cabernet Sauvignon), and price tags.

The wine regions of Bordeaux have districts within districts as the wines get better.

A Legend is Born

In the Bordeaux region, several hundred châteaux (vineyards) produce the outstanding wines that have made Bordeaux a legend. They send their liquid treasures to brokers and shippers in Bordeaux.

A few names—Château Lafite-Rothschild, Château Mouton-Rothschild, Château Latour, and Château Margaux—have come to mean "superlative wine" throughout the world. These names have endowed Bordeaux with a certain mystique. But let's not get carried away. The region also makes prodigious quantities of ordinary wines for local consumption. But far fewer of these lesser wines ever appear on our shelves or tables; so the Bordeaux legend remains intact.

Heard it Through the Grapevine

Of the 3.5 billion bottles of wine produced annually in France, Bordeaux produces 850 million of them, and an astounding 25 percent of all AOC wine. Most Bordeaux wines are dry reds. About 11 percent are dry white wines, and 2 percent are sweet white wines, most notably the Sauternes.

Bordeaux wines range in price from cheap to outrageous. Some noble wines from great vintages have sold for thousands or dollars. But don't worry: You needn't be Donald Trump to enjoy a fine Bordeaux! Many good-quality Bordeaux, both red and white, begin at about $15 a bottle when they are young.

Many of the Bordeaux you will hear about are super-premium or noble quality. These are the wines vintners aspire to imitate. When they are young, the typical Bordeaux classified growth will have a deep ruby hue with aromas of black currants, spice, cedar, fine leather, chocolate, and cassis.

For the first five to 10 years, these finest wines can be very vinous and austere, with puckering tannins. As they age, their colors change to garnet, with a gem-like brilliance. These will develop an extraordinarily complex bouquet and flavor with more agreeable tannins. On rare occasions, the very best will develop an unusual scent that is almost devoid of flavor, like the air after a rainstorm. The subtle nuances of bouquet will be delicate and beautiful. I call this marvelous quality "vaporous."

Tasting Tip

The greatest Bordeaux châteaux develop wines of power, yet that exhibit the softest nuances of flavor, like the piccolo coming through the orchestral tutti at the end of Beethoven Fifth. The very best also develop an extraordinary refinement, one we have described as finesse and breed.

The greatest classified red Bordeaux wines may take 20 years or more to reach maturity. (Some even continue to improve after 50 years in the bottle!) As you may expect, the greatest of these wines, from extraordinary vintages, command a king's ransom. In 1985, a bottle of 1797 Château Lafite-Rothschild alleged to have belonged to Thomas Jefferson sold at auction for more than $150,000, although during the last decade of economic recession, Bordeaux prices and exports have dropped considerably.

The Best Come from Médoc

The Médoc is a district—our second tier of wine quality within the larger AOC of Bordeaux. The most famous—and definitely the best—red-wine vineyards of the Bordeaux district lie within the Médoc, north of the city along the Gironde estuary.

The best vineyards are situated along a narrow strip of gravely soil, about 10 miles long and no more than seven miles wide. In this small area, extraordinary conditions of climate and soil meet centuries of winemaking tradition and dedication. Here thrives the noble Cabernet Sauvignon grape.

The wines of the four major communes of Médoc have distinct characteristics and subtle nuances, described in Table 10.1, as do the red wines of Graves, a district to the south, known also for its high-quality wines.

Table 10.1 The Four Major Communes of Médoc and Graves

Commune Example	Distinct	Characteristics
Margaux	Château Lascombes	Moderately tannic; medium-bodied; fragrant, perfumed aromas; complex, generous, elegant, and long-lived.
St.-Julien	Château Léoville-Poyferré	Softer tannins; rich, flavorful; medium/full-bodied; sometimes fruity; earlier maturing; elegance and finesse.
Pauillac	Château Lafite-Rothschild	Firm tannins; rich, powerful,yet with delicate nuances of flavor; firm backbone; full-bodied; extraordinary finesse and elegance (First Growths) black currants and cedar aromas; extremely long-lived.
St.-Estèphe	Château Cos d'Estournel	Tannic hard, firm; full-bodied earthy and vinous; rarely elegant but pleasingly masculine; slow to mature.
Graves	Château Haut-Brion	Moderately tannic; vinous with (ironically) a gravely mouthfeel; earthy; early to mature.

The 1855 Overture

I'll bet you're still wondering about that word "Cru" on the label! I think I can help out, but you have to indulge me as I give a brief history lesson. We need to go back to 1855, the year of Napoléon III's Exposition Universelle de Paris. France was about to put itself on display for the whole world. And Bordeaux wines would be featured. (Mais naturellement!)

So the organizers of this exposition asked the Gironde Chamber of Commerce to create a classification of the region's wines to accompany their display. The Chamber assigned the job to the wine brokers of Bordeaux, who selected 61 superior red wines, dividing them into five categories or crus (the cru, or growth, refers to the wine estate), based on price.

Price? Well, in those days, price really was a sound indicator of quality. While the classification was supposed to be limited to the districts of the Médoc, one wine of the Graves, Château Haut-Brion, also was listed because of its excellence and fame.

Heard it Through the Grapevine

If you are confused about our four tiers and the crus of the top one, you are not alone. A cru is a separate classification within an appellation or district in our quality-ranking system. Some appellations have classifications; others not so worthy do not.

Actually, some less deserving appellations do have their own classifications now. It's very political and confusing. But all you need to know is that crus are classifications within a district in Bordeaux. Thus a classified wine has both an appellation and a designation that reflects that fact that within a particular district some wines are better than others.

Here's what's amazing: In the nearly 160 years since that 1855 Classification of the Médoc, they have made only one change! A decree of June 21, 1973, upgraded Chateau Mouton-Rothschild from deuxieme (second) cru to premier (first). Table 10.2 shows the chateaux of the first and second crus.

Table 10.2 The First Two Growths of Bordeaux

Château	**Commune**
First Growths	
Château Lafite-Rothschild	Pauillac
Château Latour	Pauillac
Château Margaux	Margaux
Château Haut-Brion	Graves (Pessac)
Château Mouton-Rothschild*	Pauillac
Second Growths	
Château Rausan-Ségla	Margaux
Château Rauzan-Gassies	Margaux
Château Léoville-Las Cases	St.-Julien
Château Léoville-Poyferré	St.-Julien
Château Léoville-Barton	St.-Julien
Château Durfort-Vivens	Margaux
Château Lascombes	Margaux
Château Gruaud-Larose	St.-Julien
Château Brane-Cantenac	Margaux
Château Pichon-Longueville Baron	Pauillac
Château Pichon-Lalande	Pauillac
Château Ducru-Beaucaillou	St.-Julien
Château Cos d'Estournel	St.-Estèphe
Château Montrose	St.-Estèphe

*** Elevated from Second Growth in 1973**

For a listing of the 3rd, 4th, and 5th crus, see Appendix A.

The 61 ranked wines also are known as Grands Crus Classés. While some vineyards have deteriorated or been incorporated into others, these rankings seem firmly set in stone, with only one growth, Château Mouton-Rothschild, ever changing its status. Today there are rumblings about this rigidity as several château have upgraded through big-dollar investments both in winery and vineyard. Now they are politicking for elevation to a higher status.

As you may expect, there is considerable controversy over the 1855 classification. Many lesser classified growths feel worthy of promotion. To understand fully the honor of being one of the 61, remember, even in 1855, there were thousands of wine producers in Bordeaux.

Also, you've noticed that with the exception of Château Haut-Brion, all of the wines listed are from the Médoc. Château Haut-Brion was included because in 1855 it was considered one of the finest wines of Bordeaux (as well as one of the most expensive). No one dared ignore it.

Only two regions were classified in 1855: the Médoc and Sauternes (a sweet wine area in southern Graves). Over the years, other Bordeaux regions, such as St.-Emilion and Pomerol, have been classified. But with the exception of Château Pétrus and a few others, none measures up to the first growths of the 1855 Médoc classification.

Saint-Emilion and Pomerol

The districts of Saint-Emilion and Pomerol lie to the east of the city of Bordeaux. Tiny, picturesque Saint-Emilion has many cafés that look out over the vineyards, but if you travel there you might be shocked that the hilly, stone-street town itself is inhabited by only a few hundred residents. It's amazing that so much phenomenal wine can come from such a small spot! But it's the surrounding vineyards, not the town of St.-Emillion itself, in which all that delicious juice lies. There, you can sip your wine and watch it grow at the same time.

Thousands of small châteaux cover the district, although only a few enjoy the best soils and microclimates for producing great wines. St. Emilion produces many fine wines from a variety of conditions that differ from those of the Médoc and Graves. The district does have its classified first growths now. However, with few exceptions (La Mondotte and Valandraud among them), these first growths do not measure up to the first growths of the 1855 Médoc classification. I count at least 40 excellent estates here.

In the Pomerol district, several estates rival those of the 1855 Médoc classification, and

Tasting Tip

Smaller and lesser known, Pomerol has gained recognition from wine connoisseurs over the past three decades. Rightly so, as its best wine, Chateau Pétrus, commands the highest price in Bordeaux, and with up-and-comers like Le Pin and L'église Clinet turning heads.

many others produce very fine wines. The soil here contains large amounts of clay in which Merlot grapes grow merrily. This gives the wines of Pomerol a distinct character from their Cabernet Sauvignon-producing neighbors.

Graves

The district of Graves, located along the southern limits of the city of Bordeaux, gets its name from its gravely soil. (I'm not making this up!) I find it interesting that the wines of this district also seem to present a gravely, stony sense on my palate.

Graves produces both red and white wines, but it's most renowned for its fine whites from the sandy soils to the south in this appellation. Dry and sweet wines are divided pretty much into north and south parts, respectively. Northern Graves, specifically the district of Pessac-Léognan, an AC that was created only in 1987, is home to some of the world's most prestigious dry white wines. The best dry white Graves are refreshing, crisp, and delightful when young. With age they become mellow, developing complexity and richness.

The Sommelier Says

Despite its offering some of the world's greatest white wines, Graves still ships a quantity of mediocre, overly sulfured product. You have to be careful when buying white wines from this district, choosing only from those producers who make the better wines. Still, modern winemaking techniques, like use of stainless steel tanks for fermentation, has upped the ante considerably on the general quality of vin from this spot.

Heard it Through the Grapevine

The principle white-wine grape varieties of Graves are Sauvignon Blanc and Semillon. As a blend, they are well matched. The Sauvignon Blanc grape offers immediate flavor, charm, and great acidity, while the Semillon adds body, softness, and depth to the wine.

Sauternes—Sweet and Noble Rot

Within the larger district south of Bordeaux are the Sauternes and Barsac districts. (Yes, there are district within districts!) These produce sweet wines, mostly—thanks to a particular micro-climate and a family of fungi that thrives in it.

Fungi of the genus Botrytis are responsible for much disease in vegetables and fruits. But on the skins of grapes, under loving attention and control, they create wonders—what vintners call "the noble rot." And nowhere is this rot nobler (nor more prolific) than in the Sauternes and Barsac districts of Graves on the western bank of the Gironde!

The best Sauternes wines owe their unique and luscious flavor to Botrytis—and to the labor of vineyard workers who hand-pick the grapes. Grape by grape! Each berry is selected and harvested by hand, ensuring that only the fully mature berries be chosen. At the best châteaux, a vineyard may be harvested ten times or more.

This is one reason why the best Sauternes—like its most famous, Château d'Yquem—are so expensive. And (you've heard it from me before) this is where it pays to know your vineyards. Some properties are more meticulous and obsessive with these procedures than others. The most outstanding (and expensive) Sauternes are produced by only a few in the district. Still, Sauternes wines are never produced in sub-par vintages, and have very strict controls over the yields and production methods. The top chateaux will sell off their lesser wine rather than try to make a silk purse from a sow's ear!

Cru Bourgeois: Pleasant and Cheap

If you're looking for a good buy in a Bordeaux wine, here's a tip: Stay away from the classified crus. Even with the economic down-turn of the early 21st century, demand for these has driven their prices high, sometimes out-of-sight high. Believe me, you don't need a wine from the 1855 classification to enjoy Bordeaux. In fact, you can drink the non-classified wines, and even the second labels of fabled producers, long before you can their classified cousins and at an nth of the price. And often they're nearly as good.

Tasting Tip

There are several red and white Bordeaux called "petits châteaux" that have no formal classification. Selling for $10 or less, these are light-bodied wines that you can enjoy immediately. They're perfectly fine for any informal dinner at home.

There is a newer classification just below that of 1855. This is the Cru Bourgeois, with roughly 400 red wines to choose among. Cru Bourgeouis was introduced to recognize more of Bourdeaux's high-quality chateaux that weren't among the 1855 classification. The designation was created in 1932 with around 400-plus estates, but after that things got a little sticky. The classification updated in 1978, and then a new three-tier Cru Bourgeois system was further demarked to create a tiny little hierarchical system within the classification in the early aughts. This, it seems, didn't sit well with the powers that be (e.g., the French government), who tossed the tiers in the trash. By 2010, a newer version of the classification was re-introduced—and back to the original single-tier Cru Bourgeois designation. Such drama!

Generally, these sell for less than $30 (sometimes less than $20!), and several can be comparable to or even better than the lower-end classified growths!

To Cellar or to Sip?

Think about it: You might have to wait a lifetime to drink a Premier Cru, unless you pay a fortune for an aged bottle (or you have very, very generous and wealthy friends!). But many fine Bordeaux mature much sooner. Many lesser 1855 Cru Classé wines will be ready in five or 10 years, though others can take longer. Most petit châteaux, commune wines, and négociant blends are made for early consumption.

Generally, you can tell from the price of your wine and its classification (or lack of classification) whether it is made for early consumption or yearns for solitude in your wine cellar. A wine that needs aging will taste unpleasantly tannic if you drink it too soon. Drinking such a wine before its time is a form of infanticide. Any wine that needs long cellaring will not display its extraordinary qualities too young. In fact, it can be rather unpleasant.

CHAPTER 11

The Noble Wines of Bordeaux

In This Chapter

- The greatest appellations
- The greatest châteaux
- Where to find values

In the last chapter, we discussed the Bordeaux region generally. In this chapter, we're going to take a very close look at the Bordeaux region's most distinguished districts and châteaux—those capable of producing wines that belong to that rarefied class that I call "noble."

In this chapter, I've provided many lists and tables. You'll find these useful when you go shopping for a great, noble Bordeaux.

Tasting Tip

There's a good reason a quality ranking from 1855 might remain useful, even today. The conditions of soil and microclimate that distinguished these chateaux back then still exist.

Very few wines from the 1855 have fallen in quality. But many others from outside that classification have improved and now compare favorably with their honored cousins.

The Classiest Classifications

In Chapter 10, we looked at the 1855 Classification of the Wines of the Haut-Médoc, which considered the wines of the Médoc (and one of Graves, Château Haut-Brion). At that time, these rankings represented a local consensus (as reflected in price). In all those years, only one change has been made.

The 1855 Classification was, by far, the most prestigious. But it was not the only such ranking of Bordeaux wines. There have been others, including another from the year 1855. While the Médoc classification looked only at red wines, the 1855 classification of the châteaux of Sauternes-Barsac ranked this region's unique sweet white wines.

The 1855 Classification of Sauternes-Barsac set Château d'Yquem above all the rest. The other 23 châteaux then were divided among Premiers Crus (First Growths) and Deuxièmes Crus (Second Growths).

First Growths of Sauternes-Barsac:

- Château Guiraud
- Château La Tour Blanche
- Château Lafaurie-Peyraguey
- Château de Rayne-Rabaud
- Château Sigalas Rabaud
- Château Rabaud-Promis
- Château Haut-Payraguey
- Château Coutet
- Château Climens
- Château Sudruiraut
- Château Rieussec

Second Growths of Sauternes-Barsac:

- Château d'Arche
- Château Filhot
- Château Lamothe
- Château de Myrat
- Château Doisy-Védrenes
- Château Doisy-Daëne
- Château Suau
- Château Broustet
- Château Caillou
- Château Nairac
- Château de Malle
- Château Romer

Wine label of Chateau d'Yquem

As with the 1855 Médoc classification, these remain fairly reliable, though not perfect.

Heard it Through the Grapevine

Just like all AC wines, those of Sauternes-Barsac are tightly controlled, but the parameters for making the sweet, luscious dessert wines of this area can seem even more restrictive. In addition to limitations placed on the amount of acres you are allowed to plant, what varietals you are allowed to plant, and how far apart your vines must be, Sauternes is extraordinarily costly to produce (hence the generally high price tags on only a half-bottle!). Add to that the notion that the best producers won't even release a wine if they deem the vintage subpar, and you've got just about the riskiest, extreme-winemaking example in the world.

A hundred years passed before any other Bordeaux regions were classified. In 1955, the production of St.-Emilion was put into two classifications: Premiers Grands Crus Classés (First Great Growths) and Grands Crus Classés (Great Growths). These were corrected in 1959 and revised in 1969 and 1996. We will look at the very best of these later this chapter.

Graves lies due south of the city of Bordeaux. Under the 1959 classification of this region, 13 châteaux that produce red wines achieved Cru Classé (Classified Growth) status. These were joined by eight châteaux that produce white wines.

The Sommelier Says

The market value of a high classification is enormous. So you can imagine the pressures on those who are responsible for wine rankings!

Though a few classified wines may not be worthy of their official status, it's more likely there are several unclassified wines that are. This is where you look for bargains, if you are more interested in wine than prestige.

Table 11.1 Graves Classified Growths of 1959, Red Wine

Estate	Commune
Château Haut-Brion	Pessac
Château Bouscaut	Cadaujac
Château Carbonnieux	Léognan
Château de Chevalier	Léognan
Château de Fieuzal	Léognan
Château Haut-Bailly	Léognan
Château La Mission-Haut-Brion	Pessac
Château La Tour-Haut-Brion	Talence
Château La Tour-Martillac	Martillac
Château Malartic-Lagraviére	Léognan
Château Olivier	Léognan
Château Pape-Clément	Pessac
Château Smith-Haut-Lafitte	Martillac

Table 11.2 Graves Classified Growths of 1959, White Wine

Estate	Commune
Château Bouscaut	Cadaujac
Château Carbonnieux	Léognan
Domaine de Chevalier	Léognan
Château Couhins	Villaneve-d'Ornon
Château Laville-Haut-Brion	Talence
Château Malartic-Lagraviére	Léognan
Château Olivier	Léognan
Château La Tour-Martillac	Martillac

Haut-Médoc on High

The northern third of the Médoc Peninsula is called, simply, Médoc (sometimes Bas-Médoc). The southern two-thirds is called Haut-Médoc (Upper Médoc), ending in the south at the city of Bordeaux. This is geography, though, not wine! The AOC appellations don't follow that scheme exactly.

Heard it Through the Grapevine

In the Médoc, there are two regional appellations, Médoc and Haut-Médoc. And there are six communal appellations, St.-Estèphe, Pauillac, St.-Julien, Moulis, Listrac and Margaux. These communal appellations, geographically, are part of the Haut-Médoc. However, the appellation Haut-Médoc applies only to those parts of that region that are not part of those six communal appellations.

Four communal appellations of the (geographic, not appellation) Haut-Médoc—Pauillac, Margaux, St.-Julien, and St.-Estèphe—account for all the First and Second Growths of the 1855 Classification (except for that one from Graves). However, five châteaux from three communes within the regional appellation, Haut-Médoc, appear in the 1855 Classification among the Third, Fourth, and Fifth Growths:

- Château La Lagune, in Ludon (Third Growth)
- Château La Tour Carnet, in St.-Laurent (Fourth Growth)
- Château Belgrave, in St.-Laurent (Fifth Growth)
- Château de Camensac, in St.-Laurent (Fifth Growth)
- Château Cantemerle, in Macau (Fifth Growth)

Vino Vocab

Let's review French ordinal numbers. The 1855 classification ranked wines into five growths:

- Premiers Crus, **First Growths**
- Deuxièmes Crus, **Second Growths**
- Troisièmes Crus, **Third Growths**
- Quatrièmes Crus, **Fourth Growths**
- Cinquièmes Crus, **Fifth Growths**

The AOC Haut-Médoc region is enormous, with more than 11,500 acres in grapes in 15 communes. The soils here are sandy-gravely, but with considerable local variation. Principle grapes are Cabernet Sauvignon, Merlot, and Cabernet Franc, with Merlot increasing its share in the mix.

Saint Emilion Superiority

This large district lies along the right bank of the Dordogne River, almost due east of Bordeaux. The St.-Emilion appellation is centered on the picturesque medieval town of the same name. The St.-Emilion region is divided into two parts: "Côtes" and "Graves" ("slopes" and "gravel").

The wines from the Côtes are nicely colored, perfumed, and medium-bodied. Yet they can display a strong tannic complexity. They age well, but you can drink them earlier than those from the Médoc or Graves appellations.

Wines grown in the Graves region of St.-Emilion resemble those of the nearby Pomerol appellation, featuring a distinct fruitiness. You can drink these quite young, but aging doesn't harm them.

Heard it Through the Grapevine

The Côtes region of St.-Emilion comprises the slopes south of the town and the plateau beyond. A thin layer of clay and limestone soils sits on a bed of limestone. This is perfect for the Merlot and Cabernet Franc grapes.

The Graves region lies west of the town. Here the soils are deeper and gravely, with some clay and sand, which allows some planting in Cabernet Sauvignon.

Praises for Pomerol

The Pomerol appellation lies just north of St.-Emilion. It's the smallest of the Bordeaux appellations. But wine-lovers treasure the wines from this district's many small vintners. Winemaking standards here are very high, and it's remarkable that Pomerol's wines never have undergone classification.

Tasting Tip

One thing that distinguishes the wines of Pomerol from those of the other great Bordeaux appellations is that it is made mostly from the Merlot grape, sometimes entirely.

Most Bordeaux wines are based on the Cabernet Sauvignon grape, with Merlot and other permitted grapes blended. But Pomerol's soils favor Merlot, and they can favor you, too, with their remarkable plushness.

Styles vary greatly among the châteaux of Pomerol—from the powerful flavor presence favored by Château Pétrus to the silk-textured subtlety sought by Château l'Evangile.

Haut-Médoc Premiers Crus

Let's look now at Bordeaux's noblest (and most desired) wines, the Premiers Crus of the 1855 Classification:

Château Lafite-Rothschild

Wine label of Chateau Lafite Rothschild.

This famous estate is in Pauillac. (Actually, a tiny bit lies in St.-Estèphe, but for AOC purposes, it's all Pauillac.)

If you are traveling in France, you haven't seen Bordeaux until you've visited Château Lafite-Rothschild! This is the home of Bordeaux's noblest wine.

The estate is large, with over 200 acres in production. (If you're talking soybeans, that's tiny. But for fine vinifera, it's huge!) Cabernet Sauvignon accounts for two-thirds of the planting, with Merlot and Cabernet Franc, one-sixth, each. The vines are quite old, averaging nearly 40 years.

The complexity and authority of this wine is impossible to describe. It is considered the best of the Premiers Crus. All I will say is take one sip, and you'll know forever the meaning of the word "finesse." You can drink this 10 years after vintage, or set it aside for 35.

Château Margaux

Wine label of Chateau Margeaux.

Château Margaux is guess where? Margaux! What a pretty name! (And a pretty wine to go with it.)

Even if you weren't a wine-lover, you might want to visit this distinguished Château for its splendid architecture and its classical beauty. The village is self-sustaining, with Old-World craftsmen capable of any task—even barrel cooperage.

The estate's over 200 producing acres are planted three-quarters in Cabernet Sauvignon and about a quarter in Merlot, as well as a little Cabernet Franc and Petit Verdot for good measure. Like its name, Margaux's wine is delicate and refined, like a rare china teacup. The floral scents add to the impression.

Despite that delicacy, this wine ages very well. Yes, it's great young. But it only gets better!

Château Latour

Château Latour is another first-growth estate in Pauillac, not as famous as Lafite-Rothschild but most worthy of its Premier Cru status.

Latour is not the same Château it was in 1855! Since 1963, it's been (mostly) in the hands of British investors, who have put large sums of money into its modernization. For one thing, the large and ancient oaken fermenting casks were replaced by stainless steel. But this wine is no stranger to wood. After fermentation, it's transferred gently into new, small oak casks where it rests peacefully for two years before bottling.

Heard it Through the Grapevine

When it comes to fermenting a fine wine, why replace oak with stainless steel? There are two good reasons:

First, clean, non-absorbent stainless neither adds nor takes anything away from the wine. This ensures consistent quality, year after year.

Second, the thin, strong walls of stainless steel casks permit precise temperature control during fermentation, another important quality consideration.

About 160 acres are in vine, about 120 these, always, covered with older vines. Three-fourths is planted in Cabernet Sauvignon, with 15 percent in Cabernet Franc, 8 percent in Merlot, and 2 percent in Petit Verdot.

This wine "rests on its skins" for a week or more after fermentation, allowing the fullest development of color and tannins. You definitely do not want to drink this one young! But do consider buying some from a vintage year for your grandchildren, or future grandchildren! Age brings out this wine's breeding and authority.

Château Haut-Brion

Château Haut-Brion is in Graves. What's wrong with this picture? Graves is not part of the Médoc region. The appellation lies just southwest of Bordeaux, near the left bank of the Garonne. It's the only non-Médoc wine in the 1855 Classification. (Its fame was so great, they didn't dare exclude it.)

What makes Haut-Brion great? Its soil, unique to the region, gravel covered with sand. And perfect for Médoc-style wines.

The estate's 119 producing acres are planted 44 percent in Cabernet Sauvignon, 45 percent Merlot, about 10 percent in Cabernet Franc, and 1 percent Petit Verdot. (Actually, a little plot is dedicated to Sauvignon Blanc and Sémillon for this estate's dry white Haut-Brion Blanc.)

In flavor, this wine shows a strength and depth, with no harshness. And of course, it improves greatly with age.

Château Mouton-Rothschild

Château Mouton-Rothschild, the third First Growth from Pauillac, may be remembered best as the only estate to have been upgraded in the 1855 Classification. That was in 1973, and with the consent of the other four Premier Crus.

This change only formalized what had been be a de facto classification since the 1920s. Château Mouton-Rothschild readily commanded the same market prices as the then-four First Growths.

The estate has about 200 acres in production. Cabernet Sauvignon accounts for around 75 percent, with nearly 10 percent Cabernet Franc and Merlot each, as well as little Petit Verdot. The favor is big, as you would imagine with that much Cabernet Sauvignon, displaying lots of fruit. And yes, let's not be too impatient. Set some aside for drinking in your old age.

Distinguished Districts

Four communes produce wines of such distinctions that they are appellations separate from the remainder of the Haut-Médoc regional appellation. These distinguished districts—Margaux, St.-Julien, Pauillac, and St.-Estèphe—lie south to north along the western shore of the Gironde estuary, north of Bordeaux.

Generally, the slopes face the morning sun, but innumerable east-flowing streams provide small slopes with southern exposure. The soils here are deep and very permeable, being sand, gravel, and limestone. For most agriculture, these are very poor soils. But for the wine grapes grown in the Médoc, they're perfect.

The soils hold the day's heat very well, moderating nighttime temperatures. Daytimes don't become excessively hot, either, because of the estuary and the nearby Atlantic.

Cool days; temperate nights; clear, sunny skies; long summer days; and thick, porous soils conspire to create winegrowing conditions found nowhere else on earth.

The Graves district sits apart, adjoining Bordeaux to the southwest. But its gravely soils and similar micro-climate provide an environment similar to that of the four districts along the Gironde.

Margaux

Margaux has the honor of supplying 21 growths to the 1855 classification. As we move up the wide Gironde (toward the south), the wines become supple, smooth, and elegant. Ruby in color, they are full, without being overpowering.

The soils here have a high portion of white gravel, with some chalk. Subsoils vary from sandy to gravely, accounting in some of the variety we observe among the châteaux.

St.-Julien

St.-Julien is the smallest producer among the four Haut-Médoc communes. In addition to the 11 wines this region contributes to the 1855 Classification, you will find several châteaux represented in the Cru Bourgeois classification.

These wines are similar to those of Pauillac, but perhaps lacking in the latter's power, particularly from those situated closer to Margaux. You can drink these young, yet they do age well.

The terrain is very gravely, with subsoils of sandstone and clay. Most of the châteaux lie close to the Gironde estuary. With its excellent drainage, St.-Julien can produce excellent wines even in wetter years.

Tasting Tip

It's hard to generalize about the noble wines of Pauillac. Subtle differences in soil, drainage, and sunlight bring about wonderful differences you will have no trouble distinguishing.

Pauillac

Pauillac means prestige! Three of Médoc's four First Growths come from here (along with 15 other classified wines)! But prestige comes at a price: The three Premiers Crus—La Tour, Lafite-Rothschild, and Mouton-Rothschild—can put a strain on your wallet. But don't despair. This commune seems incapable of producing a poor wine.

To the three Premiers Crus I would add Chateau Pichon-Longueville, for unique flavors and excellent aging potential.

St.-Estèphe

Of the communal appellations of the Haut-Médoc (geographically), St.-Estèphe is the largest producer. This district lies closest to the mouth of the Gironde. Its soils have less gravel and more clay than those further south. These heavier soils drain slowly, leading to very robust wines. Some might say too robust. And indeed, there has been a trend since the sixties to grow and blend more Merlot, which is fruitier and less tannic than the Cabernet Sauvignon.

Although only five St.-Estèphe wines made the 1855 Classification, you will find several worthy rivals among the Crus Grands Bourgeois Exceptionnels.

St.-Estèphe lacks the prestige of Margaux, St.-Julien and Pauillac. That's good for you, because with careful shopping, you can get some great values from here. While it's true, the commune earned only five places in the 1855 Classification, several wines from the lesser Cru Bourgeois classification have achieved genuine greatness in recent years.

The commune's vineyards, planted over 3,000 acres, have been slow to mature, developing lots of tannins and overall toughness. This has been less of a problem since growers switched much of their production from Cabernet Sauvignon to the juicier Merlot.

Heard it Through the Grapevine

The Graves region takes its name from its gravely soil, overlaid with a fine sand. In the southern part, there's a bit more clay and limestone. The drainage is excellent; so drought years can present quality problems. However, in wet years, these wines can be sublime!

Graves

The wines of Graves were the first of Bordeaux to be exported, going back to the 12th century! And Thomas Jefferson was no stranger to these wines.

The best white wines of this region are among the best in France. But it's the red wines that have made Graves famous. The Premier Cru Haut-Brion has been famous for centuries.

Deuxièmes Crus

Remember that old Avis slogan, "When you're Number Two, you try harder."? The Deuxièmes Crus (second growths) from the 1855 Great Classification of the Médoc are no slouches when it comes to careful winemaking. Here are some of the most popular:

- Château Rauzan-Ségla. Formerly known as Rausan-Ségla, this 130-acre estate is located in Margaux. It's planted about two-thirds Cabernet Sauvignon, a third Merlot, with small amounts of Petit Verdot and Cabernet Franc. Set this aside seven to 30 years.
- Château Léoville-Las Cases. This estate is in St.-Julien. Its over 200 acres are planted 85 percent Cabernet Sauvignon, 14.5 percent Merlot, and 0.5 percent Cabernet Franc. Age it eight to 30 years to do it justice.
- Château Léoville-Poyferré. Also in St.-Julien, this estate is planted over about 200 acres. The grapes are 52 percent Cabernet Sauvignon, 28 percent Merlot, 12 percent Cabernet Franc, and eight percent Petit Verdot. Keep this 8 to 20 years after vintage.
- Château Lascombes. The 210 acres of this Margaux estate are planted 50 percent Merlot, 45 percent Cabernet Sauvignon, and 5 percent Petit Verdot. Good for drinking six to 20 years after vintage.

Heard it Through the Grapevine

Lascombes managed to nearly double their acreage in 2008 when they began renting vineyards from Château Martinens. It's a neat trick for classified growths who can only expand their vineyard holdings within their classification via vineyards in their appellation—pretty tricky in a place where land isn't given away easily!

- Château Gruaud-Larose. About 200 acres of this large St.-Julien estate are in vine, with an average vine age of 45 years! The grapes are 57 percent Cabernet Sauvignon, 30 percent Merlot, 8 percent Cabernet Franc, 3 percent Petit Verdot, and 2 percent Malbec. (Yep. It adds up to 100.) You should age this 10 to 35 years.
- Château Brane-Cantenac. Here, in Cantenac-Margaux, 230 acres are planted in 62.5 percent Cabernet Sauvignon, 33 percent Merlot, 4 percent Cabernet Franc, and 0.5 percent Petit Verdot. You can drink this relatively young, about five years after vintage.
- Château Pichon-Longueville-Baron. (This also is known as Pichon-Baron.) This Pauillac estate is planted with 170 acres that are comprised of 60 percent Cabernet Sauvignon, 35 percent Merlot, and the rest divided between Cabernet Franc and some Petit Verdot. Drink it in eight years, or let it age for 25.
- Château Ducru-Beaucaillou. These 125 acres in St.-Julien are planted 70 percent Cabernet Sauvignon, and 30 percent Merlot. Age this 10 to 30 years.
- Château Cos d'Estournel. These 170 acres in St.-Estèphe are planted 60 percent Cabernet Sauvignon and 40 percent Merlot. You can age this eight to 30 years.

Autres Crus

What about the Autres Crus (other growths): third, fourth, and fifth? Some of these are quite well known and very highly regarded. They represent a fine way to add wines from the Haut-Mèdoc to your collection at affordable prices. Here are some I would recommend.

Wine label of Chateau Langoa Barton.

There are 14 Troisièmes Crus (third growths), from which I recommend (communes in parentheses):

➤ Château Giscours (Labarde-Margaux)

➤ Château Langoa-Barton (St.-Julien)

➤ Château Palmer (Cantenac-Margaux)

➤ Château Calon-Ségur (St.-Estèphe)

Of the 10 Quatrièmes Crus (fourth growths), you can't go wrong with:

➤ Château Talbot (St.-Julien)

➤ Château Duhart-Milon-Rothschild (Pauillac)

➤ Château Beychevelle (St.-Julien)

➤ Château Prieuré-Lichine (Cantenac-Margaux)

And finally, don't neglect these from among the 18 Cinquièmes Crus (fifth growths):

- Château Pontet-Canet (Pauillac)
- Château Grand-Puy-Lacoste (Pauillac)
- Château Haut-Batailley (Pauillac)
- Château Lynch-Bages (Pauillac)

Saint Emilion

Although the wines of St.-Emilion do not meet the lofty standard set by those of the Haut-Médoc, they are very highly regarded. The district is planted mainly in Merlot, and this is reflected in the grape blends of its wines. These are round and fruity and a little more alcoholic than those from the Médoc.

Premiers Grands Crus Classés

The 1996 classification of St.-Emilion lists 13 Premiers Grands Crus Classés (First Great Growths). Of these, I feel the noblest are:

- Château Ausone. This estate's 17 acres are planted in vines 40 to 50 years old! The grapes are Cabernet Sauvignon and Merlot, half and half. You can put these away as long as 50 years, but don't drink them younger than 15.
- Château Cheval Blanc. The vines average 40 years in age on this 90-acre estate. It's planted two-thirds Cabernet Franc and one-third Merlot. You can drink this superb wine as young as five years after vintage. (Or cellar it for 20 years.)
- Château Canon. Here we have 45 acres planted 55 percent in Merlot, 45 percent in Cabernet Sauvignon. Age this seven to 25 years.
- Château Figeac. Large by St.-Emilion standards, this estate plants its 100 acres about equally in Cabernet Sauvignon, Cabernet Franc, and Merlot. You can drink this as young as three years, but after 15 it may have passed its peak.
- Château Trottevielle. The vines average 40 years old on this estate's 25 acres. The grapes are half Merlot, with 45 percent Cabernet Franc, and 5 percent Cabernet Sauvignon. Age this five to 20 years.

The Sommelier Says

Since the wines of St-Emilion were first classified in 1955, the inductees, and potential new classified estates, are evaluated about every 10 years for inclusion or, sacrebleu!, declassification. Because a few desclassified chateaux made a big, ol' fuss over the 2006 list, it was deemed null the following year, keeping the latest (as of this writing) list of classified St.-Emilion producers as they were in the '90s. Talk about a flashback.

Grands Crus Classés

There are 57 Grands Crus Classés (Great Growths) in St.-Emilion. Often a lesser classification means a greater value for you. The following wines will satisfy your desire to sample from among the best Bordeaux without too much damage to your bank account:

- Château Bellevue
- Château Cadet-Piola
- Château Canon-La-Gaff
- Château Clos de Jabob
- Château Dassault
- Château Soutard

Pomerol

The wines of Pomerol are 80 to 100 percent Merlot. Their fruitiness is plummy, and they are as smooth as velvet. Their rich ruby colors provide further joys. You can drink these much younger than those made predominantly from the Cabernet Sauvignon grape.

Here are some wines I would recommend without hesitation:

Best of the Best

- Château Pétrus. This is the best of the best of the best! Some wine experts rate this wine alongside the great Château Lafite-Rothschild, at the top of the first-growth list in the Haut-Médoc 1855 Classification (and that's reflected in its sky-high price). This small (28 acres) estate is the only one that features a clay topsoil. That and its very old vines account for this wine's noble attributes. It's planted 95 percent Merlot, 5 percent Cabernet Franc. Set this one aside 10 to 30 years.
- Château La Conseillante. This 30-acre estate is planted 80 percent in Merlot and 20 percent Cabernet Franc.
- Château La Fleur de Gay. The tiny (7.5 acres) estate is planted 100 percent Merlot, with a 40-year average age of the vines, the same as at Château Pétrus.
- Château Lafleur. This cozy estate, 11 acres, is planted equally in Merlot and Cabernet Franc.
- Château Le Pin. Here, the grapes (92 percent Merlot, 8 percent Cabernet Franc) are grown on a minuscule 5-acre plot. Drink four to 12 years after vintage.
- Château Trotanoy. The 18 acres of this estate are planted 90 percent Merlot and 10 percent Cabernet Franc.

Second Best

The wines from these Pomerol châteaux will not disappoint you:

- Château Clinet
- Château l'Eglise-Clinet
- Château l'Evangile
- Château Certan de May
- Château Latour à Pomerol
- Château Petit Village
- Château Vieux-Châteaux-Certan

Old Standards; Modern Smarts

It's funny that so many wine drinkers think of Bordeaux as being the epitome of old-school. Yes, as we've seen in this chapter, it is home such rich tradition and history (as to make

California look like a twinkle in ma mere's vinous eye), but that doesn't mean that the Bordelaise rest on their First Growth laurels—far from it. Here are some of the modern techniques great Bordeaux producers use these days to keep on top of their game one the world wine stage:

- Heeding the Harvest. Years ago, hand-harvesting and hauling in up to 5 tons of grapes in large bins lead to the grapes on the bottom getting crushed and that juice starting to oxidize before it even got to the sorting table. Today, producers not only use smaller bins with a perforated bottom to catch the juice from any incidental crushing occurs.
- Chillin' Out. Many producers are using the technological side of temperature control to perform cold macerations which put fermentation in a stasis, yet allow the enzymes present to begin to extract color, aroma, and flavor. When the must is warmed (see below), this "pre"-maceration has succeeded in softening the tannins, thus making the wine more drinkable, more quickly.
- Adding warmth. Producers are trying out warmer, longer macerations to encourage more overall fruit/tannin/acid balance than the previous stemminess, bitter qualities, and astringency that sometimes used to be a problem, especially in poorer vintages.
- Punching v. Pumping. In what can be viewed as a return to the old, many modern Bordeaux producers have found that a gentle cap punch-down is a far better way to extra color and create consistency than the agitation of pumping over, a technique where the juice is violently sucked from the bottom to the top of the tank.
- Fermentation Techniques. Another way that Bordelaise producers have found the can keep up with the global market and make their wines more approachable sooner is performing malolactic fermentation—the process of changing harsher, lactic acid to softer, malic acid—entirely in new, French oak barrels, so that the wine isn't as overtly affected by the new wood (e.g., the leaching of more harsh tannic structure).
- Seeking Softness. Along the same lines as the above, more Bordeaux producers are looking for that sweet spot between immediate market approachability and age-ability, making their wines more drinker-friendly out of the gate via aging their wines after malolactic fermentation on the lees, and doing so via the modern Oxoline technique, which more quickly simulates the effects of lees stirring without having to open the barrel.

You also shouldn't be surprised to find some pretty high-tech monitoring equipment in most of the better chateaux. Of course, there is no replacement for a winemaker's judgment, but many ensure the fine reputations of their houses by using special computer software to monitor everything from phenolic compounds to acidity to temperature during fermentation, assuring that winemakers are alerted to even so much as an nth of a percentage difference of change.

CHAPTER 12

Burgundy – La Reine de Vin

In This Chapter

- What makes Burgundy special?
- The complex organization of Burgundy
- The "cru" of Burgundy
- Where are the values?

Burgundy wines can be very frustrating. To be sure, your wine-seller stocks many good, if not exceptional Burgundies. But price isn't a reliable guide. Some of the most expensive Burgundies can be downright awful when produced by low-quality négociants or careless estates.

So why bother? Because Burgundy's very best wines truly are vins extraordinaires. They stand among the most fascinating and interesting of all wines. Unfortunately for the consumer, they also bear price tags displaying their stratospheric status, and many importers and wine merchants refuse to handle such expensive wares in small lots.

Unless you happen to be touring Burgundy, have Christie's on speed dial, or you've hit that lottery number, the ultimate Burgundies may be beyond your grasp. But don't be dismayed. It just happens you can enjoy some very pleasant red and white Burgundy wines without much outlay.

In this chapter, we'll visit Burgundy's five wine districts, each home to a number of small estates. You'll find out how the terroir affects the grapes grown on each estate, producing distinctively different wines. And you'll learn the characteristics of fine red and white Burgundies. Also, you'll learn about a very refreshing Burgundy bargain—Beaujolais (no, not just the nouveau you drink during the holidays), the inexpensive, refreshing, light-bodied red wine that you serve lightly chilled.

Part of the problem with selecting fine Burgundies lies in the fact that the Burgundy region produces much less than Bordeaux, only about a quarter. And of that smaller yield, the selection of superior wines is disturbingly meager—however, it is spread out among hundreds of vineyard names recognized and protected under the AOC system; Bordeaux has around 60 appellation names recognized under the AOC regulations. (We hardly can count the Beaujolais district. Though, technically, part of Burgundy, it produces a very different type of wine.)

The Domain of the Domaine

The vineyards of Burgundy are much smaller than those of Bordeaux. An estate of 50 or 60 acres represents a very large holding, and such a vineyard owned by only one proprietor is an exception. Here's an example: Clos de Vougeot consists of 125 acres, but it's owned by more than 80 different individuals! This can make it somewhat complicated to judge the quality of a wine by reading its label. More on that later.

The citoyens of the French Revolution had a hand in this vineyard fragmentation. Before the Revolution, the majority of vineyards were owned by the First and Second Estates (nobility and clergy). After the revolution, these vineyards were distributed among the peasants. With the institution (1804) of the Code civil des Françaises, which required that land be divided equally among all heirs, vineyard ownership was divided even further.

Vino Vocab

There's another difference between vineyard holdings in Burgundy and in Bordeaux. A Burgundian estate is called a domaine, while in Bordeaux, we have the majestic château.

Burgundy comprises five districts, all of which produce distinctive wines. These five are, from north to south, Chablis, the Côte d'Or, the Côte Chalonnaise, Mâconnais, and

Beaujolais. The Côte d'Or (literally golden coast, or river bank) is again divided into two parts: the Côte de Nuits and the Côte de Beaune, separated by the Sâone River.

Burgundy's climate is marked by hot summers and cold winters. Spring frosts are an issue at times, rot caused by summer rain, as well as a few localized hailstorms during été that can damage delicate grapes. Limestone and calcareous clay are the prevalent soil types.

The prime varietals of this region are Pinot Noir, for red Burgundies, and Chardonnay, for white. Burgundy is where that fussy vinifera, Pinot Noir, is on its best behavior, displaying its most regal and charming character.

As you head south into the Beaujolais district, the soil becomes granitic. This is where we find the red Gamay grape. You also find another white varietal, aligoté, grown throughout the region and used for two-dimensional white table wines, as well as for sparkling.

The terroir of Burgundy (location, soils, climate, topography) is highly variable, which is what makes the region so fascinating for many wine lovers. Soils vary from one site to the next. Within one vineyard, two plots of the same grape varietal growing only a short distance from each other may yield two distinctively different wines. This is where knowledge of the Burgundy label becomes important. Owners even within the same small vineyard will not necessarily produce the same qualities or styles of wines.

The AOC structure for Burgundy takes this notion of terroir into consideration. There are AOC Burgundy appellations for individual vineyard sites that are of exceptional quality.

In Burgundy, the terms Premier cru (first growth) and Grand cru (great growth, the very highest quality) are official designations under AOC law. This is in contrast to Bordeaux, where the same terms designate status imparted outside of AOC legislation.

The Sommelier Says

It's very easy to confuse the Bordeaux term Grand Cru Classé with the Burgundian Grand cru. The first, not part of the AOC system, applies to all 61 classified wines of Bordeaux. The second, AOC official, is awarded only to Burgundy's very finest vintages. (It's almost as though the French wanted to confuse us.)

Table 11.1 provides examples of AOC names in Burgundy from the most general to the most specific, the individual vineyard. The two broadest categories—regional and district—

account for over 60 percent of all Burgundy wines. These run from $10 to $20 per bottle. Commune or Village wines, such as Gevrey-Chambertin, make 25 percent of Burgundy's production, and they retail for $25 to $40 per bottle. There are 53 communes in Burgundy with their own appellation.

Getting more distinguished, we have the Premier crus, such as Puligny-Montrachet Les Pucelles. These make up approximately 11 percent of total production. Five hundred sixty-one vineyards carry the Premier cru appellation. These wines sell for $25 to $80 per bottle.

And at the rarest level, we have the 32 Grand crus, such as Corton-Charlemagne or Le Montrachet. These account for a mere 1 percent of Burgundy's production. Grand cru prices begin around $60 or $70, and they can soar to upwards of $1,000 a bottle for, say, Romanée-Conti. (Or how about $5,000 for a bottle of the same in a mature great vintage?)

Table 11.1—The Structure of Burgundy AOC Names

Specificity of Site	Examples
Region	Bourgogne Rouge
District	Côte de Nuits Villages; Mâcon-Villages
Village or Commune	Nuits St. Georges; Gevrey-Chambertin; Fixin
Premier Cru;	Puligny-Montrachet Les Pucelles; Beaune Clos-des-Ursules; Nuits St. Georges—Les Perriéres
Grand Cru Le	Chambertin; La Romanée; Le Montrachet

The last two classifications refer to specific vineyards.

The classification of your Burgund) ven appear! Grand cru Burgundies

Heard it Through the Grapevine

You may have read in some wine books that the labels for Premier cru wines bear the name of the commune plus the name of the vineyard in the same size type, that if the vineyard name appears in smaller lettering than the commune name, the wine is not a Premier cru. Not true!

In practice, most Premier cru labels actually do display the vineyard name in smaller type than the commune name. But not always. The vineyard name may appear in the same size or even larger type. Just remember: if there is a vineyard name on the label of a Burgundy wine, it's either a Premier or Grand cru.

with their own appellation may choose to display only the vineyard name, with the term 'appellation controlée' below, without the esteemed 'Grand cru.' I suppose this is because they are very snooty about their reputations, figuring that those who appreciate their product will know exactly who they are.

So how do you tell these quiet Grands crus from lesser "village wines" with commune appellations (for example, "appellation Meursault controlée")? The best way is to know your cru domaines, or consult a wine encyclopedia or Burgundy book. But there's a simpler way: If it's cheap, it's not a Grand cru.

Some vintners will blend the grapes from two or more Premier cru vineyards in the same commune. These wines still are Premier crus, but the label will not have the name of a specific Premier cru vineyard. Instead, the label will have a commune name with the words "Premier cru" or "1er cru." These wines generally come from négociants (wine brokers who buy wine and sell it under their own name). However, some growers with several tiny, lesser-known vineyards may blend their product and sell it simply as Premier cru. Good marketing, I suppose.

Ne Plus Ultra White

White Burgundy combines a silky mouthfeel and fullness of flavor with lively acidity. The better appellations have a touch of oak. These develop complexity and finesse with age. Grand crus may require up to 10 years in the bottle, but most white Burgundies are ready to drink after two or three years.

Tasting Tip

White Burgundies often delight us with an aftertaste that's a lingering kaleidoscope of flavors—both from the initial taste of the wine and some that develop. The world offers us some great Chardonnays, but there's nothing like a great white Burgundy (except a great red Burgundy).

Is It Burgundy or Bordeaux?

A fine red Burgundy is as different from its Bordeaux counterpart as night and day. Since they are made from the Pinot Noir grape, Burgundies are lighter in color. They are medium- to full-bodied, they are relatively low in tannins, and often feel silky or velvety on the palate.

The Burgundy aroma is unique, with flavors that may defy description. Not uncommon are flavors resembling cherries and ripe berries, or moss and woodsy mushroom scents. With age, a superior Burgundy develops great complexity with subtle nuances of flavor and finesse that can be memorable. A red Burgundy requires seven to 10 years to mature, the greatest can continue to improve for decades. Bordeaux reds, on the other hand, tend to be much more tannic, full-bodied, and often with the aromas and flavors of black fruits, bell peppers, and even tobacco.

Navigating the Export Maze

Let's look at the principle wine districts of Burgundy. Wines from these districts are the ones that you most likely will find in the U.S.

The Sommelier Says

Pouilly-Fuissé became the darling of wine importers during the 1960s. This meteoric fame was matched by meteoric prices. But that's no concern to us today. Priced way beyond its worth during its 15 minutes of fame, Pouilly-Fuissé long ago returned to being a pleasant, unpretentious, and reasonably priced white wine.

Mâcon-Villages

The Mâconnais district lies directly south of the Chalonnaise and north of Beaujolais. The overall climate is sunny and mild, and the winemaking center is the city of Mâcon. The hills surrounding this area are replete with the chalky limestone loved by Chardonnay grapes.

Mâcon-Villages wines are whites of excellent value at $10 to $15 a bottle. To be sure, they lack the complexity and distinction of the more expensive Pouilly-Fuissé wines. But these wines are lively and crisp, meant to be enjoyed young. Most are soft, round, and fruity. Made from 100 percent Chardonnay grapes, their unoaked freshness contrasts with the oaked majority of Chardonnay wines.

The label will read Mâcon or Mâcon-Villages. Mâcon-Villages is a cut above mere Mâcon, and the best wines are those that come from a specific village. You can tell by the name of the village added to the appellation (for example, Mâcon-Viré or Mâcon-Lugny).

Pouilly-Fuissé

Pouilly-Fuissé and Saint-Véran are two inner appellations within the Mâcon district made from Chardonnay grapes grown on rolling hills with a soil that imbues them with a unique quality, the foremost being the whites tend to be rich and robust, with slightly higher alcohol than other parts of the region. Both wines are similar to Chablis, but softer and less steely, as they often see barrel aging.

Pouilly-Fuissé wines are mid-premium quality, usually selling for $15 to $30 a bottle. They are distinctly Chardonnay and have a crisp apple aroma, with a smooth texture and slight depth of flavor. Unlike the simple Mâcon wines, they often are oaked, rendering them richer and fuller in body. The best of these wines come from the villages of Solutré-Pouilly, Davayé, and Fuisse. They display more fruitiness and depth than Chablis, and the finish reveals a clean, earthy flavor. After three or four years' aging, Pouilly-Fuissés develop a subtle degree of finesse. Saint-Véran wines are a decent value at $18 to $25 a bottle.

Beaujolais

Every year around Thanksgiving, you will see the signs in wine shop windows: "Beaujolais Nouveau is here!" This has nothing to do, actually, with our American holiday. It's just fortuitous timing.

Beaujolais wine, nouveau or not, is made from the red Gamay vinifera, not Pinot Noir. Gamay thrives in Beaujolais, though it does poorly elsewhere in France. In fact, there once was a royal decree that banned this grape from vineyards outside Beaujolais.

Beaujolais and Beaujolais Supérieur (which has one more percentage alcohol) are district-wide AOC appellations. These wines come from the southern area of Beaujolais. The clay soil in this district produces simple, light-bodied fruity wines that sell for less than $10 a bottle and are best served no more than a year or two after their vintage. Unlike most other red wines, they go well with light foods and are great to drink slightly chilled in warm weather.

Tasting Tip

Beaujolais nouveau is only six weeks old when it appears on Thanksgiving tables. Its vinous and fruity quality is very low in tannins and makes it a refreshing beverage by itself, or with your favorite snacks. Don't even think of storing it! It's meant to be enjoyed within six months of its vintage.

Several communes in the north of Beaujolais produce wines with potential mid-premium quality. These are the crus Beaujolais, which are distinctly better than Beaujolais-Villages.

Only the name of the cru appears on the label, so you have to know the names of 10 cru villages to know that they are Beaujolais wines. Here they are: Brouilly, Chénas, Chiroubles, Côte-de-Brouilly, Fleurie, Juliénas, Morgon, Moulin á Vent, Regnié, and Saint-Amour.

Wines from Brouilly and Fleurie tend to be elegant in style and very fragrant. Those from Moulin á Vent and Morgon offer rich flavor and style and are capable of longer aging. Over time, the best may resemble a village red Burgundy. Table 11.2 reviews the crus of Beaujolais.

Table 11.2—The Cru of Beaujolais

Cru	Description
Brouilly	The lightest and fruitiest of the cru. Drink within two years.
Côte de Brouilly	A step better than Brouilly, fuller with more concentration; drink within three years.
Regnié	This is the newest addition to the Beaujolais cru. It is very similar to Brouilly in style and flavor.
Morgon	This cru resembles a red Burgundy more than a Beaujolais. It is full, rich, and earthy. Can age up to five to eight years.
Chiroubles	Very delicate, flavorful, and perfumed. They are often super-premium wines. Drink within four years.
Fleurie	Rich and flavorful with a medium body and velvety mouthfeel. Drink within four years.
Moulin á Vent	This is the richest and most concentrated of the cru. Powerful with the capacity to age up to 10 years or more.
Chénas	Rich and flavorful. Similar to a Moulin á Vent. Drink within four years.
Juliénas	Rich, full-bodied and full-flavored. One of the best of the cru. Drink within four years.
Saint-Amour	Light to medium body, soft and delicate. Drink within two years.

Beaujolais generally are sold by large négociants—companies that buy grapes and/or wines from growers to crush themselves or blend, bottle, and sell under their own labels. Two Premier négociants are Georges Duboeuf and Louis Jadot. These names on the label are reliable indicators of quality, as they do more than just buy finished wine. They work with the growers and set high standards for what they will buy. There are also some new faces on labels these days, like the well-respected importer Kermit Lynch, who now bottles and sells his own high-quality Beaujolais as well. There also are some better estate-bottled Beaujolais available, primarily imported by Alain Junguenet, Louis/Dresner Selections, Neil Rosenthal, Kermit Lynch, Louis Latour, and Weyngandt-Metzler.

Chablis

As luck would have it, the village of Chablis shares its name with what may have become the best-known generic wine mediocrity from the U.S. (This is where your new wine knowledge comes in very handy.) The vineyards of Chablis are the northernmost in Burgundy, situated on the hills of the Serein River valley. The locale's limestone soil and layers of marine fossils beneath impart a special character to the Chardonnay grape and combines with the cooler climate to give Chablis Chardonnay a distinctive quality.

Heard it Through the Grapevine

Chablis wines undergo a somewhat different processing than do other Burgundy whites. While the white wines of the Côte d'Or generally are fermented and aged in oak barrels, most Chablis winemakers have switched to stainless steel.

The best Chablis wines come from a relatively small vineyard area. Chablis wines are light, austere, crisp wines with a characteristic bouquet and a steely taste resembling gunflint. The finest Chablis, ranked as Grand crus, develop a degree of elegance and style, and sipping them alongside a plate of freshly shucked oysters is just about the most wonderful thing you can do.

The Côte Chalonnaise

The Côte Chalonnaise is a Burgundy lover's dream. These lovely wines are both enjoyable and reasonably priced. They lack the refinement of the Côte d'Or wines, being somewhat coarser and earthier and with less perfume, but they are perfectly drinkable. (Moreover, you won't have to skimp on your meal to pay for it.)

The district lies to the south of the Côte d'Or and has five appellations that produce good wines for $15 to $40 per bottle.

- Mercurey. These wines are mostly reds, some whites. This is the home of the best Chalonnaise wines ($20 to $30).
- Rully. About evenly divided between reds and whites. The earthy white wines are far superior to the reds.
- Givry. Mostly red, some white. Here the reds are superior, although quite earthy.
- Montagny. All white wines, which are pleasant and enjoyable.
- Bouzeron. Wines from this district frequently are labeled Bourgogne Rouge, Bourgogne Blanc, or Bourgogne Aligote (the only other white grape permitted in Burgundy).

The Great Wines of the Côte d'Or

Without question, wines from the Côte d'Or are the most costly. Alas, this fact too often is a reflection of pricing zeal, rather than of outstanding quality.

When they are on target, Côte d'Or wines are superb. When they miss, they can be very bad, even dreadful, suffering from indifferent winemaking or an overly ambitious quest for big production. These should be subtle, replete with nuances, supple in texture, and unique in style.

The Sommelier Says

The Côte d'Or quality depends on the skill and integrity of the grower. The temperamental, tightly clustered Pinot Noir grape tolerates no error. One mistake and good-bye, Charlie! So sometimes the result can be very disappointing. One way to avoid surprises is to acquaint yourself with the best growers and producers. For a list of the most reliable producers and négociants, see Chapter 13 and Appendix A.

The Côte d'Or, where wine legends are made, is a narrow 40-mile strip consisting of two main subdivisions. The northern part is the Côte de Nuits, named for its commercial center, the city of Nuits-Saint-Georges. This is the origin of some of the finest red Burgundies. The southern part is the Côte de Beaune, named for its most important city, Beaune. The Côte de Beaune is famous for both red and white wines, but its white Burgundies are especially celebrated.

You'll find mid-premium Burgundies from the Côte d'Or have two general appellations. Those from the larger place names will either be called Côte de Nuits or Côte de Nuits-Villages, or Côte de Beaune or Côte de Beaune-Villages. Wines with village names usually are of higher quality, although all fall within the same general range.

The red wines have a recognizably fruity, vinous aroma of Pinot Noir with the regional character of red Burgundies. With experience, you'll come to recognize this distinctive flair and aroma. The wines are straightforward, simple, and reasonably well-balanced, with soft tannins and a lingering finish. Though sometimes coarse and lacking in finesse, they exhibit amply the character of the Burgundy region.

Côte de Nuits

The red wines from the Côte de Nuits tend to be fuller-bodied, firmer and more sharply defined than their southern counterparts from the Côte de Beaune.

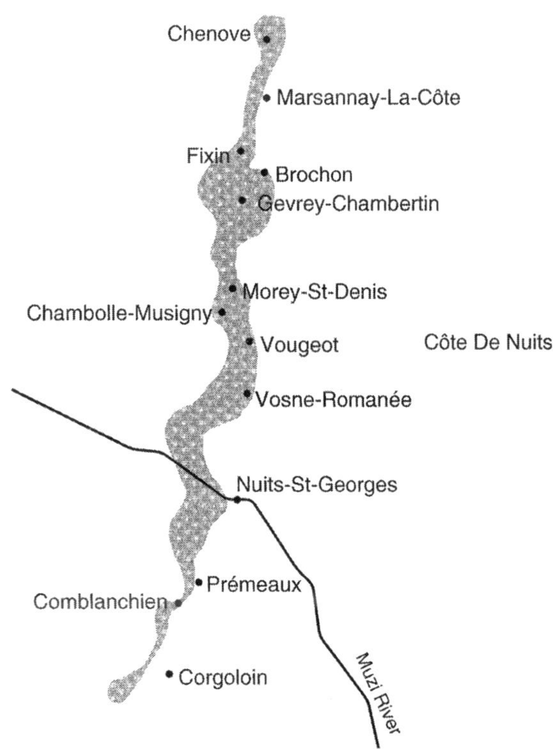

Each wine district of the Côte de Nuits produces a unique wine.

Let's look at the wines of the Côte de Nuits:

- The village of Gevrey-Chambertin in the Côte de Nuits is rightfully famous. Its Premier cru wines are super-premium quality, offering great intensity of flavor with balance. The Grand crus (of which there are eight) are labeled "Chambertin," sometimes hyphenated with a vineyard name.

Chambertin and Chambertin-Clos de Beze, its neighbor, are outstanding examples. Complex, rich, harmonious, and beautifully structured, they combine power with finesse as they age. The other Grand crus vineyards of Chambertin don't offer quite as much complexity, but they still rank highly in quality.

- Chambolle-Musigny lies further south. Its wines tend to be delicate, feminine, soft, and elegant, possessing great finesse. This area is typified by the Grand cru vineyard, Le Musigny, a noble wine of uncommon breed. Unlike most of the vineyards of the Côte de Nuits, Le Musigny is noted for its superb white as well as red Burgundy.
- Vougeot is the home of the immense Grand cru vineyard (by Burgundy standards) Clos de Vougeot. Although quality varies (remember, this one domaine has beaucoup owners), Clos de Vougeot wines are enormously aromatic, sturdy, and complex. They are medium-bodied, not as muscular as those of Chambertin. The finest offerings of the vineyard have unquestionably noble bearing.
- Flagey-Echézeaux is the name of a commune, but it's not used as an appellation. It contains two Grand cru wines, Grand Echézeaux and Echézeaux, each of which has several owners. These are super-premium wines: aromatic, with a slightly more refined style than their Vougeot cousins.
- Vosne-Romanée is a village associated with many of Burgundy's most famous and revered wines. Its Grand crus—La Romanée-Conti, La Romanée, La Tache, Richebourg, and Romanée-Saint-Vivant—are giants in the world of wine. These rich, velvety wines combine a depth and complexity of flavor from truffles, herbs, and berries, in a style that epitomizes finesse and rare breed.

The Grand crus—with the exception of Saint-Vivant, which is slightly lighter—usually achieve noble quality status. Their aging potential is tremendous. Bottle-aging accentuates these wines' harmonious character and finish.

- Nuits-Saint-Georges contains no Grand cru vineyards at all, but has many Premier crus. Stylistically, these wines are strongly aromatic, earthy, and often more tannic than the wines of other communes. They possess a sturdy, full-bodied, very vinous flavor that comes into full harmony with long aging. If they are not noble wines, they are not far off the mark.

- Fixin is the northernmost district in the Côte de Nuits. It produces sturdy, earthy red wines that do not develop finesse.
- Morey-Saint-Denis produces full-bodied, sturdy, rich red wines. Grand crus include part of Bonnes Mares, Clos des Lambrays, Clos de la Roche, Clos Saint-Denis, and Clos de Tart. These wines provide good value for the high quality they offer.

Côte de Beaune

The Côte de Beaune produces fewer Grand cru wines, but it gives us numerous Premier crus and super-premium red wines. The red wines from the northern part of the Côte de Beaune, around Aloxe-Corton, are softer, fuller-bodied, and richer in flavor than the wines from the Côte de Nuits.

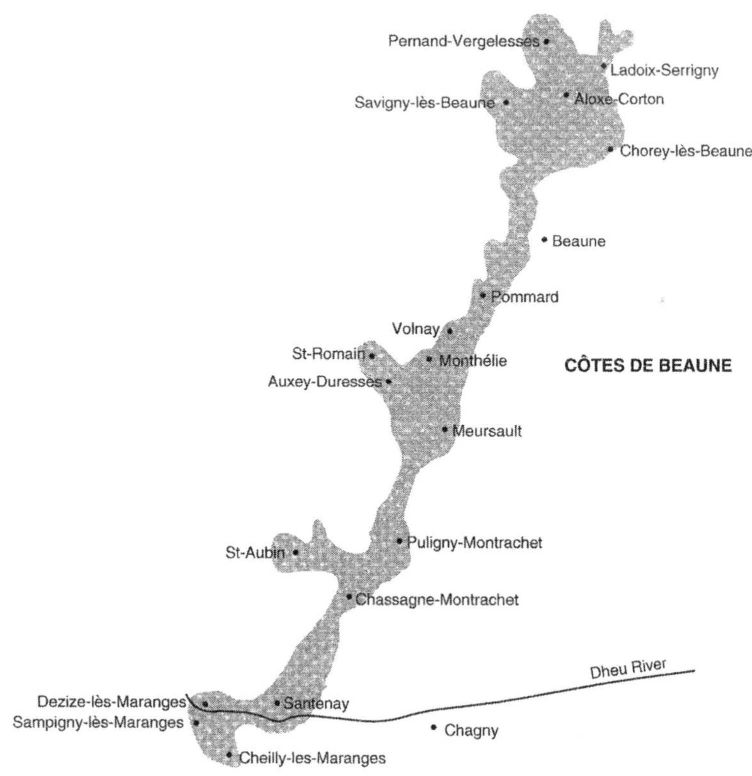

Like the Côte de Nuits, each wine district of the Côte de Beaune produces a unique wine.

The following is a list of the wines of the Côte de Beaune:

- Aloxe-Corton produces full-bodied, sturdy, mid-premium wines labeled under the simple "Corton" appellation. The better, Premier cru Le Corton, Corton-Clos du Roi, and Corton-Bressandes are super-premium wines.

Heard it Through the Grapevine

Aloxe-Corton offers two superlative white Grand cru vineyards—Corton-Charlemagne and Charlemagne. These Chardonnay wines are of noble quality. Stylistically, they offer a rich, perfumed aroma of complex fruit and butter with classical proportion. The texture is oily, like butterscotch, but with fine acid balance for structure and longevity.

- Savigny-les-Beaunes wines offer good value. Five of the wines are Premier cru appellations. The wines labeled under the Savigny-les-Beaunes appellation are mid-premium quality. The Premier crus possess superior delicacy and finesse.
- Beaune, Côte de Beaune, and Côte de Beaune Villages are wines from the village of Beaune, which is entitled to use one of three appellations. Beaune wines are medium-bodied, gentle reds and whites.

Tasting Tip

Côte de Beaune Villages wines generally are mid-premium quality, with some finesse and moderate aging potential. The Premier crus are complex wines, capable of combining great depth with a distinctive aroma, and lightness of body with a firm structure.

- Chorey-les-Beaune has red wines, similar to the Côte de Beaune wines. These offer good value.
- Pommard is a village that produces many mid-premium wines under its appellation. These can be village bottlings or from specific vineyard sites, and are full-bodied masculine reds. The Premier crus are fairly rich in aroma and body, with a typical earthy characteristic finish. They age reasonably well and may aspire to super-premium status. Three recommended Grand crus are Les Grands Epenots, Clos Blanc, and Les Rugiens.
- Volnay are the lightest in style of all the Côte de Beaune wines, almost to the point of being fragile. Delicate and early maturing, the Volnay Premier crus are soft and elegant red wines with delicacy and finesse that place them in the super-premium division.
- Auxey-Duresses, Monthelie, Saint-Romain, and Saint-Aubin are little-known villages producing mostly red with some good white wines; they provide good value as they are not in much demand.
- Pernand-Vergelesses is another little-known district that provides good value in red and white wines.
- Santenay, in the south of the Côte de Beaune, are lighter and more delicate wines and have less aging potential in bottle.
- The Meursault place name offers some red wines. However, it's better regarded for its white wines, which range from mid- to super-premium. Those labeled simply "A Meursault" are the mid-premiums—floral in character and streamlined in body with high, crisp acidity. The Premier crus of Meursault are the super-premiums, which display a silky texture, full body, assertive aromas, and complex flavors.
- Puligny-Montrachet white Burgundies are wine perfection! The Grand crus—Le Montrachet, Bâtard-Montrachet, Chevalier-Montrachet, and Bienvenue-Bâtard-Montrachet—are legendary single-vineyard appellations capable of noble quality. Some of the vineyards, namely Le Montrachet and Bâtard-Montrachet, cross over into Chassagne-Montrachet. The wines have a rich, complex fruity aroma, often buttery in character, and combine depth of flavor with a hard veneer that is intense yet austere. They achieve unusual power and finesse for white wines, and require upwards of 10 years of cellaring before they reach their peak.

Heard it Through the Grapevine

The Premier crus of both Puligny and Chassagne tend to be super-premium wines. Some, such as Les Combettes and Les Pucelles have, on occasion, rivaled the Grand crus in noble quality. However, as the vineyards are owned by so many different proprietors and these appellations are used by so many shippers, the names of owners and shippers become your crucial quality determinants.

- Chassagne-Montrachet offers some red wines, but it's most famed for its stylish white wines, particularly the Premier crus, which are full and firm in structure, with a distinct earthy flavor and character. Often they are super-premium wines. Chassagne-Montrachet are somewhat sturdier than Puligny, but with less finesse.

Value? It's All Relative

In Burgundy, value is a relative term. Value-priced wines such as the village and lesser-known appellations offer good value, but these do not display the qualities and subtleties that make Burgundian wines so revered (and, oftentimes, pricey!).

The Sommelier Says

Eager, no-credit-limit wine hobbyists have driven the price of the most desired wines into the stratosphere, even during the recent recession. Wines from the best growers, as well as most revered vineyard sites, command such a high price that they offer little value relative to their costs.

When it comes to the Premier crus and Grand crus, you should look to the vineyards and growers that currently are less fashionable among collectors. Finding the best values requires a familiarity with the numerous growers, their properties, and reputation. (Did I ever say learning about wine would be easy?) Burgundy presents the greatest challenge for the wine lover.

The Intricate Ages of Burgundy

While there are guidelines for aging Burgundy, there also are exceptions to these. The techniques of the different growers in any quality tier can make for either early- or late-maturing wines.

Generally, you can consume red or white wines labeled from the Bourgogne or village appellations three to five years from their vintage. Red wines from Premier cru vineyards mature five to 10 years from their vintage, with notable exceptions that can age for decades.

You should drink the Premier cru whites three to seven years from their vintage. But make sure you cellar Grand cru reds at least seven years, because it takes time for them to develop their nuanced, intricate qualities. These peak, generally, in 10 to 15 years, with some having aging potential of decades. Grand cru whites should have a minimum of three years aging, preferably five years. Many even improve for 10 years or more.

CHAPTER 13

A Closer Look at Burgundy

In This Chapter

- Burgundy's unique terminology
- A tour of the Côte d'Or
- Selected growers and producers

As you learned from the previous chapter, the Burgundy wine region comprises five districts: Chablis, the Côte d'Or, the Côte Chalonnaise, Mâconnais, and Beaujolais. In this chapter, we'll explore genuine nobility, which takes us through only one of these five, the inimitable Côte d'Or.

Burgundy and Bordeaux might as well be from different planets, as two very distinct wine regions from the same country. They have very little in common. Their grapes differ, the languages of their classifications differ, as do their bottle shapes, as do their characteristics and their aging qualities. It's apples and oranges. Or maybe even bananas and pomegranates.

Their differences are also notable in prices. Some of the noblest Burgundies are produced in extremely small quantities, sometimes as few as fifty cases a year! And some connoisseurs (or collectors) want one of everything; so prices go through the roof accordingly sometimes, as do other rare, fine things in high demand.

Fortunately for us, though, not all noble Burgundies are rare, nor will they cost you a year's worth of shelter. This chapter will point you to some good values.

Burgundian Classifications

In a sense, Burgundy has been an official wine region since 1415, when Charles VI (Charles the Mad) issued an edict delimiting what rightly could be called "Bourgogne." The first modern classification of the winegrowing regions of Côte d'Or was in 1905, amended after the World War, in 1919.

Heard it Through the Grapevine

The name Côtes d'Or means Golden Slopes. And any traveler who has viewed these picturesque hillsides in the autumn could not deny that they are golden, indeed! But according to a négociant of that region, the name actually is shortened from Côte d'Orient, so called after its many east-facing slopes (the most desirable).

This classification looked at individual crops, usually single vineyards, called climats. These have been assembled into appellations, such as Beaune and Meursault.

Grand Cru

Only 30 climats (vineyards) were declared Grand Cru, or Great Growth. Of these, 23 are in the northern Côte de Nuits, and seven in the southern Côte de Beaune.

Look on the labels, and you'll see only the name of the vineyard. (And the Appellation Contrôlée, of course.) That's how you know it's a Grand Cru.

Vino Vocab

What we call Grand Cru formerly had been called Tête de Cuvée, literally "head of the class."

Premier Cru

From among thousands of climats, about 560 or so were designated Premier Cru, or First Growth. (Note the distinction between the same designation in Bordeaux!)

On the labels of these bottles, you will read the name of the commune, followed by the name of the vineyard in lettering of the same size, color, and style. (And also the Appellation Contrôlée assurance.)

Village Appellations

The vast numbers of vineyards of the Côte d'Or are neither Grands Crus nor Premiers Crus. These account for the largest share of the region's production. On the label, you will read the village name, but no vineyard designation. Though none of these is anywhere near to noble in quality, many of these are quite good and fairly priced.

Visit Côte de Nuits and See

Named for the small, but important, village Nuits-Saint-Georges, this is the part of the Côte d'Or that's responsible for the color we associate with the word burgundy—because of its red wines. Twelve miles long and one mile wide, this magical wine kingdom featured some of the most famous vineyards of France.

Nuits-Saint-Georges

The largest town between Dijon and Beaune has just a little over five thousand people. (They are called Nuitons.) Yet it gives its name to this northern part of the Côte d'Or. Like the larger Beaune, Nuits-Saint-Georges is an important commercial wine center, home to many important négociants and cellars. Six of this village's vineyards are Premier Cru. None are Grand Cru.

The following Premiers Crus come from vineyards 12 to 21 acres in size. If you're lucky enough to find one of these, buy it:

- Les Damodes
- Aux Boudots
- La Richemone
- Aux Murgers
- Les St.-Greorges
- Les Vaucrains

Tasting Tip

Although there are no Grand Cru climats here, some of the commune's 41 Premiers Crus compare favorably with those of the upper classification. The better vineyards here are very small, though, and you'll have trouble finding some of these tannic, full-bodied, and strong wines that are characteristic of this commune.

Gevrey-Chambertin

Here near its northern limit is the flagship commune of the Côte de Nuits. About 1,300 acres are under vine, including nine Grands Crus (215 acres) and 26 Premiers Crus (212 acres).

The nine Grands Crus are:

- Mazis-Chambertin
- Ruchottes-Chambertin
- Chambertin Clos-de-Bèze
- Chapelle-Chambertin
- Griotte-Chambertin
- Charmes-Chambertin
- Chambertin
- Latricières-Chambertin
- Mazoyères-Chambertin

The soils here exhibit wide variety, with further variety of slope and sunlight. These famous wines are highly regarded for their earthy, meaty style. The Emperor Napoleon liked these wines especially, which played no small part in the development of their reputation.

Chambolle-Musigny

This commune lies between Gevrey-Chambertin and Nuits-St.-Georges. Of its 550 acres, 65 are dedicated to two Grands Crus, 137 to 25 Premiers Crus. These are the lightest, most delicate reds of the Côte de Nuits. You can attribute this to the commune's limestone soils.

The two Grands Crus are:

- Bonnes Mares
- Le Musigny

Of the 25 Premiers Crus, the most respected are:

- Les Armoureuses
- Les Charmes

Vosne-Romanée

This commune lies just north of Nuits-St.-Georges. Together with tiny, adjacent Flagey-Échezeaux to the east, we have six Grands Crus and 15 Premiers Crus. The two communes total only 465 acres. In this commune lie the finest of Burgundy's vineyards; tiny Romanée-Conti is considered probably the very finest wine produced on earth followed by La Tâche, Richebourg, and La Romanée. Naturally, they command a king's ransom for a bottle.

The Grand Crus from here are the most expensive, being praised for their finesse.

- Romanée-Conti
- La Grande Rue
- La Romanée
- Richebourg
- La Tâche
- Romanée-St.-Vivant

Heard it Through the Grapevine

The miniature village of Flagey-Échezeaux, associated with Vosne-Romanée, literally is on the "wrong side of the tracks." Separated by the north-south running railroad, its slopes of this lie to the east of its larger sibling.

Vougeot

The walled, 125-acre Clos de Vougeot vineyard sits on a steep hillside a mile south of town. This Grand Cru climat dominates this commune's total acreage.

Grand cru red Burgundy

More than 80 proprietors make wine from this single vineyard! Who's to say any one is characteristic? I recommend Alain Hudelot-Noëllat as an excellent and affordable example from this property.

Some others you might consider are:

- Chopin-Groffier
- J. Confuron-Contidot
- Gros Frère et Soeur
- Haegelen-Jayer
- Leroy
- Méo-Camuzet
- Mongeard-Mugneret
- Georges Roumier
- Jean Tardy

Morey-St.-Denis

Just southeast of Gevrey-Chambertin is this tiny village surrounded by 370 acres of vineyards. These include five Grands Crus, which are:

- Clos de la Roche
- Clos St.-Denis
- Clos des Lambrays
- Clos de Tart
- Bonnes Mares

These are among the very finest Grand Cru Burgundies, and yet they sell for something less than those of the neighboring communes. These wines are firm, rich, and fragrant.

Now for Côte de Beaune

What a difference a few miles to the south makes! Well, it's not the latitude, actually, but differences in soils, slope, and drainage. This southern part of the Côte d'Or is where we find most of the white Burgundies, which many wine-lovers consider to be the best white wines on earth. This 15-mile strip presents a kaleidoscope of vinous color.

Corton

About four miles north of Beaune sits the village of Corton, at the base of an imposing, south- and east-facing hill, one covered with viticulture. The climat Le Corton covers 360 acres, some in two adjacent communes. These are planted in the Pinot Noir grape. This gigantic Grand Cru property actually is made up of 21 individual vineyards. You'll recognize them on the labels, as each vineyard name is attached to the name "Corton."

Tasting Tip

The colors match! The soils of the Côte de Beaune are lighter in color than the reddish earth of the Côte de Nuits, having more limestone and less iron. This favors the Chardonnay grape, which has made the Côte de Beaune famous for its white Burgundies.

Adjacent to this large collection of red-wine property, on the southwest, is the Corton-Charlemagne vineyard, an additional 177 acres. It's a separate Grand Cru climat called Corton-Charlemagne, and this is the Chardonnay you simply must drink—white Burgundy at its very best!

Beaune

Beaune is the capital of Burgundy—and its winemaking heart and soul. This medieval walled city of about 22,000 is a popular tourist destination. Though it gives its name to the Côte de Beaune and though its headquarters to much of the Côte d'Or's wine trade, it offers no Grand Cru climats of its own.

Premier Cru red Burgundy

Beaune does feature 42 Premiers Crus planted over about 780 acres. Three of my favorite producers are Louis Latour, Joseph Drouhin, and Maison Louis Jadot, which I write about later. About 85 percent of the commune's production is red wine. These wines are not gigantic in flavor, but their smoothness, fruitiness, and harmony make up for this amply.

Pommard

This well-known commune just south of Beaune has 795 acres, all Pinot Noir. Although it has no Grand Cru climats, its 27 Premiers Crus (288 acres) offer some of the fullest wines of the Côte de Beaune. It's not so tannic as it is concentrated and perfumy—what I call breed.

Here are some producers you might look for:

- Comte Armand
- Ballot-Millot
- Courcel
- Joseph Drouhin
- Jean Garaudet
- Armand Girardin
- Machard de Gramont
- Jaboulet-Vercherre
- Louis Jadot
- Leroy

Volnay

Moving south from Pommard, we come to Volnay. It has no Grands Crus, but its 30 Premiers Crus are worth your attention. They differ substantially from those of Pommard, being delicate and subtle, what I would call elegant.

I am especially fond of Marquis d'Angerville, with its Premier Cru Clos des Ducs, which I mention later in this chapter. Other growers you might look for are:

- J. M. Bouley
- Comte Lafon
- Hubert de Montille
- Domaine de la Pousse d'Or

Meursault

This village lies a mile or so due south of Pommard. The gentle slopes to the south of the town all are planted in Chardonnay. These White Burgundies are big and exhilarating.

Premier Cru white Burgundy.

Heard it Through the Grapevine

Don't write off a commune like Meursault because it lacks Grand Cru vineyards. It takes more than a great grape to make a great wine. Many of Burgundy's domaines have produced Premier Cru wines that approach or reach nobility. Considering the prices Burgundy's Grands Crus fetch, it's worthwhile getting to know a few of the Premiers Crus. But most important, as always: Know your grower!

There are no Grands Crus, but there are 13 Premiers Crus. Some producers you might consider are:

- Robert Ampeau
- Bitouzet-Prieur
- Coche-Debord
- Ballot-Millot

Puligny-Montrachet

This tiny village six miles south of Beaune features four Grands Crus. Its name nearly is synonymous with White Burgundy. Subtle differences in soil, drainage, and slope provide considerable variation, but not in overall quality, which is quite high.

The four Grands Crus of Puligny-Montrachet are:

- Montrachet
- Chevalier-Montrachet
- Bâtard-Montrachet
- Bien-Venues-Bâtard-Montrachet

The total acreage for these Grands Crus is only 76; so these can be hard to find—and very expensive.

Chassagne-Montrachet

This tiny hamlet, near the southern limit of the Côte de Beaune, features three Grands Crus. Unfortunately, these cover only 28 acres of the 1,100 acres of vineyards in the commune.

About half of Chassagne-Montrachet's output is red wine, and these fine wines tend to go for moderate prices. The Grands Crus all are white wines. They are:

- Le Montrachet
- Bâtard-Montrachet
- Criots-Bâtard-Montrachet

The last named Grand Cru is only 3.9 acres!

These white wines are big and opulent—with lots of fruit.

Santenay

Santanay lies at the southernmost part of the Côte de Beaune, but it's still only half an hour by car from Beaune. Surprising, this is a red-wine commune, producing white wine in minuscule quantities—about 15 percent of their total production.

There are no Grands Crus here, but 11 Premiers Crus occupy about half of the commune's 810 acres of vines. These are:

- La Comme
- Clos de Tavannes
- Les Gravières
- Passetemps
- La Maladière
- Grand Clos Rousseau
- Clos des Mouches
- Beauregard
- Clos Faubard
- Beaurepaire
- Clos Rousseau

Growers and Producers

The Grands Crus and the Premiers Crus of the Côte d'Or generally are apportioned over large numbers of growers. A single vineyard can yield a number of rather different wines. It all depends on the grower! (Well, not all. Sometimes there are small differences in soils and other growing conditions that account for some of the variability.)

The Sommelier Says

Why do Burgundies cost so much? Considering the scarcity of some Grands Crus, sometimes only a few dozen cases a year, you might wonder why some don't cost more.

But with a little knowledge and a little experience, it is possible to get some pretty good Burgundies for reasonable (though never cheap) prices. But you have to know your domaines!

Here is a list of growers I like. Not all their grapes come from Grand Cru climats, and some Burgundy-drinkers will argue whether this one or that one belongs on this small list. But as I have said many times, the appreciation of wine is an individual experience.

Once you have begun sipping Burgundies—red, white, or both—you're sure to develop your own list of favorites:

The Very Best

- Philippe Leclerc (Gevrey-Chambertin). Here 20 acres are planted with vines 40 to 60 years old. The domaine produces red wines from eight holdings, including four Premier Cru. These are Champonnets, Les Champeaux, Les Cazetiers, and La Combe Aux Moines.
- Dujac (Morey-St.-Denis). With holdings spanning 30 acres, this domaine harvests from 13 vineyards. Five have Grand Cru status: Clos de la Roche, Clos-St.-Denis, Bonnes Mares, Charmes-Chambertin, and Échezeaux. Four are Premier Cru. They are: Clos de la Roche, Clos-St.-Denis, Bonnes Mares, and Charmes-Chambertin.
- Georges Roumier (Chambolle-Musigny). These nine holdings, about 30 acres of Pinot Noir feature four of Grand Cru status: Bonnes-Mares, Musigny, Corton-Charlemagne, and Clos Vougeot.
- Jean Gros (Vosne-Romanée). About nine tiny holdings over 29 acres, with the smallest amount of Chardonnay (about a half acre). The two Grands Crus are Richebourg and Clos de Vougeot.
- Domaine de la Romanée-Conti (Vosne-Romanée). This remarkable domaine has just over 60 acres of holdings in seven Grand Cru climats. They are Romanée-Conti, La Tâche, Richebourg, Romanée-St.-Vivant, Grands-Échezeaux, Échezeaux, and Montrachet. A fine selection of red Burgundies!

- Faiveley (Nuits-St.-Georges). This giant domaine spans 300 acres, with nearly 30 holdings, all red wines. Seven have Grand Cru status: Chambertin Clos de Bèze, Mazis-Chambertin, Latricières-Chambertin, Musigny, Clos de Vougeot, Échezeaux, Rougnet et Corton, and Corton-Charlemagne.
- Domaine des Comtes Lafon (Meursault). This great White Burgundy domaine of about 30 acres is predominantly Premier Cru, with the exception of a holding, less than an acre, in Montrachet. But don't neglect the Premiers Crus Les Charmes and Les Perrières, which should be a little easier to find and a lot less expensive.
- Leflaive (Puligny-Montrachet). This 55-acre domaine has four distinguished Grand Cru holdings: Montrachet, Chevalier-Montrachet, Bâtard-Montrachet, and Bienvenues-Bâtard-Montrachet. The first of these is a minuscule one-fifth acre! Leflaive produces one Premier Cru red, Sous de Dos d'Ane.
- Ramonet (Chassagne-Montrachet). This distinguished domaine has three Grand Cru holdings among its 34 acres of vineyards. These are Le Montrachet, Bâtard-Montrachet, and Bienvenues-Bâtard-Montrachet. They all are Chardonnays, of course.
- Comte Georges de Vogüé (Chambolle-Musigny). This domaine has about 30 acres from five holdings, three of which are Grand Cru. These are: Musigny, Bonnes-Mares, and Musigny (blanc). That last, the white wine, yields only 160 cases a year, a rare Chardonnay grown on Côte de Nuits soil.

The Next Best

- Bruno Claire (Marsannay). With 20 holdings totaling 57 acres, this domaine produces both red and white wines—and a distinguished rosé. One small plot has vines that are more than 90 years old! The two Grands Crus are Clos de Bèze, red, and Le Charlemagne, white. Six vineyards are Premier Cru status.
- Armand Rousseau (Gevrey-Chambertin). This remarkable domaine of 34 acres produces its distinguished red wines from 11 vineyards, six of which are Grand Cru. These are Mazis-Chambertin, Charmes-Mazoyères, Clos de Bèze, Chambertin, Ruchottes Chambertin, and Clos de la Roche. Four other vineyards are Premier Cru.
- Ponsot (Morey-St.-Denis). Here we have 10 holdings totaling about 22 acres. These are red wines, except for the output of the tiny Clos des Monts-Luisants, which is planted in a blend of Chardonnay and the rare Aligoté, from vines planted in 1911! The Grand Cru holdings are Griotte-Chambertin, Chambertin, Chapelle-Chambertin, Clos de la Roche, and Clos St.-Denis.

- Barthod-Noëllat (Chambolle-Musigny). This domaine has nine holdings totaling only 14 acres. Seven are Premier Cru. Perhaps the finest, and rarest, is the one from Les Charmes, a holding less than an acre.
- Michel Chevillon (Nuits-St.-Georges). About 20 acres over nine holdings are all planted in Pinot Noir. Four wines are Premier Cru: Les St.-Georges, Les Porets, Champs Perdrix, and Crots, Bousselots.
- Robert Chevillon (Nuits-St.-Georges). This domaine has 13 holdings totaling 30 acres, nine of which are Premiers Crus. Two that you might find are Les Vaucrains and Les Chaignots.
- Jean Grivot (Vosne-Romanée). Now run by Jean's son, Etienne, here we have 15 holdings over only 25 acres, including three Grands Crus: Échezeaux, Clos de Vougeot, and Richebourg. All are red wines, from vines averaging more than 50 years old.
- Joseph Drouhin (Beaune). This large domaine, 62 acres, has 10 Grands Crus among its holdings, all reds, except for a small amount of white from the Clos des Mouches, a Premier Cru. Most of the Grand Cru holdings are very small, the largest being a two-acre parcel in Clos de Vougeot.
- Maison Louis Jadot (Beaune). This 182-acre domaine is one of the largest in Burgundy, has 90 holdings (and is now even dabbling in the New World, with a winery in Willamette, Oregon), including five Grands Crus. These are Chambertin Clos de Bèze, Chapelle Chambertin, Bonnes-Mares, Musigny, and Clos de Vougeot. Jadot produces one village-appellation rosé and a few regional whites.
- Leroy (Auxey-Duresses). In this 55-acre, biodynamically farmed domaine, we span the full range from the ordinary to the exquisite. Along with regional and village appellations and several Premiers Crus, Leroy produces red wines from nine distinguished Grands Crus. These are Corton-Charlemagne, Corton Renardes, Romanée-St.-Vivant, Richebourg, Clos de Vougeot, Musigny, Clos de la Roche, Latricières Chambertin, and Chambertin.
- Michel Colin Deleger (Chassagne-Montrachet). Except for some regional and village reds, this domaine produces white Burgundies, predominantly from Premier Cru vineyards. Once 48 acres, Michel split his vineyards between his sons, now farming a few small parcels, including his notable white, the Grand Cru Chevalier Montrachet "Les Demoiselles," from a holding of less than one acre.
- Jean-Marc Morey (Chassagne-Montrachet). This 20-acre domaine has no Grand Cru holdings, but produces both reds and whites from 10 Premiers Crus. Jean-Marc Morey is proudest of his Les Champs Gains red and its Les Caillerets white.

- Bernard Morey (Chassagne-Montrachet). Bernard Morey, who now works with his daughter, Caroline, produces both reds and whites from Premiers Crus over his 28 acres of holdings. I recommend the Les Charmois white.

Good and Reliable

- Louis Trapet (Gevrey-Chambertin). The domaine produces red wines over 30 acres from seven holdings, a few with vines more than 80 years old. Three vineyards are Grand Cru: Chambertin, Chapelle-Chambertin, and Latricières-Chambertin. One is Premier Cru.
- Domaine des Lambrays (Morey-St.-Denis). These holdings comprise 32 acres, all red wines, with two Grand Cru and four Premier Cru vineyards. The Grands Crus are Clos de Lambrays and Corton, Clos des Maréchaudes. The Premiers Crus are Le Village-La Riotte, Corton, Clos des Maréchaudes, Les Maillerets, and Les Folatières.
- Le Clos de Tart (Morey-St.-Denis). This remarkable Grand Cru vineyard has existed intact for more than 800 years! This 19-acre plot, the domaine's only holding, produces a wine that's complete, without being big and strong.
- Alain Hudelot-Noëllat (Vougeot). Here we have nearly 30 acres over 11 holdings, all red. Three of these are Grand Cru: Clos de Vougeot, Romanée-St.-Vivant, and Richebourg.
- Henri Gouges (Nuits-St.-Georges). This domaine has 35 acres over nine holdings. Six are Premier Cru, including La Perrière, which is planted in Chardonnay. Another white Burgundy is grown on a regional appellation vineyard. The rest are reds.
- Louis Latour (Beaune). This large (125 acres) domaine has 20 holdings, including seven Grands Crus, both red and white Burgundies. The reds are Corton Bressandes, Chevalier-Montrachat, Chambertin, and Romanée-St.-Vivant. The whites are Le Charlemagne, Les Languettes, and Le Corton.
- Marquis d'Angerville (Volnay). Yes, he's a real marquis! And his domaine of 33 acres includes nine Premiers Crus and one village appellation, nearly all planted in Pinot Noir. Of special note is the Clos des Ducs.
- Jacques Prieur (Meursault). This domain, about 50 acres, features both reds and whites from eight small Grand Cru holdings. The whites are Montrachet and Chevalier Montrachet. The reds are Corton Bressandes, Corton Charlemagne, Clos de Vougeot, Le Musigny, Chambertin, and Chambertin Clos de Bèze.

CHAPTER 14

The Tour de France

In This Chapter

- The Loire Valley: fresh and fruity
- The Rhône Valley: wines of substance
- Jura: Louis Pasteur's homeland is also home to some unusual vin
- Alsace: German wines of France
- Provence: land of sunshine
- Champagne: where the bubbles sparkle
- Languedoc and Rousillon: simple wines, improving all the time

We've lingered long in the Bordeaux and Burgundy regions. In Chapter 21, we'll call on France's Champagne region, as well. But in this chapter we'll visit all the rest of France.

I mean that literally. The French grow their wine grapes simply everywhere. We'll begin with the Loire River Valley. In that winegrowing region, the longest in the world, grapes, flavors, and styles vary with the scenery. They offer us many distinctive, enjoyable, and affordable wines.

Then we'll explore the Rhône Valley with its hearty, full-bodied wines. Then on to Alsace, where three centuries of contention between France and Germany have left us a French wine region with a decidedly German flair. This is where the noble Riesling varietal shares its fame with the spicy Gewürztraminer.

Next, we'll travel south, near the Riviera, to sunny Provence. There we'll find large quantities of straightforward, refreshing wines.

Finally, you'll learn how modern technology has transformed the once-inferior wines of Languedoc-Roussillon, which run from central France all the way south to the Mediterranean, into table wines of excellent value.

The Loire River Valley

In its winding peregrination, the Loire River extends nearly 650 miles. Along its lower reaches, this river nurtures the world's longest viticultural region. The area is rich in picturesque vineyards, vast amounts of farmland, magnificent castles and châteaux, and wines that range from pleasant and inexpensive to complex and fascinating.

The Loire is France's longest river. It rises in the Cévennes mountains in the southeast. Flowing north, it cuts through the high plateau region of the Massif Central before turning west and widening into a broad valley, France's agricultural heartland. The Loire widens into an estuary at Nantes before flowing into the Atlantic at the northern part of the Bay of Biscay.

If you want to savor wine in its homeland, this is a fascinating region to visit. The cool climate produces light-bodied, refreshing white wines and minerally, medium-bodied reds. Now let's look at the districts of the Loire region.

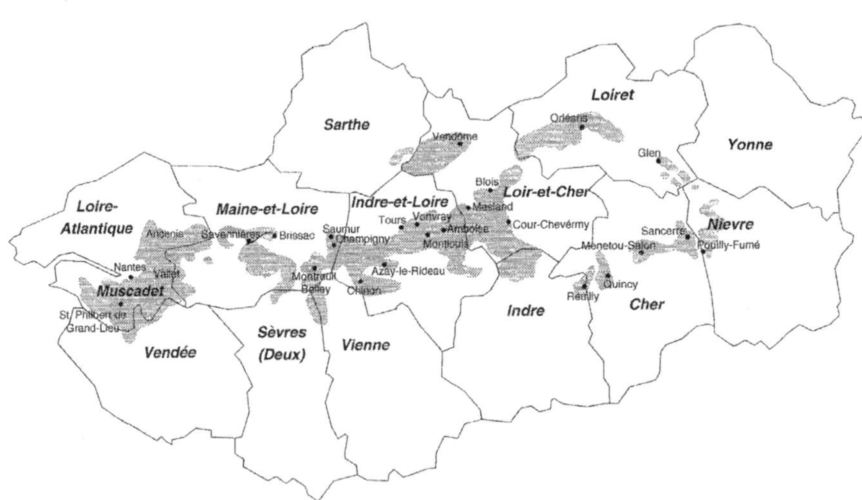

The Loire River nurtures the world's longest viticultural region.

Muscadet

Tasting Tip

The best Muscadets are crisp and bone dry. Muscadet is an excellent companion to oysters, clams, and delicate fish. It's also a great summer drink.

Let's begin at the river's mouth, near the city of Nantes, where the Loire forms a large estuary. Here vineyards produce the Muscadet, or Melon de Bourgogne grape. Muscadet wines are light-bodied, pleasant, and at times slightly fruity wines.

Muscadet wines are refreshing, and their prices are too. You can find a good Muscadet for $10 to $15 a bottle. Buy it while it's still young—at its best. It retains a zesty effervescence and piquant vinous character for about one year from its vintage date.

The best Muscadet wines will bear the name of the Sèvre-et-Maine region on the label. Also look for the term "sur lie" (from the lees). These are bottled right from the cask with no racking. This procedure gives the wine freshness, and sometimes a lively little prickle of carbon dioxide on the tongue. The most refreshing and flavorful Muscadet is bottled sur lie, best drunk as early as possible.

Pouilly-Fumé

Pouilly-Fumé is a wine made from the grape Sauvignon Blanc in the vicinity of the town of Pouilly-sur-Loire. It is somewhat fuller than Sancerre and can have aromas of gun flint and spicy flavors.

Pouilly-Fumés range from slightly thin and ordinary wines to more aromatic, slightly complex premium wines. Pouilly-Fumé can be quite a fine wine when made by a good producer like Ladoucette. Richer than Sancerre, Pouilly-Fumé complements poached salmon, veal, or chicken.

Pouilly-Fumé wines range in price from $15 to $35 per bottle. It is best enjoyed young, within three or four years of the vintage.

Sancerre

In the eastern end of the region, about 80 miles south of Paris, are the towns of Sancerre and Pouilly-sur-Loire, on opposite banks of the river. Here thrives the Sauvignon Blanc grape, which makes lively, dry wines. These offer spicy, green-grass flavors that can range from ordinary to outstanding and can be very distinctive.

Compared with Pouilly-Fumé, Sancerre is somewhat lighter in body, extremely elegant, and more refreshing. It's a good match with shellfish or delicate fish like rainbow trout. In recent years, Sancerre prices have risen, and fetch bottle prices from $20 to $35 or $40 a bottle. They are best drunk within three or four years of their vintage.

In much smaller quantities, you can find Pinot Noir produced here as well, and while it isn't the same complexity that you might find in its nearby neighbor, Burgundy, and the reds of Sancerre are far less famous than the whites, they are worth seeking out, with their tendency toward medium-light bodied wines with bright, fresh red cherry, strawberry, and fresh herby flavors and aromas.

Vouvray

The central part of the Loire Valley region, near Tours, features both Vouvray wines and several palatial châteaux. Most Vouvray wines are white, made from the Chenin Blanc grape, which does well in this terrain, once trod by royalty.

Heard it Through the Grapevine

The wines of Vouvray are produced in three distinct styles—dry, medium-dry, or sweet (called moelleux). These last are luscious and at their best, super-premium. These sweet wines can be made only in vintages of unusual ripeness, which occur infrequently. That makes these both rare and costly. Vouvray also produces sparkling wines that are pleasant and inexpensive.

The best Vouvray wines are agers. These require several years to develop. With their high acidity, they can last years without risk of becoming salad dressing. These begin in the $12 to $30 range.

Chinon and Bourgueil

While the Loire may be most famous for its whites, reds produced from the Cabernet Franc grape varietal have become more and more noteworthy with wine geeks and value-seekers looking for interesting, food-friendly reds that defy the long-time trend of big, oaky California wines. Chinon and Bourgueil lie on the south and north sides, respectively, of the Loire River and producer reds that range from light and gently fruity to dry, lip-smacking reds that taste of pencil lead and dried herbs, and range in price from around $15 to $35.

Rosés of the Loire

The Loire Valley produces rosé wines in huge quantities. Most come from an area around Anjou. These popular Anjou rosés are a lovely pink-orange color, and are made from Grolleau, Cabernet Franc, and Gamay. They are low in acidity, appealingly fruity, and sometimes slightly spritzy. They range from dry to medium-sweet in style.

The Rhône River Valley

Just south of Beaujolais, stretching between the city of Lyon in the foothills of the Swiss Alps all the way south to Provence, is the warm, sunny, and wine-rich Rhône Valley. But while the region is referred to in one, fell linguistic swoop, it is distinctly divided into northern and southern parts.

These regional reds are full, robust, and hearty with good color and a ripe, fruity character. The whites age well and are oftentimes spicy, medium-bodied, rich, and earthy.

The Sommelier Says

The Rhône Valley wine region is split into northern and southern divisions. Strangely, the part of the Rhône Valley that lies in between—which totals about 40 miles of land—does not afford growing conditions suitable for wine production.

Northern and southern Rhône divisions produce distinctively different wines. The greatest distinction, however, may be in amount of wine produced (and, possibly, the prices charged for them): About 95 percent comes from the southern Rhône. The prime red varietal in the northern Rhone is spicy Syrah; for whites, it's Viognier, Marsanne, and Rousanne. The southern Rhône's main grapes is Grenache, with other reds like Mourvedre, Cinsault, and Syrah in the mix producing wines high in alcohol and juicy, red fruit flavors and aromas. Most southern Rhône wines are simple, inexpensive to medium priced, and accessible and enjoyable for a great, informal evening at home. The section that follows describes the different districts of the northern and southern Rhône.

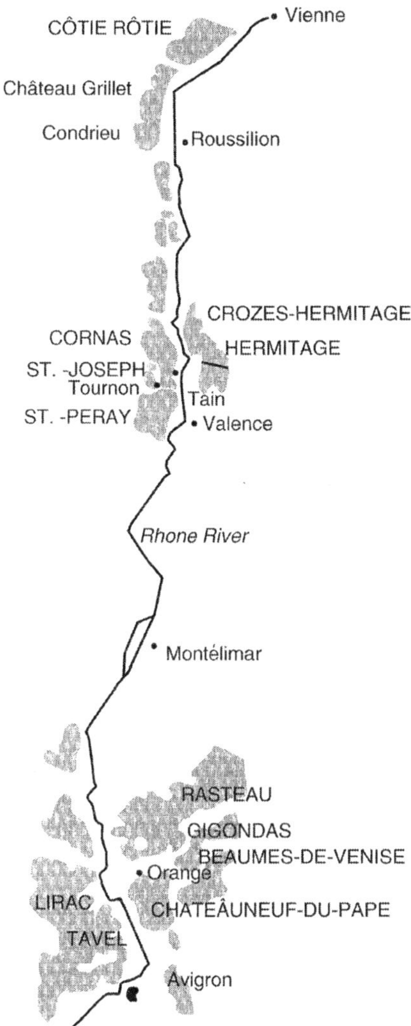

The Rhone River Valley produces some superb wines.

Côtes du Rhône

The Côtes du Rhône and Côte du Rhône-Villages appellations of the southern Rhone offer a number of highly drinkable red and white wines. Reds are more available in the U.S., ranging from $9 to $20 per bottle. Wines from the higher appellation—the 19 villages that make up Côtes du Rhône-Villages—are fuller and occupy the higher end of the price spectrum.

Heard it Through the Grapevine

France's Rhône River, its second-longest, originates high in the Swiss Alps. In Switzerland, it's punctuated by the Lake of Geneva (near where those watches are made). The Rhône enters France east of Lyon where it turns southward. Then it flows through its eponymous wine region and into the Mediterranean at Marseilles, where the French wines had their origin.

The reds generally are fruity and light-bodied, similar to inexpensive Beaujolais. Uncomplicated by nature, they can withstand a slight chilling to bring out their fruity vinosity, low acidity, and light tannins. The result is thoroughly pleasant drinking. The less common white Côtes du Rhône bottlings are mildly fruity, somewhat coarse and rough—earthy wine at its best!

Gigondas, Vacqueyras, and Beaumes de Venise

Gigondas, Vacqueyras, and Beaumes de Venise are three former members of Côtes du Rhône-Village that now merit their own appellations. Gigondas, especially, is robust, rich, and a good ager. A superior vintage can thrive for 10 years or more in the bottle, and they range in cost from $20 to $35 a bottle.

Chateâuneuf-du-Pape

Chateâuneuf-du-Pape is the pride of the southern Rhône Valley. Its intriguing name evokes the 14th century, when the popes resided in nearby Avignon. The vineyards with this venerable appellation extend over 8,000 acres, producing more than a million cases of wine.

Chateâuneuf-du-Pape is a robust red wine made from a blend of up to 13 grape varieties. The primary grapes are Grenache, Mourvedre, and Syrah. Quality ranges from mid-premium to an occasional super-premium. At the upper levels are slow-maturing, hard, sturdy, and tannic wines. The best have a full body and are rich, complex, and high in alcohol. Some more accessible wines are fruitier, less complex, and rounder.

Tasting Tip

The best Chateâuneuf-du-Pape vintages age well in-bottle for 15 to 20 years. One of the very finest, Château Râyas, differs from type by being 100 percent Grenache, made from very old vines. Château Beaucastel is a notable wine that can mature for 20 years or longer.

Tavel and Lirac

A close neighbor of Chateâuneuf-du-Pape, Tavel excels in producing the world's best—and most expensive—rosés. Less celebrated than Tavel, Lirac produces both reds and rosés, though the latter do not equal the quality of their Tavel cousins. However, these offer tasty, refreshing wines, reasonably priced. The wines from both areas are made primarily from Grenache and Cinsault grapes.

Hermitage

Hermitage reds from the northern Rhone are mid- to super-premium wines, rich and full-bodied, and with great aging potential. They are made from the noble Syrah grape. They are not quite up to Côte-Rotie wines in finesse, but are high in tannins and alcohol, and they develop complexity and vigor when fully aged.

The best vintages will mature in-bottle for 30 years or more (1988, 1989, 1990, 1991 and 1995, 1998, 1999, 2003, 2006 and 2009 were stellar years for the northern Rhône; 2009 was one of the finest ever for Hermitage). The three best producers of Hermitage are Chapoutier, Jean-Louis Chave, and Paul Jaboulet Ainé. The best Hermitages range from $35 to $60, but you can find Hermitages from lesser producers for as little as $20 to $30 a bottle.Hermitage also produces a small quantity of white wine, made from the Marsanne and Rousanne grape varieties. White Hermitage is a full, rich, earthy wine that needs six to 10 years to really develop.

Condrieu

Condrieu is made 100 percent from the Viognier grape variety, and it's another excellent white wine from the northern Rhône. This is one of the most fragrant and floral wines you can find. It has flavors that are delicate yet lush, with fragrant fresh apricot and peach nuances. Drink it young. Condrieu sells for $25 to $70 a bottle.

Côte-Rotie

Côte-Rôtie—which translates to mean "roasted hills" for the vineyards' full-on exposure to sunlight—are wines almost uniformly high in quality, with many reaching super-premium status. They are more subtle than Hermitage wines, in part due to the up to 20 percent of the white Viognier grape that may be added, which lends itself to rather perfumed and pretty aromatics. Firm and long-lasting, they develop a berry and truffle flavor with aging, and their smooth texture gives them finesse as they mature.

Peak vintages of Côte-Rôtie possess aging potential of 20 years or more (1991 was a great year, as was the recent 2009). The most celebrated producer of Côte-Rôtie is Guigal. La

Mouline, La Landonne, and La Turque, Guigal's single-vineyard wines, are superb (although quite expensive). You can find most Côte-Rôties for $30 to $80 a bottle.

Jura: Unusual Wines Worth Your Time

Tucked between Burgundy and Switzerland, Jura is known (well, when it is known at all—it is definitely more the darling of the wine-geek crowd than the crowd-pleaser set) for a few things: for its dino-dwellers of 210 million years ago and the Jurassic Era that took its name from the eponymous mountains; from being the homeland of Louis Pasteur and some great cheese to boot, fittingly; and fossil-laden soils that make for some pretty interesting Chardonnay, Pinot Noir, Savagnin (or the vin jaune), and Poulsard, a red varietal that makes light-bodied, slightly orange-hued reds.

Jura is France's smallest wine-producing region,with less than 5,000 acres of vineland, Jura (which, if you're unsure about how to say that first letter, it's pronounced like the "z" in that famous Gabor sister's name) is a unique little spot, for sure. Its fossil-laden soil became famous where cool-climate loving varietals grow in the foothills.

The wines of Jura (especially the whites) are not for everyone—they are extremely dry, slightly briny, and highly unusual. Still, if you can keep an open mind, and an open palate, the slightly oxidized Chardonnays and sherry-like Vin Jaunes are phenomenal food-friendly wines. Pay special attention to the wines from the area known as Arbois, where you will find fascinating examples of Chardonnay and Poulard on the market.

Alsace—the German Wines of France

Located in France's Northeast, bordering Germany, Alsace is separated from the rest of France by the Vosges Mountains. Wines from Alsace differ in several ways from those from all other French regions. First, they differ in character and style (not to mention the grape varietals that thrive), bearing a closer kinship with the wines of Germany. Next, most Alsatian wines carry a grape variety name and bear the appellation "Alsace." Finally, Alsatian wines come in a tall, thin, tapered bottle, called a flute, unlike any other French wine bottles.

The Alsatian vineyards are situated on the lower slopes of the Vosges Mountains, west of the Rhine River. These are among the most beautiful in the world, dotted with picturesque villages and impressive cathedrals. Despite the northern latitude of the Alsatian region, the climate is temperate, sunny and dry, the kind of climate grapes (and grape growers) love.

Alsatian vineyards largely are planted in German varieties—Riesling, Sylvaner, Gewürtztraminer—along with some Pinot Blanc, Pinot Gris, Pinot Noir, and Muscat varieties. The small quantity of light-bodied Pinot Noir is vastly outnumbered by the 93 percent of Alsatian wines that are white. The climate and vinification endow the Alsatian whites with a fuller body, stronger alcohol content, and greater austerity and dryness than their German counterparts. The Alsatian whites, Gewürztraminer especially, have a spicy character unique to the region.

Heard it Through the Grapevine

Until the close of World War II, the territory and people of Alsace have been variously French or German. Originally part of the Holy Roman Empire, Alsace lands were acquired by France in bits and pieces over a span of several hundred years. But the entire Alsace-Lorraine region was annexed by the German Empire in 1871, after the Franco-Prussian War. The territories reverted to France after the First World War, only to be taken over by Germany during the Second.

Those few periods of German rule and affiliation seem to have left a mark on the style of Alsatian wines. These fine wines are far closer in character to German wines than to their French counterparts. As in Germany, most Alsatian production is white wine.

Riesling

In Alsace, the Riesling is king of wines (as it is in Germany). Here, however, it is produced in a relatively dry style. Alsace Rieslings have a flowery bouquet, but with a firmness that belies its flavors.

Most Alsatian Rieslings are made to be consumed young. But certain wines from outstanding vintages are made in the late-harvest style, and can they be aged for a decade or more. Rieslings show up here in the $15 to $30 a bottle price range, with late-harvest bottlings going for upwards of $60 a bottle or more.

Gewürztraminer

For dry, spicy Gewürztraminers, Alsace has no equal. The Gewürztraminer grape has a personality all its own—pungent and intense, with a unique spicy flavor. Either you like it, or you don't!

High in alcohol and low in acidity, its impression is rich and mellow. Gewürztraminer goes well with strong cheeses, spicy Asian cuisine, and your favorite fruit. Also, it's fine all by itself, before or after a meal. It sells in the same price range as Alsatian Riesling, but it doesn't age well.

Pinot Blanc

Alsace Pinot Blanc is the lightest of the Alsatian wines, with a mellow, fruity character. While it generally is dry, some producers make it medium-dry to appeal to wine drinkers who do not like an austere style. You cannot tell from the label which style is which; so you should ask your wine merchant. In either style, these wines are best drunk young. Alsatian Pinot Blancs range from $10 to $20 a bottle.

Other Varieties

The Sylvaner grapes make slightly fruity, highly acidic table wines. Only a small quantity is sold in the U.S. Similarly, Muscat d'Alsace, a slightly bitter, usually dry white wine is found here only in small quantities. Tokay d'Alsace, made from Pinot Gris, is a full-bodied, rich, and spicy wine with a lot to offer. Like Gewürztraminer, it is low in acidity and high in alcohol. It sells in the $10 to $20 category, and makes a good complement for spicy meat dishes.

Les Autres

Les Autres means simply "the others." The two areas in this section—Côtes de Provence and Languedoc-Rousillon —produce simple, affordable wines. However, those of the latter are gaining in quality and attention.

Côtes de Provence—Land of Sunshine

Côtes de Provence is located in the south of France, bordering the French Riviera in the hilly region between Marseilles and Nice. It produces vast quantities of refreshing and simple red, white, and rosé wines, along with tiny amounts of sparkling wine.

The white wines are labeled either "Côtes de Provence" or "Cassis." When well-made, these relatively dry wines are fruity and pleasingly refreshing, with some amount of distinction. White wines from the Appellation Controlée Cassis tend to be more austere and richer in flavor. The numerous rosés from this region are uncomplicated and dry to slightly off-dry. The red wine from Bandol, made primarily from the Mourvedre Franc varietal, is tasty and pleasant. (But it tends to be overpriced.)

Languedoc-Roussillon—Gaining in Quality

It used to the be that the Mediterranean-rimming regions of Languedoc and Rousillon were, like southern Italy, the country's bulk-production smorgasbord. But growers here began to see that there is money is quality (and exports), and with funding from the EU, the quality here has improved by leaps and bounds. In late 2007, Languedoc was elevated to an AOC, with subregional AOCs like St.-Chinian, Minervois, and Corbières producing wines from red varietals such Carignan, Grenache, Cinsault, Mourvedre, and Syrah making waves for quality wines at inexpensive prices.

In the past, many districts in the large Languedoc-Roussillon region of France were known only for very cheap vins ordinnaires. However, thanks to innovation and technology (and some strong motivation on the part of the region's winemakers), these wines have improved in quality—and that includes the wines designated as Vins de Pays, too, where plantings of varietals like Cabernet Sauvignon, Merlot, and Chardonnay has increased and yielded interesting results. For the most part, these are straightforward, simple wines that are very reasonably priced and perfect for everyday drinking. They range in price from $7 to $15 a bottle and frequently offer fine value.

CHAPTER 15

Wines of Italy

In This Chapter

- Italian wine laws
- What's on the Italian wine label
- The wine regions of Italy

Italy is the largest wine-producer in the world, beating out France, Spain, and the U.S. Practically all of this mountainous country supports winegrowing, from the Alpine soil in the north to the sunny shores of the Mediterranean to the south.

Wine is an essential part of any Italian dinner. So perhaps you won't be surprised to learn that people have made wine on the Italian peninsula for three millennia. But guess how long Italy has had a formal system of wine classification? For just slightly less than 50 years, having begun in 1963 when the Italian government decided to use the French system as a model. And even today, Italy still lacks anything like the French "cru" system of vineyard classification, but it has—and continues—to make some of the finest, most terroir-driven, utterly unique wines in the world.

Italian grapes are not only provincial, they're patriotic! Even the finicky Pinot Noir has conceded grudgingly to perform outside of France (and with some pretty good success with producers like Hofsatter in Alto Adige, for instance). In contrast, the Italian grape varieties—such as Sangiovese, Nebbiolo, and Barbera—are outstanding performers only in their native soils, despite efforts everywhere from South America to California to imitate.

But the Italian growing environments are unique, as well as varied. Some vineyards thrive high in the mountains. The altitude seems to protect the vines from the withering heat of the lowlands. In fact, the only wines in the world made on the slopes of an active volcano are the whites and reds of Mount Etna, a spot that has seen a doubling of winemakers putting down roots in the dry, volcanic soil in the last decade.

Italy has 20 wine regions, corresponding to its political jurisdictions. These wine regions here are called zones, to avoid any particular political connotation.

For generations, Italians kept the best premium wines for their own consumption, but today it's possible to find great Italian wines—wines with breed and finesse. It takes just a little homework. Begin by reading this chapter.

The best wine districts of Italy.

The Basic Three

For purposes of this book, I'm going to rank Italian wines into three categories:

1. Inexpensive red and white wines for everyday drinking.

2. The better wines, which range from simple to mid-premium quality.

3. A small, select number of wines that are of super-premium quality, and on occasion, noble quality.

Tasting Tip

If you've avoided Italian wines—in favor of those from France or California—because you think they are inherently inferior, think again! Italian vintners have been turning out many new products that have enjoyed worldwide acclaim, not to mention old stunning standbys like Barolo, Barbaresco, and Amarone!

In the first category we find one of the best-known Italian wines for casual drinking. I mean Lambrusco, that effervescent, slightly sweet red wine that rose to popularity in the U. S. in the 1970s. It continues to please drinkers who want a pleasant, undemanding wine.

In the second category are most of the wines I'll describe in this chapter, plus many others space doesn't allow me to discuss.

The third category includes wines the Italians have created to emulate the finest wines of Bordeaux and California as well as the very best homegrown wines—Barolo, Barbesco, Gattinara, and Brunello.

What's up, DOC?

Long ago, when most people heard the term "Italian wine" we pictured a cheap and largely undrinkable product in a straw-covered flask, with "Chianti" on the label. (Some of these wines actually were from Chianti, but many were not.)

As you might imagine, a number of Italian winemakers who took pride in their creations felt they were unfairly stigmatized. So they set about to correct things, to provide a viable structure for their national wine industry. And they got the government to help them.

So Italy enacted a body of laws called the Denominazione di Origine Controllata (DOC). Introduced in 1963, the DOC went into effect in 1967.

DOC laws control the quality of Italian wines through legal definition of viticultural districts, regulation of yields-per-acre, specification of grape varieties, specifications for alcohol content, and minimum requirements for cask aging. The terms "Superiore," "Riserva," and "Classico," which appear on wine labels, took on legal significance.

Vino Vocab

In Italy, DOC stands for Denominazione di Origine Controllata, the exact Italian equivalent of the French Appellation d'Origine Contrôlée, which means, simply, "controlled place name."

The lowest category of Italian wines, rarely imported, is simple table wine, which does not fall under DOC regulations. The second, most of what we see in the U.S., is DOC (Denominazione di Origine Controllata) wine. This runs from simple everyday wines to super-premium. Look for the phrase Denominazione di Origine Controllata on the label.

At the very top is Denominazione di Origine Controllata e Garantita (DOCG). This elite, mostly in the super-premium quality category, must meet additional standards for winemaking and taste-testing, such as the wines must be grown, produced, and bottled all in their respective designated area.

Heard it Through the Grapevine

Currently there are over 300 DOC-designated (Denominazione di Origine Controllata) districts in Italy. An appellation of a Classico region, with more stringent standards than the broader DOC, provides a second tier at this level. (Chianti Classico is an example.)

Over 50 Italian wines have earned the respected Denominazione di Origine Controllata e Garantita (DOCG) designation. DOCG wines that fail to pass the tasting test are declassified as ordinary table wine, rather than DOC wine. This motivates winemakers to produce a superior product.

All Roads Lead to Wine

Italy has hundreds of wine districts, too many to cover in this book. Instead, we'll look at those that produce wines readily available in the United States.

Italy's Main Wine Regions

Red Wine	White Wine	Grape Variety
Piedmont		
Barbaresco		Nebbiolo
Barbera d'Alba and similar DOCs		Barbera
Gavi		Cortese di Cortese Gavi
Roero Arneis		Arneis
Barolo		Nebbiolo
Gattinara		Nebbiolo, Bonarda[1]
Tuscany		
Brunello di Montalcino		Sangiovese Grosso
Chianti, Chianti Classico		Sangiovese, Canaiolo, and others
Vernaccia di San		Gimignano Vernaccia
Vino Nobile di Montepulciano		Sangiovese, Canaiolo, and others[1]
Carmignano		Sangiovese, Cabernet Sauvignon[1]
Super-Tuscans2		Carbernet Sauvignon, Sangiovese
Veneto		
Amarone della Valpolicella		Corvina, Rondinella Molinara[1]; semi-dried
Bardolino		Corvina, Rondinella, Molinara[1]
	Bianco di Custoza	Trebbiano, Garganega, Tocai[1]
	Lugana	Trebbiano
Soave		Soave Garganega, Trebbiano, and others[1]
Valpolicella		Corvina, Rondinella, Molinara[1]
Trentino-Alto Adige		
Pinot Nero		Pinot Nero/Noir
Lagrein		Lagrein
Schiava		Schiava
	Chardonnay	Chardonnay (various DOCs)
	Pinot Grigio	Pinot Gris (various DOCs)
	Pinot Bianco	Pinot Blanc (various DOCs)
	Sauvignon	Sauvignon Blanc (various DOCs)

Red Wine	**White Wine**	**Grape Variety**
	Kerner	Kerner
	Sylvaner	Sylvaner
	Riesling	Riesling
	Traminer	Gewurztraminer
Fruili-Venezia Giulia		
	Chardonnay	Chardonnay (various DOCs)
	Pinot Blanco	Pinot Blanc (various DOCs)
	Pinot Grigio	Pinot Gris (various DOCs)
	Sauvignon	Sauvignon Blanc (various DOCs)
	Tocai Friulano	Tocai Friulano (various DOCs)
Umbria		
	Orvieto	Trebbiano

1 Blended wines, made from two or more grapes

2 Non-traditional wines produced mainly in the Chianti district (see Tuscany)

Tuscany—Where It All Began

Tuscan winemaking began 3,000 years ago with the Etruscans who inhabited this northern piece of Italy. Now that's what I call tradition!

The name of the region's most famous wine, Chianti, appears in records from 1260 B.C.E. (only then it referred to a white wine). In an interesting twist of fate, white wine from Tuscany may not legally be called Chianti.

The Sommelier Says

DOCG tasting requirements do not always guarantee superior quality. Too much depends on the qualifications of the taster, tasting methods, and taste standards employed. When it comes to selecting a superior Italian wine, there is no substitute for knowledge.

The best wines of Tuscany come from near Florence, a city known for its Renaissance art. The vineyards of Chianti, the largest DOC zone, are situated among olive groves, stone farmhouses, and an occasional castle. It's only a short hop from bucolic, picturesque vineyards to some of the world's most impressive art and architecture.

Chianti is divided into eight sub-districts: Classico, Colli Fiorentini, Montespertoli, Montalbano, Rufina, Colli Aretini, Colli Senesi, and Colli Pisani. All of them turn out good wine (in fact, all hold DOCG status), but Chianti Classico is the undisputed numero uno. Second in quality is Chianti Rufina.

Heard it Through the Grapevine

Chianti wines may carry the name of the district, or may appear simply as "Chianti." The name Chianti by itself may mean the wine was blended from grapes from two districts. The cépage (blending of grape varieties) in Chianti is carried out at the producer's discretion, but only certain grape varieties are permitted, and certain ones are required by DOC law.

Sangiovese is the dominant grape, with a requirement of 50 to 80 percent, and the other red grape—Canaiolo—at 10 to 30 percent. The blend also requires from 10 to 30 percent from the white grapes Trebbiano or Malvasia. Many producers make their Chiantis almost entirely from the Sangiovese grape, which is not consistent with the DOC regulations, but I think it makes for a better wine.

Chianti wines vary according to sub-district and, to a lesser degree, grape blending. They also vary in style and quality. Ordinary Chianti, at the lower end of the price range, is a prickly, fruity wine, made to be drunk young. The middle range embraces simple to mid-premium wines, Classico or otherwise. These age well in the bottle for several years, but you can enjoy them and their lovely cherry-fruit flavors when you buy them.

The highest quality is the Riserva, the product of a special selection of vines or harvest, greater care in winemaking, and longer aging before release (at least three years). Riservas frequently are aged in French oak for a minimum of 10 years. Many will age well for 20 or 30 years.

Chianti is a very dry red wine that goes well with food. It is a vinous wine that frequently has an aroma of cherries and sometimes hints of violets. Its taste sometimes is similar to that of tart cherries, but for the most part Chianti is best described as, well, tasting like Chianti. The best Chiantis are high in acidity and do not reach their peak until four to eight years after the vintage. Some of the better Chiantis, particularly the single-vineyard examples, can age for 10 years or more in great vintages.

Chianti is not the only red wine of Italy. (It just seems that way!) One important Tuscan red wine, currently taking bows, hails from the town of Montalcino, south of Florence in the Sienna hills. It emerged from a clone or variant of the Sangiovese, known as the Brunello, or large Sangiovese. The resulting wine, Brunello di Montalcino, brings some of the highest prices of any Italian wine.

Brunello di Montalcino is one of those overnight successes that's been around for ages—literally. In 1970, the Biondi-Santi family (the leading producer in Montalcino) decided their wines could use some publicity. So they invited some leading wine writers to a tasting of rare vintages. Needless to say, these 1888 and 1891 vintages were a smash!

Brunello immediately became one of the most sought-after wines in Italy. Twelve years after its harvest, the 1971 reserve bottling retailed in the U.S. for $130 a bottle. Even by the extravagant standards of the '80s, that was pretty pricey for a young wine in no way ready to drink.

The publicity for this DOCG wine has been mixed. Not all bottlings deserved the prices they demanded. Now that the rage has died down, however, there is general agreement that Brunello di Montalcino has the potential to be one of the world's most superb and long-lived red wines. Prices begin at $40 to $80 a bottle and scale upward.

The Sommelier Says

The Brunello variant on Chianti is a huge, full-bodied, and intense wine, with concentration and astringent tannins. But to enjoy its qualities, you may need to age it up to 20 years. Now, some producers in Montalcino are making a more accessible version of Brunello, one that is ready to drink in about five years.

From vineyards surrounding the hilly town of Montepulciano comes another red wine, Vino Nobile di Montepulciano. Vino Nobile is close to a Chianti Classico, but responds better to aging. Its minimum age is two years; a Riserva must have three years, and with four it can be designated Riserva Speciale. Just as there is a younger and lighter version of Brunello, there's a younger Vino Nobile as well: Rosso di Montepulciano.

The Carmignano district west of Florence produces a red wine that owes a good part of its high quality to the incongruous (but welcome) presence of Cabernet Sauvignon. Essentially a Chianti with a French flair, Carmignano can be made with up to 10 percent of the noble Bordeaux grape.

Possibly descended from the white wine of the ancient Etruscans, Vernaccia di San Gimignano bears the name of a medieval walled village west of the Chianti Classico zone. Vernaccia is vinified to be drunk young. It is a refreshing white wine with a slightly viscous texture with hints of almonds and nuts. Most Vernaccias sell in the $12 to $20 price range.

Super-Tuscans—Triumph of Technology

During the 1970s, certain visionary winemakers decided to transcend the limits of traditional winemaking and experiment with unorthodox blendings in a quest to make wine of Bordeaux classified-growth stature. Producers like Piero Antinori gained worldwide attention by creating new wines (for example, Tignanello and Solaia) that became known collectively as super-Tuscans. Like Carmignano, these blends were usually Sangiovese and Cabernet Sauvignon.

Tasting Tip

The super-Tuscans are not cheap! But you can be sure of one thing: They all are of superb quality—super-premium or better. The most famous super-Tuscan wines, Sassicaia and Solaia, are much sought after by wine aficionados, costing upwards of $200 in great vintages.

Today, there's considerable variabilityin the blends of the super-Tuscans. Some producers use Cabernet Sauvignon; others use Merlot or Syrah, while others stick to native Tuscan varieties. There's a considerable range in price, too: from $30, up to $200 per bottle.

Piedmont—Alba and Asti

Situated in the extreme northwest, at the base of the Swiss Alps, bordering France and Switzerland in an area that combines agriculture, industry, and mountaineering, Piedmont is the site of two very important wine zones: Alba (which means "white") is known for its red wines. Asti is famous for its sparkling wines (see Chapter 21).

Heard it Through the Grapevine

The red Nebbiolo grape lies at the heart of three of Italy's best DOCG wines: Barolo, Barbaresco, and Gattinara. (In Gattinara, Nebbiolo is known by its local name, Spanna.) A decade ago, Barolo was the undisputed king of the mountain, followed by Gattinara. These days, Barbaresco seems to have gained in popularity, but Gattinara remains a superb (if underrated) wine.

Piedmont produces some of the greatest Italian red wines. Some wine lovers call it the noble wine region of Italy, a reputation it owes to the distinguished Nebbiolo varietal. This sensitive grape is the pride of the Piedmont. Nowhere else does it really express itself.

Barolo and Barbaresco both come from the central part of the Piedmont region. Made entirely from Nebbiolo grapes, they hail from the Langhe hills near Alba. Both Barbaresco and Barolo are full-bodied, robust wines—high in tannin, acidity, and alcohol. Their aromas evoke hints of tar, violets, strawberries, and black truffles. Barbaresco tends to be less austere than Barolo and slightly lower in alcoholic content. It is softer and more delicate, and can be consumed earlier.

Traditionally made, Barolo and Barbaresco are agers—some (Barolo especially) need 10 years of aging or more before they are ready to drink. And you should open these a few hours before drinking to give them adequate breathing. Some producers make these wines in the Bordeaux style; so you can enjoy them sooner. The vintners use French oak barrels for aging to give the wine an oaked character.

Barolo, Barbaresco, and Gattinara all are excellent complements to a meal. Fine Barolos and Barbarescos are a bit pricey: $30 to $60 a bottle. But from a good producer and a good vintage, they are worth the ticket. You might want to start with Gattinara. It offers Nebbiolo style and verve at a more manageable price: $12 to $25 a bottle.

Tasting Tip

Roughly half of Piedmont's wine production comes from the Barbera grape. This is the everyday table wine of the Piedmont. Drink Barbera while it's young, though you might age a good vintage. This is a rich, fruity, rustic wine with high acidity but little tannin. You'll find Barbera d'Alba is somewhat more rich than the more austere Barbera d'Asti.

Dolcetto is another favorite everyday red wine. If you know some Italian and you think "Dolcetto" means this is a sweet wine, you're wrong. Actually, it's the grape that's sweet. The wine is quite dry. It's vinous in quality, low in acidity, and rich in soft tannins. I find it easy to drink, even with its slight bitter undertone.

Heard it Through the Grapevine

You will find two types of Barbera on the market. The traditional style is aged in large oak casks, but they impart only a minimum of oak flavor. These wines retail in the $10 to $25 range. The more modern method is aging in barriques (French oak barrels). These smaller containers offer more wood-wine contact, in proportion to volume, than those giant casks. This endows the wine with more oaky flavor, but at a higher price: $30 to $60 per bottle. Oaky is in, but don't be afraid to go for tradition. You and your wallet, both, may prefer the old style.

Nebbiolo d'Alba is another Piedmont red you might try. Lighter in body than Barolo or Barbaresco, it often has a sort of fruity, sweet undertone. It retails at $15 to $30.

The Red Queen in Lewis Carroll's *Through the Looking-Glass* would love Piedmont, no doubt about it! Here reds dominate. However, there are two whites you might try.

Gavi is a very dry, refreshing wine with high acidity, named for a town in southern Piedmont. Most Gavis sell for $12 to $20 a bottle; however, some of the best examples go for as much as $40 a bottle and are worth the price.

The second white wine is Arneis, from the Roero zone near Alba. Arneis is named for its grape variety—Arneis. Arneis is a medium-dry to dry wine with a rich flavor and texture. It reveals its best qualities when consumed within a year of the vintage. It sells for $12 to $25 a bottle.

Friuli—Putting Whites on the Map

The Friuli-Venezia Giulia district is nestled up againstAustria and Slovenia in the northeast. This prolific zone has notified the world that Italy's wines come in two colors. In this zone, white bottles outnumber red four-to-one. Over the past 25 years, white wines from Friuli-Venezia Giulia (better known in the U.S. simply as Friuli)—have made their way to New World shores and stores.

Tasting Tip

And now for something really different: One Friuli wine that falls into no category is Picolit, an unusual (and expensive) white dessert wine. It makes a good conversation piece when wine lovers gather.

The districts of Collio and Colli Orientali del Friuli are the top winemaking districts in Friuli. The cool climate produces wines that are crisp and clean. The grapes of Friuli include Riesling (both Rhein and Italico), Müller-Thurgau, Chardonnay, Sauvignon Blanc, Pinot Bianco, and Pinot Grigio. Add to this impressive collection of white varietals two local winners, Tocai Friulano and Ribolla Gialla.

Umbria—Volcanic Vineyards

Umbria lies to the south of Tuscany, almost in the center of Italy. According to legend, its best-known wine, the white Orvieto, has been planted since Etruscan times.

The vineyards grow on volcanic rock, which gives the wine a distinctive, earthy character. Made from the Trebbiano grape, Orvieto also has a Classico zone, and is produced as both a dry and a semi-dry wine. You can find a good Orvieto for around than $10.

Sicily and Sardinia

Although Sardinian wines have achieved some popularity in the U.S., most are no more than ordinary. However, Sicily has seen quite a surge in popularity among American wine drinkers, and produces some interesting wines, notably from Regaleali's vineyards (intriguingly situated on the slopes of Mount Etna). The white DOC wines of Etna have a (I don't have another word for this) volcanic character that makes them particularly interesting.

Regaleali produces red, white, and rosé wines; these range from mediocre to extraordinary, reds that are among Italy's finest. As one producer of note in Sicily, Count Regaleali's best red wine is called Rosso del Conte. He makes a Chardonnay that rivals those of the Côte d'Or. Regaleali also makes a dry rosato (rosé) that sells for about $13 made from the indigenous Nero d'Avola grape.

Sicily sends us some good sparkling wines, ranging from the brut to the sweet, muscat-flavored spumantes from the Island of Pantellaria (see Chapter 21). This Mediterranean island also produces a fortified wine known as Marsala, which ranges in style from dry to very sweet, and in quality from average to very refined. Marsala is used both as an apéritif and for cooking (see Chapter 22).

Interestingly, Sicily has become a bit of a hotbed for forward-thinking winemakers, like Frank Cornelissen, Andrea Franchetti, and Marco de Grazia, who are seizing the opportunity to vinify solely or blend native varietals, like Nerello Mascalese, Nerello Cappuccio, Carricante, and Catarratto.

Three Gentle Wines of Verona

Veneto lies just to the west of Friuli in the north. The best wines from this zone come from vineyards surrounding the beautiful city of Verona. Verona's three leading wines are among the most well-known, widely available in here. These are two reds, Valpolicella and Bardolino, and a white, Soave. (It's too bad the Montagues and the Capulets didn't raise a glass of one of these to settle their differences!)

Valpolicella and Bardolino both are made primarily from the Corvina grape. The Valpolicella district resides on a series of hills, some of that overlook Verona. Bardolino is named for the charming village situated on Lake Garda. It also has a Classico zone where the better wines are made. Bardolino is a light, fruity wine, pleasant when young. It's closer in style to Beaujolais than to its Corvina cousin, Valpolicella. Try a chilled Bardolino on a hot summer evening (and imagine you're on the beautiful lake in the Italian countryside).

Heard it Through the Grapevine

Valpolicella is fuller in body than Bardolino, with more color, alcohol, durability, depth, and complexity. Those labeled Classico come from the best growing area. An exception is Valpantena, made from a valley to the east. It doesn't have the Classico label, but its quality is as good as Classico, sometimes better. If you see Superiore on the label, it means a minimum of one year's aging. Some Valpolicellas improve in the bottle for several years.

Another classification of Valpolicella is Recioto. It's made from grapes grown high up on the hillside and dried on straw mats in lofts or attics to concentrate their sugars and fruits before vinification. Recioto contains 14 to 16 percent alcohol, and it's made in three different styles.

The first is a sparkling wine, rarely seen in the U.S. The second, labeled simply Recioto, is sweet because fermentation stopped before all the sugar was fermented. Finally, there is Amarone Recioto (or Amarone della Valpolicella, or just Amarone), which has fermented

Vino Vocab

When fermentation ceases before all the sugar is converted, it's said to be stuck. One reason for this is development of high alcohol, which kills the yeasts.

completely. Amarone is one of those special wines of Italy that deserves super-premium classification. Amarone is velvety, round, soft, well-balanced, and full of character. You can age the best of these 10 to 15 years, though most are delightful after five years.

Soave is an easy-to-drink white wine that's grown near Valpolicella. Made predominantly from the Garganega grape, along with some Trebbiano, Soave is available as both Classico and non-Classico wine. Most of the better Soaves come from the Classico zone, an area to the northeast of the picturesque town of Soave itself.

We Americans love the pleasant flavors of Valpolicella, Bardolino, and Soave. And we like their prices, as well. Most retail in the $5 to $8 range. Two other white wines of the region, Bianco di Custoza and Lugana, fall into the same range.

Heard it Through the Grapevine

Bardolino Superiore, Soave Classico, and Recioto di Soave (a sweet wine that employs the same drying technique as Amarone) were given DOCG status around the turn of the 21st century. For Bardolino, the blend must be made up of 35–65 percent Corvina, 10–40 percent of Rondinella, and up to 20 percent other red varietals, including the non-native Cabernet Sauvignon and Merlot (which were formerly not permitted). For Soave Classico, the main Garganega grape varietal may be blended with Chardonnay and Trebbiano.

The Top of the Boot

Trentino-Alto Adige, located at the most northerly "top of the boot," actually comprises two very distinct zones. To the south, we have the Italian-speaking Trentino; to the north, the German-speaking Alto Adige (or South Tyrol). These interesting wines differ no less than the languages of their vintners.

Most of the red wines from this border region go to Austria, although it isn't too difficult to find some here, too. The white wines rival those of Friuli. Pinot Grigio, Chardonnay, and Pinot Bianco from Alto Adige retail in the $10 to $30 range.

Lombardy—Master Wine Craftsmen

Once famed for its expert craftsmen, Lombardy is less renowned for its wine. To be sure, the region offers some delightful red and white wines.

The best white is Lugana, produced from the slopes bordering Lake Garda. Four mid-premium reds come from the Valltellina region, high up in the pre-Alps, just below the Swiss border. The predominant grape is Nebbiolo, known here as Chiavennasca. The four light-bodied red wines are Sassella, Inferno, Grumello, and Valgella. All are highly drinkable and affordable too: usually less than $15. Drink them while they're young.

Latium—Near the Coliseum

Latium (or Lazio) occupies the west-central part of Italy, around Rome. Its best-known wine is Frascati, made from the Trebbiano grape and produced on the volcanic slopes of the Colli Romani southwest of Rome. Named for the town Frascati, this wine should be light, fresh, charming, and fragrant.

Most of these wines are dry (labeled asciutto or secco), but there also are sweeter versions (cannellino, dolci, or amabile). Enjoy these while they're young. Vast quantities of Frascati are produced and quality can be variable.

The Sommelier Says

Latium turns out prodigious quantities of Frascati, both red and white. Quality varies greatly. If you find one not to your liking, it's worth your while to try another.

Emilia-Romagna

Emilia-Romagna lies in the northeast, along the Adriatic, south of Veneto. It's best known for the city of Bologna and from the ocean of soft, effervescent Lambrusco wine it produces each year, which has seen a bit of a Renaissance in America the last few years, with slightly dryer styles of the often-sweet semi-sparkler becoming a popular.

Abruzzo

Abruzzo lies along the Adriatic, just south of Emilia-Romagna. In the U.S., we know this region for its red Montepulciano d'Abruzzo. This inexpensive wine is easy to drink, with low tannins and low acidity, and makes a great choice for an everyday table wine. Bottles can be found for as low as $7 or $8 on up to $15.

Marche (The Marches)

Moving further south along the Adriatic, we come to Marche. This region lies outside most tourist routes, offering few historical attractions. But it's very much on our wine map!

Heard it Through the Grapevine

What's in a name? Marche, in English, means "the Marches." The what? Well, this old term refers to the borderlands of a country or empire, what we call "buffer states." In the third century B.C.E., long before Rome had encircled the Mediterranean with its empire, the ancient city had annexed the land to the east, still called Marche.

The region's white wine, Verdicchio, gives Marche some distinction. The most famous zone here is the large Verdicchio dei Castelli di Jesi. The grapes used here are the Verdicchio, with up to 20 percent of Trebbiano Toscano and Malvasio Toscano permitted. This is a dry, simple wine to be enjoyed young, within two years at most.

On the Slopes of Mt. Vesuvius

Campania lies to the southwest, just south of Latium, the land of Naples and Mount Vesuvius. Just northeast of Naples we find some outstanding wines, ranging from mid-premium to (sometimes) noble quality. These are the work of Antonio Mastroberardino. It's worth your while to negotiate the six syllables of this name to sample some of his superb product!

Greco du Tufo, Fiano di Avellino, and Falanghina are Mastroberardino's unique whites. Greco is viscous and quite strong in bouquet and flavor. Sometimes it can be a bit strong in alcohol, but it's always well balanced. Its flavors have a bitter almond edge that increases with bottle age. It retails in the $15 to $70 range. Fiano has greater elegance of body and texture and a sort of toasty bouquet. Falanghina has a rich, full body and spicy undertones.

Apart from the excellence of these two whites, Mastroberardino's masterpiece is his rich, full-bodied, and tannic Taurasi. This DOCG wine is made from the red Aglianico grape, grown at 1,000 feet or higher. The great vintages of Taurasi age well for 10 or 20 years and can attain near noble status. The single-vineyard Taurasi, named Radici, is especially recommended.

A Sea of Wine

Apulia and Basilicata, along with Calabria, lie at the extreme south of "the boot" (the shoe part) of Italy. These dry, sunny regions produce a veritable sea of wine.

Apulia, the heel of the boot, essentially is one gigantic vineyard. But only over the past two decades have vintners there invested in the modern winemaking technology necessary to make good wines. In the past, these wines had been heavy in alcohol and often sun-baked. Today, the wines of Apulia—notably, Primitivo and Negroamaro among the reds, and Malvasia in the whites—are fruitier, fresher, and lighter. The Aleatico di Puglia grape is used for a red DOC dessert wine.

Basilicata, the toe of the boot, has achieved its distinction through Aglianico del Vulture, a superb red wine that improves with age, recently achieving DOCG status in 2011. This is a mid-premium wine, quite smooth, with a caramel background and lots of fruit.

CHAPTER 16

Wines with a Spanish Spirit

In This Chapter

- The wines of Spain
- The wines of Portugal
- The wines of South America

Spain ranks third, behind Italy and France, in wine production, but since the death of dictator Francisco Franco in 1975, and a subsequent embracing of democracy, wine in this nation of 46 million people has utterly flourished.

And speaking of an increase in creativity, quality, and enthusiasm, the table wines of Portugal, Chile, and Argentina have had a similar arc of success. And while you might find some similarities in the robust style of some of these wines, there are more than a few surprising differences beyond borders and continents. But while they (mostly) share the same language, the biggest thing these fantastic wine-producing nations share is that they offer excellent values for what you get in the bottle. You should consider these wines not just for your everyday drinking, but as a great opportunity to line your cellar with age-able, complex bottles for the future.

In this chapter, we'll survey the traditional wines of Spain and Portugal, as well as some of their more recent, exciting exports. Some examples are the gorgeous Riojas from Spain and the Daos from Portugal. Then we'll visit the eclectic wines of Chile, Argentina, and Uruguay. This New-World viticulture, introduced by Spanish colonists, has undergone centuries of change, as successive generations of immigrants have played their parts. All the countries covered in this chapter produce substantial quantities of agreeable wine of good value. I think they all deserve the greater worldwide visibility they've been catching as of late—and much more.

Olé! Red Wines—Red-Hot Value

Spain evokes images of bright sunlight on distant mountains, Flamenco dancers, brave toreadors, gently strummed guitars, and (if you're up on your architecture) the Guggenheim in Bilbao—that shiny-ship of an art center that famed architect Frank Gehry designed in the sweet, little port city near San Sebastian. Wine? Red, of course, with quality ranging from ordinary to superb.

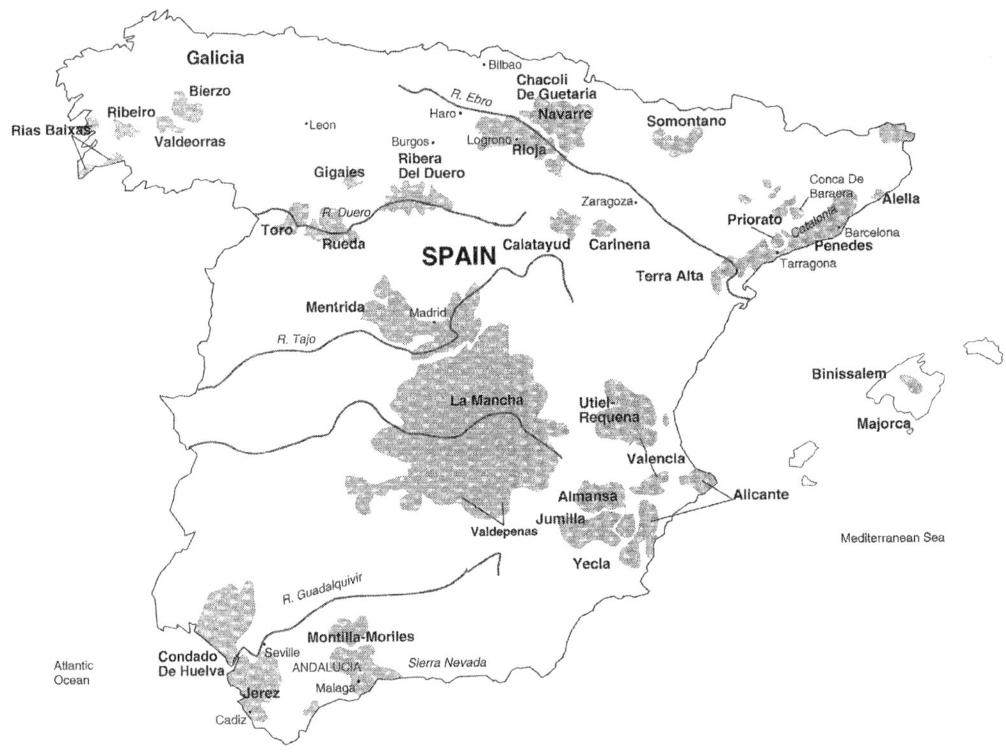

The finest wines of the regions of Spain.

Spanish wine has seen an amazing amount of progress in everything from winemaking techniques to exports to its wine laws. Since joining with the European Union, its classification system is in line with the more recognizable designations of France, starting with Vino de Mesa (e.g., table wine), Vino de la Tierra (which are comparable to the French Vins de Pays), Denominaciones de Origen (DO), which means "place name," and the higher classification, Denominación de Origen Calificada (DOC).

The higher tier was added only in 1991, and so far, its two occupants are Rioja, the popular tempranillo-based red wines from that region, and Priorat, the lusty, rich garnacha-based blends that hail from this once nearly barren land.

Rioja—Fame and Fashion

Located in north-central Spain, Rioja is the one region we're most likely to have heard of. Rioja is divided into three districts: Rioja Alavesa and Rioja Alta, which have a cool climate; and Rioja Baja, which has the warmer climate more typical of Spain.

In the Riojas, the predominant grape is the red Tempranillo (although you will also find more and more of the white grape of this area, Viura, on shelves these days, too). Rioja wine traditionally is a blend, however, more modern producers have been making mono-varietal versions with some good success. The fruity Garnacha (known in France as Grenache) is one of the better-known varieties used in blending, and another you might see is Mazuelo. The best Riojas usually are made of grapes from the two cooler districts, or it may contain grapes from all three.

In earlier years, Rioja reds had been aged in small oak barrels (from America). Nowadays, stainless steel- and bottle-aging have been added to the more traditional method of cask-aging, resulting in fresher, crisper, fruit-forward wines. While American oak remains traditional, there is some movement toward French oak, which imparts a spicier character to the wine. Is one better than the other? That all depends on your own, individual taste.

Before modernization and DOC classification, Reserva on a red wine label meant only the wine was aged. No hint of quality. Today, Reserva, used exclusively for red wines, denotes a minimum quality as well as aging.

There are several types of red Riojas. Some Riojas are young wines with little to no oak aging, or jovens. Others, labeled crianza, are aged by the vintner in oak for a minimum of one year and in bottle for a minimum of one year as well; reservas are aged for three years (and now, quality is demanded). The finest Riojas are aged five years or longer and bestowed with the status gran reserva.

Red wines make up 85 percent of Rioja's total output, with full-bodied rosé wines made from Garnacha accounting for 15 percent, and whites the final 10 percent. Prices, generally, are reasonable: Crianza reds begin at about $10 to $12 per bottle. Reservas start at around $15, and Gran reservas will begin at around $30 to $40 on average with some renowned labels selling for hundreds of dollars. The top recent vintages from Rioja are (in order): 1995, 1999, 2005, 2007, 2008, and 2009.

Catalunya—Reds to Pour, Sparklers to Pop

Catalunya was deemed a D.O. only in 1999, but seems like a veritable fruit basket of reasonably priced, delicious Spanish wines. The Penedes in Catalunya, southwest of Barcelona, is far less famous than Rioja, but this is where you go for robust table wines made from the red varietals Garnacha and Monastrell. It is also where you will find the lovely sparkler, Cava, made from the native varietal Paralleda as well as Chardonnay. Its two leading producers, Torres, Allemany, and Jean Leon, are known for their outstanding red wines, which start in the $7 to $8 range, with the better wines going for up to $30 a bottle. These wines are made in both varietal renditions as well as blends. For Cava, look for Sumarroca, Freixenet, and Llopart among many others.

Ribera del Duero: Muscled Red Muscling to the Forefront

Ribera del Duero, north of Madrid, has made quite a splash over the last 30 years. Dozens of new vintners have brought their wines to market from there, and you might want to look for these. As in Rioja, the main varietal here is the red Tempranillo, but some producers also mix a little Cabernet Sauvignon in as well.

Until recently, the legendary Vega Sicilia winery dominated this region. They produce Spain's most renowned wine, Unico (which means "unique"). Made from Tempranillo, with a little Cabernet Sauvignon, Unico is an intense, tannic, and concentrated red wine that requires long aging after its 10 years in the cask and several more years in-bottle at the winery. It sells for more than $300 a bottle. But there are many other producers from Rioja offering reasonably priced options, like Bodega Perez Pascuas, Emilio Moro, Cepa, and Vina Sastra.

Rueda—Young and Fresh

Located west of Ribera del Duero, the Rueda region is known for one of Spain's best white wines. Made from the Verdejo grape, crisp, aromatic, refreshing wines with a stylish, fruity character. The price is attractive, from $8 to $12 a bottle.

Galicia Means Crisp Whites

Galicia, on the Atlantic coast in northwestern Spain, has one specific district, Rias Baixas, that boasts an exhilarating wine. This is a white made from the varietal Albariño, which displays an intense acidity, flowery aromas, and delicate flavors reminiscent of a Condrieu (See Chapter 14, The Rhône River Valley). Albariños range in price from about $15 to $25 a bottle.

Valencia, Jumilla, La Manhca: Up and Coming

Three regions that used to be far more well known for their bulk-wine production than for bottling decent everyday table wines are Valencia and Jumilla on the Mediterranean coast, south of Penedes, and just slightly right of center in the middle of the country, La Mancha. More and more, you will see bottles of Tempranillo coming from each of these spots, although La Mancha is also known for its Monastrell.

Sherry Central

Jerez is a large wine region in southern Spain best known as the home of Sherry. The wines from Jerez are subject to the country's highest regulatory standards. The predominant grape here is the Palomino, a delicious variety that undergoes a unique process to produce the fortified Sherry.

Sherry is proof of the importance of soil and climate to wine production. As a viticultural area, Jerez is divided into three sections, all based on soil type. The most prized (but least productive) regions have soils characterized by albariza, a soil that is mostly chalk, lots of limestone and magnesium. The topsoils (which actually are white) bear the best Sherry grapes. By law, at least 40 percent of the grapes used in Sherry must come from these famed albariza soils.

Barro, another soil division (literally "clay"), is more productive. Finally, árena, the third region (it means "sand"), bears vines that are immensely productive, but weak in character.

Sherry is made in large volume by modern, efficient methods of crushing and vinification. But Sherry is a fortified wine; so I'll have much more to say about it in Chapter 22.

Deciphering the Spanish Wine Label

These are the most important terms you will find on a Spanish wine label.

- Crianza. For red wines, the wine has been aged for at least two years, including a period of oak aging; for white and rosé wines, Crianza means that the wines are a minimum of one year old.
- Reserva. Red reservas must be aged in oak and bottle for a minimum of three years; white and rosé reservas must be aged for a minimum of two years, including six months in oak. Reservas are produced only in good vintages.
- Gran Reserva. Red wines must be aged in oak and bottle for a minimum of five years; white and rosé gran reservas must be aged a minimum of four years with a minimum of six months in oak. Gran Reservas are made only in exceptional vintages.

- Cosecha or Vendimia. The vintage year.
- Bodega. Winery.
- Tinto. Red.
- Blanco. White.
- Viejo. Old.
- Viña. Vineyard.

Portugal—More Than Porto

If you came of age in the 1970s, there's a good chance your first wine either was Mateus (which nobody seems to pronounce correctly) or Lancer's. These two medium-dry, somewhat effervescent rosés in their distinctive bottles were for quite some time Portugal's most familiar wines, although the country has been taking great pains to change that.

If you know anything at all about Portugal, it's in all likelihood the country's most famous quaff, the dark dessert wine, Port.

But Portuguese table wine is making its way into the American market, and for very good reason. While much of it doesn't exactly roll off the American tongue just yet (loureiro or touriga nacional, anyone?), and some of it can be a little bit on the pricey side in today's economy, the current trend of modernization, stronger quality control, and better marketing is gaining higher status and visibility in the ever-expanding world wine market.

Within the Portuguese classification system, the highest tier is the Denominação de Origem Controlada (DOC). Right now, 26 wine regions have received this distinction.

The next tier, the Indicação de Proveniencia Regulamentad (IPR), has been awarded to four regions, many of which aspire to elevation to DOC status. IPR corresponds roughly to the VDQS status of France.

The designation, Vinho de Regional (regional table wines), corresponds to the Spanish Vino de la Tierra and the French Vins de Pays. All remaining wines are known simply as Vinho de Mesa.

Wines of Portugal.

Green Wine!

Vinho Verde means "green wine." The color refers to the grapes, not the wine! This DOC region, between the Minhos and Douros Rivers, is the country's largest wine-producing region.

The most widely available Vinho Verdes are the brands Quinta de Aveleda, and Casal Garcia, which sell for $6 to $10 a bottle. These are medium-dry wines, meant to be served chilled and consumed young. Rarely are they any better than ordinary. Slightly more expensive Vinho Verdes are made from the Alvarhino grape (as in the Spanish Albariño) from the sub-region of Monção. These retail for $12 to $20 a bottle. The higher quality Vinho Verdes are more complex, with some potential for aging. They may be hard to find but are worth the effort.

Dao—The Best Table Wine

The best Dao wines are the reds, although there are some good whites as well. Most of these wines are blends from within the region, and some are vintage-dated. Those that are aged in wood casks are entitled to Reserva status. This cask-aging makes them soft and mellow. Dao reds typically are smooth and full-bodied, while the whites are light and simple. Few stand out as distinctive, but they offer pleasant drinking at equally pleasant prices.

Douro—Porto, and More…

Located in northeastern Portugal, the Douro River region produces Portugal's most renowned wine, Port, officially known in Portugal as "Porto." The steep and hilly terrain, with hot summers moderated by cool evenings, are ideal for growing the deep-colored, full-flavored grape varieties needed for Port. (See Chapter 22, Porto—The Real Thing)

More and more, the region is increasing production of some interesting table wines from the same grapes used to make port. These wines can range in style from medium-bodied and fruity to intense and robust, requiring years of aging.

Alentejo

In the southern part of Portugal, this warm, dry grape-growing region has seen more and more vineyard action in recent years, with producers like Esporao creating palate-pleasing blends using native varietals, like Trincadeira and Aragonez, with classic varietals like Cabernet Sauvignon and Syrah.

Sweet, Strong, and Misunderstood!

The excellent fortified sweet wines of Moscatel de Setubal still suffer from an erroneous and unfortunate association with the inferior, American-made "Muscatel." To be sure, the two are fortified wines. But there the resemblance ends!

Setubal wines are deeply colored with a strong, complex Muscat character, and they improve with long aging. I find it interesting that the producers sell both six-year-old and twenty-five-year-old bottlings. You will find these in fine wine stores, often at an attractive price for a wine of such high quality.

Unlocking the Language

These are the important terms you will need to know to be comfortable with Portuguese wines:

- Reserva. A vintage wine of superior quality.
- Garrafeira. A reserva that has been aged a minimum of two years in cask and one year in bottle for a red wine; six months in cask and six months in bottle for a white wine.
- Quinta. Estate or vineyard.
- Colheita. Vintage year.
- Seco. Dry.
- Adega. Winery.
- Tinto. Red.
- Vinho. Wine.

Chile—Old World and New

Chilean winemaking displays a cosmopolitan tradition. The first vineyards were planted in Chile by Spanish colonists in the mid-16th century. Then, in the 19th century, a wave of immigrants, mostly Italian, brought with them their own winemaking legacies.

To this we add Chile's unique soils, terrain, and climate that sometimes favor grapes we associate with France. Many Chilean vineyards are planted in Bordeaux grape varieties, like Cabernet Sauvignon and Merlot. A few regions seem perfect for the Riesling, yielding wines that are delightfully fresh, dry, and austere—similar in style to the German Steinwein (see Chapter 17).

Geographically isolated on that long, narrow strip between the formidable Andes and the broad Pacific, Chile is one of the only wine regions of the world that escaped the dreaded phylloxera, a tiny but deadly pest that nearly wiped out the greatest vineyards in Europe during the nineteenth century. Indeed, its unique terrain seems to be made for grape-growing: High coastal ranges protect much of the growing land from excess humidity, and the soothing Pacific protects it from excess heat.

Chile at a Glance

From south to north within the Chile, the wine regions are:

- Aconcagua – near the sea and slightly north of Santiago, here is where Chile's famed, warm Casablanca Valley lies, home to fantastic Chardonnay and Sauvignon Blanc, as well as some surprisingly lovely Pinot Noirs.
- Central Valley – Just south of Santiago lies this, the most prolific wine-producing area in the country—over 90 percent of Chile's wine comes from here alone. Here, we have a few important spots to keep on your radar: 1) Maipo. Though relatively small, this is where many of the major wineries are located and is known for its well-balanced, easy-going Cabernet Sauvignon. 2) Rapel. This is where the Colchagua district is located. It is a cooler region than Maipo and known for its production of classic red varietals, like Cabernet Sauvignon, Merlot, and Carmenere. Maule. This is where the Curico district is located. It is cooler and less dry than Rapel, and it is here that producers like Montes, Concha y Toro, and Casa Lapostelle have had great success with red varietals like Cabernet Sauvignon, Syrah, and Carmenere.
- Southern Valley – In recent years, many Chilean producers have been exploring the fertile, hilly seaside land of this cooler spot. Subregions to keep in mind are Bio Bio and Itata, which have both showed promise for aromatic whites, like Riesling and Gewurtztraminer.

While the Pais grape, which locals have enjoyed for centuries, is hardly a household word outside of its native land, Chile has become one of the belles of the ball in terms of affordable, quality wines made from European varietals.

Chilean producers of Cabernet Sauvignon, Merlot, and Chardonnay wines have modernized their winemaking facilities and techniques and, in doing so, captured a share of international markets. Today, the number of vines bearing these varietals has multiplied, and so has the number of bottlings designated for export.

Foreign investment has had a great influence. The Miguel Torres winery in Curico has a Spanish owner. Even a California winemaker, Augustin Huneeus of Franciscan Vineyards, has become a developer of the new Casablanca wine region.

Finally, it was inevitable that Chile's reputation for French-style reds would inspire the interest of Bordeaux's best. Château Lafite-Rothschild now owns the Los Vascos winery. Also, the Vina Aquitania is a collaboration of the noted Bordeaux châteaux, Château Cos d'Estournel, and Château Margaux. In Chile, Si! Si! is turning into Oui! Oui!

Chilean reds have easily become contenders as world-class wines, with lots of unexplored potential still to pluck, exemplified by the outstanding Don Melchor made from Cabernet

Sauvignon by Concha y Toro, one of several wineries known for its excellent, inexpensive varietal wines.

Argentina—Smoothing the Rough Edges

Argentina is the fifth largest wine-producing country in the world. In Argentina, the historical pattern of grape-growing and vinification is similar to Chile's. Spaniards planted the first vineyards in the 16th century. In the nineteenth century, immigrants, mostly Italian, influenced and expanded this industry. Today, Argentinean winemaking is under strict government control.

Most of Argentina's vineyards are concentrated in the hot, arid Mendoza region, in the west, shielded from the ocean by the Andes. The next largest wine-producing area is San Juan, in the hotter and drier lands north of Mendoza. La Rioja (which you are more likely to see labeled as Famatina Valley) lies further north, still. Beyond that, there is also Cafayette in the sky-touching climes of Salta, which has become known for the very aromatic native white varietal, Torrontes. To the south, there is also the moderately cool region called Rio Negro, where Malbec reigns supreme.

Most grapes grow in the flatlands, though the better vineyards (and a growing number of them) are situated at higher elevations where the climate is more temperate. Daytime temperatures during maturation can exceed 110 degrees F, which encourages high sugar content, but can give the wines a peculiar sun-baked flavor.

Argentine winemaking has come a long way, with projects like Cheval des Andes, which began in 1999 as a project between famed St. Emilion producer Chateau Cheval Blanc and Moet property, Terrazas de los Andes that are making outstanding Bordeaux blends. With the trend toward modernization, the once rough wines of Argentina have mostly become a thing of the past, and as far as value goes, you can shop Argentina for a cornucopia of good-value reds between $8 and $20 a bottle.

Argentina at a Glance

Well, that's actually kind of a misnomer—it's hard to glance at Argentina, with its thousands of miles of terrain covering seven different wine regions from top to tip. Let's take a closer look:

Reason and Region

Stretching over 2,000 miles from north to south, Argentina's seven striking wine regions are rich with so much more than the mighty Malbec.

Salta

Spend a few days in Salta and you will know why its name means "the most beautiful." The sky-high striking scenery in this northernmost wine region is like nothing you've ever seen, from the rainbow-colored mountain ranges of Humahuaco, to the 18th-century colonial architecture, and the silent ancient volcanoes, Salta's beauty will stop you in your tracks easily and often.

Part of that natural loveliness can be also be found in the breathtaking Calchaqui Valley vineyards and wineries, an area that produces only 5 percent of Argentina's wines, but one whose growth and quality have many wine aficionados betting that it will soon rival Mendoza.

Salta is home to the highest vineyards in Argentina—and some of the highest in the world—reaching nearly 5,000 feet above sea level. Local winemakers here are crafting stand-out Torrontes, with bright acidity balancing this grape's sometimes fruit-forward tendencies. Other grape varietals to pay particular attention to here: Syrah, Tannat, Cabernet Sauvignon, and Malbec.

Catamarca

The road to Catamarcan wine is paved with archeological gold. The 31-mile route that heads right to the heart of Catamarca wine country holds a fascinating view of pre-Columbian ruins and adobe architecture dating back as far as the 15th century. Up until recently, though, Catarmarcan wineries were known more producing local table wine and raisins, but this has changed as drastically as the world surrounding the old adobe huts. Boutique wineries in the area are upping the ante with promising showings of Syrah, Malbec, Cabernet Sauvignon, and Bonarda from small-scale vineyards from the Fiambala Valley.

La Rioja

Its name hints not only at its rich red cliffs and sand-blasted desert canyons, but at two of the grape varietals that explode from the vines that thrive in the dry, windy area of the Famatina Valley—Malbec and Syrah. But this is not to say that the lighter shade of things should be overlooked. In fact, the Chilecito Valley is considered inarguably the most important Torrontes-producing area in the country, having been declared Argentina's first D.O.C.

San Juan

Bigger hasn't always meant better. Until recently, San Juan was Argentina's second-largest wine producing area, but most of the resulting quaff was relegated to the table jug. No more. In fact, the last decade has seen such a promising showing of world-class Syrah from this region, that the buzz on the street is San Juan has officially stepped into the ring as a contender. Other grapes to check out: Bonarda, Cabernet Sauvignon, Tannat, and Malbec for the reds, and Viognier (a grape often used to describe the qualities of Torrontes), Chardonnay, and Pinot Grigio for the whites.

Mendoza

There's no denying that Mendoza is the most vibrant, vital winemaking region in all of Argentina. It's the area that put this South American country on the winemaking map; the one that produces 80 percent of all their wines; the place that the laid-back locals call the land of "sol y vino" (sun and wine). And Mendoza's charm only seems to grow—over the last few years, it has seen a 30 percent jump in wine exports and an influx of wine-loving tourists, eager to lose themselves in these mid-Andean wineries that thrive thanks to an incredible, intricate irrigation system of aqueducts and dykes that feed the vineyards and olive groves.

Lately, Mendoza terroir is proving itself to be even more valuable than was already established, showing potential for greater things to come. For now, their stunning Malbecs remain the juicy giant of this fascinating wine-producing region, but a host of other grape varietals (Cabernet Sauvignon, Merlot, Bonarda, Syra, Tempranillo, Semillon, Chardonnay, among others) are proving an interesting lot to watch.

Neuquén

The wine region of Neuquén marks a couple of important geographic occurrences: It's the end of the Andes and the beginning of the northernmost section of Patagonia, a vast, wild natural wonder of wide-open grassy pampa, ice fields, and glaciers. It's a place that can humble the most ardent nature lover—and up until 1990, one that seemed an unfriendly spot for vines.

Fast forward almost two decades, and it seems that man might have conquered Mother Nature in order to reap the benefits of Neuquén's sunny days and cool nights. Through creative means (e.g., much-needed irrigation and the use of poplar trees to shield vines from the sometimes vicious winds) fledgling, ambitious young winemakers have made Neuquén their Mecca, building sleek, modern wineries and using state-of-the-art winemaking techniques. From great value Cabernet Sauvignons, Malbecs, and Merlots to Pinot Noirs showing interesting potential, Neuquén is proving itself to be a fruitful one to watch.

Rio Negro

In many ways Neuquén's next-door neighbor, Rio Negro, couldn't be more different. Ever synonymous with the fruit trade, this fertile wine region, fed by the river of the same name, has long had the benefit of a vast irrigation system set up by British engineers over a hundred years ago. Since then, the land here has been rife with apples, pears, peaches, and all other varieties of fruits and vegetables. Grapes have grown here, too, since the early 20th century, with producers crafting outstanding old-vine Malbecs. Pinot Noir and Merlot, too, have made a decent showing, with winemakers leaning toward a more European style.

Uruguay and Brazil

While not as readily and easily available as their two South American cousins above, both Uruguay and Brazil have been making small steps into the global wine market, too. From Uruguay, keep your nose and palate peeled for robust reds from the grape Tanat (initially brought to the country by Basque settlers in the late nineteenth century). In Brazil, Italian immigrants brought their techniques and know-how, and in the Serra Gaucho region, off-dry, aromatic sparkling wines are made.

CHAPTER 17

From the Rhine to the Aegean

In This Chapter

- The many wines of Germany
- Wines of Austria
- Wines of Switzerland
- Wine of England
- Wines of Greece
- Wines of Hungary

Germany offers some of the most varied and enjoyable experiences the world of wine has to offer. Some of the driest and some of the sweetest wines come from this country. (Even wines made from grapes that have become frozen raisins!)

German wine labels, with their strange, long words, may seem intimidating. However, German wine laws are logical (you expected otherwise?), and these labels can tell us quite a lot. That is, once we recognize a few terms, which is one reason for this chapter.

Later, we'll discover that German-speaking Austrians have some very original (and delicious) ideas about wine. And the German-Italian-French-speaking Swiss have several notions of their own. And while you may have though Jolly Old England was full of ale-centric sippers, you'll see that the burgeoning sparkling wine industry might have you exclaiming, "God save the Queen!"

Then we visit a bit of the ancient world, Greece, where we can sample some unusual beverages made in a very, very old-fashioned way.

We'll finish with some wines that made the Hapsburgs happy, the distinguished products of Hungary, as well as a quick peak at how robust Romanian wines are making a showing.

Zum Wohl! (To your health!)

The finest wine regions of Germany.

Germany—Süss und Trocken

Regardless what you've heard, not all German wines are sweet. Some even carry the word Trocken on the label, which means dry. In general, though, German whites run medium-dry to sweet. They are floral and fragrant, refreshing, full of bright, balancing acidity—and never oaked.

Microclimates and More

Germany's wine districts differ from those of other countries in one regard. Instead of having one generalized climate, each German wine district may comprise several microclimates. These vary with every turn of the winding rivers (principally the Rhine and the Mosel) on which they locate their choicest vineyards. The flowing rivers temper the harsh extremes of weather and help protect the vulnerable grapes.

The best vineyard slopes face south. Every element of topography can affect the wine: the steepness of the slope; the amount of sun reflected from the adjoining rivers; the nearness of a wind-sheltering forest or mountain peak; altitude; and as in other winegrowing areas, the soil constituents. German wine conditions not only vary place to place, but (more than in other lands) year to year. With German wines, vintages do matter!

Where Riesling Reigns

Germany is the first home of the noble Riesling, which unlike most vinifera, is no sun worshipper. It is, however, something of a snob. Only in Germany's best vineyards does it ripen consistently. As a result, it represents only 21 percent of all viticultural plantings.

The most prolific German grape is the Müller-Thurgau. Some say this varietal is a cross between Riesling and Silvaner. Other say it's the marriage of two Riesling clones. It ripens earlier than Riesling, yielding a soft, round, fragrant wine. However, it's not in Riesling's exalted class.

Müller-Thurgau loves the cool German climate, just as German winegrowers love it. Germany cultivates other white varietals. These include Silvaner, Kerner, Scheurebe, and Ruländer (Pinot Gris). Still, between Riesling and Muller-Thurgau, these two German powerhouse white varietals account for more than 35 percent of Germany's nearly 260,000 acres under vine.

And true enough, Germany is renowned for its whites—but don't discount the red stuff. In the last decade, you may have noticed a few bottles full pretty ruby-hued juice with oddball German names, like Spätburgunder – which, actually, is one to pay attention to. You might know the red varietal Spätburgunder better by its Sideways-centric name, Pinot Noir, and plantings of it have increased slowly but surely, with nearly 12 percent of Germany's fertile vineland bursting with the persnickety red grape.

But before we start color-coding, let's break the ultimate code first—the language of the German wine label!

German Wine Laws Simplified

One very striking thing about the German language is the length of some of its words. This occurs through compounding, the cementing of several words to form a new one. German wine label designations are somewhat the same, building from separate elements until some become quite long. (At least, there are spaces between these words.)

Let's begin with the place of origin, the town. Bernkastel is a good choice. (To this name Germans add the suffix -er, for reasons of German grammar.) Next comes the name of the vineyard, say Badstube. Then comes the name of the grape. How about Riesling? So now we have Bernkasteler Badstube Riesling. Isn't that easy?

Now we come to something that's unique to German wines, at least to the finer wines: a measure of ripeness dictated by when the grape was harvested. This is a real quality assessment. It's called Prädikat (the same word Germans use for report-card grades). But before we continue, let's look at the broadest quality designations under the 1971 German wine laws.

At the bottom, we have Tafelwein (table wine), or Landwein (table wines with some regional designation). These are everyday stuff, not good enough to export. Then comes Qualitätswein, short for Qualitätswein bestimmter Anbaugebiet (QbA), which means, "wines of quality from a specified region."

Heard it Through the Grapevine

The Qualitätswein designation describes most of the lower-price German wines that are exported. Some popular and colorful generic names you might see are Liebfraumilch (see Milk of the Virgin), Naktarsch (bare bottom), Schwatze Katz (black cat), and Black Tower.

Now we return to Qualitätswein mit Prädikat (QmP), "wines of quality with special ranking," the highest level.

Heard it Through the Grapevine

While you may well still see Qualitätswein mit Prädikat (QmP) on many labels on shelves, it's a term that is no more! In 2006, the German federal cabinet switched Qualitätswein mit Prädikat to the easier-for-us-to-say Prädikatswein, which took effect during the 2007/08 vintage.

This system of assigning rank to ripeness isn't so strange, actually, when we consider the cool German climate in which ripeness is the desired, but sometimes elusive, goal. There are five Prädikat levels, the higher usually indicating a higher (riper) quality. From the lowest to the highest, these are:

- Kabinett
- Spätlese (late harvest)
- Auslese (select harvest)
- Beerenauslese (selected grape-by-grape)
- Trockenbeerenauslese (selected grape-by-grape, with the grapes on their way to becoming raisins).

Vino Vocab

There is a category within Beerenauslese called Eiswein (ice wine). It's very rare, as the temperature condition must be just-so according to German law. The grapes freeze on the vines, and then are harvested individually. It is a very risky, time-consuming, expensive, and cold endeavor, which is why these wines tend to cost upwards of $40 a half bottle and then some. But when you sip their honeyed nectar, you will understand why this nectar of the Gods is worth the effort and price!

Now there's no need to be intimidated by such a descriptor as "Bernkasteler Badstube Riesling Trockenbeerenauslese." In the case of German wines, word count is a reliable indicator of quality.

The finest wines at each level are made from the Riesling grape, although the quality of wines made from other grape varieties improves as riper grapes are used. Kabinett wines generally are somewhat dry and fruity, though well-balanced. Wines graded from Spätlese, upward, indicate some degree of selection. Spätlese wines are made from grapes ranging from fairly ripe to greatly mature, and can come to us from fairly dry to slightly sweet.

Tasting Tip

Prädikat is assigned according to the Oechsle scale, a measure of sugar in the grape juice prior to fermentation. Not all finished product will be sweet, though. At the two lower Prädikat levels, the grape juice may be fully fermented to dryness. Above these, the amount of sugar in the ripe grapes guarantees us a sweet wine—but remember, Germany's great ability for acidity generally manages to keep the sweet from becoming cloying.

The 1971 German wine laws also define viticultural areas as follows:

- Bereich is an enormous region, which may be subdivided into one or more Grosslagen.
- Grosslage means "large locale." It's essentially a large vineyard that contains smaller vineyards (Einzellagen), sometimes several hundred acres with thousands of vineyards, all of which produce wines of similar quality and character. A wine from a Grosslage is identified on the label with a generic name that look just like a vineyard name. To tell the difference you need to know the Grosslagen names.
- Einzellage, literally "single-cell locale," is the smallest defined region, an individual vineyard that is at least twelve acres. The Einzellage is indicated on the label after the village name.

Milk of the Virgin

Liebfraumilch, which means "milk of the Virgin," originates from an old vineyard that had surrounding the Liebfraustift (institution dedicated to Our Lady) at Worms in the

Rheinhessen region. Sweet and simple, Liebfraumilch may be the best-known German wine in the U.S. (and for many people, their first taste of Vitis vinifera)—however, you might know it better by its more popular exported name, Blue Nun, which had its hey-day in the 70s and 80s. Today, the Blue Nun brand was bought up and dusted off for a modern-day market, but for some of us, that ol' woman of the blue cloth forever symbolizes low-quality Riesling.

Heard it Through the Grapevine

Liebfraumilch and many other inexpensive German wines are produced using a method called süss Reserve (sweet reserve), which helps maintain a desired level of sweetness. The wine is fully fermented to create a dry wine of low alcohol and high acidity. But here's the trick: Before fermentation, a small quantity of grape juice is withheld, to be blended later with the fermented wine.

The unfermented grape juice, or süss Reserve, adds its natural, sweet, fruity flavor to the finished wine. Wines produced in this style are termed lieblich, which means lovely or gentle. They are fruity, light-bodied, sweet wines.

Yellow in color, with a slight greenish hue, Liebfraumilch is a blend of several grape varieties, primarily Müller-Thurgau with Riesling, Silvaner, and/or Kerner. It's produced generally in the Rheinhessen or the Pfalz region, with lesser quantities produced in the Nahe and the Rheingau. Liebfraumilch is ranked Qualitätswein, (or QbA). Typically low in alcohol, it is medium-dry, with a refreshing acidity, and a pleasant fruity flavor. It is definitely meant to be enjoyed young. Liebfraumilch sells from $6 to $12 a bottle.

Germany: the Dry Side

In recent years, Riesling in all its styles—but especially the dry versions—have become oh-so trendy outside of their homeland. The driest category in German wines is *trocken* (dry). Trocken wines have virtually no residual sugar and range in taste from austere to tart. Halbtrocken (half-dry) wines are midway between trocken and lieblich. More mellow than trocken wines, they have a certain amount of residual sugar and a fairly dry taste. They are somewhat higher in alcohol than Kabinett or Spätlese wines.

Heard it Through the Grapevine

In an effort to help consumers better understand the differences in Riesling styles, the International Riesling Foundation was formed in 2007 as a joint project between members in America, Germany, South Africa, Australia, and New Zealand. One of the helpful things the group created was the Riesling Taste Profile– a graph called small enough to fit on the back label of a bottle that shows the consumer that particular bottle's level of sweetness.

Overripened, Rotted, and Expensive

Wines from the Auslese category on up, are made from grapes that may be over-ripened, rot-infected, or even naturally frozen. Remarkably, these are among of the world's finest wines. And unique in their aromas and flavors.

Tasting Tip

Auslese (and higher) wines are made from overripe grapes that endow the wine with a fuller body and a higher concentration of flavor. Their sweetness usually is balanced by sufficient acidity.

Beerenauslese (grape-selected) wines are made from grapes that have over-ripened and generally display the noble rot, Botrytis. This gives them a honeyed and luscious opulence when vinified. Winemakers choosing to make a Beerenauslese are gamblers. They risk losing their entire crop to frost as the grapes are left on the vine to ripen. As a result, only small numbers of Beerenauslese are produced each year. Yes, it can be expensive.

Trockenbeerenauslese (dried on the vine) wines are at the very top of the hierarchy. These berries are harvested individually and usually show signs of Botrytis (although it's not a legal requirement). These wines possess a concentrated lusciousness like nectar. (This, I understand, is Wotan's favorite beverage in Valhalla.)

The intense lusciousness is the combined effect of the grape's essence, the flavor of noble rot, and the high level of residual sugar (which may approach 20 percent). This wine is a killer to make. It's not only risky, it's a difficult wine to vinify and requires superior skill and loving dedication throughout the process. Prices easily can run into the three-figure range.

Maybe it is the cool climate—or maybe it's the same spirit that gave us Zeppelins, dachshunds, and lederhosen—but the German winemaking industry has some truly strange offerings. Perhaps the strangest is Eiswein (ice wine), made from grapes left on the vine to freeze. (Talk about turning a liability into an asset!)

Once harvested, the grapes are crushed gently to retain the sweet, concentrated grape juice, minus the ice. The juice left to undergo fermentation is richly concentrated in sugar, flavor, and acidity. Depending on the skill of the winemaker, this opulent wine can better the late-harvest German wines. You'll find these rare wines in half-bottles, sometimes at obscene prices.

Das Rheingold

In Das Rheingold, the first of Wagner's four-opera Ring Cycle, a gold hoard, fashioned into a ring, grants its owner ultimate power. (The remaining 13 hours of the plot are too hard to explain here.) Some of the Rhine River's most golden treasures come in tall, amber-colored bottles. And you don't have to blackmail the gods to obtain them. (Admittedly, they're not as easy to find in wine shops as their French or Italian counterparts.)

Vino Vocab

Four of Germany's wine regions bear the name of the renowned river: Rheingau, Rheinhessen, Pfalz (formerly called Rheinpfalz), and Mittelrhein.

Rheingau

The Rheingau is a tiny wine region (only one-quarter the size of the Mosel, which we'll get to in a moment), but along with the the latter, it is the most important in Germany. It's divided into 10 Grosslagen and 120 einzellagen (individual vineyards) among 28 communities that jut quaintly along the river's banks. Riesling grapes account for more than 80 percent of the vineyard planting, producing the finest wines of the region. The Rieslings tend to be round, soft, and deep in color.

The following are the leading Grosslagen:

- Hochheim produces full-bodied and fruity wines, often with a trace of earthiness. The best vineyards include Domdechaney, Hölle, and Sommerheil, whose wines fall within the mid-premium quality range and are comparable in quality to wines from Johannisberg (see below). The finest estate is Schloss Eltz, followed by the vineyards of Taubenberg and Sonnenberg.
- Erbach is noted for its sturdy wines, with full-bodied flavors and long life. Erbach gained its stature primarily on the reputation of the wines produced by the Marcobrunn estate; in the best vintages, these noble wines rank with the world's best.
- In Hattenheim, the Steinberg estate produces superlative wines. The wines of other Hattenheim vineyards are somewhat more delicate and less firm than the noble class Steinbergers.

- In Winkel, the Schloss Vollrads vineyard eclipses all others. Its wines are characterized by ripeness and great fruit—unquestionably noble quality material. Their Kabinett and Spätlese rank in the mid- to super-premium range.
- Wines from Rauenthal are characterized by a distinctive sense of fruit and an almost spicy flair. Most of the wines fall into the mid-premium range, but some of the better Lagen—Baiken, Wülfen, Langenstrück, and Nonnenburg—are capable of producing wines of noble stature.
- Eltville produces wines that are pleasing, fine, soft, and have good bouquet. Although less distinguished than the wines of the Rauenthal, they are highly drinkable, simple to mid-premium quality wines.
- Johannisberg, the village, is the most famous name of the Rheingau. The wines made here range from simple to super-premium in quality, with the Schloss (castle) Johannisberg standing out for its noble wines from the great vintages. Johannisberger wines are distinguished for their finesse and fine bouquet. Schloss Johannisberg wines have an extra dimension of breed, placing them among the world's great wines.

Rheinhessen

The large Rheinhessen region produces a greater variety of wines—ranging from small table wines to spritzenwein (wine you mix with soda)—than any other German wine district. Its most famous export is Liebfraumilch, which is made by nearly all of the region's 167 villages. The Rheinhessen accounts for 50 percent of all German wine exports, and while it used to be almost entirely white grapes, today white grape varietals account for about 70 percent, with growing acreage now being devoted to reds.

Heard it Through the Grapevine

Rheinhessen wines tend to be soft, with a pronounced character that makes them the easiest to identify of all German wines. But because of a temperate climate, the wines lack the character they might have had if they had to fight for their lives.

The initial popularity of the Rheinhessen wines probably is based on their intense bouquet and straightforward sweetness. Most Rheinhessen wines are made from the Müller-Thurgau grape, which produces juicy, soft, fruity wines. The next mostly widely used vine is the Silvaner, which produces full, round wines.

The Rheinhessen comprises three Bereichs: Bingen, Nierstein, and Wonnegau. The highest quality wines come from Nierstein (and its towns, Oppenheim and Nierstein). Its long-lived Rieslings are unquestionably the best Rheinhessen wines. They are soft, full-bodied, and elegant, with a unique, easily identified, marvelous bouquet.

In the Bereich of Bingen, the village of Bingen, itself, produces wines similar to those of the Nahe (see Leaving the Main Road), which are fuller, heavier, and more concentrated than the average Rhine wine. The wines here profit from warmer microclimates that give them a special fullness and ripeness. With time, Riesling wines develop elegance and style, and Silvaner wines gain in distinction.

Tasting Tip

On the whole, wines from the town of Nierstein have more elegance than those from Oppenheim, although in some vintages (particularly hot, dry years), Oppenheim wines reign superior. Remember, in Germany, vintages count.

Wines from the finest vineyards of Nachenheim have great bouquet and are remarkable for their elegance, finesse and class. The best wines combine depth, fire, spiciness, and delicacy in marvelous and noble harmony.

Wonnegau is where the city of Worms is located. Alzey, the center of the inland area, and its surrounding towns, produce good, clean-tasting lieblich wines.

The Pfalz

The Pfalz region is close in size to the Rheinhessen. Situated along the Rhenish wine road (the Weinstrasse), its enchanting and scenic vineyards grow on a high plateau above the river's western bank.

In the finer vineyards, the soil contains large amounts of Schist (slate), which retains the day's heat during the cool evening hours. A long, warm fall fosters grape maturity, which enables the area to produce intense, sweet wines ranging from Spätlese to Trockenbeerenauslese. Some of these high-ranked Prädikats achieve super-premium or noble status.

As in other areas, the finest wines come from the noble Riesling, though this grape accounts for only 14 percent of all vineyard plantings. Pfalz Rieslings offer an attractive and remarkable balance. They're fuller than those of the Mosel, less mild and soft than those of the Rheinhessen, and less overwhelming in bouquet than those of the Rheingau. This region produces some of the world's finest Auslese and Beerenauslese wines.

The predominant grape here is the Müller-Thurgau, which yields pale, fresh wines. The Silvaner accounts for 20 percent of vineyard production, ranging in quality from simple premium to mid-premium. A small amount of spicy wine is produced from the Gewürztraminer. Recently, Kerner, Scheurebe, and Spatburgunder (Pinot Noir) have gained in importance.

Mittelrhein

Mittelrhein, along the banks of the northern Rhine, is one of Germany's smallest wine regions. It is noted mainly for its Rieslings.

The Mosel (Moselle)

The Mosel region comprises the vineyards dotting the slopes of the serpentine Mosel and its tributaries, the Saar and Ruwer. Until 2006, it was officially known as the Mosel-Saar-Ruwer (or MSR), however, German law now dictates the region is simply referred to as Mosel (much easier for you and me!). Divided in two, the area includes the Mittelmosel (Central Mosel), which produces the greatest wines of the region, and the Saar-Ruwer, which produces good, if not necessarily distinctive, wines.

Vino Vocab

Sometimes you will see and hear the River Mosel (MOH-zl) as Moselle (moh-ZELL). The river rises in France; so either is correct.

More than half (55 percent) of the plantings are Riesling. Mosel Rieslings are light in body, delicate, and refined. They often are described as floral wines, evoking images of flowers in spring meadows. They have a lively and refreshing taste; low in alcohol, often exhibiting a slight effervescence. These are wines that you must be drink while they're young.

Bereich Bernkastel is the best known region in the Mittelmosel, and premium and noble wines are produced by four of its six Grosslagen: Michelsberg, Kurfürstlay, Münzlay, and Schwarzlay. The two others, Probstberg and St. Michael, produce simple-premium wines.

The Sommelier Says

To be filed under The Cutting Off of One's Nose to Spite the Face: In the late aughts, Germany began a project to built a four-lane, mile-long bridge right through the beautiful vineyards of the Mosel wine region. The Mosel High Bridge (aka, the Hochmoselbrücke) would rise 518 feet on stilts above the vineland and is planned to be operational by 2016, despite enormous public outcry. The result? The sure destruction and pollution of some of the oldest and finest vineyards in the region.

- The villages of the Grosslage Michelsberg produce some of the most distinctive wines in the Mosel. There are the fresh, light wines of Trittenheim and the more intense wines of Neumagen. The best and most famous village in this Grosslage is Piesport.
- In the Grosslage Kurfürstlay, the two best wine-producing villages are Brauneberg and Bernkastel. Brauneberg wines are very full-bodied, rich in flavor and long-lived. When from the best vineyards, such as Juffer, they can reach super-premium class.
- In the Grosslage of Munzlay, the three villages of Graach, Wehlen, and Zeltingen yield wines capable of achieving super-premium or noble status. These wines are well-balanced and fragrant, although the style can vary from vineyard to vineyard and range from fine, fragrant, and delicate to full-bodied and big. Wehlen is the home of some of the finest Mosel wines, many of which come from the renowned Prums estate. The fuller-bodied wines of Zeltingen range from ordinary quality wines to super-premiums, ranking alongside Graach and Wehlen.

Tasting Tip

Piesporter Michelsberg is the name of the district's Grosslage wines—do not confuse it with an individual vineyard wine. The Kabinett wines usually are mid-premium quality, with typical Mosel delicacy. Those of Auslese and above, from the better vineyards, can achieve super-premium quality—richly sweet, complex, and flavorful.

- The Grosslage of Scharzberg is where we find the Saar, a tributary of the Mosel. The quality of wine from here varies greatly, depending upon the whims of Mother Nature. Scharzhofberger is the noble estate and wine of the Saar.
- The tiny Ruwer Valley gives us the lightest and most delicate of the Mosel wines. The top-quality names are Maximin Grünhaus and Eitelsbach.

Vino Vocab

That squat green bottle on the shelf may not be the Portuguese Mateus. If it has a German label, this is a Boxbeutel (BOX-boy-tl), the distinctive flask for the wines of Franconia.

Leaving the Main Road

The Nahe River region, west of the Rheinhessen, produces agreeable, pleasant wines which are somewhat fuller, heavier, and more intense than most German wines.

Baden, the southernmost, and consequently the warmest, region, produces fairly full-bodied, pleasant, straightforward wines. The wines of Franconia are unlike other German wines. They are fuller in body, higher in alcohol, and have an earthy and steely character that replaces the typical flowery, fruity wine profile.

Heard it Through the Grapevine

Eighty percent of Austria's wines are white. The most popular are made from the indigenous white Grüner Veltliner—a grape varietal that has gained in popularity in the United States over the last few years. These wines are medium-bodied and refreshing, with herbal and, occasionally, vegetable flavors. Austrian growers plant Müller-Thurgau, along with Welschriesling, a grape frequently used to make ordinary table wines in Eastern Europe. These wines excel in quality in Austria, tending to be light, soft, and aromatic.

Silvaner, the noble Riesling, and Ruländer (Pinot Gris) also are planted here. The wines made from these grapes are similar in style to German wines. Though they rarely reach the same flavor heights, Austria's sweet, late-picked, berry-selected, and dessert style wines have received international acclaim. Austria's crisp, dry whites, which range from light- to full-bodied, are just beginning to gain recognition.

Wines from the Land of Waltzes

The Austrian people enjoy their native wines! Annual per-capita consumption is roughly about eight gallons. Strangely, no Austrian wines come from near its borders with its wine-producing neighbors, Germany, Italy, or Switzerland. The best wines of Austria come from Langenlois, Krems, and Wachau, all in its eastern provinces. Baden, near Vienna, produces light, fruity-style wines.

Most of Austria's red wine is produced in Burgenland, one of the country's warmer regions bordering Hungary. The red wines are medium- to full-bodied, with a fruity character and moderate tannins.

Austrian wine laws follow the German model. Better wines are divided into Qualitätswein and Prädikatswein classifications. The only difference from the German laws is that, in Austria, Prädikat begins with Spätlese. The minimum ripeness required for each level is higher in Austria than in Germany, and Austrian wines typically are higher in alcohol.

The German system of labeling also applies to Austrian wines, including linking the varietal name with the place-name. There are some exceptions. For example, in Burgenland, the wines generally carry varietal names followed by the region.

Tasting Tip

Switzerland is well situated for winemaking—nestled among Germany, France, and Italy. Vineyards dot all regions, German-speaking, French-speaking, and Italian-speaking.

Switzerland—Interesting, but Rarely Exported

Like the Austrians, the Swiss enjoy their wines. Annual per-capita consumption is close to 12 gallons. Unfortunately for the rest of the wine world, the Swiss enjoy their wines so much that they keep most of them at home—only about 2 percent make it outside their borders.

The canton of Vaud is the largest winegrowing region. To the south is the Valais. Switzerland used to be similar to Germany, with roughly two-thirds of their wines white, but since 2001 that has flip-flopped: Today, more reds (Pinot Noir, in particular) are grown and vinified here than white. On the white side, the grape Chasselas is the most widely planted. Swiss wines tend to be expensive for their quality and, not a good value. They do, however, offer a certain unique character.

Vaud

Most of the vineyards here are located on slopes surrounding beautiful Lake Geneva. The two major sub-regions are Lavaux and La Côte. (Guess which language they speak here!)

With its southern exposure, Lavaux enjoys the tempering effect of Lake Geneva. The predominant grape variety is the Chasselas, which yields a grapey, if neutral, white wine. Chasselas wines tend to be fairly full-bodied, with dry and straightforward earthy flavors. La Côte, on the northern shore, produces similar wines to Lavaux.

Valais

The Valais has a few warmer growing sites, particularly on the slopes near the Rhône River. Chasselas is known here by its local name, Fendant. In the temperate (for Switzerland)

Valais, it develops full body and offers good balance. Dôle is the local name for red wine, made from either Gamay or Pinot Noir. Petit-Dôle is another name for Pinot Noir.

Heard it Through the Grapevine

Rèze has some historical—or mythical—importance: It was once (according to the story) used to produce a wine, vin de glacier, made by mountain peasants reputed to remain fresh for decades when kept at high elevation.

In Valais, wines from the Müller-Thurgau grape are called "Johannisberg." Malvoisie is a soft, sweet dessert-style wine made from the Pinot Gris grape. The area still cultivates several local wines such as Arvine, Amirgne, Humagne, and Rèze.

Neuchâtel

The region of Lake Neuchâtel in the northwest corner is adept at producing good quality in both red and white table wines—something a bit unusual this far north. Remarkably, the fussy Pinot Noir yields a delicate, fruity style of wine. The village of Cortaillod offers some of the better, light Pinot Noirs.

Ticino

Ticino is located in the southern corner, known as Italian Switzerland. Most of the vineyards here are planted in red varieties. Nostrano is the name for a light, blended red. Viti is the name for fuller-bodied reds made from the Merlot variety.

Bubbly Ol' England

Bubbles aren't just for beer anymore in England—they're showing up in the most sophisticated of flutes. There are about 350 wineries giving it a go in Great Britain, with most of them concentrated in the southeast around Kent, Surrey, and East and West Sussex. Here, grapes like Chardonnay, Pinot Noir, and Pinot Meunier are gaining favor for traditional Champagne-centric sparklers. And while their exports linger around 1 or 2 percent, the quality and recent notoriety among the wine press may well create a rebel yell on this side of the pond for more British-style bubbly.

Greece—Dionysus Country

Greece is one of the oldest winegrowing regions in the world. In fact, ancient Greeks honored their own wine god, Dionysus. No wonder they have more than 300 indigenous grape varietals!

The Greek wine palate is rather different from ours, stemming perhaps from the traditional red-and-black clay vessels from Attic times. In those ancient days, the Greeks kept their wine from spoiling by adding preservatives such as herbs and spices—even goat cheese! A few vestiges of this practice remain. (I don't know of any wines today with goat cheese!) Resin flavorings still are added to the white Retsina and the rosé, Kokkineli.

Retsina is a favorite wine for many Greeks. If you're planning some travel in Greece, you may want to sample this in its home territory. A word of caution: Many similarly inclined wine lovers have been so unnerved by their first taste of Retsina, they have forgotten their desire to sample other native Greek wines.

There are some pleasant and fruity wines produced in Greece. Most are not distinguished, but they don't taste like Retsina. (Incidentally, Retsina is flavored with resin, a plant substance used in the manufacture of varnish.) But hey! Greek olives are an acquired taste, too!

Tasting Tip

Some pleasant fruity Greek table wines, red and white, are exported to the U.S. They're very drinkable and relatively inexpensive. The largest producers are Achaia-Clauss and Andrew Cambas. Boutari is a name linked with quality.

Attica, the home of the Parthenon, is a leading wine-producing area in Greece—and where most of the Retsina is made. The Peloponnese, an area of Sparta, is the largest wine district, producing mostly sweet wines. Wine is made also on many of the Greek islands, including Crete, Samos, Santorini, Rhodes, and Corfu. Little of it is exported to the U.S., but if you're planning a trip to Greece, there's plenty of it waiting.

Fortified dessert wines are the second most important Greek wine type. First in prestige is the dark red Mavrodaphne, similar to California Port, although lower in alcohol.

Hungary—the Blood of the Bull

Despite a momentary affair with international grape varietals late in the last century, Hungary continues to uphold a centuries-old tradition of turning out many good to fine wines from indigenous varietals. In fact, many of its grape varieties are indigenous. Others, like the Silvaner and the Walschriesling, have been adapted successfully to the area.

Hungarian wines are quite distinct in style, made to suit the tastes of the local populace. But unlike that of the Greeks, Hungarian taste is not so different from ours. The result is a variety of good wines, many of them reasonably priced and a good bargain. And they're easy to find.

The most important Hungarian wines are the whites. Some pleasant white wines come from the region of Transdanubia (across the Danube), near Lake Balaton. They're usually labeled Badacsonyi, followed by a grape name, such as the widely planted Furmint.

The most distinguished wines are made from Botrytis-infected Furmint. These are the legendary whites from Tokay, in the Northern Massif region. Unsweet versions of Tokay, otherwise known as dry to off-dry wines, are labeled Tokay Szamorodni. They have a slightly nutty, slightly oxidized character.

Heard it Through the Grapevine

For the wines of Tokay, you'll see the word aszu (AH-soo) as the descriptor for sweet. Tokay varies from slightly sweet to the richly concentrated, celestial wine, Tokay Eszencia (Tokay essence), which is made from Botrytis-infected grapes in a manner similar to the German Trockenbeerenauslese. Rare and always expensive, Eszencia can be close to 50 percent sugar! Alcohol levels, though, often are very low. Over the centuries, it has been the preferred beverage of the European nobility and was once considered to have curative, therapeutic powers.

On a Tokay Eszencia wine label, you'll see the term puttonyos, which refers to the measure of sweetness as determined by the quantity of Botrytis-infected, overripe grapes that were added to the wine. Wines labeled 3 Puttonyos are moderately sweet; those labeled 5 Puttonyos are very sweet and concentrated.

Probably the best-known of Hungarian wines is the red Egri Bikaver, which literally means "Bull's Blood of Eger." The name comes from its deep color; so don't expect it to have some hemoglobular property. It's a dependable, full-bodied red wine with some potential for aging. Eger also makes a sweet-style Merlot, with the local name Médoc Noir, but it's seldom seen outside of the country.

CHAPTER 18

Go West!

In This Chapter

- Discovering winegrowing regions in the North America west
- Choosing varietal wines from California
- Fine wines from Oregon and Washington

America doesn't share Europe's long tradition for wine. Wine, older than history, is relatively new in the Western Hemisphere. You could say an American wine industry dates from the nineteenth century, when European immigrants transplanted vines into the U.S., Chile, and Argentina. However, it wasn't until the 1970s, thanks to California, that the U.S. had large enough commercial output to sit among the world's great wine producers.

Those pioneer wine growers arrived in the New World with their native grapes, their skills, and their respect for wine. But they left behind the rigid Old World laws that had regulated their craft.

Vintage Laissez-Faire

American vintners face fewer rules than those of other wine-producing countries. To be sure, the U.S. does have a system to let us know where the wine was grown. These are the AVAs, standard names (appellations) designating the American wine-growing regions. However, there are no rules regarding which varieties may be planted where and no limits on yields-per-acre.

American wines displaying a varietal name must be made at least 75 percent from the juice of that grape. But some of these varieties offer quantity for the producer, rather than quality for us consumers.

An AVA on the label means at least 85 percent of the grapes came from the specified place. That doesn't tell us much, because some AVAs may include areas that produce only mediocre grapes along with some that yield the very finest.

Vino Vocab

AVA stands for American Viticultural Area. This is like the French word, appellation, which means, simply, "name."

Some other words on the label have standard meanings. The terms "Grown, produced, and bottled by" and "Estate bottled" mean the producer owned or controlled all the grapes that went into that wine. If you see "Produced and bottled by," that means the vintner actually made and bottled at least 75 percent. Now watch out! The phrase "Made and bottled by" means the winery may have produced as little as 10 percent of that wine. (Pretty tricky, huh!)

Tasting Tip

If the bottle says "California," you can be sure 100 percent of the grapes were California-grown. (Other states require only 75-percent content.)

Vintage date, where listed on the label, is pretty reliable. At least 95 percent of that wine must have been grown and fermented that year. But watch out! There are no rules whatsoever for the use of such nice-sounding embellishments as "reserve", "special reserve," or "vintner's reserve." Producers often add such promising descriptions to their mediocre, large-volume production as a marketing gimmick, while their superior wines are shipped with no extra words on their labels. Other wine-producing countries are quite strict about the meaning of every word, but as you can see, such regulation in the US is quite spare.

The Sommelier Says

"Estate bottled" and "Grown, produced, and bottled by" sound pretty impressive. However, those can be applied to some of the least distinguished and interesting wines. So these terms are no assurance of quality.

For us wine-consumers, I suppose, that's both good news and bad. On the plus side, we buyers of American wines face an amazing selection from among thousands of producers. On the minus, the label can't tell us much about the quality of what's inside.

Sure, there's a varietal name on the label, but that's no real help. Both a region's very best wines and its very worst actually may show the same information on their labels. So when you buy American, you simply have to know your producer!

A California Peregrination

In France, each wine-growing region specializes in wines made from only one or no more than a few grape varieties. But in California, most AVAs produce wines from most grapes. In the following California appellations, you will learn which varieties to seek in which AVAs.

Tasting Tip

Just as you would expect, some varietals excel in certain areas, but flop in others. Many of the latter represent some grower's failed experiment. You shouldn't have to pay for these! Learn to associate AVAs with those grapes that do best in them.

California, Here I Come!

This is one giant category! The grapes may have been grown anywhere at all in the Golden State. (You can be sure the contents are 100 percent California, though.) Wines falling under this broad appellation range from ordinary everyday to simple-premium in quality.

Appellation North Coast

You can be sure the wines designated "North Coast" are from one of the better wine-growing regions of the state. These range in quality from everyday to mid-premium. This popular AVA includes wines from:

- Napa Valley
- Sonoma Valley
- Mendocino County
- Lake County

Operator, Get Me Central!

Welcome to the Central Valley! This hot, fertile, sunny valley, about 100 miles long, used to be jug-wine country and featured lots of so-so, high-yielding grapes that fed California's bulk-wine pipeline (and, to a certain extent, still do). But don't reject the Central Valley out of hand! Many producers have upped the ante on quality in this region that has started make a mark with Zinfandels, Cabernet Sauvignon, and for its Rhone varietals like Syrah and Viognier, as well as for its efforts in spearheading more responsible, sustainable farming practices. Names like Tablas Creek, J. Lohr, Bonny Doon, Chalone, Qupe, Au Bon Climat, and Ridge, for instance, now grow craft beautiful wines in Paso Robles, San Luis Obispo, Lodi, and Santa Barbara up further north to Monterey and Carmel.

California's Best

Now let's zoom in closer and explore those particular California AVAs that give us the best (or most interesting) wines.

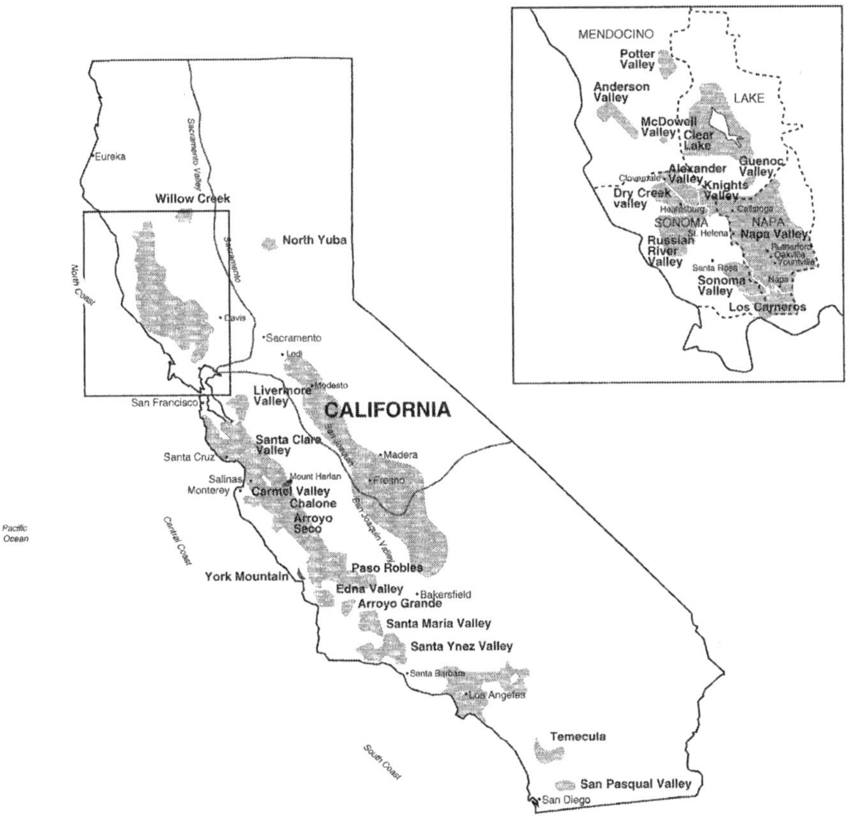

The best-known wine regions of California.

Growers Don't Nap in Napa

Ask anybody to name a California wine-growing region, and chances are good the response will be, "Napa Valley." But for all its fame, this modest region accounts for not quite five percent of California's production. Some say this is California's "Bordeaux Region." Maybe not. Some pretty mediocre vintages have been bottled here, along with some of the finest.

Heard it Through the Grapevine

Higher is better; elevation, that is. Napa wines from vineyards on the slopes of the Mayacamas Mountains to the west or the Howell Mountains to the east generally are superior to those from the Valley floor.

The Napa Valley lies just northeast of cosmopolitan San Francisco. In this small growing region, more than 450 wineries compete for precious acreage. Its picturesque character makes this region a popular tourist destination.

Napa was the second U.S.-declared AVA, and now this small region contains 14 sub-appellations, plus the Carneros AVA (see below) that is shared by Napa and Sonoma. These are:

- Calistoga, Diamond Mountain, Spring Mountain, and Mount Veeder, in the western mountains.
- Howell Mountain, Stags' Leap District, Atlas Peak (which are all hilly or mountainous), Oak Knoll, Yountville, and Wild Horse Valley—all in the eastern portion of Napa.
- Rutherford, St. Helena, Chiles Valley, and Oakville—on the valley floor.

The Sommelier Says

A "Napa Valley" appellation alone cannot guarantee greatness. Napa Valley wines range from mediocre to sublime. So there's no substitute for doing your homework. You need to know your growers and what they produce.

Let's begin with the white wines and with the varietal most closely associated with Napa, the Chardonnay. The very finest of these have a ripe aroma and flavor, frequently spicy, offering a mélange of apricot, pineapple and citrus. The texture is rich, and the alcohol high—13 percent or more—giving these fine wines a certain headiness when young.

Some of these may be fermented in oaken barrels, in the true Burgundian fashion, or even in small, French, oak casks. This endows these vintages with a slight oaky spiciness and a vanilla character that goes well with its varietal personality. Mid-premium Chardonnays may be made from less-ripe grapes or have spent less time aging. They are fruity, appley, but less complex. There also has been a trend as of late to eschew barrels altogether, fermenting in stainless steel and bottling from there, for a clean, more crisp and citrusy style of the grape.

The Sauvignan Blanc is Napa's second most famous white varietal. The very best of these resemble their French namesakes, but rarely can they rival the finest from the Graves or the Médoc. (Then again, Sauvignon Blancs from other French regions can't, either.)

These distinguished Sauvignons range from subtle, light, and steel fermented, to moderately oaked, to powerful, warm and heavily oaked. It all depends on the winery. In general, the Napa style lies in the direction of full ripeness, counterbalanced by assertive oak flavors. Don't worry about age. Though capable of good bottle-aging, they're fine when they're young.

Heard it Through the Grapevine

Have you ever hear of Fume Blanc? It was the term for Sauvignon Blanc coined by California fine-wine country pioneer, Robert Mondavi. Mondavi admired the French style of Sauvignon Blanc, especially that of the Loire Valley, whose terroir lends smoky, minerally characteristics in its Pouilly Fume. Mondavi had a whole lot of Sauvignon Blanc on his hands from the growers he'd contracted with, and wasn't sure what to do with it. In a moment of inspiration, he decided to use a little barrel aging to add a bit of complexity that reminded him of the Pouilly Fumes he'd tried, and, voilà, Fume Blanc was born.

The Napa Valley is not well known for its Rieslings (usually labeled "Johannisberg Reisling"). Few of Napa's drier Rieslings can match the charm of the authentic Rhines and Mosels from Germany. But they easily equal those from elsewhere.

When we come to the late harvests, Napa's Rieslings can stand up against Germany's very best. These Napa grapes, along with some from Sonoma and Monterey Counties, can develop the "noble rot" (see Chapter 17, Overripened, Rotted, and Expensive) that allows the production of late-harvest wines in the true German tradition.

Heard it Through the Grapevine

There are no direct U.S. equivalents to the German mit Prädikat designations; so just look for the term "Late Harvest" on the label. These rare wines can achieve super-premium or even noble status. With them, you enjoy the characteristic Riesling floral together with the Botrytis complexity—honeyed aroma, hint of almonds, with acid balance to the innate sweetness.

Now let's sample Napa's red wines, beginning with that region's Cabernet Sauvignon. When Napa producers go for it, this wine can rank among California's very best. Well-made Napa Cabernets present a berryish, herbal aroma. They are full of body, with ample tannins and some warmth. The super-premiums have a riper character that's reminiscent of cassis, dried sage, and black currents. These wines often develop a cedary "cigar-box" characteristic with bottle-aging. The very best of these can be set aside a decade or more.

Tasting Tip

Napa Valley Cabernet Sauvignons made from grapes grown north of Yountville, generally fall in the mid- to super-premium range. A select few from vineyards in Rutherford, Oakville, or the Stags' Leap District, can achieve noble status.

Merlot is another popular grape varietal from the West Coast. Its tannins are less harsh, less astringent than Cabernet's. And Napa is on top when it comes to excellent Merlots! The best are very ripe and herbaceous in aroma and flavor. In character, they are round, soft, and voluptuous. With some, you may notice a finish that's slightly sweet.

The Zinfandel grape thrives in Napa Valley when grown on hillside sites and allowed to develop high sugar levels. It does less well on the valley floor. Super-premium Zinfandels come from hillsides or from very old vineyards. Zinfandel reigns in the Calistoga region, the area's warmest sub-region.

Most Napa Valley Zinfandels are berry-like and medium-bodied, with moderate tannins, a tart finish, and higher alcohol levels that can easily start at 13 or 14 percent. That's red Zinfandel we're talking about! The blush wine called White Zinfandel is quite different. It's a light, sweet, and fruity wine, made from the red zinfandel grape.

Heard it Through the Grapevine

Bordeaux-style blended wines are showing up now in greater numbers. The reds usually are made from the red Bordeaux varieties (Cabernet Sauvignon, Cabernet Franc, Merlot, and sometimes Malbec and Petit Verdot). The whites usually are made from the white Bordeaux grapes (Sauvignon Blanc and Semillon). Some of these blends are known by the name Meritage, although rarely does this name appear on the label.

Some Place, Sonoma!

The Sonoma wine-growing region is not the picturesque tourist trap Napa is, but it's home to some of California's most successful wineries. This region is much larger than Napa. Its climate is similar, except along the cooler coast. The grape varieties grown here mostly are the same as in Napa, but the style and character of the finished product often are quite distinct. Sonoma earned AVA status in 1984, and since then many more sub-appellations (plus Carneros, shared with Napa) have grown among the 15,000 vineyard acres in Sonoma County. These are the designated AVAs of Sonoma:

- Sonoma Valley
- Sonoma Mountain
- Sonoma Coast
- Dry Creek Valley
- Alexander Valley

- Russian River Valley
- Green Valley—contained within Russian River Valley
- Chalk Hill—contained within Russian River Valley
- Knights Valley
- Bennett Valley
- Knights Valley

Tasting Tip

Sonoma Chardonnays tend to be fruitier and leaner than Napa's, and long bottle aging improves them.

To make things just a bit confusing, Sonoma County contains parts of two other AVAs: Northern Sonoma, encompassing Russian River Valley, Alexander Valley, Dry Creek Valley, and Knight's Valley; and Sonoma Coast, which includes land situated along the coast in western Sonoma.

Sonoma offers mid- and super-premium Chardonnays. The Dry Creek and Alexander Valley districts feature a fruity varietal aroma with a lemony flavor; they have a medium-bodied, slightly viscous texture. Only the Dry Creek district is noted for its Sauvignon Blancs.

Sonoma is the home of many mid-premium Cabernet Sauvignons. Most are vinous and straightforward, medium-bodied, moderately tannic, early maturing, with a slightly weedy, peppery character. These traits are especially evident in wines from Dry Creek, Alexander Valley, and the Sonoma Valley.

Heard it Through the Grapevine

Not many California wineries can manage the finicky Pinot Noir grape as well as some do in Sonoma, particularly in the Russian River Valley. In these wines, you will discover the characteristic Pinot Noir fruitiness, a slightly cherry, smoky character, medium body, and slight tannins. Successful California Pinot Noirs are the result of continuing experimentation, which has grown wildly in popularity.

Super-premium Zinfandels come from a number of hillside vineyards in Dry Creek (see below) and Alexander Valley. Alexander Valley Zinfandels range from mid- to super-premium and offer a distinct, ripe cherry, blackberry character, along with richness and depth.

Wines Flow at Dry Creek

The Sonoma appellation "Dry Creek Valley" gets its own listing. Dry Creek is celebrated for its Chardonnays, Sauvignon Blancs, Cabernet Sauvignons, and Zinfandels. In fact, Dry Creek Valley is Zinfandel Heaven! These grapes are noted for richness and depth. The best of the Dry Creek red Zinfandels have an earthy, peppery character that distinguishes them from others.

Carry on, Carneros!

Carneros is the single most important wine growing district in California. It runs from the southern part of Napa Valley into Sonoma County. Temperatures there are moderated by cooling breezes from the Pacific and by the mists that roll in from San Pablo Bay. So look here for cool-climate grapes, such as Chardonnay, Pinot Noir, and several white varieties that make high-quality sparkling wines.

As in Sonoma, many winemakers in Carneros have tamed the Pinot Noir grape, creating a few mid- to super-premium wines. The Pinots typically are deep-colored, with herbal, cherryish, and slightly roasted aromas and flavors, a velvety texture, some depth and a long finish.

Leaping Cabernet!

Two words sum up the Stags' Leap District in Napa: Cabernet Sauvignons! This is where you will find the most exceptional examples of this renowned grape.

Mendocino Vino

The name Mendocino has a lyrical ring, evocative of the quaint, picturesque town itself. This AVA lies due north of Sonoma and has two main subdivisions: Ukiah is a large, rural area with a prolific growth of vineyards. The smaller Anderson Valley has a cool climate and the highest level of rainfall of all winegrowing regions.

All the popular varietals thrive here. Initially best known for Zinfandel and Cabernet Sauvignon, they've been joined by Chardonnay, Riesling, Sauvignon Blanc, Gewürztraminer, Pinot Noir, and grapes for sparkling wines. Parducci was the first winery to operate in the area; today it shares its renown with Fetzer.

The Anderson Valley recently has made a name for itself in the sparkling-wine industry, featuring such operations as Roederer Champagne, Scharffenberger, and Handley.

Mendocino Chardonnays usually are lemony and crisp, characterized by a firm, lean style. They don't pretend to be anything more than enjoyable beverages, and their quality is consistent. Mendocino-style Sauvignon Blanc is early-maturing; it's soft and light-bodied, its grassy, black pepper varietal flavor somewhat muted, but very refreshing. The Rieslings are slightly sweet, like the German Kabinett, with low acidity.

There's a lot of Zinfandel grown here, and the range is extensive. They are berrylike, medium-bodied, with moderate tannins and a tart finish. The regional Pinot Noirs offer varietal fruitiness, a slightly cherry, smoky character, medium body, and slight tannins.

Heard it Through the Grapevine

Mendocino-grown Zinfandels vary from simple and berrylike to riper and excessively tannic, depending on climate. They often have an appealing ripe fruit aroma, redolent of berries and herbs, but more astringent and tannic. In the mid-premium category and above, they have a fresh violets and plum-like character, and moderate (around 13 percent) alcohol.

Another Great Lake

Lake County, to the north of Napa, recently has gained in popularity. It's primarily planted in red wine grapes, Cabernet Sauvignon and Zinfandel. The regional versions of these varietals tend to be light-bodied, but with straightforward flavor. A few strongly varietal Sauvignon Blancs are made from Lake County grapes.

Adorable Amador County

Amador is located in the Sierra foothills, where weary prospectors once panned for gold. Few of them found any, but the winegrowers who discovered the native Zinfandel did much better. Zinfandel grapes reach full ripeness in this region. They're generally warm, fruity, and very tannic.

The foothills are located southwest of Sacramento, where Amador shares some of its winemaking fame with El Dorado County. The most prominent grape-growing areas are

Shenandoah Valley and Fiddletown in Amador. Vineyards in hot, dry El Dorado are planted at high altitude to counteract the summer heat.

Tasting Tip

Amador County grows and bottles small amounts of Cabernet Sauvignon, Sauvignon Blanc, and Riesling, but its Zinfandel is tops.

Cruisin' in Santa Cruz

Santa Cruz is a beautiful, mountainous area that runs from San Francisco south to the beachy town of Santa Cruz. Decades ago there were only a dozen small wineries here, but the numbers have grown, some now the very best in California, like Ridge, Calera, and Bonny Doon. This is a cool growing region, with sea breezes on both sides. Pinot Noir grows happily on the Pacific side, while Cabernet Sauvignon prefers the San Francisco Bay area. Chardonnay likes them both.

The appellation Santa Cruz appears on many big-styled, ripe Chardonnays and Pinot Noirs.

Goin' to Monterey!

A few hours south of Napa and Sonoma, this scenic coastal area in the North Central Coast is a haven for writers and artists in Carmel, the little town at the end of the Monterey Peninsula. And it's home to many superb vineyards and wineries. Monterey has two centers: the Salinas Valley near Soledad, and King City in the southern portion. The northern half is dry, cool, and windy—ideal for growing white grapes.

The Sommelier Says

If you had sampled some of Monterey's Cabernet Sauvignon in the 1970s, you might have complained it tasted like uncooked asparagus and smelled like bell peppers. (And it did!) But no longer, as Monterey growers have learned how to create great wines.

Monterey is a microcosm of contemporary California viticulture: modern science in service to winegrowing. Through careful experimentation, growers and winemakers here have eliminated many faults that had beset their product in the 1970s. For instance, Monterey Cabernet Sauvignon has managed to shed its vegetable-garden image as innovative winemakers have learned to cope with their unusual regional trait, and even use it to advantage. Today these Cabernets have an herbal, spicy flavor; a moderate, peppery overtone; and good varietal character.

Heard it Through the Grapevine

Monterey vintners have applied the techniques of Burgundy winemaking to coax their Chardonnays to their full potential. These Chardonnays tend to have more varietal character in aroma and flavor than those from further north, with an accent on fresh, varietal fruitiness. Many display a unique, green or grassy character, medium body, and a sharp, crisp finish.

Monterey is a great place for Sauvignon Blanc. At mid-premium quality status, they yield a characteristic grassy, weedy, or black pepper flavor.

Monterey offers some dry-styled or slightly sweet Rieslings; flowery yet firm, they're similar to the German Kabinett harvest. These "Soft Rieslings" can be opulently fruity and flowery; they're low in alcohol and meant for simple sipping.

Meet Me in San Luis!

San Luis Obispo is another area that continues to gain in importance. Its main sub-districts are the warm and hilly Paso Robles—featuring Zinfandel, Cabernet Sauvignon, and Pinot Noir—and the cool, breezy Edna Valley and Arroyo Grande, planted in Chardonnay and Pinot Noir. Its Cabernets and Chardonnays are similar in style to those from Santa Barbara (see Magnificent Santa Barbara).

Tasting Tip

Gewürztraminer is an important varietal in Monterey. These wines are characteristically spicy in fragrance and fruity in flavor. Some retain a slight degree of Muscat character, which adds complexity. The best are well structured for bottle aging.

Magnificent Santa Barbara

Some of California's very first vineyards were planted by Spanish missionaries in Santa Barbara County. This area of beautiful rolling hills earned its place on our map in 1975, when pioneering Firestone Vineyards began producing their famous Pinot Noirs, Rieslings, and Chardonnays.

Initially, most of the region's wines used the Santa Ynez Valley appellation, but the Santa Maria and Los Alamos Valleys now are gaining notice.

Heard it Through the Grapevine

Santa Barbara Chardonnays mature early, and they are similar in style to their cousins from San Luis Obispo. They have a unique grassiness and, depending on sugar development, they range from very firm and hard in style, to rounder and softer (although few have the rich texture that earmarks Napa Chardonnays). They have excellent acidity and a slight silky texture.

The Sommelier Says

Collectors find value beyond what's intrinsic to that which they collect. Wine collectors know that some small California vintages, in a few years' time, will bring ridiculous prices at wine auctions. So if you're a collector, go for it! But if you buy fine wines only for their drinking pleasure, better look elsewhere.

Some Sauvignon Blanc is produced in Santa Ynez. It tends to have an aggressive, pronounced aroma of grassiness, black pepper, and fruit that need to be tamed and rounded by cask aging, bottle aging, or blending with a small percentage of Semillon. (Remember, in California wines are often blended with grapes from other regions.)

Santa Barbara Cabernets also share some traits with the San Luis Obispo version. Both have moderate, Bordeaux-like alcohol levels (around 13 percent, give or take), and a rich, herbal, berrylike aroma and flavor made complex by a weedy overtone. In some cases, we notice an oakiness from long-aging in small casks. These tend to have a short finish, compared with the regal, lingering aftertaste found in the Cabernets of Napa and the middle Médoc of Bordeaux.

A good part of Santa Barbara's growing wine reputation is founded on the affinity of the Pinot Noir grape for its soil and ocean air. The Pinots often are deep-colored, with herbal, cherryish, and slightly roasted aroma and flavors, a velvety texture, some depth, and a long finish. Some producers also blend a little bit of Syrah into their Pinot to add a spicier, richer component.

California's Best Wine Deals

It's easy to shop smart among California wines. Just remember, the very best values lie in that state's everyday and simple- to mid-premium wines. California vintners turn these out in great quantities, and you benefit from the savings. On the other hand. California's best—the super-premium and noble wines—are not priced competitively with their counterparts from Bordeaux, Burgundy, Italy, and elsewhere.

Heard it Through the Grapevine

Don't be in a hurry to remove that cork! While many California wines are meant to be consumed when bottled, the super-premium and noble quality wines benefit from bottle aging.

Chardonnays benefit from two to four years' bottle-aging. Red varieties, like Cabernet Sauvignon, Merlot, and the better Zinfandels, can benefit from five to 10 years' aging. (Sometimes even more.)

Don't Forget the Pacific Northwest!

Guess what! California isn't the only source of fine wines from the West Coast! Just to the north, in Oregon and Washington, there's a thriving wine industry. The Cascade Mountains cut through both states, and give rise to their distinctive climates.

Washington Never Slept Here

Growers in Washington State began growing vinifera varieties in the 1960s, although few commercial wineries existed until two decades later. Most of these are situated in the East, where the climate is agreeably dry.

There are currently 12 AVAs in Washington state, which are:

- The Yakima Valley in the Southeast has cool summer weather and a long growing season. It's not the biggest region, but it has more wineries (60) than the larger Columbia Valley. Chardonnay is the most widely planted varietal here.
- Columbia Valley has the most sizable grape-growing terrain, supporting 11 million acres, which hold 99 percent of the state's total grapes grown! Puget Sound wineries often use grapes from this region. Here, you find lots of Washington's famous Riesling, as well as Chardonnay, Merlot, and Cabernet Sauvignon.
- The Walla Walla Valley has grown quite a bit over the last few decades, and now has over 100 wineries in this Oregon-bordering spot where the vines were initially planted by Italian immigrants. Here, look for Cabernet Sauvignon, Syrah, and some pretty version of Pinot Gris, among others.
- Puget Sound – With around 45 wineries and a scant 69 acres of land under vine, this mild, dry, sunny spot is home to lovely, aromatic Pinot Gris and delicate Pinot Noir.
- Red Mountain – Sitting pretty on the eastern edge of the Yakima Valley, this AVA came online in 2001—aptly for its name, it is known for its classic red varietals.
- Columbia Gorge – This spot's nearly 200,000 acres under vine actually dips over the border in Oregon, and its hodge-podge of micro-climates has made it a bit of a mixed bag of varietal variety.
- Horse Heaven Hills – This windy spot rimmed by the Columbia River to the south is home to some stunning Riesling and Syrah, as well as well-rounded Cabernet Sauvignon and Merlot.
- Wahluke Slope – Merlot and Syrah hold strong here in this dry, warm spot that holds about 15 percent of the state's total vineyard land.
- Rattlesnake Hills – The steep slopes here can shoot sky-high to over 3,000 in elevation, and the terraced, rocky soil makes for some fine reds, with particular success growing Cabernet Sauvignon, Syrah, and Merlot.
- Snipes Mountain – The rocky, almost pudding-stone-like soil here in Snipes Mountain is home to some of the oldest Cabernet vines in the state, spreading out across some 760 hilly acres.
- Lake Chelan – The drama of the ice age left behind sandy soil here filled with quartz and mica, and the warming effect of the lake keeps things moderately temperate in the Lake Chelan AVA. Here, aromatics reign supreme in grapes like Gewurztraminer, Pinot Gris, Riesling, Syrah, and Pinot Noir.
- The newest AVA in Washington State (it was just added in early 2012), holds about 40 acres of clay soils where Pinot Gris, Riesling, and Syrah grow.

Choice Washington State Offerings

Gewürztraminer, Riesling, and Pinot Gris do well here, with excellent varietal character, with a less-sweet style than their California cousins. Riesling grapes thrive in the few vineyards located west of the Cascades, in the Puget Sound area.

Washington State Sauvignon Blancs are noted for their powerful character. The ubiquitous Chardonnay is widely grown, although its quality can be inconsistent. Chenin Blanc, Cabernet Sauvignon, and Merlot round out Washington's more common varietals. Washington's Columbia Crest Merlot currently is the biggest selling Merlot in the U.S.

Busy in the Beaver State

Oregon's wine industry has grown considerably, with over 400 making a $2.7 billion impact on the state—double what it was in only 2005. Its beautiful wines are not only sought-after by many an Old World wine fan who favor the state's cooler growing conditions' effects on its grapes, but they're also fetching quite a premium price. Oregon's main winegrowing region is the Willamette Valley, followed by 15 other AVAs, including the Umpqua Valley, the Rogue River Valley, Chelhalem Mountains, Yamhill-Carlton District, Ribbon Ridge, Dundee Hills, McMinnville, Eola-Amity Hills, Red Hills Douglas County, Applegate Valley, Southern Oregon, Columbia Gorge, Columbia Valley, Walla Walla Valley, and Snake River Valley.

- Willamette – The Willamette AVA is a sizable area—150 miles long and 60 miles wide—south of the city of Portland, and the state's most important wine-producing area. Its summers are quite cool, with plentiful rainfall during the harvest. Pinot Noir favors cool climates, and Oregon winemakers has made their name on this most finicky of grapes. In Willamette's winery-rich Yamhill County, all of the wineries produce Pinot Noir. Oregon Pinot Noirs first received acclaim in the early 1980s, and its reputation has soared. Recently, Pinot Noir has been joined in Oregon by two other Pinots, Pinot Gris and Pinot Blanc, as well as Chardonnay.
- Umqua – The Umqua Valley is warmer than Willamette, though still rather cool. This AVA is the home of Oregon's pioneering winery, Hillcrest Vineyards, and so deserves a bit of a special mention. Pinot Noir thrives in Umpqua, along with Riesling, Chardonnay, and Cabernet Sauvignon.
- Rogue River Valley – The Rogue River Valley is one of the warmest of the Oregon growing regions, ideal for Cabernet Sauvignon and Merlot and, of course, Chardonnay, which really took the advice, "Go West!" The Pinot Gris now is finding a happy home there, too.

Tasting Tip

Historically, Rieslings have been Oregon's second most important varietal, after the Pinot Noir. Hillcrest, which began Oregon's wine industry in 1962, is noted for its fine Rieslings.

- Chelhalem Mountains – This spot 19 miles southwest of Portland became an AVA in 2006, and is home to some of Oregon's great winemaking pioneers, like David Erath and the Adelsheims. Here, you'll find excellent examples of Pinot Noir, Chardonnay, and Pinot Gris.
- Yamhill-Carlton District – This is Pinot Country, with the not-far-off cooling Pacific Ocean influences and great drainage in the silty soil.
- Ribbon Ridge – The sedimentary, volcanic soils here along with the slightly warmer temperatures from the protective hillsides produce lush, minerally Chardonnay, Pinot Gris, and Pinot Noir.
- Dundee Hills – Cool in climate, this Pinot Noir-friendly sub-region became an AVA in 2005, and is now where about 25 vineyards grow, spread across 1,200 acres.
- McMinnville – The loamy, silty soil here in this historic fruit-farming region is 40 miles southwest of Portland, and has a microclimate that gets considerably less rainfall than some of its more regularly doused neighbors. Here, white varietals like Pinot Gris and Pinot Blanc reign supreme, and Pinot Noir does well, too.
- Eola-Amity Hills – A stone's throw from the state's capital, Salem, the warm summer and moderate winter seasons and volcanic soils here produce Pinot Noir, Chardonnay, and Pinot Gris.
- Red Hills Douglas County – The very first vineyard was planted in this single-vineyard AVA back in 1876. Today, the 220-acre Red Hill Vineyard is the only winery here—which is very unusual indeed! The iron-rich, volcanic soils are rife with 220 acres of Pinot Noir, Riesling, and Chardonnay.
- Applegate Valley – Another pioneering grape-growing spot, the Applegate Valley saw its first vineyards in 1852 when Peter Britt put down vines and opened Oregon's first official winery, Valley View Winery. With its high-elevation vineyards at around 2,000 feet and its warm, dry temperatures during the growing season, Applegate is one of the rare spots in Oregon where Cabernet and Merlot thrive, as well as Syrah and Chardonnay.
- Southern Oregon – This AVA encompasses the sub-appellations of Umpqua Valley, Rogue Valley, Red Hill Douglas County, and Applegate Valley, and in chilly Oregon has the warmest grape-growing conditions in all the state, which is why you find late-ripening reds like Cabernet here, as well as varietals like Viognier, Tempranillo, and Syrah.

- Columbia Gorge – Straddling both Oregon and Washington States for 15 miles, this river region was initially famous for being the scene of Lewis and Clark's pass-way to the Pacific Ocean in 1805, but now has become a bit of a fruit-basket for many grape varietals that thrive in its distinct microclimates of high desert in the east and cool-climate maritime influences in the west.
- Columbia Valley – The large Columbia Valley area also crosses borders between Washington State and Oregon, with the latter encompassing about 50 wineries, who grow Merlot and Cabernet Sauvignon among other high-desert-loving varietals.
- Walla Walla Valley – Snuggled at the base of the Blue Mountains, these 750 stony, silty acres of vines are home to elegant Cabernet Sauvignon, Merlot, and Syrah.
- Snake River Valley – Encompassing an area almost as large as New Jersey, the Snake River Valley AVA straddles Idaho and has vineyards that reach as high as 3,000 feet in elevation. In the dry, high air up there and volcanic, sandy, silty soil, Riesling thrives, as well as some Chardonnay and Gewurztraminer.

The Empire State's Wine Empire

To most people, New York State is the home to the Yankees, the Adirondacks, and Niagara Falls (the American side, at least). But did you know that the Empire State realize that New York is second only to California in wine production?

The western states are relative newcomers to the wine industry, but they dug right in with vitis vinifera, experimenting and cloning, and figuring out how to overcome their regional peculiarities. By contrast, New York's wine staple always had been Vitis labrusca, which is great for jams and jellies and unfermented beverages, but not so great for fine wines.

It wasn't until the 1950s that the first vinifera grapes were cultivated in New York, in the Finger Lakes region, by a Ukrainian immigrant, Dr. Konstantin Frank, who put New York on the map for its ability to grow fine Riesling, as well as other northern-thriving European grape varietals. In 1961, the first of these wines emerged from his winery, called (guess what?) Dr. Frank's Vinifera Wine Cellars. So in 1961, New York already was ahead of California, but it couldn't have held that lead.

The reason? Climate. Harsher growing conditions mean more labor, and more labor means higher costs. There are no warm Pacific zephyrs blowing across New York! So except for some low-priced sparkling wines, Empire State wines cannot compete successfully with those from the Golden State.

Heard it Through the Grapevine

America's oldest winery, the Brotherhood Winery in New York's Hudson Valley, was founded in 1839. And the second-oldest? That would be the Canandaigua Wine Company in the Finger Lakes region of New York, which also is the country's second largest.

Linger at the Finger Lakes

The cold climate of the Finger Lakes district in western New York is tempered somewhat by these four large bodies of water. About 85 percent of the state's wines come from this district, and more and more are planting vitis vinifera. Riesling and Chardonnay are the two most successful varietals. During the 1980s, wineries like Glenora and Hermann J. Weimer began paving the way toward high-quality vinifera wines. Today, newcomers like Thirsty Owl, Ravines, Heron Hill, and Red Newt Cellars have all raised the bar, and some eyebrows, for the Finger Lakes ability to grow and craft outstanding noble wines.

Not Just The Hamptons!

Wow, has Long Island grown since Louisa and Alex Hargrave, who planted the first commercial vineyard on a wing and prayer in 1973 on an potato farm. Since then, more than 40 vineyards have popped up, mostly cropped onto the North Fork AVA at the end of Long Island, as well as a few on the South Fork, and they continue to show great promise with several vinifera grapes, notably Merlot, Chardonnay, Sauvignon Blanc, Cabernet Franc, and recently white varietals like Friulano and Muscat. Notable producers include Paumonok, Lenz, Channing Daughters, Wolffer, Bedell, and McCall, who has had surprising success with Pinot Noir, a grape that has historically not done as well here.

Rip Van Winkle Did Sleep Here

The Hudson River Valley, a mere 40 miles north of Manhattan, is home to Benmarl, Clinton, and several other wineries, including the historic Brotherhood, which caters to the regions many tourists. They have shown good progress with the better French hybrids, like the red Baco Noir and whites like Seyval Blanc and Vidal, and they succeed occasionally with these vinifera grapes. This region also grows labrusca varieties, which may be sold to wineries in the Finger Lakes district.

CHAPTER 19

Wines of Canada

In This Chapter

- The rebirth of Canada's wine industry
- The Vintners Quality Alliance
- Wines of Ontario
- Wines of British Columbia

Canadian wine? Absolutely. North of the U.S. border, summer days are longer (though at the expense of longer winter nights). And in a few special regions, soil and climate conspire to produce wines of the highest quality, some unique in the world.

Canada has had commercial vineyards for more than a hundred years, but the Canadian wine industry we're going to explore has existed little more than 20 years. The 1980s were a big decade for Canadians. In 1982, there was the Canada Act (1982), under which Canada obtained complete national sovereignty. And in 1988, there was the U.S.-Canada Free Trade Act, which stimulated the rebirth of Canadian wine. In this chapter, we'll look at that remarkable renaissance, and we'll visit Canada's wine regions, both east and west. At that time, there were a handful of wineries that today has grown to over 700.

Canadian Wine? Yes!

Historically, Canadian wineries used native American grapes, Vitis labrusca, rather than the European Vitis vinifera. The labrusca sort make wonderful jams and jellies. And grape juices, too. But fine wine grapes, these are not!

Heard it Through the Grapevine

In 1853, horticulturist Ephraim Bull exhibited a new variety of the native American grape species, Vitis labrusca at the Massachusetts Horticulture Society. This was the first Concord grape. Within 10 years, this grape was planted throughout eastern North America.

In 1869, a dentist in Vineland, N.J., Thomas Welch, began manufacture of a pasteurized grape juice from the Concord grape he grew in his back yard, as a substitute for the alcoholic wines used in his church's communion service.

(Canada is recovering only now from the success of the commercial Concord and other labrusca varieties.)

Yes, the 1980s were a time of change. The world became more aware of fine wines, but these did not include wines from Canada. The Canadian wine industry was quite aware of this situation. And these growers, vintners, and shippers decided to do something about it.

VQA You Can Trust

Canada's biggest handicap to entry into the market for fine wines was that they had cultivated the wrong grape species, Vitis labrusca, instead of the traditional European Vitis vinifera. But would they be willing to uproot (in some cases) a hundred years' worth of growing tradition and start over? Yes. But with a little help from Ottawa.

In 1988, Canada signed a Free Trade Agreement with the U.S. That meant no more price protection for wines from the inferior labrusca grape. Now they would have to face competition from wines of higher quality, fairly priced.

The Canadian government began a five-year program to subsidize those labrusca growers who decided to plant something else. In Ontario, this meant other grapes, the noble vinifera. In British Columbia, it meant, mostly, replacing labrusca with other crops. However, in that province about a third of the original vineyard acreage was kept in grapes, but switched to the better European varietals.

New grapes meant new winemaking technologies—and heavy capital investment. Canadian vintners proved their dedication to the new opportunities the new grapes provided. These savvy business folk had planned their rebirth very carefully. In 1989, the Ontario growers organized the Vintners Quality Alliance (VQA), under which they would show the world they could make fine wines.

The VQA provided regulations to cover everything from the grape to the glass. They regulations went into effect nationwide in 1990. And in 1998, the VQA introduced a new labeling system, one that the world has come to respect.

The VQA name and symbol on a Canadian wine label is your assurance that:

- The wine is made from 100-percent Canadian-grown grapes.
- The wine has been made to VQA standards set by the provinces of Ontario or British Columbia.
- The wine has been sampled by a provincial panel of tasters.

This change in Canadian wine labels made them much easier to read. As Joe Friday, the police detective in the 1950s TV show *Dragnet* said, "Just the facts, ma'am."

In addition to bottle-size, alcohol content, and vintage (where applicable), Canadian labels show:

- The producer's name (though sometimes in code)
- The producing region
- Where the wine was bottled
- Quality level

I'll discuss that last, quality level, as we look at Canada's two main wine-producing provinces.

Vino Vocab

When you see the words Vintners Quality Alliance (or the letters VQA), think of the French AOC or the German QmP. This is Canada's strict code for wine production and a reliable mark of quality.

Big Province; Big Wine!

Ontario is a very large province, of about 400,000 square miles. However, its three Designated Viticultural Areas (DVAs)are found on that tiny bit of the south that nestles along Lakes Erie And Ontario. These lie at the same latitude as the southern wine districts of France, the northern winegrowing regions of Italy and Spain, and the West Coast region of the U.S. between the Mendocino Valley of California and the winegrowing regions of Washington State.

Compared with France's wine regions, Ontario wine country experiences hotter summers, but colder winters. This allows Ontario (and also British Columbia!) to produce icewines (see Chapter 17, German Wine Laws) on a consistent basis. Soils in this glacier-scraped region range from sandy loams to gravel, sand, and clay.

Ontario accounts for the largest percentage of Canada's wine production, with more than 125 wineries producing to VQA standards. Many vintners of this cosmopolitan province were trained in France, Italy, Germany, Austria, and the United States. Growers plant most of the leading European varietals, including Chardonnay, Sauvignon Blanc, Pinot Gris, Riesling, Gewürztraminer, Cabernet Franc, Pinot Noir, Gamay, Cabernet Sauvignon, and Merlot.

Heard it Through the Grapevine

More than 200 years ago, in the German duchy of Franconia, Icewine (Eiswein) was discovered quite by accident, when winemakers tried to rescue their crop by pressing grapes that had frozen on the vine. Germany has produced it ever since, but only in small batches, because conditions that allow it are rare.

Not so in Canada's winegrowing provinces! Long days of hot summer sunshine allow grapes to develop high sugar and complexity. But the days shorten drastically in the fall, and temperatures fall readily into the freezing range, with a maximum of 17.6 degrees F required by law for an icewine harvest . Ontario and British Columbia now lead the world in production of this rare and wonderful dessert wine.

In Ontario, the VQA recognizes two levels of quality. (Both are superior.) The first is the Provincial Designation. To use the term Ontario on the label, the wines must meet four requirements:

- Wines must be made from approved grapes—classic European varietals and hybrids.
- If labeled as a varietal, the wine must be made from no less than 85 percent of that grape.
- Whether varietal or blend, all grapes must have been grown in Ontario.
- All varieties must meet stipulated minimum sugar levels.

The higher VQA level is Geographic Designation. Ontario has three Designated Viticultural Areas (DVAs), which we will discuss later in some detail.

In addition to those for the Provincial Designation, these wines meet certain additional requirements:

- Only classic European varieties are allowed.
- If the vintner wishes to designate a vineyard, it must be in a DVA, and all the grapes must come from that vineyard.
- Wines labeled "estate bottled" must be made entirely from grapes from one DVA that are owned or controlled by the winery.
- Minimum sugar levels are set for vineyard-designated, estate-bottled, dessert wines and icewines.

All VQA wines are evaluated and sampled by a panel of wine experts before they may display the VQA symbol.

Now let's take a look at Ontario's four DVAs.

Tasting Tip

The Ontario Vintners Quality Alliance, VQA, sets standards and checks all VQA candidates for compliance with these standards for production and labeling.

Additionally, the VQA issues vintage reports for each Designated Viticultural Area (DVA). Wine consumers benefit greatly from this information.

The Niagara Peninsula

This Designated Viticultural Area lies between the southwestern shore of Lake Ontario and the Niagara Escarpment. This latter is the amazing geological feature responsible for Niagara Falls. It's a wall of granite, 100 to 150 feet high, that runs west-to-east between Lake Erie and Lake Ontario.

The most interesting aspect of the Niagara Peninsula is the microclimate interplay between the Lake Ontario and the Escarpment. In the fall, the lake still holds summer heat. Warm air rises from the lake and moves inland, but when it hits the Escarpment, it falls and returns to the lake for further warming. This unique circulation allows an extended season for the development of sugars in these grapes.

Here, you will find around 80 wineries (way more than half of Niagara's total!) spread across nearly 14,000 acres under vines that bust with Riesling, Chardonnay, Merlot, Cabernet Franc, and Cabernet Sauvignon. Here, you'll find 12 sub-appellations, which include:

- Beamsville Bench
- Short Hills Bench
- Creek Shores
- St. David's Bench
- Four Mile Creek
- Twenty Mile Bench
- Lincoln Lakeshore
- Vinemount Ridge
- Niagara Lakeshore
- Niagara Escarpment
- Niagara River
- Niagara-on-the-Lake

Heard it Through the Grapevine

When the Ice Age glacier receded, it left behind minerals and trace elements from many rocky strata, which have become part of the soil. These contribute to the development of complexity in the flavors of the area's wines.

Lake Erie North Shore

This area lies along Lake Erie's northwestern shore. The vineyard slope cultivation enjoys a southern exposure and the moderating effect of the lake on temperatures. Lake Erie is the shallowest of the Great Lakes; so its surface temperature tends to be the warmest. Here, there are around a dozen wineries producing Riesling, Cabernet Franc, and Merlot.

Pelee Island

Pelee Island, situated in Lake Erie about 15 miles south of the mainland, is Canada's southernmost point—and its smallest viticultural area. Because of both latitude and the warming effect of the lake, this DVA enjoys a growing season 30 days longer than on the mainland.

The soil here is similar to that of the mainland, glacial deposits of sand, loam, and clay over limestone bedrock. There is only one winery on the island, and while it is Burgundy's main grapes of Chardonnay and Pinot Noir that thrive, there have also been some promising experiments with varietals like Tempranillo, too.

Prince Edward County

Designated as a VQA region in 2007, Prince Edward County is the latest addition on Ontario's wine-producing map. The low-yielding vines that struggle in the solid limestone bedrock and stony soils here make for some lovely, concentrated Cabernet Franc and Pinot Noir, as well as some intense Chardonnay. About 20 wineries are spread across lake-rimming DVA with over 500 miles of shoreline.

Tasting Tip

Ontario's Lake Erie North Shore climate is very similar to that of France's Bordeaux region. So it's not surprising that some of Ontario's finest wines come from this DVA.

America's Other West Coast

The mountainous far-west province of British Columbia (B.C.) has its own Vintners Quality Alliance (VQA). This was established through a law of 1990. Under this law, the British Columbia Wine Institute establishes regulatory controls for growing, production and naming. Some highlights:

- The designation "Product of British Columbia" means all the grapes were grown in that province.
- Wines bearing a viticultural name contain a minimum of 85 percent grapes grown in that area.
- Wines designating a grape variety must be made at least 85 percent from the juice of that grape.
- A vintage date on the label guarantees no less than 85 percent of the wine came from that harvest.
- Wines labeled "estate bottled" must be produced entirely from grapes grown in a vineyard owned by the winery, with all steps—from crushing to bottling—done at that winery.

Heard it Through the Grapevine

Pelee Island is the site of Canada's first commercial winery, the Vin Villa, which opened in 1866.

Of course, through most its history, this winery had used the native labrusca grapes. But in 1980, all of Pelee Island was replanted in the European vinifera.

There are over 175 VQA wineries in B.C. The very first vineyards were planted in the 1860s at a mission located in the Okanagan Valley. The first commercial winery dates from 1932, in the same locale—and you might say that growth has gained quite a bit of momentum: 20 years ago, there were 1,000 acres under vine. Today, it's nearly 10,000 and growing.

The Sommelier Says

Many thought the Free Trade Act of 1988 would put an end to British Columbia's wine industry. In that year, acreage in wine-grape production crashed—from 2,500 to only 800.

Now, with vineyard renewal in vinifera and superior quality control through the VQA, B.C. has increased its wine cultivation to where it's planting more acres than ever before.

Most of B.C.'s wine industry lies in lowland areas guarded by coastal mountains to the west and the Rockies to the east. This makes for summers that are surprisingly sunny, hot and dry. Such conditions allow good development of sugar and flavors.

The leading varieties cultivated by B.C.'s best wineries are Chardonnay, Pinot Blanc, Pinot Noir, Merlot, Riesling, and Gewürztraminer.

British Columbia has five Designated Viticultural Areas: Okanagan Valley, Similkameen Valley, Fraser Valley, Vancouver Island, and Gulf Islands.

Heard it Through the Grapevine

Colona Wines has operated in British Columbia continuously since 1932, western Canada's oldest commercial winery. It is situated in the northern part of the Okanagan Valley, near the town of Kelowna.

Okanagan Can!

The Okanagan Valley is B.C.'s oldest wine-producing region. This area features more than 70 wineries that produce from premium grape varieties, and provide about 95 percent of British Columbia's total vinous output.

The south end of the valley has an annual rainfall of less than six inches, making it the only part of Canada classified as desert. Growers must use some irrigation as they plant this part of the valley in classic red viniferas.

The northern end of this long north-south valley offers a cooler and wetter climate. This favors the French and German white varietals that are planted here among the area's five sub-regions, Kelowna, Naramata, Okanagan Falls, Golden Mile, and Black Sage/Osoyoos.

Assimilating Similkameen

Through the mountains, just west of the southern part of the Okanagan Valley, lies the high-desert cattle range that's the Simulkameen Valley winegrowing area. The small plots are planted along the banks of the Similkameen River, with some irrigation.

Here the summer days are long, and the rainfall sparse. The microclimate of the area and its soils, mostly gravel and clay, provide superb conditions to grow both red and white grapes, Merlot, Pinot Noir, Chardonnay, and Vidal, among the area's 13 wineries.

Fraser's Praises

In the southwestern corner of British Columbia, a short drive up the Fraser River from Vancouver, you will find about 10 small vineyards that enjoy a climate somewhat different from that of the interior.

Here along the coast hot, dry summers are followed by warm, rainy winters. Growers here need to irrigate their plots of award-winning Chardonnay, Pinot Blanc, Riesling, and other white varietals.

Vancouver Island

Lying just off the southwestern coast of B.C., Vancouver Island is the province's newest winegrowing region. Most of these few acres of grapes are located near the town of Duncan.

Here you will find Pinot Gris, Pinot Noir, Muscat, and Müller-Thurgau. Look for some of their late-harvest Botrytis-infected bottlings. Its 25 wineries and 200 acres under vine account for a slender 3-plus percent of B.C.'s total wine production.

Gulf Islands

Settled by European gold miners in the mid-nineteenth century, the Gulf Islands sit just southwest of the Strait of Georgia on Vancouver Island's eastern coast, nestled between the Campbell River to the north and Victoria to the south. Just shy of making 2 percent of British Columbia's wine production, this tiny region has right wineries, which often supplement their smallish supplies with grapes from the Okanagan Valley.

Awards? Yes!

It's reasonable to say the Canadian wine industry began only in 1989 (Ontario) and 1990 (British Columbia), as wines from these provinces came under the VQA insignia of quality.

Canadian vintners have entered their wines in international competition—in Europe, Asia, and the Americas. And in less than a decade, they have scored hundreds of medals, including many golds. Canadian wines occupy a secure position among the greatest wines from France, Italy, Germany, and the U.S. And in what was one of the most exciting nods of the twenty-first century for Canadian wine, the esteemed producer Jackson Triggs was the very first North American producer to win the Rosemount Estate Trophy at the International Wine & Spirits Awards in London for their outstanding Syrah. Not bad for the kids from Canada!

Let's Visit Canadian Wineries

Though its wine industry is fairly new, Canada's appeal to tourism is quite old, particularly in the country's two wine provinces, Ontario and British Columbia.

If you plan a trip to Niagara Falls or to Toronto, you're quite close to Ontario's viticultural areas. All you need to do is get a list of VQA wineries. Then call a few up! Most will be delighted to meet you and let you sample their finest.

You can get a list of Ontario VQA wineries from:

Wine Council of Ontario
4890 Victoria Avenue North
P.O. Box 4000

Vineland Station, Ontario
Canada L0R 2E0
www.winecouncilofontario.ca

The winegrowing regions of British Columbia are well worth a visit (and there's lots of info on Wine Country Ontario's website, www.winecountryontario.ca), even without the wine. They offer some of North America's most spectacular and memorable scenery.

But do visit the wineries!

Most of them do offer tours. And if you are driving up the Okanagan Valley, be sure you visit the Wine Museum at Kelowna.

You can get a list of B.C.'s VQA wineries from:

British Columbia Wine Institute
1726 Dolphin Road
Suite 107 Kelowna, B.C.
Canada V1Y 9R9
www.winebc.org

CHAPTER 20

From the Lands Down Under

In This Chapter

- The Wines of Australia
- The Wines of New Zealand
- The Wines of South Africa

G'day! Yes, I know, mate. The term "Down Under" refers to Australia and New Zealand. But I'd like to extend it (just here) to include another English-speaking wine-producer from beneath the Southern Cross, South Africa. Y'got a problem with that, mate?

Australian wines are far from Outback plonk—they are positively refined! Once a bit on the rough-and-tumble side, today's Australian sippers are respectable, good-quality whites and reds with grace and style that will do well on any table.

Australian wines often offer good value, as does its southeastern Kiwi neighbor, New Zealand, which has created its own exciting antipodean wine industry, well in tune with current export markets.

Then there's South Africa. With its revolutionary change in government in 1993, lifting the long-standing international boycott on its goods, this African nation has become a significant player in the export market. And believe me, they have some wines worth exporting!

Wine from the Outback

Since the mid-80s, Australia has been on a hungry (well, maybe thirsty is more apt) track to a veritable wine renaissance, more than doubling its exports, and the quality of them. You might find it surprising now with such great Aussie option on shelves from coast to coast here, but not too long ago all we could find from Kangaroo Country were cheap, fortified wines. Today, we see a brand new Australian wine industry, one that's earned itself an honorable standing in the world wine market.

Tasting Tip

Those raunchy reds and hot-tasting whites that made up Australia's first varietal efforts now are tamed, tuned, and styled into wines of refinement, balance, and charm.

This turn-around is not unlike California's. In California, we used to have screwcapped jug wines. In Australia, it was "bag-in-box" which, along with the screwcap, is actually another concept that's coming back around these days, too! It's also something the Aussies and their Kiwi neighbors are very passionate about: embracing of technology with an eye on the future.

There's one difference between Australia and California: California is Zinfandel's first home. Australia has no wine it can call exclusively its own, although it's found a way to put its own mark on a varietal or two that have become the mark of Aussie pride.

Vinifera vines first made their appearance in Australia in the late 18th and early 19th centuries from Europe by way of the Cape of Good Hope. Fortified wines were a common thing in warm climates, especially in the days when spoilage was a serious problem. So it's not surprising that rich, sweet wines dominated Australian production. (Even today, Australia makes some of the best Sherry outside of Spain.)

Those Aussie Blends

The predominant grape used in Australia's better wines is Syrah, known there as Shiraz. Shiraz is the name you'll see on the label, which, in New World, California-style, bears the grape varietal name. The named grape must make up at least 85 percent of the bottle's contents.

Australian vintners commonly blend two vinifera and use both varietal names. The dominant grape comes first. Examples: Shiraz/Cabernet Sauvignon or Cabernet Sauvignon/ Shiraz. You may find these blends a bit unusual. Most winemakers follow the classic French prototypes, such as, Cabernet Sauvignon with Merlot and Cabernet Blanc or Semillon with

Sauvignon Blanc. But with no special tradition, Australia has created two original styles of wine: Shiraz with Cabernet Sauvignon and Semillon with Chardonnay.

Other important Australian varietals are Chardonnay, both oaked and stainless-steel styles, and Semillon—or a combination of the two. Some of the Semillons are also aged in oak, similar to Chardonnay, with tastes of vanilla and oak with complexity. Others are unoaked, which produces simple, crisp white wines when young. These same wines become complex and honeyed with bottle age.

Tasting Tip

The ever-popular Shirazes are made in several styles, from very light, quaffable, simple-premium wines to serious, complex wines that require bottle-aging. They deserve your attention.

Heard it Through the Grapevine

Sprawling Australia is a long way from historic France in style no less than geography. The majority of Australian wines carry the appellation "South Eastern Australia." This means the grapes could have been grown in any one of the three states in this immense territory. You will find others that reveal wines from several appellations, with the percentage of each frequently listed. If you're looking for distinctive, stylistic, regional nuances, you must look for wines from a single, more narrow appellation.

For all their idiosyncrasies, Australian wine labels are very informative and easy to read. Most blended wines list their grape varieties on the label, and the percentages of each grape usually are included. There is one catch, though: There's no restriction on where the grapes used in blended wines are grown, so there are many trans-regional blends.

Southern Hemisphere Napa-Sonoma

Australia's main viticultural regions are geographically and climatically similar to California's Napa and Sonoma Valleys: dry, not too humid, and ranging in temperature from moderate to fairly warm in some parts.

The most important wine-producing state is South Australia, which accounts for approximately 40 percent of Australia's wine. It has two distinctly different faces. The

Riverlands region in the Lower Murray Zone, which produces the inexpensive jug-style wine that is the staple of the bag-in-box industry. Closer to the state capital, Adelaide, are the vineyard regions, which are gaining renown for their fine wines. These include the following:

- Barossa Valley lies north of Adelaide and was one of the first regions to be associated with fine wines. It is a place to find Shiraz, Grenache, and Cabernet Sauvignon that are solid, consistent, and continually improving.
- Eden Valley lies just due south of the Barossa Valley. This is one of the coolest vineyard regions, highly influenced by the German settlers who first came here in the mid-nineteenth century. Here, you will find high-acid, dry and off-dry Rieslings of excellent quality.
- In Coonawarra along the Limestone Coast, the climate is cool, and the region is esteemed for its classic reds, Cabernet Sauvignon and Shiraz. There can be wide vintage variations, but in fine years, the Cabernets have been standouts!
- Clare Valley – The cool climate here yields crisp Rieslings and graceful Chardonnays.
- McLaren Vale – Located south of Adelaide and cooled by the ocean, this is red wine territory, known primarily for its Shiraz, which accounts for 50 percent of the area's production, along with Cabernet Sauvignon, Merlot, and more recently Tempranillo.
- In Padthaway, which has the same distinctive red terra rossa soil that Coonawarra does, Cabernet Sauvignon takes up about half the planting and production here. The rest? Shiraz and Chard!

New South Wales was Australia's first viticultural state. Today, it accounts for approximately 20 percent of the country's wine. Its main wine region is the Hunter Valley. During the 1980s, Hunter Valley attracted wealthy investors and lifestyle-seekers, making it sort of a Napa-Down-Under. The Hunter Valley consists of two distinct districts:

- Lower Hunter Valley, close to Sydney, is warm and humid, with heavy, rich soils, where Semillon and Shiraz thrive.
- The Upper Hunter Valley is drier and further inland, and here the classic varietal Chardonnay is queen of all the land. Riesling and Pinot Noir have also yielded some impressive efforts.

The other winemaking state in New South Wales is the Central Ranges. Here, the Mudgee, Orange, and Cowra regions, situated inland near the mountains due west of Hunter Valley, offer intense Chardonnays, Merlot, and Cabernet Sauvignon.

Victoria, in eastern Australia, is the site of many small wineries that account for about a quarter of Australia's total wine production. It offers quantities of everyday white, red, and sparkling wines and remains a center for fortified wines. The wines produced here range from stylish Pinot Noirs to rich, fortified dessert wines. Among the key winegrowing regions in the state of Victoria are:

- Rutherglen, Glenrowan, and Milawa – Situated in the northeast, the warm climate lends itself to the making of fortified wines including fortified Muscats and Tokays.
- Goulburn Valley – This central area is known for its Shiraz and Marsanne.
- Great Western – This is the mainstay of Australia's sparkling wine industry.
- Yarra Valley – This cool region located close to Melbourne yields some fine Pinot Noir, Cabernet Sauvignon, and Chardonnay.
- The Pyrenees and Grampians regions in Western Victoria are home to high-acid, tannic, muscled Shiraz, as well as sparkling wines.

What Are Australia's Best Values?

Australian bag-in-box wines are Australia's best values; inexpensive, and they provide good value. You can find them in some stores, and with the outpour in popularity of eco-conscious sipping, they're starting to gain popularity in the U.S.

Australian Chardonnay, Shiraz, and Cabernet Sauvignon, priced around $9 to $11 (U.S.), provide good value in well-made wines. The more expensive Australian wines, $20 or more, compare with their counterparts from other parts of the world. However, these are not the bargains their lower-priced mates are.

Wine Under the Ocean Spray

Think of Australia, and the next country that comes to mind usually is New Zealand. Somewhat behind its larger neighbor, New Zealand has emerged and stuck a small but mighty flag in the ground of the world wine market.

New Zealand lies a little farther south than Australia, where it's cooler. Actually, New Zealand is two large islands, both of which are subject to the effects of the ocean spray.

The warmer North Island is known for its red wines, particularly Cabernet Sauvignon, which come from the area around Auckland and Hawkes Bay. These are produced along with Chardonnay in Gisborne and Pinot Noir in Martinborough. The South Island contains Marlborough, New Zealand's largest wine region, which is had gained acclaim for its white wines, notably Sauvignon Blanc and Chardonnay.

New Zealand's whites generally are unoaked, with rich flavors and sharp acidity. Its reds are similar to those of Australia. The wines of New Zealand tend to be priced higher than comparable wines from Australia and elsewhere, but they do provide an interesting wine experience.

New Beginnings in South Africa

Tasting Tip

South Africa's rich, dessert-style Muscat wine, Constantia, became legendary during the early history of South Africa. It was considered a delicacy in the royal courts of Europe.

Since Dutch settlers introduced the first European vines more than three hundred years ago, South Africa has produced a good variety of wines. Later, the Dutch were joined by French Huguenots, who contributed their Gaelic winemaking knowledge and techniques.

Aside from a continental regard for South Africa's Constantia dessert wine, few countries other than Great Britain displayed any interest in this country's wines. Up until 1918, quality regulation was poor to nonexistent, and overproduction resulted in inferior wines. To combat this effect, the government adopted a regulating body, the KWV (a cartel-like winegrowers' association), to control an anarchic industry.

The strict quota system of the KWV has come under a lot of criticism, especially in recent years. In 1992, the KWV finally loosened controls, permitting independent wineries greater production. In 1973, the government implemented a type of appellation system, granting an official "Wine of Origin" seal to certain wines and certain estates to ensure accuracy of label information.

With the death of Apartheid, the writing of a new constitution, and the election of Nelson Mandela, South Africa gained new esteem in the world. More important, it was able to reenter markets that had been close ernational boycott.

Heard it Through the Grapevine

Despite changes, both in winemaking and in government policy, the giant KWV cartel still runs the show. The growing table-wine industry is dominated by the Stellenbosch Farmers' Winery Group (SFW). The Nederburg Estate, regarded as one of South Africa's most esteemed properties, is part of SFW. Another important table wine producer is the Bergkelder Group. Eighteen wine estates, including some of South Africa's best, are affiliated with this firm.

Although it used to be that few of the country's 5,000 grape growers were wine producers. They deliver their grapes to one of the 70 cooperatives run by the KWV, the country's largest winery. Approximately half the crop is turned into distilled alcohol or grape concentrate. Most of the remaining grapes are used for Sherry or Port. However, more and more of this production is being used to make dry, unfortified wines. New independent wineries are cropping up, and South Africa is gaining a reputation for higher-quality, estate-grown wines.

Although South Africa ranks eighth in worldwide wine production, around 20 percent is exported. The U.K. remains its biggest customer.

Wine of Origin

The implementation of the Wine of Origin (WO) appellation system resulted in the creation of 10 wine districts (and their subdistricts). Most of South Africa's viticultural land is located in Cape Province near the southeastern coast (in the vicinity of Cape Town). The vineyards are known collectively as the Coastal District vineyards. The two most prominent districts are Paarl and Stellenbosch, but several others are emerging (including one subdistrict). Currently the five key wine districts are:

- Stellenbosch – This region is the largest in area and production, and is renowned for its high-quality wines, particularly reds. It's situated east of Cape Town.
- Paarl – Located north of Stellenbosch. It's the site of the KWV and the impressive Nederburg Estate. Paarl is recognized for its high-quality white wines.
- Franschloek Valley – This subdistrict of Paarl is a center for experimentation and innovation in winemaking.
- Constantia – Located south of Cape Town, this historic region created the luscious dessert wine that wowed the nobility of Europe.
- Durbanville – Located north of Cape Town, this region is noted for its rolling hills with well-drained soil.

South Africa's WO legislation is modeled after the French Appellation Contrôlée system. That is, it includes strict regulation of vineyard sites, grape varieties, vintage-dating, and so on. Under South African law, varietal wines must contain at least 75 percent of the designated grape. (Those produced for export to the European Union, however, must have at least 85 percent of the named grape.) Roughly 10 percent of South Africa's wines now earn the WO seal.

Steen Rules

Chenin Blanc, called Steen in South Africa, is the reigning grape variety. And no wonder: It's one versatile vinifera! Though used mainly to make medium-dry to semi-sweet wines, it also makes dry wines, late-harvest Botrytis wines, rosés, and sparkling wines. Sauvignon Blanc and Chardonnay also are gaining in popularity.

The predominant red grape traditionally has been Cinsault—or, Cinsaut, as they spell it in South Africa—the same as the Rhône variety (formerly called the Hermitage in South Africa). The Cinsault grape produces an ever-popular wine by the same name. It's been getting a few rivals lately, notably Cabernet and Merlot, and to a lesser degree Pinot Noir and Shiraz.

The table wines of South Africa always have included a few crossbreeds. The best known is the distinctive Pinotage, a hybrid of Cinsault and Pinot Noir. Pinotage combines the berry fruitiness of Pinot Noir with the earthy qualities of a Rhône wine, producing an easy-to-drink, light- to medium-bodied, simple-premium wine, and many are worth seeking out.

CHAPTER 21
A Bit of Bubbly

In This Chapter

- Styles of sparkling wine
- How sparkling wine is made
- True Champagne
- Sparkling wines of the world

His first name wasn't really 'Dom.' That's a title attached to the names of Benedictine monks. His name was Pierre, Pierre Pèrignon. He was blind.

In 1688, Dom Pèrignon, was put in charge of the wine cellars at the Abby of Hautvillers, near Reims in France's Champagne province. It was he who first decided to quit worrying about those annoying bubbles that developed in the bottles of the abby's wines and to start perfecting this strange, 'mad' wine. The world of celebration and mirth hasn't been the same since!

From those old Fred Astaire and Ginger Rogers movies to the latest James Bond, we know what sophisticates do, don't we? They sip Champagne! And so does everyone else, it seems—at weddings, birthday celebrations, and of course, New Year's Eve bashes.

Most of us have experienced Champagne (or imagine we have). But no one has described this lively beverage better than the blind monk, himself. They say he held his glass and exclaimed, 'I am drinking stars!'

In this chapter, we'll explore the science and the art that allow vintners to create those stars.

Champagne Is a Province

If bubbles, alone, were the key to Champagne's opulent image, we could celebrate our triumphs and delights with soft drinks. But Champagne is much, much more than bubbles.

In Champagne, the French province east of Paris, vintners apply the most exacting standards and costly procedures to create that sumptuous beverage we find just right for special occasions. With its precisely delimited growing region, authentic French Champagne is very limited in production, and even with the recent recession, ever-rising prices reinforce its image as a luxury wine that weathers even the toughest economic storms.

The Sommelier Says

When designer Yves Saint Laurent created a perfume he named "Champagne," the Interprofessionnel du Vin Champagne (the trade organization for Champagne wines) took him to court. And won.

The vintners of Champagne guard their distinguished name very carefully!

Yet, there are many other sparkling wines we may endow with at least some of Champagne's mystique and pleasant associations. Of course, we shouldn't call these "Champagnes." Countries like Chile, Australia, and Canada have signed agreements with the EU voluntarily limiting the use of the term "Champagne" on labels in their countries only if that wine was produced, in fact, in the Champagne region. In the U.S., mostly wines from the Champagne region bear "Champagne" on the label, however this is very recent. American wineries who had approval to use the word "champagne" prior to 2006 may still do so (unfortunately for disgruntled and sincere Champagne producers), but they may only do so with their geographical area of origin (e.g., "California Champagne"). Still, even those American producers who fit squarely into that loophole are increasingly eschewing the term "Champagne" out of respect and using sparkling wine or vin mousseux.

And as far as the term méthode champenoise goes, it was deemed forbidden on labels in the EU after a court deemed it so in 1994. After some tussle back and forth, the ruling was revised in 2005 to allow other sparkling wine producers to use the term méthode traditionnelle.

Heard it Through the Grapevine

Under French legislation, Champagne is a sparkling wine produced only within the defined geographic boundaries of that district and made under the strict regulations of the Appellation Côntrolée.

To make Champagne, only certain grape varieties may be used, and only one procedure—the Méthode Champenoise. Sparkling wines from elsewhere in France are called vin mousseux and, more commonly, crèmant, and never Champagne, even if the same grapes and same methods are used.

You can get sparkling wines of good quality at reasonable prices, comparable to those for good table wines. So it's easy to enjoy some effervescence before dinner. Or with dinner. Or to celebrate some special occasion (like finishing that report or giving the dog a bath).

It's no harder to select a sparkling wine than any other type of wine. A little knowledge, some label-reading, and maybe a few phone calls, and that's it! Remember, you're the one drinking the stuff, not some wine snob who wants to tell you what you ought to buy. If you enjoy it, it's the right selection.

Extra Dry; Slightly Sweet: Huh?

The hardest part of selecting a Champagne is figuring out the label. Why, you might ask, is Extra Dry sweeter than Brut (which means "crude" or "raw")? When we discuss still (not sparking) wines, drier means less sweet!

The word "brut" is not very precise. Brut can range from 0 to 2 percent residual sweetness. Then there's Demi-Sec (half-sweet), which suggests half as sweet. But in the case of Champagne, it means twice as sweet!

Confused yet? Well, before I confuse myself, let me lay them all out for you, from driest to sweetest:

- Extra Brut, Brut Nature, or Brut Sauvage: Bone dry
- Brut: Dry
- Extra Dry: Medium dry
- Sec: Slightly sweet
- Demi-Sec: Fairly sweet
- Doux: Very sweet

Tasting Tip

Sweetness in Champagnes can easily mask defects—either a weak cuvée (blend) or a winemaking flaw. The drier a Champagne is, the more perfectly it has to be rendered. Its flaws and weaknesses can't be concealed. The most delicate Champagnes, particularly those called Grand Marks or Tête de Cuvée by the producer to signify the best, must be flawless.

Whether your palette judges it dry or semi-sweet is a matter of personal judgment. And preference. But there are some things you can look for to assess the quality of a sparkling wine or Champagne:

- Look at the bubbles (known as the bead). They should be tiny, bursting somewhat above the surface of the wine. (Think of those cartoon depictions where the bubbles float skyward from the glass.) The bead should endure in your glass for ten minutes, at least.
- Check the mouthfeel. The finer the wine, the tinier the bubbles. These will be less aggressive on your palate.
- Assess the balance between sweetness and acidity. This marks the difference between a good-tasting sparkling wine and one that is unpleasant.
- Sparkling wine made by the Méthode Champenoise (I'll explain shortly) will have a slightly creamy mouthfeel, the result of their extended aging on the lees.
- Now the finish: It should be crisp, refreshing, and clean. Bitterness on the finish of a sparkling wine is a sign of poorly made wine.

The Night They Invented Champagne

What Dom Pérignon described as stars actually was no more than carbon dioxide retained in the bottle following a second fermentation of residual sugar gobbled up by live yeast that had remained from the original fermentation. In the case of that abby near Reims, it was unintended. Short growing seasons meant late harvests. Early cold weather stopped the fermentation before it was complete. This resumed in the warming spring, after winter bottling.

Heard it Through the Grapevine

How many bubbles are in that bottle of bubbly? Yes! This is a serious question! American scientist, Bill Lembeck, wanted to know. So he found out.

First, Lembeck established that the average gas pressure in a bottle of Champagne was about 5.5 atmospheres (typical inflation pressure for the tires of a large truck). Then he measured the sizes of bubbles in the glass using an optical comparator. (They run about a fiftieth of an inch.) Finally, subtracting the gas that lies above the liquid, he divided the remainder by the volume of these tiny bubbles. The answer? Forty-nine million bubbles!

Dom Pérignon didn't discover Champagne. He exploited its virtues and eliminated its imperfections. In doing so, he turned what had been considered a failure into his region's greatest success. Pérignon was a fastidious monk, who devoted years to experimentation with grape blends and to developing superior methods of clarifying his wines. Champagne, like the Germans' first Eiswein, is an example of defeat converted into triumph.

The fermentation gases added sparkle to wine, and high pressures. Many of Pérignon's bottles exploded. So the Dom substituted stronger glass bottles developed by the English. And he experimented with improvements on the wooden or oil-soaked hemp bottle stoppers in use at the time.

Tasting Tip

For U.S. wines, believe it or not, the term "sparkling wine" on the label is a better indicator of quality than the word "champagne."

Sparkling wine is a perfectly respectable wine term. Beware of cheap imitation champagnes from California and New York State that sell for less than $10 and have the nerve to describe their contents as "champagne."

About a hundred years later, in 1805, Barbe-Nicole Cliquot Ponsardin took over her husband's small winery after his death. Madame Cliquot was a remarkable woman, totally dedicated to perfecting what Dom Pérignon had begun. It was she who developed the mushroom-shaped champagne cork we know today. Madame Cliquot's winery still turns out excellent Champagnes, under the name "Veuve (widow) Cliquot."

France's Champagne province wasn't the only part of the winegrowing world that experienced incomplete fermentation in its wines. Many sparkling wines come from cool areas where vines are slow to ripen. A still wine from such a region might be excessively acidic, harsh, and thin—in a word, awful. But through the intricate processes of refermentation, this potential salad dressing becomes a winning touchdown.

In the U.S., sparkling wine and champagne (note the lowercase c) get their sparkle during a second fermentation in a sealed container. The choice of grape varieties is up to the producer, with no restrictions on growing conditions or bubble-producing technique. The only legal limitation is that these bubbles must be produced naturally and not added by artificial carbonation.

The terms "champagne" and "sparkling wine" are used interchangeably. I prefer to use the term "Champagne" the way Madame Cliquot and the Appellation Controlée intended it. So I will refer to all effervescent wines from outside the Champagne district as "sparkling wine."

French Champagne derives its quality from a series of time-proven, exacting methods. Permissible grape varieties are the noble Chardonnay, Pinot Noir, and Pinot Meunier. Even in Champagne's cool climate, these grapes develop character when picked at low sugar levels ranging between 15 and 19 degrees Brix. (The norm for table wine is 20 to 23 degrees.)

These grapes ferment conventionally into wine. Then the Champagne-maker assembles them into a base wine, or blend, known as the vin de cuvée. The blend may be entirely from one vintage, but usually it consists of wines from two or more years, acquired to suit different markets. For example, the blend may be drier for export to the U.K., or sweeter for U.S. tastes. Despite this variability, the vin de cuvée usually is made within an established house style.

The Méthode Champenoise is the original, and most involved, technique. Other, lesser methods are the transfer method and the bulk, or Charmat, process. So let's divide our hypothetical cuvée into three batches and begin with the Méthode Champenoise.

Méthode Champenoise: It's in the Bottle

The most important thing to remember about the Méthode Champenoise, or traditional method, as you might see it on a bottle produced outside of the Champagne region, is that the second fermentation of your wine took place in the actual bottle you got from your wine shop. The cuvée that was the basis for your Champagne was fermented and bottled. Then the vintner added a bit of sugar and yeast before the bottles were sealed, with either a temporary cork or metal crown cap. Then these bottles were placed on their sides for the second fermentation, of three or four months. That's just the beginning.

By law, the wine must remain in contact with the dead yeast cells at least one year. Some remain as many as five years. Time "on the yeast" adds flavor, texture, and complexity through a process of yeast autolysis (breakdown), which contributes richness and a desired yeasty character. Virtually all the top-line French Champagnes spend several years on the yeast.

The Sommelier Says

The labels of all U.S. sparkling wines must indicate how they were made. If by the French Champagne method, you will see "Méthode Champenoise," "Traditional Method," or "Fermented in this Bottle."

But be careful! Wines labeled "Fermented in the bottle" are from the cheaper transfer process. What a difference one word makes!

Once the bubbles are created and the flavors are developed, the vintner must remove the yeast sediment from each bottle. This technique is called dégorgement (disgorgement). This is what distinguishes the Méthode Champenoise from the less-costly transfer-process shortcut. Prior to dégorgement, the Champagne undergoes a laborious and time-consuming process called remuage, or riddling.

For remuage, the bottles are placed neck-down in special A-frame racks. Each day, cellar workers riddle (slightly shake and rotate) each bottle, causing the sediment to creep gradually from the side of the bottle to the neck area. After about six weeks, the sediment is lodged in the neck, up against the closure. At this stage, the bottles are carefully removed—neck down—and taken to the dégorgement room.

Heard it Through the Grapevine

Today, many Champagne and sparkling-wine houses using the traditional method have done away with the charming (and laborious!) tradition of having individual workers doing the riddling for remuage. Today, a large (and expensive!) machine called a Gyropalatte, holds hundreds of bottles into a cube-shaped container that rotates and gently shakes the bottles mechanically.

Tasting Tip

French Champagne is ready to drink at the time you buy it, no matter how long the vintner has seen fit to age it.

(A good thing, too! Who wants to wait to pop that cork?)

Dégorgement can be done either by hand or machine. The principle remains the same. The neck of the bottle is immersed in a below-freezing brine solution, which traps the sediment in a plug of ice. The bottle is opened, the plug expelled by the pressure, and voilà!—No more sediment!

Some liquid always is lost in the process, and it's replaced according to house style—either with Champagne or a solution of Cognac and a sugar syrup. This tiny squirt actually determines the sweetness of the finished Champagne. Known as the dosage, it usually contains some sugar.

Following dégorgement, a special multi-layered cork is inserted, the protective wire hood attached, and the Champagne set aside for further bottle-aging to allow dosage and wine to marry.

Transfer Method: Fake?

If you follow the steps of the Méthode Champenoise, it's not difficult to see why fine French Champagne is très cher (very expensive). A less costly method for making sparkling wine (note the distinction) is the transfer method, a time- and labor-saving shortcut to bottle-fermented wine. It differs from the Méthode Champenoise in two ways.

First, though the wine undergoes its second fermentation in a bottle, it's not the same bottle you'll find on the shelf. Second, there's no riddling or disgorging. Both steps are replaced by filtration.

During the transfer process, the wine is transferred into a large, pressurized tank via a special machine designed to prevent loss of pressure. Once in the tank, it's filtered to remove the yeast cells and all other sediment. Then it's bottled. The process ensures that the sparkling product is free from sediment, and it's far less costly than the Méthode Champenoise. The catch is that some of the character developed during fermentation may be filtered out along with the yeast.

Actually, the distinction can be quite subtle. If the cuvées are similar, the distinguishing factors are the length of time the wine spends on the yeast and the degree of filtration used. Both influence flavor. But unless you have comparable bottles in front of you, it can be difficult to distinguish between a fine sparkling wine made by the transfer method and one made by the Méthode Champenoise. (Even for a wine expert, regardless of what they may have you believe.)

The transfer method still can give us sparkling beverages with the sought-after tiny beads and persistent effervescence that are the hallmarks of a fine sparkling wine.

Charmat Process: Bubbles in Bulk

With our third batch of cuvée, we come to the Charmat, or bulk process (named for Eugene Charmat, the Frenchman who invented it). After its initial fermentation, the cuvée is poured directly into a closed tank, with an added solution of yeast and sugar. The size of the tank varies, but it's usually several thousand gallons (bigger than any bottle). The second fermentation takes three to four weeks, at which point the wine is filtered and bottled.

Heard it Through the Grapevine

What about those oversized Champagne bottles you might see at your local wine shop? You probably know that the two-bottle size is called a "magnum." But what about those bigger ones? Here's a list:

Name	Volume	Number of bottles
Jéroboam	3 liters	4
Rehoboam	4.5 liters	6
Methuselah	6 liters	8
Salmanazar	9 liters	12
Balthazar	12 liters	16
Nebuchadnezzar	15 liters	20

The bulk process makes sparkling wine, but it's unlikely Madame Cliquot would have approved. (Nor, perhaps, will you—unless, of course, you're using it to break on the hull of a ship, or dump over a sports colleague's head after a winning game—then you won't feel so bad about all those wasted bubbles!) Bulk-process sparkling wines generally form larger bubbles that dissipate quickly. They also lack the traditional yeasty character, because they spend little time, if any, in contact with the yeast.

Basically this merely is wine made bubbly—not always pleasantly so. Charmat lends itself to large volume and an efficient use of time, labor, and equipment. It's used to make inexpensive sparkling wine, often from neutral- or even poor-quality grapes.

Champagne—The True Champagne

Champagne's opulent aura may be a bit overdone, but just as in Hollywood, there is such a thing as star quality. And just as a great director brings out the best in a star, a great Champagne maker gets Academy Award nominations for all the grapes!

The Sommelier Says

Sparkling wines made elsewhere than Champagne use the same descriptors for sweetness.

Though these terms have legal definition in Champagne, they may be inconsistent in other places.

Champagne as a Fine Art

Making Champagne really is more of an art than a science. The wine artisan must create the cuvée carefully—by tasting and retasting potential components (which may be up to 200 different wines). Then there's monitoring the time on the yeast. Then riddling the bottles, with just the right touch. Finally there's disgorging the sediment. This is not mere manufacturing! It's medieval craftsmanship.

But the final product—with its small, delicate bead, persistent effervescence, subtle yeastiness, and intricate balance—justifies the extraordinary time and care demanded by the Méthode Champenoise.

Champagne is the northernmost wine growing region in France. Its cool climate makes grape-growing (especially red grapes) for table wines a real gamble. But it's ideal for achieving those sparkles. And its chalky limestone soil is perfect for the Pinot Noir that adds fullness and body to the cuvée.

Most of the major Champagne houses reside in two cities within the district. The first is historic Rheims, where Joan of Arc led the Dauphin Charles to be crowned King of France. The second is the smaller Epernay, located south of Rheims. Surrounding these historic towns are the vineyard sites where the three Champagne grape varieties—Pinot Noir, Chardonnay, and Pinot Meunier—are cultivated.

- The Montagne de Reims (south of Rheims) is where the best Pinot Noir grapes grow.
- The Côte des Blancs (south of Epernay) is where we find the best Chardonnay.
- The Vallée de la Marne (west of Epernay) favors the Pinot Meunier (a black grape). However, all three varieties are grown here.

French Champagne makers are perfectionists. (Under strict French law they have to be!) Both grape varieties and yields are closely regulated, with quality uppermost in mind. Pinot Noir contributes fullness, body, structure, and longevity. Chardonnay offers finesse, backbone, delicacy, freshness, and elegance. And Pinot Meunier provides floral scents and fruitiness. In the end, though, the proportions depend on the Champagne maker's style and vision.

Certain vineyards are esteemed for Pinot Noir, while others are cherished for Chardonnay. Except for the Blanc de Blancs, which are made entirely from white grapes (hence the name, which means literally "white from whites"), the usual ratio is two-thirds black grapes to one-third Chardonnay. Of the two black grapes, it's Pinot Noir that dominates; only a small amount of Pinot Meunier is used. There's also a Blanc de Noirs ("white from blacks"), made entirely from black grapes.

Heard it Through the Grapevine

The highest-quality product comes from free-run juice, the juice that runs off the grapes from their own weight before pressing. Pressing is an art in Champagne because it's essential to avoid tainting the juice of the dark-skinned grapes with anything more than the slightest hint of color or bitterness of flavor.

The Champagne district has about 350 crus (vineyards) that are graded for quality. The highest ranked vineyards are sought after by the prestigious houses especially for their top-of-the-line Grand Mark.

Non-Vintage Champagnes—House Style

Contrary to legend, most Champagne (85 percent of all produced) is non-vintage (NV). That is, you'll find no vintage year on the label. It's all in the blending. In addition to the myriad wines in the cuvée, NV Champagnes are allowed to contain wine from three or more harvests.

Non-vintage Champagnes are created according to the favored house style. One house may seek elegance and finesse, while another will strive for fruitiness, and a third might consider body and full flavor as paramount. Every Champagne house has its own style, and it's rarely tampered with. After all, Champagne drinkers don't differ from other consumers. Most remain loyal to their preferred style of Champagne.

As noted in our earlier discussion of the Méthode Champenoise, most Champagne producers age their product long beyond the one-year minimum. The usual time for NV Champagne is two-and-a-half to three years. This additional aging provides greater marrying time for the blend and enhances the wine's flavor and complexity as it absorbs the lees in the bottle.

Vintage Champagne—Crème de la Crème

It occurs only a few times each decade—a year when the weather in Champagne is so friendly that a good cuvée can be made exclusively from the vines of that year, without blending from reserve wines from previous harvests. When this happens, we have a vintage Champagne.

There are two categories of vintage Champagnes:

Regular vintage lies within the $50- to $100-a-bottle price range. The label will carry the name of the house, plus the vintage date.

Premium vintage (tête de cuvée or prestige cuvée). Some examples are Taittinger's Comtes de Champagne, Roederer's Cristal, Veuve Clicquot's La Grande Dame. These run from $100 to $300 per bottle (and beyond!).

No doubt you'd like me to give you some reasons for spending a substantial sum for a vintage year on the label. Okay. Here's why I feel vintage Champagne is unquestionably superior:

- The cuvée is made from the finest grapes from the finest vineyards (without exception for tête de cuvée).
- Vintage Champagne is made usually from the two noble varieties only, Pinot Noir and Chardonnay.
- Vintage Champagnes usually are aged two or more years longer than non-vintage Champagnes, giving them greater complexity and finesse.
- The grapes all come from a superior, if not superlative, vintage.

Vintage Champagne is richer in flavor than non-vintage Champagne. Also, it may also more full-bodied and more complex, with a longer finish. Whether a vintage Champagne is worth its extra cost is a question you have to decide for yourself after trying one.

Blanc de Noirs

This rare and exotic Champagne specimen (the name means "white from blacks") is made exclusively from black grapes—sometimes 100 percent Pinot Noir. It's at the upper end of the tête de cuvée price range. Bollinger's Blanc de Noirs Vielles Vignes (old vines) is the crème de la crème of these rare creations.

Blanc de Blancs

Blanc de Blancs literally translates as "white from whites." (If you're feeling artistic, think of it as white-on-white.)

The Sommelier Says

Don't pop that cork!

While it might be fun to launch that cork like a mortar shell, it's very wasteful of those expensive bubbles (not to mention dangerous and potentially damaging to everything from friends to light fixtures). There's a much better (and classier) way:

With a firm grip on the cork, turn the bottle, allowing the cork to emerge slowly. When it's nearly out, let the gas escape slowly. Then pour.

Blanc de blancs is made 100 percent from noble Chardonnay grapes. It can be either vintage or non-vintage, and it's usually priced a bit higher than other Champagnes in the same class. Blanc de blancs are lighter and more delicate than other Champagnes.

Rosé Champagne

Commonly (maybe too commonly) known as pink Champagne, rosé Champagnes actually are a cut above average. Unfortunately, being pink and sparkling makes people take them less seriously. They're usually made from Pinot Noir and Chardonnay only. Like blanc de blancs, they can be either vintage or non-vintage, and they cost a bit more than regular Champagnes in the same category.

The Premier Producers

As I explained earlier in this section, all of the best Champagne houses develop their own signature style. Here's my list of premier producers categorized according to style:

Light and elegant

- Billecart-Salmon
- Charles de Cazanove
- de Castellane
- Jacquesson
- Laurent-Perrier
- Perrier-Jouet
- Philipponnat
- Ruinart
- Taittinger

Medium-bodied

- Charles Heidsieck
- Deutz
- Hiedsieck Monopole
- Möet & Chandon
- Mumm
- Pol Roger
- Pommery

Full-bodied

- Bollinger
- Gosset
- Henriot
- Krug
- Louis Roederer
- Salon
- Veuve Clicquot

If you're in the market for tête de cuvée, here's a guide to some of the best, so you'll know you're getting superior quality for your investment:

- Billecart-Salmon: Blanc de Blancs (1986, 1985)
- Bollinger: Blancs de Noirs Vielles Vignes (1997, 1985)
- Cattier: Clos du Moulin (the only non-vintage on the list)
- Charbaut: Certificate Blanc de Blancs (1985)
- Charles de Cazanove: Stradivarius (1989)
- Charles Heidsieck: Blanc des Millenaires (1989, 1983)
- Gosset: Grand Millesime and Rosé (1985)
- Hiedsieck Monopole: Diamant Bleu and Rosé (1985, 1982)
- Jacquesson: Signature (1995, 1985)
- Laurent-Perrier: Grand Siecle (1988, 1985)
- Louis Roederer: Cristal (1988, 1986, 1985)
- Möet & Chandon: Dom Perignon (1988, 1985, 1982)
- Mumm: Rene Lalou (1985, 1982)
- Philipponnat: Clos de Goisses (1992, 1986, 1985, 1982)
- Pol Roger: cuvée Sir Winston Churchill (1986, 1985)
- Pommery: cuvée Louise Pommery (1988, 1987, 1985)
- Ruinart: Dom Ruinart Blanc de Blancs (1988, 1985)
- Salon: Le Mesnil (1983, 1982, 1979)
- Taittinger: Compte de Champagne (1988, 1985)
- Veuve Clicquot: La Grande Dame (1998, 1988, 1985, 1983)

Crèmant/Vin Mousseux—Not Quite Champagne

As I've mentioned, most sparkling wines made in France outside of the Champagne region are called crèmant or vin mousseux. The most popular of these wines come from the Loire Valley, with a few appearing from the Rhône, Alsace, Burgundy, and Midi regions.

The Loire sparklers can be quite good and relatively inexpensive. The difference is they are made from different grape varieties than Champagne, and spend less time on the yeast. Saumur is the Loire Valley's biggest appellation for crèmant, which may or may not be made by the Méthode Champenoise. A word of caution: It tends toward over-sweet, and quality varies.

Note that when made by the Méthode Champenoise, the wine may be labeled crémant. Grape varieties do not have to be the ones used for true Champagne (and those appropriate for the region—which, in the case of the Loire Valley, is Chenin Blanc, Chardonnay, and Cabernet Franc), and usually will be those typical of the region. Most sell in the $12 to $25 price range.

Good Taste Without the Designer Label

You've probably imbibed California sparkling wine, and chances are you've had some Italian sparkles from the famous Asti wine zone, or the incredibly popular Prosecco. Or maybe you've tried some of the Spanish sparkling wine that's also become increasingly popular in recent years. These may not be Champagne, but they're worthy beverages in their own right.

The Cavas of Spain

Spain's sparkler, cava, has made quite a pop in the sparkling wine market, and most of its bubbly is available for less than $15. The best of it comes from the Penedes region near Barcelona.

Tasting Tip

Cava made by the Méthode Champenoise can be well-balanced with a fine, steady bead. The distinction is in the grapes. Most Cavas use local Spanish varieties—namely, Macabeo, Xerel-lo, and Paralleda), although the finer cuvées contain Chardonnay. Cava production is dominated by two huge wineries, both of whose catchy commercials have made them well-known to U.S. consumers: Freixenet and Codorniu.

German Sekt

Theoretically, the cool German climate makes it the perfect place for sparkling wines. Unfortunately, this theory does not translate into practice. Germany produces some of the finest white wines of the entire wine world, but Sekt just isn't one of them.

Sekt is produced by the Charmat method, which can make it coarsely bubbly. The better brands can be fruity and fresh, but only a handful of brands make a decent Sekt. The best are made from Riesling grapes, which can provide an interesting taste experience. If you see a bottle with the words Deutscher Sekt, however, this guarantees that the grapes are German grown (regular Sekt need not be) and produced within the country. The best are made from Riesling.

Spumante from Italy

Italy is one of the leading volume producers of sparkling wines, formerly known as spumante (literally, sparkling).

Heard it Through the Grapevine

Before Dom Pérignon and Madame Cliquot tamed that bottle-fermented product that became Champagne, the French had some interesting names for it.

One was saute bouchon (cork-popper), because of the numbers of accidental openings (before the corks were tied in place). Another was vin diable (devil wine), after the tendency of numbers of bottles to explode in their cellars.

Unfortunately, the term spumante came to be associated with a fruity, oversweet beverage resembling a soft drink. So sparkling wines now bear the regional name without any mention of spumante. The Italians do prefer their sparkling wines sweet, so even those labeled Brut tend to be on the sweet side. But it's not impossible to find good Italian sparkling wines that are bone-dry.

The major production center is the Piedmont, which gives us Asti. This well-known Italian sparkler is made from the Muscat grape, which has a musklike or pinelike aroma that's attractive but not overpowering in a well-balanced wine. A good Asti is delicious and fruity, with flavors reminiscent of pine. Made by the Charmat method, Asti is non-vintage and is meant to be consumed when purchased.

Some very good-quality sparkling wine is produced by the Méthode Champenoise in the Oltrepo-Pavese and Franciacorta wine zones of Lombardy. Until recently, only small quantities were exported, but now they're not difficult to find. This is where you'll find the bone-dry bubbly, the dry sparkling wines are made with little to no dosage.

Tasting Tip

The California bubbly made by the French Champagne houses is definitely a different wine than the Champagne they make in Champagne. The California versions are fruitier and more direct.

And chances are you are very familiar with Italy's wildly popular popper, Prosecco, which has been wholeheartedly embraced by American wine consumers.

Domestic Bubbles

Most of the domestic sparklers you'll find in your wine shop come from California. Happily, the West Coast producers have outlived a reputation for making inferior, mass-produced, grapey imitations of the real thing. Made by the Méthode Champenoise, the bubbles have gotten smaller and more persistent, and the quality has improved vastly.

Some of the best California sparkling wines come from French Champagne houses that have set up shop on the West Coast. Led by Möet & Chandon, which began California production in 1973, Roederer, Taittinger, and others have heard the siren call of the Golden State.

Remember, for the best quality, look for the words "sparkling wine" on the label, not "champagne."

CHAPTER 22
Fortified Wines

In This Chapter

- Porto wines from Portugal
- Ports of the world
- Sherry—sunshine from Spain
- Madeira—from the island

Historically, people added alcohol to wines to give them stability. No bottle fermentation (or bubbles) wanted! The higher alcohol killed the yeast stopped fermentation. This "fortification" ensured the survival of wines that were transported over long distances.

By definition, a fortified wine is any wine with alcohol content boosted through the addition of brandy or neutral spirits. Fortified wines usually range from 17 to 21 percent alcohol (by volume), somewhat higher than the 14 percent limit for table wines.

Portugal and Spain insist that the fortifying agents come from within their borders, often within a delineated region, and that they are made from specified grape varieties. (This has nothing to do with quality control. It's just a protectionist measure.)

In this chapter you will learn all about the fortified wines of Spain and Portugal (both mainland and the offshore island, Madeira). Fortified wines differ from table wines in style and alcohol content.

Body Building for Wine

Fortified wines are made two ways. In the first, the vintner selects grapes for their ability to develop high sugar content, with potential to ferment to high alcohol levels. The must (juice) from these select grapes is inoculated with special, powerful yeasts, capable of thriving at high alcohol concentrations. The alcohol level will reach 17 or 18 percent, which finally does stop fermentation. Sweetness can be adjusted later.

In the second (and more traditional method), the vintner adds a fortifying agent to increase the level of alcohol and, where necessary, to halt fermentation. Most Ports, Sherries, Marsalas, and Madeiras start with grapes high in natural sugars. They may be fermented to dryness, or fortified to stop fermentation while there still is some sweetness. The selection of the brandy or neutral spirits used as the fortifying agent is important to the quality of the product. Some fortified wines are aged in wood for smoothness, while others are left raw and rough.

Porto—The Real Thing

A few decades ago, the Portuguese changed the name of their Port to "Porto" to avoid confusion in a marketplace filled with "Ports" from many other countries. Only Port from Portugal may be called Porto. But in this chapter, I'll refer to Porto as Port, because here we're looking (nearly) only at authentic Port, from Portugal.

Heard it Through the Grapevine

The foremost authority on Port was H. Warner Allen, a noted wine writer from the early part of the century. He wrote, "Vintage Port has a lushness, unctuousness, delicacy, and refinement that make Port unparalleled by any wine of its type in the world."

Port long has been a favorite of the English gentry, and some swear it's a British invention. When faced with a shortage of French wine in the late 17th century, the resourceful (and thirsty) British imported wine from Portugal. To ensure its stability on the journey to England, they added a touch of brandy to the finished wine.

In 1670, the first English Port house, Warre, opened its doors in the seaport city of Oporto, Portugal. Oporto is still the home of true Port. As Port became an important commodity, the process for making it became more refined. Instead of adding the brandy as an afterthought the (mainly British) producers began to add the brandy during the fermentation process.

Today, a Port producer can make as many as six different styles of Port, depending on the taste preferences of the intended market. True Port has gotten sweeter by design to meet market demands, but the basic process remains the same.

Port is made from a blend of grapes grown on the steep slopes of Portugal's Douro region, where the soils are a gravely schist (slate), and the climate is warm to hot. As many as 15 different indigenous grape varieties may go into the making of Port. These grapes, truly, are unsung heroes. Even the most important of them these days are relative unknowns: Touriga Nacional, Touriga Franca, Tinta Cão, Tinta Roriz, and Tinta Barroca.

These local grapes are chosen for their ability to develop high sugars, good color, and when used in concert, character and finesse. After they're gathered from the terraced hillsides, the grapes are fermented and brought to Oporto for prolonged aging, blending, and bottling. The quality of Port is derived from the vintage, the aging, and the blending. Variations in these elements account for nuances in style.

Vintage Port

Vintage Port is the top of the line among ports. It's produced only in exceptional vintages, capable of producing wines of great depth and complexity. Individual producers set the standards, but a vintage year generally is declared by consensus. It's unusual to find a lone producer declaring a vintage year (although it's not impossible).

The Sommelier Says

Bottle-aging leaves a crusty sediment on the bottom and along the sides of the bottles of vintage port. You really need to exercise care when you handle and open these fine wines. And you should decant them before serving, to ensure you don't ruin your experience with the bitter deposits.

Usually made from selected lots, Vintage Port is capable of aging and developing complexity for many, many years. Once it's been fermented, fortified, and adjusted for sweetness, Vintage Port must be aged for two years in wood before bottling.

Before aging, vintage port is concentrated and rich, to the point of being undrinkable. In bottle-aging, the spirits and flavors marry, and the wine throws a heavy deposit or sediment. Ten years in the bottle represents mere infancy. It takes 20 or 30 years before Vintage Port comes into its own. Some of the best Vintage Ports are 70 years old (sometimes much older).

Most good Vintage Ports sell in the $50 to $100 range when they are young (and years away from being ready to drink). You can expect to pay $80 or more for a Port with a decade or more age. A fully mature port can cost from $300 and more a bottle in a great vintage.

Late-Bottled Vintage

Late-Bottled Vintage Port comes from one vintage that is cask-aged for six years and filtered before bottling. Most of the sediment will settle during cask-aging, making Late-Bottled Vintage Port a compromise between Vintage and non-Vintage varieties. It is less expensive, less complex, and sometimes made from young vines or less traditional grape varieties. It sells for about $20 to $30.

Ruby Port

Ruby Port is a blend of vintages, usually lacking the intense purple colors and flavors of a better-quality Port to begin with. It's cask-aged for roughly three years or less. Ruby Ports are blended for consistent color and style. Usually these are the least expensive Ports (around $10 or $15). They're the youngest of the Port family, and are full-bodied, rougher, and less harmonious than their Tawny cousins, described next.

Tawny Port

Some Tawny Ports are deep garnet or brownish in color, but they need no more aging than a Ruby. The best lie in cask for many years, until the color becomes light or tawny through oxidation. Some well-aged Tawny Ports can be marvelous and subtle. Expect to pay about $20 and up for a longer-aged Tawny; the lesser-quality Tawnies can be found for as low as $10.

The very best Tawnies state their average age (the average of the ages of wines from which they were blended) on the label—10, 20, 30, or 40 years. Ten-year-old Tawnies cost about $20 to $30, and 20-year-olds sell for $50.

Tasting Tip

Occasionally, a Tawny Port will be so outstanding that it is not blended with Ports of other vintages but aged individually. This single-vintage Tawny will be labeled either Port of the Vintage (as opposed to Vintage Port) or Colheita Port, which spends a minimum of eight years aging in cask. An exceptional Colheita can be a fine example of an aged Port, but it is distinctively different from Vintage Port.

White Port

White Port rarely is seen outside Portugal or France. Made from white-grape varieties, it has a golden color and it's usually finished dry, bottled young, and drunk as an apéritif. The sweet-finished version usually is inferior in quality. (You can find much better apéritifs.)

Vintage Character Port

Vintage Character Port is a blend of premium Ruby ports from several vintages, cask-aged for about five years. They are full-bodied, rich, ready to drink when bottled, and sell for about $15 to $20. Vintage Character Ports are sold under a proprietary name like Boardroom (made by Dow).

Port at Home

Like other fine red wines, Vintage Ports should be stored on their sides in a cool environment. Other Ports may be stored upright like liquor, because they're already fully developed. With the exception of Ruby and White, all Ports will keep several weeks after opening.

You should serve your Port at cool room temperature, 66 to 68 degrees F. Ports go well with nuts and strong cheeses. Try walnuts with Stilton.

Ports of the World

The name "Port" refers, properly, to the city of Oporto. But the term has been borrowed and used generically, like (sorry, Kimberly-Clark!) "Kleenex."

The Sommelier Says

Non-Oporto Ports simply are dessert wines made in many countries. Some are good; some are adequate; and some are cheap, baked-tasting sweet wines bearing little resemblance to the real thing.

Perhaps the best ports to be seen outside of Portugal come from Australia. Look for Yalumba, Chateau Reynella, and Lindemans.

California and South Africa have an unfortunate history of producing dull and ordinary Ports, tainted by baked qualities and coming from grapes inappropriate to a hot climate. Today, these regions have set their sights on producing high-quality Port. Now, vintners in both places plant local grape varieties as they search for finer fortifying spirits.

In California, winemakers have developed several very interesting Ports made either from blended grapes or from blends in which Zinfandel predominates. Among the Port revivalists, Amador County and parts of Sonoma County have gained attention as respected Port wine regions. South Africa, a country traditionally noted for making fortified wines, has awakened our notice with its finer Port wines. Some South African versions are nearly indistinguishable from the Oporto products.

Tasting Tip

The most prized soil in the Jerez region is albariza, a soil that is predominately chalk, with limestone and magnesium. Easily recognizable by its white topsoil layer, albariza sections bear the best Sherry grapes, and by law at least 40 percent of the grapes used in Sherry must come from this rare soil. (See Chapter 16, Olé! Red Wines, Good Value.)

From Jerez to Sherry?

Originating in the Jerez (Andalucia) region of southern Spain, Sherry is the Anglicized pronunciation of "Jerez." This ancient Moorish town is the site of many Sherry bodegas (wineries), but it is just one part of the Sherry-producing region.

The coastal village of Puerto de Santa Maria, located southwest of Jerez, also boasts several bodegas. The sea air is believed to be an important element in the making of dry fino (a type of Sherry). Ten miles northwest of Jerez, another coastal village, Sanlúcar de Barrameda, is so renowned for its sea breezes that the lightest and driest of Sherries, Manzanilla, legally can be made only there. (It does not appear possible to make wine of this quality elsewhere.)

The predominant grape variety used in Sherry is the Palomino, a prolific vine, with delicious, edible fruit, but which normally yields thin, neutral, and sometimes harsh table wines. Once again, inventive winemakers have turned a liability into a plus.

This wine oxidizes easily during aging, yielding the characteristic and desirable nutty aroma and flavor that are the hallmarks of a fine Sherry. Pedro Ximénez is a secondary grape for Sherry, yielding a very sweet wine that is often used as a blending or sweetening agent. Moscatel (Muscat) sometimes is used for dessert Sherries.

On the Flor

Sherry is a fortified wine made in large volume. Most producers use modern, efficient methods of crushing and vinification. The Sherry-to-be begins as a wine that is fermented in stainless-steel tanks.

The first-year wine is then aged at the bodega in butts (U.S.-made oak barrels with a capacity of 158 gallons), filled to about one-third capacity. What evolves over the next year or two is a drama of self-fulfillment. Some butts will reveal a propensity toward developing the unique, thick, white film yeast called flor in Jerez. Others won't.

Heard it Through the Grapevine

The appearance of the flor yeast (technically known as Saccharomyces fermenti) is unpredictable, discerned only by frequent tastings, and found nowhere else in the world. (Call it Kismet.) During the aging process, the bodega master (vintner) tastes the contents of each butt and rates it on the basis of its propensity to develop flor on the wine's surface. Essentially, the developing wine tells the experienced vintner where it wants to go.

The wine's progress in each butt is chronicled, and based on the intrinsic character and development of the flor, the wine is channeled into one of three directions:

- Wines without any flor character and with weak flavors either will be distilled into spirits or made into vinegar.
- Wines that develop only a small degree of flor, but have good body and flavors are marked as Olorosos and introduced into a solera. (You'll learn about soleras soon!)
- Wines that are light in color with a thick layer of flor are marked as Finos and sent to another solera.

Within the bodegas, butts marked Fino will be made into three different styles of Sherry: Fino, Manzanilla, and Amontillado. The Olorosos will be made into Oloroso, Cream Sherry, or Brown Sherry. The crucial factor in achieving quality in a Sherry lies in the aging process. Most Sherries are non-vintage wines, and almost all are the product of the solera system of blending and aging in butts.

The solera, itself, is a configuration (usually triangular in shape) of barrels containing Sherry of various ages. It's usually composed of three tiers or rows, with each successive tier representing a younger wine. There is a method behind this.

The system is based on the premise that newer wines "refresh" the older ones, and the union releases a host of flavors. This procedure, called fractional blending, marries old wine with newer wine from different tiers of the solera.

Vino Vocab

The word, solera, is derived from suelo, the word for bottom or ground, referring to the bottom tier of the solera.

The oldest Sherry resides in the bottom tier. Above it are the criada, sort of a nursery in which the Sherries mature. In an established solera, the butts remain. The wine moves first laterally, and then down from one tier to the next. (Think of it as one of those mechanical puzzles with the sliding wooden squares.)

When the wine is bottled, the bodega master drains off part (no more than one-third) from each butt on the bottom tier and replaces it with wine from the tier above. As Sherry moves throughout the solera, it's continually in the process of fractional blending. (Mathematically, each bottle will have at least a little of the very first wine that was present when the solera was established.)

Fino

Fino, the finest Sherry, is always produced and aged within Jerez or in Puerto de Santa Maria. It has a pale color, a yeasty, slightly nutty aroma, delicate flavors, and is usually dry, sometimes slightly bitter. Its scent is often reminiscent of almonds. The alcohol content ranges from 15.5 to 17 percent.

Heard it Through the Grapevine

Finos average about three to five years in solera before bottling. They do not develop in the bottle and once opened, lose freshness within a week or so. If you're going to keep them at all, you need to refrigerate after opening. You should serve them chilled, and try to finish the bottle within a day or two.

Manzanilla

Manzanilla is Fino produced in Sanlúcar de Barrameda. It is pale, straw-colored, delicate, and light-bodied. Some say the wine's slightly bitter, tangy, and pungent character is due to the salty flavors picked up from the sea air.

Wines made in Sanlúcar, but sent to Jerez for aging in solera, do not develop the typical character of Manzanilla. So maybe there is something to this sea spray. More likely, the temperate sea climate causes the flor to grow more thickly. Manzanilla is the driest and most intense of all the Sherries. Served it well chilled.

Amontillado

Amontillado is an amber-colored, aged Fino that's spent a longer time in the solera. It's medium-bodied with a more pronounced, nutty flavor. Amontillado is dry and pungent. True amontillado is seen often, and it's expensive. Some lesser Sherries are labeled "Amontillado." Although you find these lesser sherries far more often in the British market, some make their way here, too. If you find an Amontillado selling for $8 or less, it is not worth buying. Serve Amontillado slightly chilled.

Tasting Tip

Amontillado has been esteemed by Americans for a very long time, as you can infer from Edgar Allen Poe's classic tale of horror, A Cask of Amontillado.

Oloroso

Oloroso is deep in color and boasts a rich, full-bodied style with a scent of walnuts. Because of its prolonged aging, it lacks the yeasty flor pungency. Olorosos are customarily dry wines, sometimes sweetened to suit market demands. They usually contain between 18 and 20 percent alcohol. Serve at room temperature or very slightly chilled.

Palo Cortado

This rare breed of Sherry is the best of the non-flor Sherries. It begins life as a fino with a flor but develops as an amontillado after losing its flor. Later, it resembles the richer, more fragrant Oloroso style, while retaining the elegance of an Amontillado. Palo Cortado is similar to an Oloroso in color, but its aroma is like Amontillado. (Got that?) Serve at room temperature or slightly chilled.

Medium Sherry

Medium Sherry is an Amontillado or light Oloroso that has been slightly sweetened.

Pale Cream

Pale Cream Sherry is a slightly sweetened blend of fino and light Amontillado Sherries.

Cream Sherry

Cream Sherry is made from Oloroso wine, often of poor quality. Once sweetened, the sweetness will mask the defects. Sadly, it is an experience with this cheap, low-quality quaff that turns off imbibers to an entire world of delicious, high-quality sherry. Don't let that be you!

The Sommelier Says

Many fortified wines labeled "Sherry" are out-and-out impostors! Few made outside Spain go through the solera process. Even the best solera Sherries from California don't measure up in flavor and interest to the real product from its Spanish homeland.

The wine is sweetened and the color darkened by the addition of wines from Pedro Ximénez grapes, which are left to sun-dry for seven to ten days for extra sugar development. Pedro Ximénez is a thick, concentrated, very sweet wine; so not much is required to make a Cream Sherry. However, its character is a key factor in the quality of the finished product. Cream Sherries are very popular.

Brown Sherry

Brown Sherry is a blend of Oloroso, Pedro Ximénez, and an added sweetening agent. It's very dark, very syrupy, and very, very sweet. The style is far more common in the U.K. than the U.S. East India is a type of Brown Sherry that is even sweeter and darker in color.

Pedro Ximénez and Moscatel

Pedro Ximénez and Moscatel is an extremely sweet, dark brown, syrupy dessert wine that can be used as a sauce on desserts. It is made from raisined grapes of these two varieties and is low in alcohol.

Montilla

Montilla is located northeast of the Jerez region, the wines made here are similar to the Fino, Amontillado, and Oloroso styles of Sherry. Unlike Sherry, they are not fortified to higher alcohol levels, but derive their strength naturally during fermentation. The main grape variety is the Pedro Ximénez. The leading brand for Montilla is Alvear, usually priced at $12 to $20. Once seldom seen in the U.S., it's now widely distributed.

Ready-to-Serve

Always buy Fino and Manzanilla when you're ready to serve them. They're at peak flavor and complexity when first opened, but an open bottle can keep in the refrigerator up to a month. (After such storage, it won't taste quite like the intricate blend the bodega master intended, but it still can drinkable and delightful.)

Appendix A lists recommended Sherry producers.

Legendary Madeira

Once famous as the beverage of choice in colonial America, Madeira is named for the Portugal-owned island off the Atlantic coast of Morocco. The grapes for this legendary fortified wine are grown on very steep hillsides that ring the perimeter of the island. The wines of Madeira often are identified by their predominant grape variety. These include, principally: Verdelho, Sercial, Bual (or Boal), and Malvasia.

To say that Madeira is hardy is an understatement! It's not just its robust character, but also its ability to age. If a wine can be called a survivor, Madeira is it. The prime Madeiras are vintage-dated from 1920 all the way back to 1795 when the colonists were still around to enjoy their favorite drink. Even the rarest, most noble Château Lafite is a mere infant by comparison.

The styles of Madeira range from sweet to moderately dry. As the juice of the grapes (or mosto) is fermented in large vats, the wines destined for a dry style will complete fermentation. The sweeter versions will have fermentation arrested through the addition of brandy.

Madeira employs one unusual production technique that accounts for its unique character. It's baked. The process is called estufagem (from estufas, or ovens). But the wine isn't put into baking dishes and placed into bread ovens or anything like that. Traditionally, it was placed into large casks that were left out under the hot sun.

Heard it Through the Grapevine

The estufagem technique was discovered quite by accident. This was back in the days when Madeira was shipped in the holds of sailing vessels. En route to the East Indies, ships passed through the tropical heat. In the overheated hold, the wine changed character. The resulting heady flavor was a hit.

Today, the slightly roasted or smoky tang is achieved by aging in heat-controlled vats. In the estufas, the temperature increases gradually until it reaches about 110 degrees F, where it remains for several months. The sugars in the wine become caramelized, and some of the wine components oxidize, a process called maderization. After estufagem, the Madeira is allowed to cool and recover for the same period of time. Finally, it is fortified and aged in wood casks before being bottled.

Okay, I admit it! Madeira is an acquired taste. Technically, this is a white wine, though even the most robust Chardonnay literally pales beside it. Madeira's characteristic color is a dark, rich amber. It has a rich, nutty aroma, a sharp tang to its flavors, and a finish as long as its age.

Most Madeira is sold under proprietary names. Authentic vintage Madeira usually comes from a single cask. Many Madeiras are aged in solera, and with those that are labeled as solera, the dates refer to when the solera was established, not to the entire contents of the bottle. (Though the bottle actually does contain a little wine that really is that old.)

The Sommelier Says

With most wines, particularly whites or rosés, maderization is bad news. Both the color and the taste are destroyed, generally through age or bad storage. In the case of Madeira, though, it's the touch that brings out its best character.

Twenty years is the designated cask-aging time for a vintage Madeira, although the wines once were aged even longer. Special Reserve Madeiras are a blend of wines about 10 years old and are less expensive. Reserve Madeira is about five years old.

The styles of Madeira are differentiated both by the grape and level of sweetness. These names reflect either the grape variety or style:

- Sercial, the finest dry Madeira, has a lightness and delicacy that lends itself well to enjoyment as an apéritif. The grape is grown at the highest altitude; so it's one of the latest to ripen. It offers the most distinctive aroma and dry, tangy taste on the palate.
- Verdelho is slightly sweeter and rounder on the palate than Sercial. It has a more typical Madeira aroma that can be best described as a toasted, nutty character.
- Bual (also Boal) is sweeter than Sercial or Verdelho, much fuller in body, and darker in color with flavors of raisins and almonds. It makes for a nice wine to serve with dessert.

Tasting Tip

Are you interested in antiques? How about nineteenth-century vintage Madeiras? Yes, you can find them, and for about $150 to $400 a bottle. Not bad, for such a distinguished bit of wine history.

And don't worry—it won't be spoiled. Just remember the Madeira motto, "Nothing can keep a good wine down."

- Malmsey, made from the Malvasia grape, is the sweetest of all, dark amber in color, and with a smooth, luxurious texture and a very long finish.
- Rainwater was once well-known in the U.S. (not surprising, from its name, which was once the proprietary name given it by a shipper in Savannah, Georgia), but has lost favor over the years. It can be variable in sweetness, but as its name implies, will be rather pale in color.
- Terrantez is between Verdelho and Bual in style. It is a powerful, medium-sweet, fragrant Madeira with a lot of acidity. It is rarely seen these days.

Setúbal

Setúbal is a Portuguese dessert wine from the town of Azeitao, south of Lisbon. Made from the Muscat grape, it is somewhat similar to Port, with grape spirit added to halt fermentation. It's a rich wine with longevity.

Marsala

Italy's most famous fortified wine, Marsala, takes its name from its prime production center, the town of Marsala in western Sicily. In vogue as a chic beverage in the late eighteenth century, it has since been reduced to the status of a cooking ingredient—a common dessert wine at best.

Despite its tarnished reputation, Marsala does bear some resemblance to Madeira, and devotees (and producers) are bent on a Marsala revival to parallel that of Madeira, which many producers are trying to engender in the American market these days. It is dark in color with amber, red, or gold versions.

Marsala has a caramel aroma, tending to be very sweet, but there are dry and semi-dry versions. The sugar comes from allowing the grapes to dry in the sun prior to fermentation or more commonly, from the addition of grape concentrate after fermentation. Dry Marsala often is blended in a solera system. Dates on Marsala bottles refer to the founding of the solera, not to a particular vintage.

The best Marsalas are labeled Superiore or Vergine. Marsala Vergine is unsweetened, uncolored, and aged longer than other styles.

Vin Santo

From Tuscany comes Vin Santo, which is rich golden amber in color and also made from dried grapes, then barrel-aged several years. Vin Santo comes in dry, medium-dry, and sweet versions.

Vermouth

This flavored, fortified vermouth, derives its name from the German word Wermut (wormwood, the plant that yields a bitter extract). It's made in many wine regions throughout the world. It boasts an intriguing list of flavoring agents: herbs, juniper, coriander, and, of course, wormwood, to name but a few.

Vermouth normally begins as inexpensive, bland white wine. The herb infusion, which has been steeped in alcohol, is then added, and the whole is quickly blended, to marry. The herb formula varies from brand to brand, and Vermouths vary from fairly dry to quite sweet. It is inexpensive, ubiquitous, and used as an apéritif or mixer. (Without Vermouth, a martini would be nothing but gin and an olive.)

Vino Vocab

Actually, there are neither worms nor wood in "wormwood," the bracing bitter flavor in Vermouth. The word is a corruption of the Germanic "Wermut," which meant "man-strength."

CHAPTER 23

Organic Wine

In This Chapter

- The dirt on low-intervention wines
- Organic winegrowing
- Organic winemaking
- Serving and storing organic wine

A decade ago, words like "organic," "sustainable," "biodynamic," and "natural" were barely mentioned, let alone part of the general public's wine vernacular. But chances are, your favorite local wine shop not only has an entire section dedicated to wines that are farmed and, possibly, produced with the environment in mind, there are a lot more of them from which to choose. But what are they? What sets them apart, if anything? Do they taste different? Are they more expensive than "regular" wines? What do all these terms actually mean, anyway? And are they any better for you or the planet?

All good questions! I will answer each of these in this chapter, but to kick things off let's start with that last question. In my estimation, the general blanket answer is yes—any producer who is thinking about the quality of his or her land, and the quality of his or her wine is making a better product. But some eco-friendly wines are less-friendly than others, and there are differences in what the terms mean for you, the consumer. That you aren't sure what they are isn't surprising—the wine industry (at least in the United States) has really only scratched the surface on organically-minded wines—and we can probably thank grocery stores for that.

Ten years ago, there were less than a million acres of certified organic farmland in the United States; today, the figure has exploded to nearly 5 million, according to the latest statistics from the United States Department of Agriculture. Your average, every day, twenty-first century grocery store offers everything from organic produce to organic dairy products to organic boxed mac n' cheese and eco-friendly laundry soap and toilet paper! It's commonplace in restaurants—and even some fast-food spots, too—to see the Farmer Brown source of your steak or potatoes listed on the menu. That wine has followed suit isn't surprising—after all, grapes are an agricultural product, too.

That organic wines are mainstream now is a direct result of a greater awareness among us all on where our food comes from and how it was farmed. In this chapter, I'll clear up the confusion you may have about what these terms mean in the wine world and explore some reasons you might choose an eco-friendly bottle with your supper tonight—and why now, more than ever, it's oh-so easy sipping green.

What's in a Name? Organic, Biodynamic, Sustainable, Natural

First things first—let's get the lingo down so you know what you're pouring when you pop it.

Organic

First things first: To gain organic certification in the U.S., a vineyard must go through an expensive, three-year process and farm its grapes according to strict guidelines, which include eschewing the use of synthetic pesticides and synthetic fertilizers, among other restrictions. However, in order to label a wine "organic," the practices a winemaker uses in the winery as well as the vineyard must be organic. The biggest restriction here being the use of the preservative, sulfites—if a wine is labeled "organic," it may have a small amount of naturally occurring sulfites, but none have been added in the farming or making of the wine. Otherwise, a producer can choose to put on his label "made from organically farmed grapes." It's a distinction of which you should be aware!

Heard it Through the Grapevine

Since 2002, the USDA recognizes and regulates organic farming in the United States (prior to that, organic certification was a state-by-state issue regulated by third-party organic organizations), and even gives a handy-dandy little USDA organic seal of approval logo to appear on all products that meet certain strict standards of production. In a groundbreaking move in 2012, the U.S. and the EU came to an agreement allowing organically certified products for approved sale among each of its nation states.

Biodynamic

Biodynamic farming is similar to organic farming, in that is eschews the use of synthetic fertilizers, pesticides, and other less-than-natural plant-controlling methods, but takes it a big step further. Created in the 1920s by the Austrian philosopher Rudolf Steiner, biodynamic farming takes a much more holistic (and, some might say, spiritual) view of farming. In biodynamics, the farm is considered a living organism, and everything around it—from the farm next door to the phases of the moon—an integral part (or detriment) of its survival. Biodynamically farmed wines use organic matter, like cow manure and compost teas, to fertilize the ground, naturally occurring plants and insects as welcomed guests instead of weeds and pests, and allow the positions of the moon to dictate when to spray, fertilize, prune, and pick. The main organization that certifies a vineyard as biodynamic is known as Demeter

Sustainable

Sustainable vineyards, in their truest sense, are those that take into account organic and biodynamic farming principles, thinking carefully about how the chemicals they choose to employ effect not just the grapes and plants and land, but the people around them, too, as well as their carbon footprint and output of pollution on the planet. Unfortunately, there is no legal federal definition of sustainability, so less-than honest producers can bandy about the term with no consequence (except, of course, the loss of respect of their peers). There have been local moves to make sustainability mean something for consumers in places like the Central Coast of California, where SIP (Sustainability in Practice) has taken root, allowing producers who meet their strict guidelines to use the SIP logo on their bottles.

Natural

Possibly the most abused word in the world of eco-conscious products, at its worst natural is a responsibility-shirking word used to green-wash the unsuspecting consumer. In the wine world, though, at its best it implies a producer who is using little to no intervention in both their farming and winemaking. To wit: no artificial fertilizers, pesticides, no sulfites in the vineyard or winery, and only natural yeast to begin fermentation. While it may sound like the wild west of winemaking, in terms of how it's made and how a consumer can discern which wines are natural and which aren't, new importers like Jenny & Francois who ring the bell for natural wine producers the world 'round are a good way to identify producers making their wines in this way.

Why Pick Organic?

Since organic is the main, recognized healthy farming and winemaking distinction in the United States, we're going to concentrate our discussion on it from this point forward, as it is the most common restrictive term you will come across. For many shoppers, the word "organic" is a valuable assurance that what they consume is not tainted with man-made fertilizers, antibiotics, herbicides, hormones, or pesticides. Increasingly, this consciousness has extended to wine. The reasons are various. You may agree, or disagree, with any of these. But as a wise consumer, you'll want to understand your options.

To Your Health

Does soil management make a difference in the taste and quality of food? Some people believe it does.

What about pesticides and herbicides used in winegrowing? Do some residues linger in the wine we drink and ground where the vines are grown? Unquestionably. But harmful? Those who set limits and standards say no, within stipulated reason. But many others believe yes. Or at least, that there's a cumulative effect of strange chemicals from hundreds of sources entering our bodies through food, drink, and air.

One thing we can say for sure: Organic products don't add anything harmful to our diets. In fact, the term "organic" used to be defined more in terms of what it lacked than for what it offered.

Sulfite Sensitivity

To many American wine-drinkers, "organic wine" (as opposed to organically farmed grapes, remember!) on the wine label means one thing: lower sulfite levels (or even no added sulfites at all). These are the people who are very sensitive to sulfites, who may experience unpleasant side-effects, from mild to severe.

Heard it Through the Grapevine

What are sulfites? These are chemical compounds that contain an SO3 arrangement. They are a by-product of treating wine with sulfur dioxide gas (SO2).

The SO2 gas reacts with the water in wine to form a very weak sulfurous acid solution, H2SO3. Much of this will consume the small amount of oxygen trapped in the wine to prevent harmful oxidation in the bottle. But a little may react with some of the natural compounds in wine to form sulfites.

Sulfur dioxide gas has been used for centuries as a fruit preservative. The amount appearing in wines has fallen throughout the world, as countries impose stricter limits. These limits vary with the type of wine being treated.

Once wine is bottled for final consumption, any remaining microbes—including yeast or bacteria—could spoil that wine. Also, you might remember that many of wine's delicate flavor compounds can be ruined through over-oxidation. A small amount of SO2 gas, added to the wine at various stages of production, kills "wild yeasts" and bacteria. It also consumes dissolved oxygen, as sulfites become sulfates.

In the U.S., sulfites are limited to 350 parts-per-million (ppm), or less, with all forms of sulfur counted. European and Australian limits are similar. Organic certification typically allows sulfites up 90 ppm for red wines and 100 ppm for whites. However, most organic growers come in at less than 40 ppm.

Sulfites occur naturally in grapes, and they are a by-product of fermentation. In some cases, sulfites could reach as much as 40 ppm, with no added SO2 gas! Somehow, a very few organic vintners have managed to make a product so low in sulfites that they are undetectable.

Under Bureau of Alcohol, Tobacco and Firearms (BATF) labeling requirements, anything with more than 10 ppm of sulfites must have the words "contains sulfites." Wines with less need not display that warning, but neither may they claim "sulfite-free" (except in those rare cases that sulfite levels are undetectable). This is not "honor system." Such vintners must include a sulfite analysis from an approved testing laboratory when they apply to the BATF for approval of their wine labels.

There is an important bit of leeway in BATF-approved labeling, though. Organic vintners may (where applicable) use the words "no added sulfites" or "naturally occurring sulfites only." Those minority who make no use of sulfur dioxide in their wine production want you to know they went to this special trouble. (Also, you need to know this when it comes to storage and keeping properties.)

Tasting Tip

Most organic vintners do use a small amount of sulfur dioxide gas. Without any, most wines would soon spoil—particularly white wines, which lack the tannins of reds. But they use it in great moderation, yielding a product with lower in sulfite than most other wines.

If you are sulfite-sensitive, or if you can taste these compounds in your wines (some people can), then organic or biodynamic-labeledwines might be your best choice.

Lifestyle Choice

Organic agriculture is more than the sum of its parts. It's a philosophy, one that considers the ecological context of all human activity, that values diversity and natural biological processes of competition, growth, death, and regeneration. Although, it's skyrocketing popularity that has burst far beyond the local health-food store has also made it a bit of a marketing tool—companies with deep pockets that can afford the certification and the marketing to get the word out reap the benefits of consumer loyalty.

Still, many conscientious consumers try to reward environmental "good behavior" by selecting products produced by growers and manufacturers who share their concerns. This shows up in the strong growth we have seen in the growing market share garnered by organic vintners.

What Makes Organic Organic?

Many decades ago, the term "organic" was pretty clear. It meant, simply, growing crops without manufactured fertilizers. Organic gardening and farming used manure and compost instead of manufactured phosphates and nitrates.

Later, "organic" began to embrace other aspects of growing: pesticides, soil management, biodiversity, animal husbandry, and food processing. Several states and many countries implemented standards for labeling products "organic." But there was no U.S. national standard.

In 1990, Congress passed the Organic Food Production Act, which directed the Agriculture Department (USDA) to develop national standards for foods labeled "organic." The federal Natural Organic Standards Board (NOSB) set to work developing standards for food and wine. In 2002, federal organic standards were officially implemented.

These cover all organic crops and processed foods, including produce, grain, meat, dairy, eggs, and fiber. (To learn more about the proposed rule, visit the National Organic Program's Web site at www.ams.usda.gov/nop/.)

The Organic Grapes into Wine Alliance (OGWA), a producers' association, has been diligent in presenting model standards to both BATF and USDA..

The Sommelier Says

How can it take more than ten years to develop national standards for organic foods and beverages? Part of the answer lies in the utter complexity of the whole problem.

Another answer lies in politics. Different producers have different interests. From the grower's standpoint, the best rule would be one that embraces all that grower's practices—but no others.

When it comes to wine, regulatory authority is distributed over many agencies. The BATF regulates wine labeling. The Federal Trade Commission (FTC) governs organic food advertising. The Food and Drug Administration (FDA) decides which foods may be labeled organic. And the USDA figures out what ingredients belong in organic foods.

"Certified organic" on the label means products that have been grown and processed according to strict uniform standards, verified annually by independent state or private organizations. Certification includes inspection of farm fields and processing facilities. The label "certified organic grapes" means only that the grapes have been grown organically.

Farm-field inspections look at long-term soil management, buffering between organic farms and neighboring conventional farms, and record-keeping. Processing inspections include review of the facility's cleaning and pest control methods, ingredient transportation and storage, and record keeping.

Organic wine is more than wine made from organically grown grapes. The concept may extends to the winemaking, itself, too, as we saw earlier. In this section, we'll go a little more in-depth for both concepts.

Organically Grown

Organic farming systems avoid both pesticides and manufactured fertilizers. That doesn't mean organic growers are indifferent to soil fertility or to pest damage. Far from it!

Organic farming is very scientific, within whatever constraints organic certifying bodies, the federal government, or the growers, themselves, place on it. Organic growing requires a deep understanding of the ecology of soils and the plants that grow in them.

Tasting Tip

When we hear of organic farming, we think of California, where social and cultural trends seem to begin. But in the case of organic wine, California was a real laggard.

France was the first to get into organic wine in a big way. They were followed by Germany. California (along with Canada and Australia) is a relative newcomer. But a very quick learner!

Soil is much more than bits of rock and other mineral material. Healthy soils are teeming universes of microbial life and microscopic bits of plant debris. There are dozens of active processes—not unlike fermentation—that render dead plant material into available nutrition for living plants.

In natural settings, growth and decay are in balance. Agriculture upsets that balance, as crops are harvested and removed. Crop rotation helps delay nutrient depletion, but most modern farmers have had to turn to manufactured fertilizers to obtain good (and profitable) yields.

Heard it Through the Grapevine

The healthiest soils are those that are in constant use, with nothing removed. As nutrients are released by dead matter, they are taken up by roots of living matter before they can be washed away. Organic winegrowers grow cover crops along with their grapes. These are plowed under each season.

Cover crops also help with pest control and erosion, both wind and water.

Organic grape growing returns much of the crop (everything but the grape must) to the soil. It plants other crops (cover crops) to naturally adjust the nitrogen in the soil and to control pests. These crops will be plowed back into the soil each season. As needed, organic growers augment their soils with natural fertilizers, such as composted manure.

The organic grower's first line of defense against pests is prevention. With planting diversity, there is pest diversity. This means no particular pest develops a dense population. And overall biodiversity—in soil organisms, insects and birds—ensures that no one pest population will grow large enough to damage the wine crop.

When pests do become a problem, there are other ways than poisons to deal with them. These include introduction of insect predators, mating disruption (through the use of synthetic pheromones!), traps, and barriers. As a last resort, organic farmers will apply natural, plant-derived pesticides, only as much as needed.

Bacteria and fungi can be as devastating to a crop as insects. Organic growing certification bodies allow the application of Bordeaux mixture—lime, copper sulfate, and water—to crops and soils. It's effective and leaves no toxic residue in the must or wine. However, overuse of this mixture can add excess copper, which in acidic soils can reduce grape yields.

Tasting Tip

Bordeaux mixture is lime, copper sulfate, and water. It leaves no residue in the wine you buy. The mixture's use against plant disease was discovered a hundred years ago in the Bordeaux wine region of France.

Though Bordeaux mixture doesn't occur in nature, certifying bodies allow its use in organic growing, possibly because it's old and uses no petrochemicals.

The most effective preventive factor in plant disease is climate. Hot, dry conditions mean little disease. In fact, some winegrowers who don't seek organic certification have adopted chemical-free agriculture. In cooler or moister climates, organic winegrowing can be very difficult.

Weed-control depends on increased cultivation, along with cover crops, mulches, and flame weeding (burned plant material maintains all its mineral nutrients).

Heard it Through the Grapevine

Don't be surprised if you visit a producer with a view toward eco-friendly vineyard practices and his farm seems like a step back in time. Many smaller producers, like Robert Sinskey in California and Olivier Cousin in the Loire Valley have employed furry friends to keep the balance in their vineyards. For instance, they employ sheep as living lawnmowers to nibble on cover crops when a little weed-control is needed (and the natural resulting fertilizer, an added bonus), as well as horses to plow, instead of tractors in order to keep the harmful compacting that tractors create on the soil to a much healthier minimum.

Organic growers spend nothing on synthetically manufactured fertilizers and pesticides. But they must apply considerably more labor to meet their production goals.

Organically Produced

Just as organic growing is not primitive agriculture, neither is organic winemaking a throwback to some pre-industrial period. We could argue, in fact, that organic viticulture is the most modern of all, because organic producers are only now developing and learning methods that ensure good quality and keeping properties—a sort of ideal combination of science and nature.

Some who sampled organic wines, say, 10 years ago might have been disappointed in a product that was cloudy, sometimes with little bits of material visible in the liquid. Today's organic wines are clear, clean, and fresh.

Vino Vocab

Would you like to sample French organic wine in its country of origin? Well, don't ask for "organic wine." In France, it's called vin bio (short for "vin biologique").

Organic winemakers pay close attention to three things: Yeast, fining and filtering (clarification), and sulfur dioxide.

Many organic vintners use only the yeasts that settle and grow naturally on the grape skins. Crop sprays used in conventional viticulture sometimes kill these yeasts. In any event, many conventional winemakers prefer the predictability of cultured yeasts.

Wild yeasts do add an element of variability to organic winemaking, but I've not known this to interfere with the fermentation of any crop. On the other hand, we may see greater year-to-year variability than with more controlled uses of cultured yeasts, which some feel adds to a wine's sense of place on your palate—kind of like looking at your yearly school pictures as you grew up—same kid, but every year you change a little.

Organic vintners clarify their wine with the minimum physical handling. Such handling can introduce oxygen, which increases the need for sulfur dioxide gas for preservation. For some reason, organic certification does not permit the use of the centrifuge (See Chapter 8, High Tech). So far, no one has given me a good reason for this rule.

Filtering is common in organic wine production, often making use of sterilized cellulose material. Another effective filtering agent—and a natural, non-animal one—is diatomaceous earth, microscopic siliceous remains of certain species of algae.

Tasting Tip

Fining (clarification) processes may add trace amounts of foreign matter to the final product. For example, beaten egg white is a common and very effective fining agent. But it does leave a very small quantity of protein in the wine. Some organic vintners sell into markets that seek foods and beverages with no animal products; so egg whites are suitable in their operations.

Finally, as we discussed earlier, organic winemakers minimize their use of sulfur dioxide gas in the growing and production of their product. In fact, some organic growers have proved it's possible to produce good wines without any added sulfites, whatever. Of course, these wines have poorer storage and keeping properties.

Heard it Through the Grapevine

The words "certified organic" on the label not only mean that the methods of growing or production were certified by the USDA, but as of February 2012, that those methods are also approved and in sync with organic products produced in the EU, opening the door for organic products from the United States to be sold in Europe, and vice versa.

Serving Organic Wines

Many organic wines are quite good, and you can serve them with confidence. But also, you must serve them with a little extra care. With minimal processing and preservative (sulfur dioxide), these wines can be very fragile.

Don't Spoil a Good Thing

Did you ever cut an apple into slices and watch them turn brown before your eyes? This is oxidation—a cosmetic problem for apples, disaster for wines. Here's the reason: The parts of your wine that oxidize, generally are those that give it its flavor.

Actually, oxidation becomes a problem the instant the grape is crushed. As soon as the juice is exposed to air, oxidation begins. Oxidation can destroy the appearance of any white wine. And conversion of certain acids can cause a wine to taste herbaceous, like leaves.

The Sommelier Says

Molds present on the grape at the time of crushing hastens the chemical reactions that cause changes in color or taste. So without sulfur dioxide gas to inhibit oxidation, organic growing with extreme care is especially important.

Once wine is bottled, the only oxidation you need to worry about is from the little bit of air trapped in the bottle (or dissolved in the wine), which actually is a necessary part of a wine's development over time. But when you open your low-sulfite or no-sulfite wine, mischief begins immediately.

Of course, there's never any need to open your organic wine early to let it breathe (Chapter 2, Breathers vs. Non-Breathers). It's best to open it just before you serve it. And if reasonable, try to finish the whole bottle. (If it's dinner for one, that would be a bit too much. But read the next section…)

Saving for a Rainy Day

Sometimes you have to store your organic wines. Before opening, that's not too hard. Where sulfites have been added, even below the lower limits imposed on organic vintners, your bottled organic wine should keep for months, even years. That assumes you are quite careful. The same rules apply as with most other wines: Keep it away from heat, bright light, and vibration. And avoid rapid temperature changes.

Once your wine is opened, though, you do have to take special care. Refrigeration slows the processes of oxidation or spoilage, but it cannot stop them altogether. Try to drink the remainder of your low-sulfite wine within a day or two. Or you can put your organic leftovers into your freezer (See Chapter 2, Will It Keep?) and keep it a little longer.

CHAPTER 24

Kosher Wine

In This Chapter

- The why and how of kosher wine
- Why you should consider kosher wine
- Who makes it and where

Jewish or not, you have kosher foods in your house. Check the packages or the labels. See that little letter U inside the circle? Or that little letter K? These are registered symbols of two organizations that certify foods as kosher. You might see one (or both) of these symbols on a bottle of wine, too.

No, kosher is not another grape varietal. And from the standpoint of grape, winemaking style, or country of origin, kosher is irrelevant. Kosher wines come in many varieties and styles and from many lands. Many of these are superior wines in every regard. And a few are, well, unusual—resembling certain wines that were popular in the U.S. 50 years ago.

Kosher? Whazzat?

"Kosher wine? Oh, yeah! It's that purple pancake syrup in the fat bottle." Want another guess? "Okay. It's wine that's blessed by some rabbi." Uh, not quite. Actually, the concept of kosher wine is quite simple.

Heard it Through the Grapevine

If kosher wines are just like other wines in grape varietals, style, and origin, how can you tell what's kosher and what isn't? The easy answer is to check the label for the symbols of either of two organizations that certify food and beverages as kosher.

One is the Orthodox Union, a nearly 90-year-old international body. Their symbol is the letter U inside the letter O. The other is Kosher Overseers Associates of America, which uses a stylized letter K. Producers of food and drink may submit their products to one (or both) of these organizations for kosher certification, for which they pay a small fee.

This is smart marketing, because many observant Jewish families purchase only dietary products that are certified kosher.

Kosher wine, like any kosher food, is wine prepared according to kashrut, the body of Jewish law and tradition that's concerned with dietary practices. Any wine made in accordance with kashrut is kosher.

The strictest Jewish dietary observance doesn't permit consumption of meat and dairy products in the same meal, nor even the use of the same dishes and utensils for both. If even the smallest amount of meat or dairy product is present in the production of food or drink, this will be noted with the kosher symbol, sometimes with just an M or a D.

Tasting Tip

About a third of the food and drink we consume is certified as kosher. That is, it's prepared from ingredients that are themselves kosher using equipment that only comes in contact with ingredients that are kosher.

Kosher foods that are neither meat nor dairy are labeled pareve, which is Yiddish for neutral. (The word pareve may or may not appear on the label.)

There is only one other important restriction: During the eight days of Passover, certain leavened grains and legumes may not be eaten. Foods that are absent these may be labeled "Kosher for Passover" or with the letter P.

What Makes Wine Kosher?

Wine is a special case in Jewish law and tradition. Wine is an integral part of rituals in synagogues or households, such as the Kiddush, a sanctification spoken over wine on the eve of the Sabbath or of a holiday.

For this reason, the kashrut for wine is somewhat stricter than that for other foods and beverages. Wine consumed for sacramental purposes must meet certain very strict requirements.

Special Handling

Kosher certification requires attention to all parts of the wine production process. Certifying bodies inspect wineries to ensure continued compliance.

- All equipment used in growing, fermentation, aging, and bottling must be used exclusively in the production of kosher products.
- The grapes and wine may be handled only by Sabbath-observing Jews. If the wine is mevushal, i.e., pasteurized, this requirement is waived.
- Only kosher-certified products may be used in the winemaking process. These include yeasts and filtering agents.

Mevushal Does the Trick

Jewish commentators believe the Torah (the books of the Bible attributed to Moses) excludes non-Jews from the winemaking process as a means of preventing intermarriage. After all, wine in all is aspects is a great socializer.

The Sommelier Says

The temperatures of pasteurization destroy bacteria, but also they can destroy the flavor components in the wine. Fortunately, technology has come to the rescue.

It's called flash pasteurization. Now it's possible to run wine through special apparatus that heats it and returns it to its original temperature in a fraction of a second—enough time to kill microbes, but not enough to destroy flavor.

Mevushal (pasteurization) is a different issue. Observant Jews may not drink any wine that could be used in pagan worship. Tradition dictates that wine that has been boiled is unfit for such use, making it okay for Jewish use.

Wines that are pasteurized need not be handled only by observant Jews. However, all other requirements of kosher certification must be met.

Not Just for Sacramental Purposes

Fifty years ago many Americans, regardless of religion, could name only two brands of wine: Mogen David and Manischewitz, both kosher wines. Today, many wineries from several countries offer certified kosher wines, in great variety, often of very high quality.

So the best reason to drink a kosher wine is the best reason to drink any wine: because you like it. Remember, you already buy dozens if not hundreds of certified kosher foods through your everyday shopping. The kosher certification has nothing to do with quality or value.

Another reason you might consider kosher wines, particularly if you have a cellar and do much entertaining, is to have some on hand to serve guests who are kashrut-observant. They'll appreciate your consideration no less than you'll appreciate their joining you in wine toasts.

Heard it Through the Grapevine

Most kosher wines are flash pasteurized, or mevushal. Under kashrut, these wines need not be handled exclusively by observant Jews.

This is a practical consideration considering how many hands a bottle of wine might pass through on its way to your table at home or in a restaurant.

Vino Vocab

Kosher is from the Hebrew word that means fitting or suitable.

Kashrut (kash-ROOT) is the Jewish law and tradition of kosher diet.

Pareve (PAH-reh-veh) is Yiddish for neutral, neither meat nor dairy.

Wide Choices

Kosher wines are made in most major wine-producing countries. They range in quality from the most ordinary to the genuinely extraordinary. But you may have trouble finding any in that little wine shop in Smallville.

The nice thing about finding one kosher wine is that you likely will find several in that same wine store. Some importers specialize in locating kosher wines from all over. One with a worldwide reputation is the Royal Wine Corporation in New York City.

Kosher wines are produced in the U.S., France, Italy, Israel, Chile, Canada, and Australia. Not all make it into export markets.

New York

New York State is the original home of the American kosher wine industry. Grapes for these wines come from both the Finger Lakes district and the Hudson Valley. In both regions, the superior vinifera grape is harvested as well as the more traditional labrusca species.

Heard it Through the Grapevine

Owned and operated by members of the Herzog family, the Royal Wine Corporation has made kosher wines since 1848. After the upheavals of war in their native Czechoslovakia and the communist takeover in 1948, the family relocated to the U.S., where they produce, import, and distribute the finest kosher wines from around the world.

The Royal Wine Corporation operates vineyards and a winery at Milton in the Hudson Valley, where they produce some excellent vinifera-based wines as well as the older-style sweetened wines. The Shapiro Wine Company of New York City is America's oldest kosher winery, with their vineyards located in the Finger Lakes region.

They also started the annual, sophisticated Kosher Wine & Food Festival in New York, shining a light on some of the best producers making quality kosher wine the world 'round.

California

The Royal Wine Corporation is a major presence among the kosher wine producers of California, under the Baron Herzog brand. In the Golden State, this house makes wines ranging from good through superb. Their Alexander Valley Special Reserve Cabernet Sauvignon of 1995 is very highly regarded. In 2006, they upped the ante on Herzog, leaving their formerly rented wine-making digs and opening a brand, spanking new winery, education center, tasting room, and restaurant in Oxnard an hour north of Los Angeles, where visitors can tour (on all days except the Sabbath, of course) and learn not just about how wine is produced, but what kosher means and the how winemaking fits into its religious restrictions.

Other major players in California's kosher wine trade are Hagafen Cellars, Weinstock Cellars, Covenant Wines, and the more boutique Four Gates. Also, there are many small-but-dedicated vintners supplying demand for kosher wines.

Celebrating? Look for the kosher symbol on some bottles of non-vintage Korbel Brut sparkling wine.

France

When you think of France, you think of Bordeaux. And Bordeaux evokes the name Rothschild. Yes, that distinguished name has been on a kosher wine since 1986 (after an absence of 100 years), thanks to the efforts of U.S.-based Royal Wine. This is under the label Barons Edmond et Benjamin de Rothschild.

Royal Wine also is responsible for Château de la Grave Herzog Selection Dry Red, a Bordeaux. There are many other kosher Bordeaux, some quite good, such as Château Giscours (Margaux) and Château Yon-Figeac (St.-Emilion). Also, you will find some excellent kosher wines from the Alsace, including the Arbarbanel Gewürztraminer, and even Laurent-Perrier offers a few kosher sparklers in their Champagne portfolio.

Italy

In the Tuscan hills, there is a very old Jewish community at Pitigliano. Near the village is a kosher winery that markets a red and a white under the name La Piccola Gerusalemme, which means Little Jerusalem, Pitigliano's nickname.

From Asti, we find the kosher Bartenura Asti and Bartenura Moscato d'Asti. And while non-kosher wines far and away outnumber the kosher, several more Italian producers are making kosher wines that you can find on shelves here, such as Giordano, Feudi de San Gregorio, Cantina Gabriele, Borgo Reale, and Falesco.

Israel

Let's not forget: Israel is a Mediterranean country, and its semiarid climate and harsh soils make for some pretty good wines.

Tiny Israel has more than 150 wineries across its five official winegrowing regions. They are Galilee, Golan Heights, Samaria, Samson, and Negev. These regions grow popular European varietals, according to the regional conditions of soil, drainage, rainfall, and temperature.

The country's largest producer in the Sansom region is Carmel, a brand that has been around since 1882 and imported for many decades. Many years ago. these wines closely resembled those oversweet kosher wines of the U.S., and many in their line still do. (They know their market well!) However, Carmel's varietal wines are similar to those inexpensive ones from California.

Tasting Tip

You don't even need to look on the label. All Israeli wines imported into the U.S. are kosher for the Passover.

The Yarden Gamla winery of the Galilee region sells more than a few good wines from vitis vinifera—in particular, a Sauvignon Blanc that's quite good. Also look out for Domaine du Castel, Banheim, Barken, and Binyamina.

Your Grandfather's Kosher Wine

To many people, the term "kosher wine" means wine that's excessively sweet. Indeed, Americans of a certain age remember when wine meant bottles of Manischewitz or Mogen David, both nationally advertised brands.

The association of kosher with sweetened wines made from the unsuitable labrusca grape species is one of history and geography, unrelated to Jewish dietary laws.

Heard it Through the Grapevine

The Shapiro Wine Company of New York is America's oldest kosher winery—more than 100 years old. Yes, they still make syrupy-sweet fermented Concord grape products in fat bottles. But now they also make lighter and drier wines (also in fat bottles) for more modern tastes.

Around the turn of the century, America took in large numbers of Jews who had fled pogroms in Russia and central Europe. A large portion settled near their port-of-entry, in and around New York City. And what kinds of grapes were grown then in the American Northeast? That acidic and ubiquitous Concord grape!

Today, even the oldest kosher wineries produce a variety of fine wines from the superior European vinifera grapes, wines no one would be embarrassed to serve. And yet, the old sweet stuff in the fat bottles remains in these wineries' catalogues. Why? Tradition! Many old-timers (not necessarily Jewish) will drink nothing else.

PART FOUR

Let's Go Wine Shopping!

CHAPTER 25

Decoding a Wine Bottle

In This Chapter

- Basic wine bottle shapes
- How to read a label
- Bottling terms that describe origin, style, and quality

At one time, the shape of a wine bottle told us exactly what was inside. Each part of the world and each style of wine had its own distinctive bottle. But bottles have become somewhat standardized, and the information they communicate has become rather fuzzy.

I find it interesting that the most unusual bottles point to wines that fall on opposite ends of the quality spectrum. The most expensive Champagnes, for instance, typically are bottled in special shapes that are unique to the brand. But then, some of the cheapest plonk attempts to disguise its lack of character with an attention-getting container. And then there are producers who eschew all the trappings of book-cover judging, and go straight for the most eco-friendly, lightweight package they can use, thinking more about carbon footprint than making a mark on the eye of the beholder.

This chapter introduces you to the things you need to know about wine bottles. Then we'll deal with the labels. I hope all this will help make you a savvy wine-shopper.

Shape Matters

Wine bottles come in several general shapes, each with its own variations. Here are the most common:

- Red Bordeaux. The red Bordeaux bottle (also sometimes called by its British term, Claret) has straight sides with sharp shoulders. This shape is used for wines made in the Bordeaux style, as well as wines grown and bottled on Bordeaux soil. Red Bordeaux, Sauternes, and Graves wines all are packaged in this squared-off bottle. So are California varietals such as Cabernet Sauvignon, Merlot, Sauvignon Blanc, Semillon (all Bordeaux vinifera), and Zinfandel, considered a Bordeaux style.

Vino Vocab

The terms claret and hock once referred, respectively, to the reds of Bordeaux and the whites of the Rhine. They both seem a bit quaint today. Neither term on a label has any legal standing.

- Burgundy. Wines fuller in body or richer in perfume than red Bordeaux-styled wines generally are bottled in the rounder, slump-shouldered Burgundy bottle. California Chardonnay and Pinot Noir—Burgundy varietals—are sold in the Burgundy bottle. Fuller-bodied Spanish wines and the sturdier Italian wines (such as Barolo and Barbaresco) find their way into variants of this shape.
- Hock (Rhenish white wine). The German Hock bottle is tall, slender, tapering, and brown in color. Its variant is the similar, but green-colored, Mosel. (The traditional rule in Germany is Rhine wine in brown bottles, Mosel in green.)

The Sommelier Says

This rule of brown for Rhine wine and green for Mosel no longer is 100-percent true. Some Rhine wines arrive now in blue bottles, but at least you won't see Mosel in brown or Rhine in Green.

The hock shape is used throughout the world, but be warned: It is not a sure indicator of the kind or quality of wine within.

Most wines from Alsace are bottled in a shape similar to the hock. So are many California Rieslings, Gewürztraminers, and Sylvaner varietals.

- Bubbly bottles. The Champagne bottle is a variant of the Burgundy bottle—sort of a fatter and sturdier cousin. It usually has an indentation, or punt, at the bottom, and thick walls to withstand the pressure of the carbonation.

Heard it Through the Grapevine

These days, there are more than a few producers who are trying to reduce their carbon footprint on ol' Mother Earth by using bottles with much smaller punts, or without the punt indentation at all. Why? They weigh less and, presumably, use up less fossil fuel in their transport from here to there.

As mentioned at the beginning of the chapter, the most expensive Champagnes usually are bottled in signature shapes. The flaring Champagne cork—the legacy of Madame Cliquot, along with the sparkling wine bearing her name—is a laminated seven-piece closure constructed to guarantee a tight seal with plenty of strength once it is in the bottle neck.

The reason for the deep green or brown color of most wine bottles is more than aesthetic: The color protects the wine from sunlight. (You wear sunglasses. Why shouldn't your wine?)

Tasting Tip

If you're the proud owner of a brand-new pleasure vessel or vehicle you'd like to christen with a magnum of bubbly, sparkling wine vintners make special christening bottles for the purpose. You would need an awful lot of muscle to smash the solid, reinforced glass of a real Champagne bottle.

Brown glass may give better protection than green, and often it's used for low-alcohol, sweet-finished white wines. But technology is supplanting tradition. With advances in winemaking and better methods of stabilizing wines for bottle aging, clear glass has become more popular. Even traditional winemakers are giving honor to the phrase, "What you see is what you get."

The varied shapes of wine bottles.

Magnums and More

In addition to different shapes, wine bottles come in varying sizes. The standard size (worldwide now) is 750 ml, which is approximately four-fifths of a quart (a fifth of a gallon). The other more common sizes are 375 ml, which is a half-bottle, and the magnum (two bottles, or 1.5 liters). A double magnum (3 liters) contains four standard bottles. A wine bottle containing six standard bottles is a Jéroboam, and a bottle containing eight standard bottles is an Impériale.

In Champagne, bottle nomenclature is somewhat different (see Chapter 21). A magnum is still a magnum, but a bottle containing four standard bottles is called a Jéroboam. A Rehoboam contains six standard bottles; a Methuselah contains eight standard bottles; a Salmanazar contains 12 standard bottles; a Balthazar contains 16 standard bottles; and a Nebuchadnezzar contains 20 standard bottles (perfect for Babylonian orgies or other big celebrations).

A Vintage—Not Just a Year

The date on the bottle is the wine's vintage. It tells you the year the grapes were harvested and nothing more. The fact that there is a date on a bottle is not an indication of quality by itself. However, most wines with a vintage are better wines.

Some everyday wines for which the vintage is of no importance might carry a vintage date to make them appear better than they are. To determine whether the region's vintage is good, great, or poor, you need to consult a vintage chart such as the one on the tear-out card in the front of this book. Or look in wine magazines or newsletters, which provide the scoop on the latest vintages.

Earlier chapters have discussed the requisites for a great vintage: the right amount of rainfall at the right times; ideal day and night temperature profiles; and sunshine. A great vintage is Mother Nature's nurturing smile on the tender succulents, allowing them to bathe, nap, and gradually reawaken refreshed and energetic, with just the right balance of acid, sugar, and flavors.

Heard it Through the Grapevine

Avoid poor vintages. The wines will be feeble, insipid, vapid—not exactly what you want to start your wine collection! There are exceptions, though.

Every poor vintage has at least some properties that can make a good wine. You can find out which wines are good by reading reviews in wine magazines, newsletters, or by surfing the online services or the Internet.

Wine drinkers tend to malign average vintages, but doing so really is unfair. True, average vintages lack the complexity and finesse of great vintages, but they're quite capable of providing a savvy consumer with some perfectly delightful wine-drinking, and usually at reasonable prices. Also, always remember that a good producer will make good wine just about all of the time (and great wine in the great years!). Get to know producers, and you'll always have a good gauge of the quality in the bottle.

There have been some great vintages! Every flavor nuance is ready and waiting to incite your nose and taste buds into a peak sensory experience. The balance is secure, the breed is bred, and the wine has a body and concentration that other wines can only envy.

How do you know what vintages have been so favored? As I said earlier, you need to consult your vintage chart. Investing in a fine wine should not be a matter of trial and error. Sometimes it's just a good idea to let someone else do some of the work.

Back Label Secrets

The back label is the one that doesn't have the picturesque scene of the vineyard or the name like Château d'Yquem with its royal crown. This label hardly seems important enough to read. However, it may contain information that is useful to you, or at least interesting. It's certainly worth a peek.

Laws control the exact content on the front label. But they say nothing about the back. That's left to the vintner's (or importer's) imagination.

The back label is where bottlers may tell you what foods are a good match for the wine or what temperature brings out its peak flavor. Or the label may offer an engaging story about the wine or the winery. Or maybe a map of the wine-growing region. Or a history of the grape. Or maybe some technical gobbledygook about pH or Brix. But you won't know if you don't look.

Bottling Terms

We've examined wine labels throughout this book. So now you're up-to-speed on your AOC, QmP, DOC, and VDQS, right? Or do you imagine the wine label is some kind of legal document or a geeky home page on the Web? Actually, it is a legal document, the purpose of which is to let you know what is in the bottle you just might take home with you.

Labels on wines sold in the U.S. are approved by the Bureau of Alcohol, Tobacco and Firearms (BATF), part of the Treasury Department. In addition to collecting alcohol taxes, BATF must ensure that the information on a wine bottle is truthful, accurate, and complete.

Tasting Tip

All imported wines must conform both to the mandatory label requirement of the U.S. and to the regulations of the country of origin. (Individual states may impose their own regulations, but these may not conflict with federal standards.)

American labels are simple. This has its good and bad points. On the plus side, more concise labeling is less likely to be misleading. On the negative side, American wine labels tell us very little about the contents of the bottle. (By law, at least. Many producers choose to provide excellent information.)

Of course, the EU (European Union) countries have strict standards for labeling, which make labels relatively easy to read—as long as you know what to look for.

Origin Descriptors

The origin descriptor tells us where the wine comes from. The descriptor starts with the country of origin. Some examples are Product of France and Product of Spain. All imported wines have these.

Next, we run through region, state, vineyard, château—whatever level of description is allowed for the particular type or quality of the wine. Not all vintners will use all the descriptors they're entitled to. Some renowned French estates, such as Château d'Yquem, list only the vineyard and the name of its producer. (Hey! What more is needed?) On the other hand, an origin descriptor on the label of a superior German wine may set a world record for syllable-count.

Quality Descriptors

Under EU regulations, a label with the vineyard name indicates better quality than one that lists only a region.

AOC, DO, DOC, and QmP are quality indicators at their most basic. In France, there are the crus: Cru Classé (classified growth), Premier Cru, and Grand Cru. These indicate both origin and quality. In Italy there is Classico—referring to a special smaller wine zone—and Riserva, which indicates extra aging. Spain has Reserva and Gran Reserva. In Portugal these words become Reserva and Garrafeira (although requirements differ somewhat). And in Germany we have Prädikat, which means the wine has something special to report of its quality and style.

The Sommelier Says

I'm a little amused when I see a label on a bottle of U.S. wine with the words Classic or Reserve. In terms of legal standards, they mean nothing, nothing at all! Except, possibly, an excuse to slap on a higher price tag.

U.S. wines carry quality descriptors like Late Harvest or Botrytis, and sparkling wines are required to state whether they are produced by the traditional method (fermented in this bottle) or the transfer method (fermented in the bottle). (Only true Champagne may use the French term Méthode Champenoise on the label.) Other than these quality descriptors, you're on your own.

Style Descriptors

Style descriptors are required legally only on German wines and on Champagne. These descriptors indicate the wine's sweetness or dryness (percentage of residual sugar). Some non-German wine labels do include style descriptors, but these are at the whim of the individual producer. (In the absence of a style descriptor, you have yet another reason for knowing your wines.)

Heard it Through the Grapevine

Since its inception in 2007, the International Riesling Foundation (www.drinkriesling.com) has worked to raise awareness among consumers of what, exactly, sweet can mean. One way they appear to be accomplishing this is via the Riesling Taste Profile chart, a chart that now appears on over 26,000,000 bottles in America alone that grades what's in the bottle from dry to sweet to help consumers better understand Riesling.

General Terms

The most basic terms are white, red, and rosé (in the language of the wine's native land). A few variations exist. For example, Italian wines may be labeled Nero (black), which means very dark red. But really, you need to judge color gradations for yourself. (In your glass—not in the green bottle!)

These general terms include most of those things that don't fall into the other categories. There's the term Table Wine, for instance, that's required on imports, optional on U.S. wines. And there are instructions to serve at room temperature or to serve chilled, which are entirely optional. The vintage also can fall into the category of general information. (If you know your vintages, it is a quality descriptor as well.)

Mandatory Information

Along with the country of origin, alcoholic content and bottle volume are imperative on all labels. Volumes of imported wines are listed in standard metric units (milliliters, ml, or centiliters, cl), and the bottles conform to approved sizes. The name and address of the importer, producer, and/or négociant are required on all labels. For California wines, the name and address of the bottler and the Bonded Winery (B.W.) license number are required.

Heard it Through the Grapevine

American labels provide the consumer with a lot of data concerning who owned the grapes and who selected, bottled, produced, and cellared the bottle's contents. But if you're looking for a quality assessment, you may feel as though you're reading a weather report for every city but your own.

Quality labeling of wines from EU countries is required, conforming to EU, national, and local regulations. These are not required for U.S. wines. (On the other hand, varietal names are mandatory only on American wines.)

The French Wine Label

The French wine label provides a lot of information that gives you clues to the quality of the wine. The label provides exacting information through its system of Appellation Controlée regulations, which are linked to carefully defined geography.

By law, the smaller the piece of property named, the more stringent the regulations are for methods of cultivation and production. Other than names of properties and estates, the names of the négociant (if any) and importer must appear on the label; so knowing the reputations of these companies is useful. Frequently, the name of the négociant or shipper is a clue to the quality of a wine from an unknown property.

French Origin Descriptors

The abbreviation AOC or AC on a label stands Appellation d'Origin Controlée. VDQS stands for Vins Délimités de qualite Supérieure, the second rank below AOC of delimited wine areas. Vins de Pays is the next rank below AOC.

Cave is the French word for cellar (easy to remember). Château-bottled, Mis au Château, Mis en bouteilles au Château, Mis au (or du) Domaine, and Mis en bouteilles au (or du) Domaine all mean estate-bottled, and they have legal significance.

The Sommelier Says

Be careful! Mis dans nos caves, Mis par le propriétaire, and Mis en bouteille a la propriete all may sound as though they describe estate-bottled wine. But they don't! Some sellers put these terms on the bottle to deceive the consumer into believing that the wine is estate-bottled when it isn't. Such terms have no legal definition.

A Négociant is a businessperson who purchases wine from growers and bottles it under a proprietary brand (or under the individual château name). An Eleveur is a négociant who buys young wine from the grower and matures it in his own cellars. Propriétaire-Récolant means owner and manager of a property.

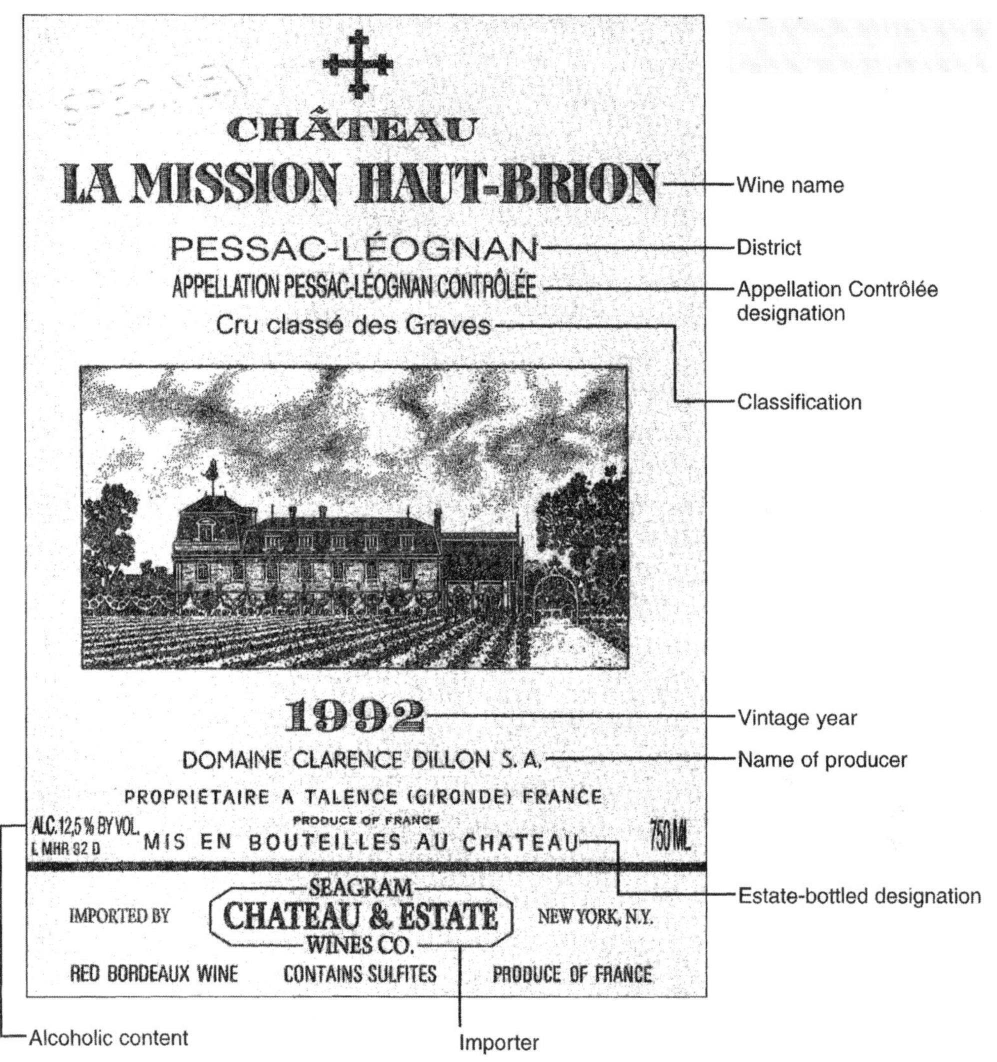

A Bordeaux wine label.

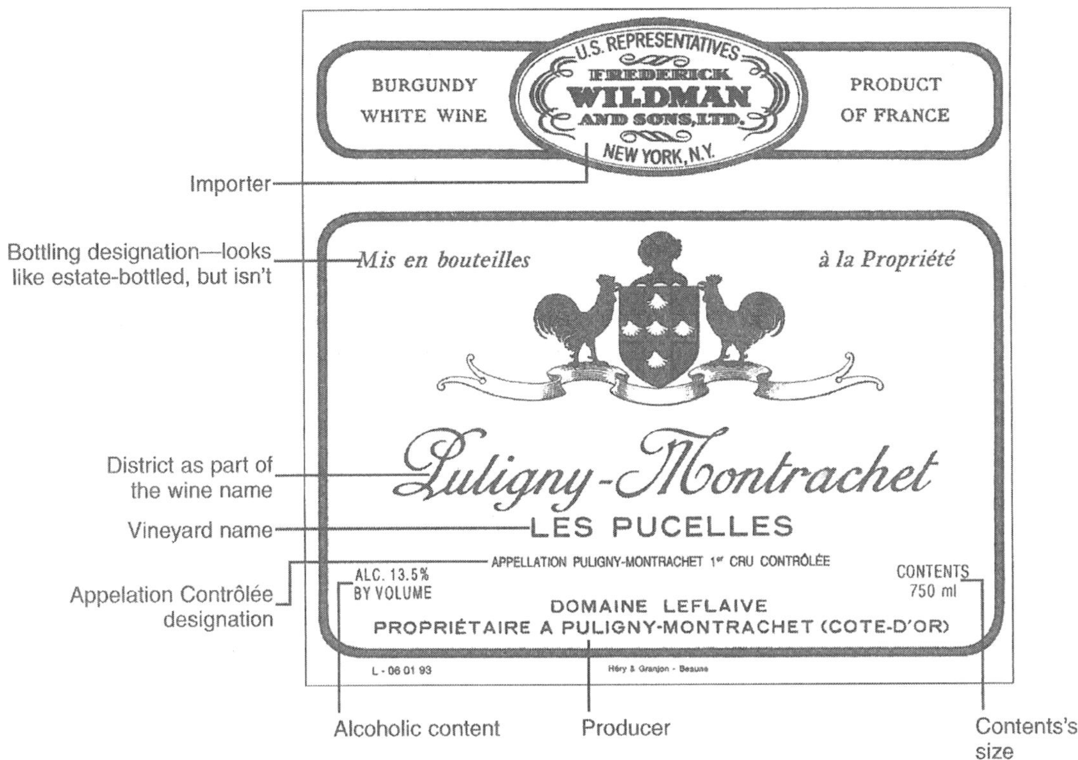

A Burgundy wine label.

French Quality Descriptors

Appellation Controlée is both an origin descriptor and a quality descriptor, as French geographical designations are linked to quality regulations. Cru Bourgeois in Bordeaux refers to the many good vineyards just below the classified growths in quality.

Cru Classé is a classified growth of Bordeaux, the most famous of which is the 1855 classification of the wines of the Médoc. (See Chapter 10, The 1855 Overture). This is preceded by the level of the cru, such as Premier Cru Classé. Cru Exceptionnel is a Bordeaux classification between cru Bourgeois and Cru Classé. Grand Cru means great growth—in Burgundy the highest level of classified vineyards, in Bordeaux the highest of the five levels of classified growths.

Grand Vin means great wine, but it has no legal definition. Anyone can use this term! Premier Cru means first growth—in Burgundy the second level of classified growth, in Bordeaux the top level of classified growths. Méthode Champenoise (fermented in this bottle) is the legally defined term for the champagne method of sparkling wine production. Supérieure indicates that the wine is at least one degree of alcohol above the minimum required for a particular AOC. (Note: The term does not mean that the wine is better or superior.) VDQS and Vin de pays relate to the quality of a non-AOC wine.

French Style Descriptors

Vin Blanc means white wine, Vin Rouge means red wine, and Vin Rosé means rosé wine. Sur lie refers to wines bottled off the lees, without racking or filtering. Pétillant means slightly sparkling or crackling. Mousseux refers to sparkling wine other than Champagne. Blanc de Blancs refers to a white wine made entirely from white grapes. (You usually see the term on Champagne bottles.) With Champagne and Mousseux, Brut means almost dry, but Extra Dry means slightly sweeter than Brut. Brut Sauvage or Sauvage means completely dry. Demi Sec means semi-sweet, which is quite sweet. Finally, Doux means even sweeter than quite sweet.

Tasting Tip

Do you like your Champagne extra dry? Then don't get Extra Dry, which is sweeter than Brut. You want even drier? Look for the word Sauvage.

French General Terms

Année means year. Recolte means crop or harvest, and Vendange means grape harvest, (used synonymously with année). A Chai is an above-ground building where wine is stored in cask. Chambré is the French word for bringing a red wine from cellar temperature to room temperature (as in Servir Chambre). Servir Frais means to serve chilled. Château in Bordeaux refers to a single estate—elsewhere it may be part of a brand name. Domaine means wine estate. Clos means walled vineyard. Côte refers to a slope with vineyards as opposed to graves or flatter, gravelly land. Cru means growth and refers to a legally defined vineyard. Cuvée is a vat or batch of wine.

The German Wine Label

The German wine label is exceedingly precise as to quality. Its descriptions are linked closely to growing regions—large down to tiny; to a designation of quality; and also to the degree of ripeness achieved by the grapes that went into the wine.

These labels appear more complicated than they are. They are less intimidating once you learn the system. The region in which the wine is produced and the ripeness of the grapes are the two main elements, and both items play important roles on the label.

The German Grosslage wine label.

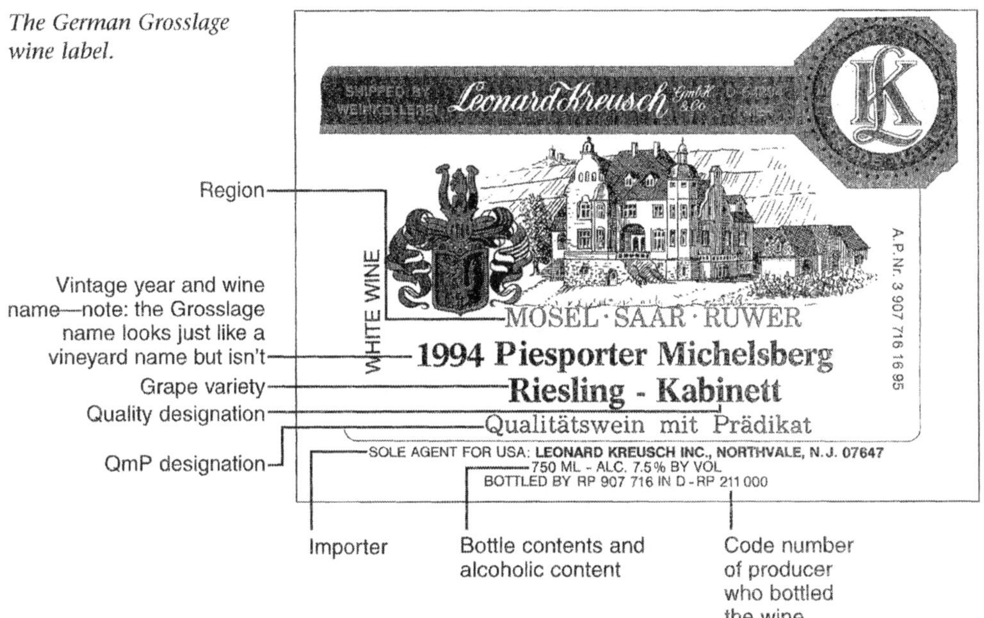

The German Einzellage wine label.

German Origin Descriptors

A Gebiet is one of Germany's 13 major wine regions. A Bereich is a large sub-region of a Gebiet. A Grosslage is a subdivision of a Bereich consisting of numerous adjoining vineyards that may span the boundaries of many villages.

Grosslage names sound like individual vineyard names. So you need to memorize Grosslage names to avoid buying a village wine when you want higher-quality wine (see Appendix A). An Einzellage is an individual vineyard site with a minimum size of approximately 12 acres. Vineyards smaller than 12 acres are given the name of a nearby Einzellage and are of similar quality and style.

Vino Vocab

The German word for still wine is pretty easy to figure out. It's Stillwein. The term for sparkling wine is not so obvious. It's Sekt. (But sometimes, Sekt means only "dry wine.")

An Abfüller is a bottler, and Abfüllung means a bottling, as from the producer's own estate. Aus Eigenem Lesegut and Erzeuger Abfüllung mean estate-bottled. Eigene Abfüllung means bottled by the producer. A Keller is a cellar, and a Weinkellerei is a place where wine is made, but not grown. (Isn't this logical?)

A Weingut is a wine estate. And a Weinhändler can be a wine shipper, wine merchant, or vintner. Winzergenossenschaft and Winzerverein both mean winegrower's cooperative. AP (Amtliche Prüfungsunummer) is the official testing number found on all better German wines. This encodes the place of origin, the producer's individual number, the individual lot number, and the year (not necessarily the vintage) that the lot was submitted for testing.

German Quality Descriptors

Tafelwein is table wine, the lowest level of quality. Tafelwein may not bear a vineyard site name. QbA (Qualitätswein bestimmter Anbaugebiete or just Qualitätswein) refers to a wine from a specific origin and is the middle level of German wine quality. QmP (Qualitätswein mit Prädikat) refers to wine with special attributes, the top level of wine quality consisting of six degrees of ripeness. No chaptalization ever is permitted for these wines!

German Style Descriptors

Kabinett is the basic grade for QmP wine that must be made from grapes with sufficient natural sugar to produce a wine with a minimum of 9½ percent alcohol. Spätlese means late picked and refers to a wine made from fully ripened grapes. Auslese is a term describing very ripe late-picked grapes that render a fairly sweet and luscious dessert wine. These are hand-selected, bunch-by-bunch.

Tasting Tip

German sweetness rankings are quality indicators, though not in the sense of one being better than another. Which one you choose will depend on how you'll serve it and on your preferences.

A cool, crisp Kabinett makes a wonderful apéritif. A rich, fruity Auslese goes well with many dinner entrées. And what better dessert wine than a perfumy, syrupy (and expensive) Trockenbeerenauslese!

Beerenauslese is a very sweet wine made from even later-picked, overripe grapes, selected grape-by-grape. Some of these may have been shriveled by Botrytis (noble rot). Trockenbeerenauslese is wine made entirely from grapes shriveled by Botrytis. During the harvest, the pickers keep these grapes separate from the others. Eiswein is a sweet, concentrated wine made from frozen grapes that may not be affected with Botrytis.

German General Terms

There are some general sweetness descriptors in use. Trocken will refer to a wine that's complete dry. Halbtrocken is half-dry or off-dry wine. Some other general terms are Perlwein, a mildly sparkling wine, and Sekt, a sparkling wine.

Moselblümchen is a generic wine from the Mosel that is in the Tafelwein class. Liebfraumilch is a generic wine from the Rhine region that is in the QbA class. A Fass is a cask, and a Fuder is a very large cask. Rotwein means red wine, and Weisswein (written in the German alphabet as Weißwein) means white wine. A Schloss is a castle, in this case, a wine estate. Staatswein refers to wine from government-owned vineyards.

The Italian Wine Label

Italian wine labels provide a fair amount of meaningful information regarding what is in the bottle. Nomenclature for certain wines is regulated under laws enacted in 1967, modeled after the French, but without the refinement of official classifications. The Italian wine-regulating system, the Denominazione di Origine Controllata (DOC) is government-approved and defines growing regions.

Heard it Through the Grapevine

For several types of wine, the DOC guarantees certain minimum standards of production. Good-quality Italian wines indicate the place, either as the name of the wine itself (Chianti, for example) or linked to a grape variety, such as Barbera D'Asti or through a DOC designation. Not all places have earned DO status, but most better Italian wines sold within the United States are DO wines.

If a grape name is not accompanied with a place (Nebbiolo d'Alba, for example), chances are the wine lacks distinction. Denominazione di Origine Controllata e Garantita (DOCG) is the highest grade of Italian wine and is granted only to regions making the highest quality wine.

The Italian wine label.

Italian Origin Descriptors

Classico refers to a wine made in a legally defined inner section of a wine district. It's supposed to denote a higher quality. IGT (Indicazione Geografica Tipica) is a classification introduced in 1992, and is the equivalent of the French Vins de Pays, and you can say was a direct result of quality producers busting out of their DOC-restrictions—namely, what grapes they could use by law. The IGT designation indicated as quality wine with grapes that are not considered part of the delimited DOC or DOCG qualifications.

DOC refers to a quality wine from specified grapes in a delimited wine district, produced in accordance with DOC wine laws. DOCG is wine made from a delimited district that has earned this highest-quality designation.

Cantina means winery or cellars. Cantina Sociale is a winegrowers' cooperative. Casa Vinicolà means wine company. A Consorzio is a local winegrowers association with legal recognition. Infiascato alla fattoria, Imbottigliato nel'origine, Imbottigliato del produttore, and Messo in bottiglia nel'origine all mean estate-bottled. Imbottigliato nello stabilimento della ditta means bottled on the premises of the company, but not estate-bottled. A Tenuta is a farm or agricultural holding.

Italian Quality Descriptors

As you know, DOC and DOCG are quality descriptors. Riserva means aged in wood for a time specified by law. Riserva Speciale means aged one year longer than Riserva. Stravecchio means very old, but you'll see that rarely.

Vino Vocab

You've heard of Spumante, sparkling wine from Italy. But what do Italians call semi-sparkling wine? Frizzante!

Italian Style Descriptors

Secco means dry, while amaro means very dry (bitter). Abboccato and amabile (literally, lovely) mean off-dry or semi-sweet, with amabile being sweeter than abboccato. Dolce means sweet. Cotto refers to a concentrated wine. Passito refers to wine made from semi-dried grapes. Vin santo is wine made from grapes dried indoors.

Italian General Terms

Vino da Tavola means tablewine. Bianco means white wine; rosso means red wine; and rosato means rosé wine. Nero is very dark red. Oh—and those funny little bottles with the woven straw? They are fiasci (plural of fiasco).

The United States Wine Label

In terms of legally defined nomenclature, very little on an American wine label helps us to tell a high-quality wine from an ordinary wine. Terms such as Reserve, Special Reserve, Vintner's Reserve, and so on, have no legal regulation, and they are used routinely on mediocre or poor wines.

American wine districts are limited solely to defining geography, with no concomitant regulations as to grape varieties that may be grown, yield, or production methods as do the French, Italians, and Germans. To tell the difference between two wines from a particular wine district (Napa Valley, for example), you must have a real knowledge of the individual producers.

With American wine, caveat emptor is the rule. The U.S. government seems to have no interest in giving us quality clues.

The Sommelier Says

Yes, it's true: Some U.S. wine districts are reputed to be better than others. However, a well-made wine from a lesser district can be far superior to a large-yield wine from a more respected district.

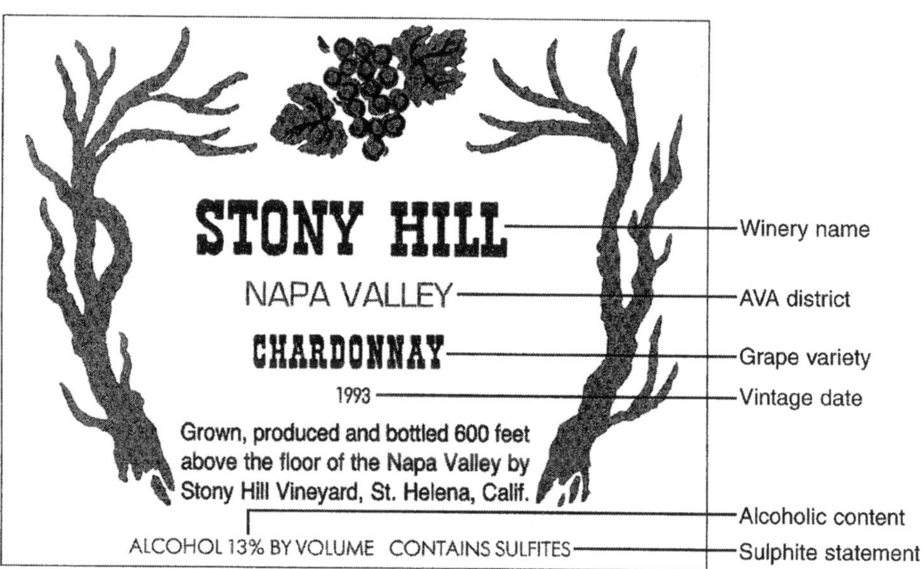

The American wine label.

American Origin Descriptors

The single word American means that the wine can be a blend of wines from different states. A state name means that 75 percent of the wine must be from the named state—unless it's California, where regulations require it to be 100 percent Californian.

A county name means that 75 percent of the wine must be from the named county. All valley, district, and regional designations on the label must be BATF-approved viticultural areas (AVAs), and at least 75 percent of the wine must come from the named area. The rule of thumb is that the smaller the geographical area specified, the better the quality. Just remember, such a descriptor provides no quality guarantee.

Something that looks like B.W. No. 0000 is the bonded winery's license number. Grown by means the grapes were grown by the named winery. Selected by means that the wine was purchased by the named winery. Made and Bottled by means that the named winery fermented at least 10 percent of the wine and bottled all the wine. Cellared and Bottled by means that the named party blended and/or aged or otherwise treated and bottled all the wine.

Produced and Bottled by, Proprietor (or Vintner) Grown, and Bottled by mean that the named party fermented at least 75 percent of the wine and bottled all the wine. Estate Bottled means that the named party fermented all the wine from grapes 100 percent from the named AVA (American Viticultural Area); that the grapes came entirely from the party's own vineyards or vineyards in which the party controls the viticultural practices; and that the wine was bottled on the same premises where it was made.

American Quality Descriptors

Reserve, Vintner's Reserve, and Special Reserve are mere label puffery with no legal definition. In some cases, these terms may appear on the best of the producer's wine. But in other cases, the wine is of the same, or maybe of lesser, quality as the producer's regular line. Rare and Classic, usually seen on the least expensive wines, has no legal definition. Such wine rarely is either rare or classic!

Nouveau refers to wines that are quickly fermented by carbonic maceration and bottled immediately after fermentation. Late Harvest means the wine was made from overripe grapes that may or may not be affected with Botrytis.

Brix is a measure of potential alcohol based on the sugar content of the grape when it was harvested. Residual sugar refers to the amount of remaining natural sugar in the wine after fermentation is completed. (More than one percent tastes sweet, although this can also depend on the acidity levels in the wine.) Off-dry refers to wine that has a little residual sugar but not enough to be sweet. Botrytis means the grapes were affected with Botrytis (noble rot). And remember, Fermented in the bottle refers to sparkling wine made by the transfer method, while Fermented in this bottle refers to sparkling wine made by Méthode Champenoise.

American General Terms

In the U.S., the term table wine refers to wine that is less than 14.5 percent alcohol (although you will see many wines these days topping that number) and made without additional alcohol. Dessert wine is more than 14.5 percent alcohol, usually a sweet wine fortified with additional alcohol. White is, well, white wine. And red is, uh, red wine. (You knew that, already. But did you know rosé wine can be called either rosé or blush?)

CHAPTER 26

Swimming in the Wine Market

In This Chapter

- Finding a good wine merchant
- Money-saving techniques for buying wine
- Wine auctions
- Secrets of the wine trade

Think of wine-buying as a challenge. If you're buying a car, a TV, a laptop, or some other big-ticket item, what do you do to make sure salespeople really know their stuff? You ask questions! Unfortunately, most purchasers of wine are intimidated by the process.

There's no need to be. In this chapter you will learn how to locate the best wine store. You'll learn, also, how to identify and use other sources of wine.

The Sommelier Says

Let's say you've found a store where the answers are quick, the advice copious, and the tone authoritative. Maybe. Maybe not. You can get all this from someone who knows little or nothing of the wines in stock! So it pays to bring a little knowledge of your own.

Finding a Good Wine Merchant

The best wine merchant is the one who understands wines and can advise you on selections that meet your budget and complement your palate. You should spend a little time finding that wine seller.

Be careful: Wine merchants aren't registered stockbrokers, who go to jail if they give you bad information or if they manipulate your account too much. They're just shop-owners, who come in as many varieties as the wines they sell.

Did someone here say varieties? The United States just became the largest wine-consuming nation in the world in 2011—a fact due in part to the notion that we can (and do) have a multitude of bottles from pretty much every wine-producing region in the world available to us. Even the real pros can't possibly know them all. Sometimes, visiting a wine store is like visiting a foreign country. Everything looks familiar, until you read the names. Then they're all different. I've had that experience more than once in wine stores that feature private brands and obscure producers.

So you ask questions, just a few strategic questions that will tell you if a merchant who is knowledgeable, honest, and accessible.

Here are a few questions I use to separate the knowledgeable from those who merely push cash-register buttons:

- What's the difference between a Bordeaux and a Burgundy?
- Why is a bottle of French Burgundy more expensive than a comparable bottle of French Bordeaux?
- What do you recommend in a bottle of dry white wine for less than $15? A domestic sparkling wine for less than $20 to go with roast chicken?

By using this tactic, you are not just testing the merchant. You also are showing yourself as a savvy wine consumer. And if all goes well, this could be the start of a beautiful friendship.

Good wine knowledge is only one criterion. You need also to consider price, service, selection, and storage.

If the Price Is Right

Price is an excellent reason for shopping around (and for knowing your wines). Prices are set by the retailer, not the producer or importer. (Yes, sometimes they are set by state governments.) Generally, you won't see a big difference from one shop to another, except in the case of those shops known for rock-bottom prices. But a couple dollars here and there can add up—especially if you're just beginning to build a wine cellar.

Heard it Through the Grapevine

If you know in advance what you want, check out one of those wine "supermarkets" or giant wine and spirits emporiums. The owners or sales help in these giants are not always knowledgeable about their wares, but the prices can be the best around. With a bit of homework, you can find substantial savings. However, don't go in assuming that everything on their shelves is the cheapest around—do a little research scanning the local paper for ads and comparison shop first.

On the other hand, if you do need advice to help with your selection, it's worth paying more for the right bottle than paying less for the wrong one. In choosing wines, as in most other items, you need to strike a balance between store loyalty and self-interest. No one retailer will satisfy all of your needs.

Service, Service, Service

When you visit a large wine shop, you may feel as though you've walked into a hotel ballroom full of strangers. You'd like somebody to greet you, introduce you around a bit. Willingness to assist is important. As customers, we have a right to cordiality from the wine shop's personnel.

The Sommelier Says

Watch out for the helpful merchant who may be too helpful. You don't need pressure. You do need to know the person who's helping you choose the right Bordeaux for the boss's party or the California white for the barbecue is someone you can trust. A willingness to give advice is great, but only if you can rely on it.

So be critical: Do the merchant's suggestions parallel your desires and requirements? Does the seller share information about new arrivals or good bargains? Ultimately, your judgment will be some combination of savvy and pure gut. By all means, enjoy the rapport you feel with a merchant who seems informed, friendly, and willing to show you around. Just be sure you're sold on more than charm.

Never be afraid to apply your own knowledge. Building your confidence is as important as building your wine cellar, and it can keep you from overspending, too.

Naming Your Price

I strongly recommend framing your questions within a particular price range to indicate you are a value hunter, not a candidate for a quick, high-profit sale. If the merchant responds with a haughty look or with an attempt to steer you to a higher price range, you'll know you're in the wrong place.

Explaining What You Need

Asking the right questions is not only the way to test the merchant's expertise and customer attitude. But I do think it's the only way to get what you need. Some people who have no problem asking for help when shopping for clothing or furnishings wilt at the thought of having to explain their wine preferences.

It's all part of the wine mystique. You may think, "What if they think my taste is gauche? Or worse yet, cheap? What if I use the wrong language? Or what if they think I'm just plain ignorant?" Forget that voice. Instead, listen to the voice that says, "I know what I want and I'm going to find it!"

When you shop, you rely on the expertise of someone who is there for two reasons—to help you and to help the store sell its goods. One way to assure yourself that you'll be explaining your needs correctly—and directly—is to make a checklist of all the points you need to cover to get the right wine:

- Informal, formal, or momentous?
- What foods (if any)?
- Personal preferences and those of guests?
- More than one wine to be served?
- Expect to have leftover bottles?
- Budget for the occasion?

Don't be afraid to use words like fruity, oaky, truffles, vanilla, or any of the things you've learned. A knowledgeable merchant won't judge your taste. (And if the merchant does not understand these terms, you are definitely not in the right place.)

Tasting Tip

Always keep an open mind. If the merchant suggests something different from the type of wine you imagined, don't dismiss the suggestion as poor listening. That wine may work, and the advice may be based on offering you value from a similar-style wine from a different region or producer. On the other hand, if the advice seems to be way off-track, you may need to be more specific.

If the suggested wine seems a bit pricey, the merchant's intent may not be to make more money, but to imply tactfully that a better wine may be more appropriate for your occasion. Buying wine is an interactive experience. Establish a dialogue with the retailer. Explain your needs, listen to answers, and don't be afraid to question advice. A good wine merchant will be as happy as you are to see you go home with the right wine.

The Importance of Selection

The type, range, and assortment of wines are important considerations in choosing your retailer. You may avoid the big emporiums when you're in the market for something special. If you're after a vintage Madeira or the right Trockenbeerenauslese to complement your Bavarian pastries, you simply won't find it in some establishments.

A good wine store will have a selection of wines to meet the needs of discerning customers. Most large wine stores stock a number of fine wines—at lower prices than you may find in a smaller shop. Many stores stock expensive and rare wines that are not on display; so make sure to inquire. (I remember that time I found a $125 Château Haut-Brion Blanc for $25 less at a discounter who kept it hidden in the basement!)

Shops with a limited selection may neglect certain important wines. These shops may have a large selection of several popular wines—Chardonnay, Beaujolais, and Pinot Noir—and quick-selling California jug wines. You may find, also, a few expensive Champagnes and big names (usually off-vintages) from Bordeaux. But beware. This merchant may not have taken the time or effort to learn about wine.

Another example is the merchant who stocks mainly well-advertised brands. Then there are the stores that feature unknown brands from producers or importers who specialize in bargain versions of well-known wine types. These wines may offer good drinking and value, but typically, they're not up to snuff.

Heard it Through the Grapevine

A good selection of wines is one that offers a variety of tastes, styles, occasions, and budgets. The shop should be both well-stocked and well-organized. Look for shops that group wines with careful thought, be it by country and wine type, or the newer trend of grouping wines by what foods they go best with, and frequently by price. And look for rack or aisle markers that can help guide you to your selection.

Some fine shops arrange wines by similar characteristics: Red Bordeaux with California Cabernet Sauvignon; German Rieslings with California Johannisberg Rieslings; Chardonnays and White Burgundies, and so on. This method makes comparison-shopping easier. It also encourages comparative tastings by type, nationality, and by smaller regions and sub-regions.

Wine Storage at the Store

Wine bottles may look good shelved upright in rows like liquor bottles, but stocking better wine this way is deplorable! Especially if the inventory doesn't turn over rapidly. Shops should store wines just as you store them at home. The bottles should be protected from direct sunlight, and bottles with corks (anything better than jug quality) should be lying on their sides.

Window dressing is a key part of selling, but no wines belong in sun-drenched windows. Better shops display only empty or sample bottles in their windows. No good merchant ever sells a bottle from a window display!

Inside the shop is another matter. Most of us like to touch and handle bottles while shopping. (How else do you read the back label?) The better shops keep a bottle of each available wine in a large rack or stacked in such a way that you can reach for it without risking an avalanche. The rest of the stock should be kept in perfect, temperature-controlled storage space.

Temperature control for wine is always important. In the main area, you should find temperature that's constant and cool. If the entire stock is not within sight, I may check to see where the cases are stored. Sometimes, the back rooms of a shop or central warehouse area are far from ideal in climate and general storage conditions. You want to know where the wine has lingered. Storage is especially important if you are buying wines by the case or purchasing old and rare wines.

Tasting Tip

If a wine has been in a cooler for weeks, chances are it's lost some of its freshness or liveliness. Some shops have a chilling machine that can chill your wine in three or four minutes without harming it. If not, buying a bottle and chilling it yourself for about half an hour is far better than taking a chance with pre-chilled wine.

Most wine shops offer a chilled-wine section featuring whites, rosés, and Champagnes. This section is offered as a convenience to customers buying wines for immediate drinking. These wines may tempt you, but you don't know how long those wines have been chilled. You're better off buying at store temperature and chilling at home.

What About Wine Ratings?

Have you ever gone to a movie that received unanimous raves, four stars in the newspaper review, only to be disappointed, dismayed, or just plain disgusted? Fortunately, rating wines is not as subjective as rating movies. Critics evaluate wines using standard criteria developed to assess acidity, tannins, sweetness, and so on.

In recent years, a 100-point system has been adopted by most wine publications and wine critics. But watch out! No one can evaluate wine on such a system with any degree of accuracy (more on this subject in Chapter 27). When reading wine reviews, look for complete and comprehensive tasting notes to guide you to the wines you like. Trouble is that many wine critics do not fully describe a wine in their published tasting notes. But their critique is better than nothing. One of the best things you can do is start to read a wine writer or two regularly. As impartial as anyone can try to be on the basic components of a particular wine, each critic has his or her own leanings that lie in the individual's palate, which you will begin to notice after reading a few reviews. Once you get to know their preference, you can better judge if a particular wine is one that matches with your own likes and dislikes in wine styles.

The Sommelier Says

Because magazines survive on advertising, they may not be your best source for wine ratings. Newsletters and updated consumer guides are more impartial and generally more thorough.

You need to look beyond the numbers. A wine may have a superlative rating, but when you go through the adjectives you may realize the wine is not going to titillate your taste for tannins or awaken your oaky aesthetic. A judicial assessment of words and numbers can help you combine your own knowledge and preferences with the critic's. Studying ratings also helps you become a better rater yourself. (For a list of wine publications, see Chapter 27.)

Saving Money

Nowadays, very few wine shops sell wine at a full markup. Some sell at better prices than others. (Not true, of course, in state-run stores.) Here are some ways to save money when you buy wine:

Discount Stores

A discount or mass merchandiser is a good source for bargains. If you're in the market for an everyday wine, don't be afraid to try unknown or private-label brands. And if you decide you like them, don't be afraid to say so! Forget the wine snobs. You may live in a state where wines are sold in supermarkets, convenience stores, or even drug stores. These places usually are good sources for everyday wines. The prices are reasonable, and you can match the wine with the food right at the source.

Private Labels

Large wine shops, or those that are part of a chain or franchise, often carry private-label wines bearing the name of the outlet or some trademark the retailer owns. Some of these can represent good value. The merchant buys a certain percentage of wines in bulk and has them bottled under the store label. Without the prestigious name of the winery, the wines can be sold for much less.

This concept is the vinous equivalent of designer fashions without the designer prices. Or more closely, supermarket "generic" products that are made by the same brand-name folks (think Trader Joe's famed "Two-Buck Chuck," made for the retailer by the large, well-known California producer Charles Shaw). Yes, quality can vary from batch to batch, but chances are that the merchant who seeks to build a reputation on the store name or exclusive trademark will choose wisely. You may come home with a great bargain.

Second Labels

When a winery selects its wines to make its brand-name wine, it frequently has some lesser-quality (but still good) wine left over. These wines may be from younger vines or vineyard sites that did not ripen to optimum maturity. Often these products are sold under another name, or second label, such as Les Forts de Latour (Château Latour's second label), or an unrelated name.

Tasting Tip

You can find excellent bargains among better winemakers' "second-labels." Keep in mind the expertise from making prime-label wines goes also into making second-label wines. Frequently these are quite good.

Second-label wines can provide excellent drinking. Some wineries also want to increase the amount of wine they sell, making optimum use of their marketing personnel, but they lack sufficient wine to meet the standards for their primary label. The winery may create a second label to market wines of a lesser quality.

Returning a Bottle of Wine

Stores' return policies fall under the heading of customer service. You've paid for your wine, taken it home, cooked the perfect meal, used your best corkscrew technique, and voilà! The odor of rancid corn chips hits you! Okay. It's rarely that obvious, but you are entitled to a product without flaws. You would return a spoiled container of milk, right? You also should return wine that is not up to your standard.

The wine merchant is in business to please consumers, not to alienate them. If the wine seems flawed or the bottle damaged, generally you'll have no problem returning it. If you are returning an unopened bottle (you've changed the menu or found out your guest hates Cabernet Sauvignon), use the same principle that guides the return of most retail items: Return it within a few days of purchase. After a week or two, the merchant is justified in refusing the bottle. (After all, how does the retailer know how you may have stored the bottle?)

Buying Old Wines

Many wine enthusiasts feel the lure sooner or later. It's like the people who start with a few nostalgic knickknacks and suddenly find themselves drawn to the finest antique shops. Someday you may survey your wine collection and think it could do with a few vintage

The Sommelier Says

Some wines from a single case of expensive old wine can be superb, while others are defective. Just remember, when you buy, buy with caution.

Ports or Madeiras. Or you may look to old and rare wines as an interesting financial investment. Or you may host a dinner that calls for a mature bottle from a great vintage. I assure you, those Grand Crus Bordeaux from an excellent vintage can provide for some very exciting wine experiences!

Yes, these wines may be quite expensive. But when you consider the value-added of careful long-term storage, the price for some of these wines may really be quite reasonable. With older wines, the storage and handling is of utmost importance. You need to ask how the wine was stored and where it came from. Inquire about getting a refund if the bottle is not what it should be, because older bottles can have considerable bottle variation.

Investment or Expensive Hobby?

Only the tiniest number of wines are good financial investments. Fortunately, you can spot them, because they share certain qualities:

- Excellent potential for longevity.
- Both press and the industry have given them unanimous commendations.
- Superlative vintages.
- A track record of appreciation.
- Rarity, such that demand drives up the price at a higher rate than with other wines. (Romanée Conti and Château Pétrus are prime examples of wines that command astronomical prices after a decade or so.)

Heard it Through the Grapevine

Even careful attention to the guidelines in this section does not ensure that you are making a good investment. No matter how careful your selections, you always face a major risk. More investment wines depreciate than appreciate in value when you factor in the cost of storage. If you are seriously thinking of becoming an investor, do the same thing you would if you were investing in stocks or commodities: Seek the help of a qualified expert. Some large retail firms can offer advice on investment wines.

Insider's Look at Auctions

Regulation of the purchase or sale of wine at auction are determined by each state. Auctioning wine is totally legal in Illinois, California (of course), and New York. Many other states permit charity wine auctions, but some states prohibit wine auctions altogether. Check with your local wine merchant to find out the story where you live.

Regardless of how modest or expansive your desires, you want assurance that you are dealing with a reputable auction house. In New York, call these places:

- Morrell & Company 212-688-9370
- Sotheby's Auction House 212-606-7000
- Acker, Merrall & Condit 212-787-1700
- Christie's 212-636-2000
- Zachy's 914-448-3026

In the Midwest:

- Chicago Wine Company 847-647-8789
- Davis & Company Wine Auctioneers 312-587-9500

In California:

- Butterfield & Butterfield Auction House 415-861-7500

Online:

- Zachy's www.zachys.com
- WineBid www.winebid.com
- Christie's www.christies.com
- Sotheby's www.sothebys.com
- Wine Gavel www.winegavel.com
- K&L Wine Merchants www.klwines.com

If you want to sell your wine, bear in mind a few facts about most auction houses and retail stores:

- They deal mainly with valuable, prestigious, or rare wine.
- They want to know where the wine comes from. Be ready to prove that the wine has had optimum storage.

- They charge a commission for their services, ranging from 10 percent to 25 percent of the sale price, depending on the deal you make. (The customary rate is 25 percent.) Some auction houses collect a 10- or 15-percent premium from the buyer.
- Some retailers pay you only after they sell your wine; others pay you when they receive the wine. Look for the best deal.

Buying wines at auction has one great advantage: You can find wines you won't find in most wine shops. In most instances, you can purchase old and rare wines only at auction or from a wine company specializing in buying wine collections for resale.

The disadvantage of buying wine at auction is that frequently you don't know the provenance (storage history and ownership) of the wine. If the wine comes from a well-known collector or an establishment known for impeccable storage and care, the auction catalog says so, and such wines usually command a premium price.

Tasting Tip

Auctions are no place to seek younger wines or mature wines that still are in the sales pipeline. With few exceptions, you'll find these wines at better prices elsewhere. (Auction fever frequently results in paying higher than market price.) And remember, at some wine auctions you may be assessed a buyer's premium, typically 10 or 15 percent.

Wine at Your Doorstep

Today, almost every wine ship—from the very boutique to the warehouse-large—sells their wine online or by telephone order (if you like the idea of actually talking to a human being). They ship to any state that subscribes to a reciprocity agreement with their state. And some may ship the wine even if your state doesn't permit it, so check out your local regulations.

Another innovation that has risen alongside our growing American thirst for wine over the last two decades is that of wine-of-the-month clubs, which ship a selection of two to six different wines each month. (If you like the wine, you usually can buy more.) Here are some worth exploring:

- Ahlgren Vineyard Wine Club 408-338-6071
- Ambrosia Wine Club 800-435-2225
- California Wine Club 800-777-4443
- California Winemaker's Guild 800-858-9463
- Gold Medal Wine Club 800-266-8888
- Oregon Pinot Noir Club 800-847-4474
- Passport Wine Club 800-867-9463

Wine Trade Secrets

A knowledge of the inner workings of the wine trade not only is useful in understanding how wines get to your store and how they are priced, but it's fascinating in its own right.

Importers

Although each state has its own regulations, the imported wine trade in the U.S. basically is a three-tiered system: Wine importers and producers sell to a distributors or wholesalers. Distributors and wholesalers sell to a retail merchant or restaurant. And shops and restaurants sell to you. (Of course, the price increases each step of the way.)

Needless to say, the wine industry loves this type of system. It provides the industry players with limited competition and guaranteed profits and debt collection, legally legislated. This system especially benefits retailers in states where minimum profits are maintained by law. Can you blame a merchant who is protected from supermarket competition for fighting to keep the status quo? Unfortunately, consumers pay millions of dollars a year for this legally sanctioned protectionism.

There was a time following the repeal of Prohibition that liquor companies concentrated on high-profit distilled spirits and left imported wines to smaller specialists. (Remember, back then there was no domestic wine industry as we know it today.) During this period, names such as Frank Schoonmaker and Alexis Lichine became famous for their high-quality imported French or German wines.

The renowned Lichine literally barnstormed the country, city to city, persuading restaurants to serve French wines. He also convinced the French to package their wines to appeal to American consumers. Other wine promoters soon joined in courting American buyers.

Heard it Through the Grapevine

During the mid-1960s and early 1970s, giant conglomerates took a serious interest in the wine business and bought several of the fabled wine companies, once renowned for excellent wines. The result was a number of liquor executives, ignorant both of wine and the wine trade, were unable to exercise control over their suppliers or choose new ones with any expertise.

With a few exceptions, the great, old-time wine importers became mere trade names submerged in an industry devoid of any real wine savvy. Today, many wine importers offer a mixed bag of goods—some bad, some good—but some superb. Ironically, the names of some of the most prestigious importers of bygone years now are associated with what to avoid rather than what to buy.

But don't get cynical! You still can count on a few importers to maintain their tradition of quality by selling only dependable merchandise. These firms are few in number, but they specialize in selecting fine wines and particular vintages on a personal level. From these importers you can buy any wine with the confidence that you are buying a superb bottle (some importers distribute domestic wines as well):

- Admiral Imports
- Bacchus Importers
- Banfi Vintners
- David Bowler
- De Maison
- Diageo
- Domaine Select Wine Estates
- Dreyfus, Ashby & Co.
- European Cellars (Eric Solomon)
- Fine Estates from Spain
- Frederick Wildman & Co.
- Jeffrey Davies/Signature Selections
- Jenny & Francois
- Jorge Ordonez

- Kobrand Corp.
- Kysela, Père et Fils
- Louis/Dressner Selections
- Marc de Grazia
- Michael Skurnik
- Neal Rosenthal
- Empson & Company
- Peter Vezan Wines
- Robert Chadderdon Selections
- Robert Kacher Selections
- Select Vineyards
- Steve Metzler/Classical Wines from Spain
- Southern Wines & Spirits
- Terry Theise Selections
- Vineyard Brands
- W. J. Deutsch & Sons
- Weygandt-Metzler Importing
- Winebow
- Wines of France/Alain Junguenet Selections

Distributors

The distributor is the wholesaler who sells the wine to the retailers and restaurants. Sometimes distributors import wine for distribution limited to their market area.

Direct Import

Some wine merchants have discovered clever loopholes in the regulations that give them an edge over their competition, provide better value for customers, and earn them generous profits. The most significant example is direct import.

Here's how it works: The merchant buys wines abroad (wines that are unavailable in the U.S.) and arranges for an importer/wholesaler to bring them into the country. Although many states rule that the wines must be "posted" at a legal resale price to everyone, these wines belong to the merchant, who is free to set the price. For doing the paperwork, the importer receives a stipend per case, sometimes as low as a dollar or two and sometimes as much as $20, depending on importing and warehousing costs.

Tasting Tip

Direct import can mean value for you. Any wine merchant who goes to all the trouble of direct import generally has a good palate—and an eye for a good deal.

The importer tells other retailers that these wines are out of stock—which they are, because the entire shipment went to only one merchant. The merchant can sell these wines for roughly 30 percent below the price of comparable wines from a national importer. Frequently these wines are even better.

Similar arrangements exist for domestic wines. This situation can complicate your comparison shopping, because a higher-priced wine can be notably lower in quality than a little-known bargain brand. If you play your cards right, however, you can emerge the winner. The two keys to bargain-finding success are an experienced palate and good book knowledge. If you have a novice palate, don't despair. Just do a little more homework (especially sipping).

Master of Wine

Master of Wine (MW) is a title bestowed by the Institute of Masters of Wine in London. To qualify, candidates must have considerable knowledge of wine and the wine trade. They need to be well-versed in the wines of the world and in each country's wine regulations and requirements. The prestigious MW is awarded only after passing a rigorous written and tasting examination. The title ensures a high level of competence. (Of course, not all MWs are created equal.)

Once the sole province of the United Kingdom, preparatory programs for the MW are currently offered in the U.S., Australia, and continental Europe. Only a small number of Americans have so far qualified for the title. Most of the 195 Masters of Wine are in the U.K.

For information on how to study for and take the test, write to Institute of Masters of Wine, Five Kings House, 1 24 Fitzroy Square, London W1T 6EP
1QS, England, +44 (0)207 383 9130 or online at www.mastersofwine.org.

Boutique Wineries

California and other states have many small wineries, called boutique wineries, that specialize in finer quality wines.

For years, many of California's finest wines rarely left the state. No, it wasn't some conspiracy by Californians to keep the good stuff from going east. Instead, the lack of national attention reflected a prejudice against domestic wines by the rest of the country. The chain of distribution was weak or nonexistent. But as the number of California wineries grew, the local market could not absorb all the wine produced, and the wineries were not equipped to market their wines nationally.

Marketing organizations quickly cropped up to fill the void. Today, many boutique wineries are promoted by these marketing firms or by national wine importers who have shrewdly recognized these small wineries as a good source of profit. Spotty distribution still remains a problem with many small California, Washington, Oregon, and New York state producers. Some wineries just do not produce enough wine to spread around. Others don't care to be involved with the regulations—which vary from state to state—imposed on the sale and movement of wine. Still others simply can't afford to pay the prohibitive fees imposed by states for registering a brand for sale within its borders.

The Sommelier Says

American wines remain one of the few domestically produced products to face severe restraints in interstate trade. With few barriers to sales of wine in the various states, we consumers would have larger choices at lower prices.

A number of these wineries sell directly to the consumer—in their tasting room or by online or telephone order. And for those of you who like to curl up with a good book, some producers still even offer their wines through mail-order organizations that feature wines in attractive and informative catalogs.

The Giants

When it comes to winemaking, domestic production once dominated by a handful of large and powerful producers in California and New York state, some of which are owned by importing firms or have their own national distribution network, are no longer the only producers that make it into the fray. Today, thanks to better and more diverse magazine coverage, online magazines, and bloggers, medium-to-smaller producers are far more likely to get their names out their these days, many, many miles far and away from where their wineries sit.

Tasting Tip

Remember when Gallo meant "cheap jug wine? No more. Gallo has enjoyed great success in achieving a more upscale image via new labels that the producer has carefully crafted over the years, with vineyards reaching far and beyond California to investments made in Argentina, New Zealand, Australia, South Africa, Spain, France, Germany, and (back where the family name began) Italy. The firm now produces some superb mid- and super-premium wines across its myriad of brand names.

You can find wines from these producers in virtually every wine store throughout the U.S. (Pretty good marketing, huh?) Gallo commands the largest share of the market. Along with a few other biggies, this group takes the lion's share of space in American wine stores. Most of these wines are ordinary jug-quality or simple-premium quality.

CHAPTER 27

The Wine Information Highway

In This Chapter

- Scoring systems
- Wine magazines and newsletters
- Wine on-line
- Books for advanced reading

You think it's hard selecting from among tens of thousands of wines? What about tens of thousands of books, blogs, magazines, articles, brochures, news columns, DVDs, and websites about wine? Actually, tens of thousands is an understatement. A quick Google search turns up 415,000,000 references to red wine, nearly 60,000,000 to white wine, and 55,600,000 to Champagne, alone! And despite the notion that magazine subscriptions are down, wine content has only increased in all the major food magazines on stands.

How can we go through this mountain of information? How can we get information that's both useful and reliable? That's what I'll try to cover in this chapter.

A Word on Scoring Systems

How many times have you heard, "On a scale of 1 to 10…" Everybody does it: Everybody rates things—from school report cards to consumer magazine tests of automobiles, home-theater systems, and computer printers.

With cars and other machines, raters measure things and convert measurements into scores. When perfect scores are added up, you get an even hundred. To read any number of wine magazines and newsletters, you'd think their 100-point rating systems were no less quantitative. But no. We're not rating Champagne bottles for their resistance to breakage under pressure. Instead, we have writers working under pressure to tell us how much they enjoyed a particular Champagne.

It's all subjective. In a blind-tasting, it's unlikely any two wine experts will give identical ratings to, say, half a dozen wines. It's unlikely a single expert will give the same product the same rating six times! That doesn't mean wine ratings are useless. Experts do reach a general consensus on the good, the bad and the downright ugly.

Heard it Through the Grapevine

The 100-point wine rating system was conceived by Robert Parker, a government lawyer who published his ratings in a newsletter, The Wine Advocate. Parker must have been aware that his system cannot be laboratory-accurate. But he bet that the system's appeal would sell newsletters. He was right. Parker's newsletter remains one of the foremost influential pieces of wine information in the field, for consumers, retailers, sommeliers, and, to an extent, producers, too.

Today, however, many experts consider the newsletter's numerical ratings unreliable and often controversial. But that's not stopped many others from emulating Parker's success. Most wine periodicals do the 100-point thing, regardless of its shortcomings.

The problem with wine rating stems from the fact that humans aren't calibrated laboratory instruments. As we wine critics taste wines, we become fatigued from the stress and effort of concentration. And (spitting aside) alcohol still gets into our systems. So wines sampled later in the tasting are at a serious disadvantage, as the palate no longer can perceive their attributes fully.

Even an extraordinary wine tasted late in a tasting of a large number of wines may be considered mediocre. As publisher of *Vintage Magazine*, I had the opportunity to test the palates of some of the A-list tasters who write for magazines and newsletters. Unknown to the participants, I put the same wine in the tasting several times. The expert critics scored the same wine vastly differently each time. In a 100-point system, some scores varied as much as 30 points!

Other experiments have shown that tasters cannot match their tasting notes or numerical ratings with any wine when it is presented a second time. The scores are all over the place.

But don't discard the scoring system entirely. Instead, think of them as helpful clues to what will be in that bottle. Concentrate on the qualitative descriptions in wine publications and see how closely your tastes match those of the writers.

Tasting Tip

For the most part, the scores you see in wine magazines like Wine Spectator, Robert Parker's The Wine Advocate, Wine & Spirits, and Wine Enthusiast are guesstimates. These are knowledgeable and experienced tasters. But none have reliable systems of palate calibration.

I advocate a letter system: A, B, C, D, F, just like school. This is a concise way for getting the point across. (A five-star system works just as well.) The Connoisseur's Guide to California Wine (www.cgcw.com) uses this type of system. The wines are evaluated in a manner similar to movie or restaurant ratings. You're given a point rating with enough information to assist you in making a decision. No pretension, no fuss. Just clear and concise information. (That is, unless you would feel comfortable rating movies or restaurants on a 100-point scale.)

Wine Magazines

Wine magazines are a good source of information about wines that are new on the market, as well as emerging wine regions, in-depth vintage reports, and even wine and food pairing guidance. Also, you get articles and commentary on topics of interest to wine enthusiasts, such as insider information like winery sales, takeovers, obituaries, new projects, and pretty much anything else you can think of. Some magazines specialize in providing lots of up-to-the-minute information. Others offer a more leisurely read. You also can find ads about wine tours, wine education programs, and wine-related equipment and products. These magazines are among the most popular:

- *Decanter*. Published in London, *Decanter* is of interest primarily in the British market. The magazine audaciously proclaims on its stationery that it is the "best" wine magazine. *Decanter* does succeed in being the most authoritative magazine, as many writers are professionals in the trade or full-time wine writers. Monthly, $56.99 a year. www.decanter.com.

- *Wine Spectator*. This publication is arguably the best wine magazine in terms of production values and graphics, with more pages, features, and wine recommendations than any other. However, it often publishes incorrect information, inaccurate vintage assessments, and wine reviews that are bizarre and laughable. The periodical has an underlying tone of arrogance and self-congratulation (which some readers will like).

The Sommelier Says

Wine Spectator employs a staff of full-time writers, both in America and Europe, to provide on-the-scene coverage. However, the writers lack professional training in wine or the wine trade. For instance, no one on the staff is a Master of Wine (MW). Wine Spectator rarely uses freelance writers for its most important coverage.

The magazine rates its wines on an untenable 100-point system that rarely is useful, and its tasting notes frequently are incomplete, though they are useful. The magazine presents the insider's view of the wine world, and for this reason everyone in the wine trade reads it.

Decanter is more authoritative, but the slick, full-color design of *Wine Spectator* has no equal. Large format, 15 issues, $49.95 a year for the print magazine; online-only, 1 year, $49.95. www.winespectator.com

- *Wine Enthusiast*. This publication is a *Wine Spectator* wannabe published by a rival of *Wine Spectator's* publisher, who was denied access to advertising in that publication and decided to publish a wine magazine himself. The main business of this magazine's publisher is wine accessories—and it shows! The features frequently are written by professional freelancer wine writers. *Wine Enthusiast's* paper quality, quality of what's on the paper, and ratings on an untenable 100-point system do not make it a worthy competitor for *Wine Spectator*, but its content has improved over the years. If you are interested in quirky wine info like under-the-radar wine regions and which celeb has a decent wine cellar, you'll enjoy reading this. I do not recommend this publication. Large format, 13 issues, $29.95 a year. www.winemag.com.
- *Wine & Spirits*. This publication covers spirits as well as wine. Its writers mainly are freelancers who are employed full-time in other professions. Wine reviews use the 100-point system. There's not much of interest here unless you are interested in wine ratings. Eight issues a year; I do not recommend this publication. $29.95 a year. www.wineandspiritsmagazine.com.

- *Imbibe*. Based in Portland, Oregon, this national bi-monthly magazine covers all things in the world of drink, but you can count on in-depth wine coverage on interesting topics from biodynamics and climate change to seasonal wine and food pairing and trendy topics like orange wine. Six issues a year; $20 a year. www.imbibemagazine.com.

Newsletters

Newsletters, once the kind of mail you'd look forward to receiving in your box, have now gone digital. But the good news is many of them have transferred their publication from paper to the screen. Newsletters offer concise, up-to-date, informative, and many reflect the opinion of one expert (with whom you may or may not agree). Others present the views of several writers. You won't find picturesque accounts of a holiday in Bordeaux or a weekend in sunny Sonoma, but you will find extensive tasting notes and buying guides. You might consider these newsletters:

Tasting Tip

One or many tasters? Some wine newsletters base all their judgments on the palate of a single taster (who also is writer, editor, and publisher). Others compile the experiences and judgments of others. If you find your tastes coincide with those of a single taster, that's the one you want to heed.

- *The Wine Advocate*. This newsletter is probably the most influential publication in the wine world. *The Wine Advocate* achieved this status by instituting a 100-point system to score the wines. Retailers quickly jumped on the bandwagon, quoting Parker's rating in their advertisements, and this name became prominently known. Despite Parker's use of the 100-point system, he does provide solid, useful information and tasting notes that are usually on the mark. Bimonthly (and still in print-version), $75 a year. www.erobertparker.com. Online, you may also use the same link to subscribe to Parker's erobertparker.com, which includes information from his Burgundy and Bordeaux books, as well as *The Buyer's Guide*, independent and extra review from Parker-approved staff writers, and wine-travel information. $99 for a one-year online subscription.

- Stephen Tanzer's *International Wine Cellar*. This is the most influential newsletter after Parker's and, in my opinion, a better read. In addition to wine reviews, Tanzer publishes interviews with important members of the winemaking community, more background information on the vintages, and guest experts writing on various subjects. This publication is a must-have if you are serious about wine. One year, $95. www.wineaccess.com.
- Jancis Robinson's *Purple Pages*. Irreverent and intelligent, British Master of Wine Jancis Robinson's influence in the wine world has grown exponentially. She is the author of *The Oxford Companion to Wine*, and her *Purple Pages* give you access to that great resource, and are peppered with her broad, studied depth of knowledge pervasive in her wine ratings, vintage reviews, and general observations on the wine world at large. Annual subscription is £60 (about $110, at the time of this writing).
- *Connoisseur's Guide to California Wine*. As its name implies, this publication specializes in California wine. Its writers tend to have a California palate (they prefer big, chewy wines). Wines are evaluated by a panel and are rated on a three star system. Bi-monthly, $50 a year. www.cgcw.com.
- *Palate Press*. From wine laws that affect your drinking and reading pleasure, to up-to-date industry and consumer-centric news, to reviews and all info in between, *Palate Press* is an ever-informative online read with a global view on the wine world. www.palatepress.com.

Free Winery Newsletters

A number of wineries, large and small, put out their own newsletters, more often than not in online form. These handy sheets contain announcements of new releases, news of happenings at the winery, and opportunities to buy wine directly from the winery. My advice is when you find a winery whose offerings you return to over and over, find their website and see if they offer a newsletter (or, more likely, a blog, where they update you on vintage, harvests, bottling, new offerings, events, etc.).

Wine in the Blogosphere

Maybe more than any other readable arena of the wine-information world, wine blogs have exploded onto the scene, with mind-boggling amounts information, photos, opinions (both informed and fairly objective to uninformed and wildly subjective), ratings, and all other bits of have-keyboard, will-spew-information bits and bites than you can shake a vine at.

Heard it Through the Grapevine

The Internet is a wonderful resource, with more information on more topics than you'll ever need (or even find). Tens of thousands of new websites and blogs are born daily, more and more on the subjects of wine and food (and, lately, spirits and cocktails, too).But easy come, easy go, they say. While some websites are offshoots of reputable and popular magazines, or the home domain of an online magazine entirely, others are maintained at the pleasure of a single individual. That superb wine site you found last week may not be around next week.

(The websites mentioned in this book have exhibited some permanence.)

- More and more wineries, wine shops, and wine entrepreneurs are creating blogs with a wine focus. Many are devoted entirely to wine. What follows are a few that are worth taking a click-through Dr. Vino. Unpretentious and utterly informed, Tyler "Dr. Vino" Colman (an actual doc of political science) focuses not only on wine's political, business, and cultural influence (and, of course, influences on the industry), but also checks the temperature on "global warming" (e.g., climate change) and how it's affecting the wine industry, trends in wine, and interviews with sommeliers in the know via his well-informed, very readable, and never off-puttingly snobby prose. www.drvino.com.
- Jamie Goode. British wine columnist for *The Sunday Express* and author of the book *Wine Science*, here you'll find thoughtful wine reviews and comparisons, up-to-the-minute industry news, vintage reports, and wine musings. www.wineanorack.com
- The Terroirist. Founded and edited by David White, a member of the Society of Wine Educators, the Terroirist offers everything from value recommendations, hidden gems, tasting notes, politics, examinations of viticultural and vinicultural techniques, to the wine industry at large. Its freelance staff mostly have wine educational backgrounds from London's WSET—but most importantly, the Terroirist is updated daily! www.terroirist.com.

Wine Accessory Catalogs

The Wine Enthusiast (www.wineenthusiast.com, 800-356-8466) and International Wine Accessories (www.iwawine.com, 800-527-4072) online and mail-order companies both produce slick, full-color catalogs and websites with a wide variety of corkscrews, wine racks, wine storage units, glassware, and other accessories. Both sell the same merchandise, pricey with high markups. International Wine Accessories tends to be less expensive than Wine Enthusiast, and it provides better service.

The Sommelier Says

Both Wine Enthusiast and International Wine Accessories promote the Vacu-Vin wine-keeping device, which scientific studies have shown to be completely ineffective.

Wine Courses

Wine courses can range from informal tastings, which are conducted by a wine expert, to professional-level courses. The latter are not restricted to members of the wine trade, but some level of proficiency is a requisite. Wine courses of various lengths and levels are conducted at numerous locations throughout the country. For information on the courses offered in your area, write to the Society of Wine Educators, 1319 F Street NW, Suite 303 Washington, D.C. 20004, 202-408-8777, www.societyofwineeducators.com. You may also consider contacting the Wine & Spirits Education Trust, a London-based wine education organization with courses for both the enthusiast and the professional in many states across the country. Check out www.wsetglobal.com for courses in your area or online.

Also, don't forget your local wine shop! More and more are offering educational courses for their consumers, often led by local sommeliers or the owners themselves when they have the proper background to do so.

Wine Clubs

A wine club is an organization where wine lovers get together at wine tastings and gourmet dinners to enjoy the fruit of the vine. A large national wine club by the name of Les Amis du Vin used to exist. The club had more than 30,000 members, but it went bankrupt. The individual chapters across the nation either disbanded or went their own way.

Tasting Tip

If you decide to start your own wine club, use your local newspaper to publish notices of your meetings so your organization can grow, or, even better (and cheaper) use social media to help you gain momentum, with sites like Facebook and Twitter as great places to get noticed. You may find a local wine retailer who wants to get involved providing wine for free or at a discount.

A wine club may exist in your locality. The best way to find out is to contact the wine and food editor of your local newspaper or your local wine retailer. If no wine club is in your area, you may want to start one, yourself. Wine clubs provide an excellent way to exchange information about wine, make new friends, and pursue your interest in wine as a hobby.

Books for Advanced Reading

In addition to encyclopedias, pocket guides, websites, blogs, phone applications, and good ol' fashioned general reading, you can find a wealth of books offering in-depth information on specific topics related to wine. Books are available on Burgundy, Bordeaux, Cabernet Sauvignon, and Chardonnay. You can find books on old wines, like Port and Madeira, and books hailing the pleasures of wine from obscure wine regions. Here is a brief list of some books that might enhance your enjoyment and appreciation of wine (for a comprehensive list see Appendix C):

- *Bordeaux* (third edition), by Robert M. Parker, Jr., 2003. This book reviews thousands of wines and vintages and provides comprehensive information about the region. (Unfortunately, this book uses the 100-point system to rate the wines.)
- *Bordeaux* (third edition), by David Peppercorn, 2006. This book offers sketches of whatever the author deems important—good vintages, history, general characteristics of the wine, and information on several hundred wineries of the region.
- *Burgundy* (third edition), by Anthony Hanson, 2006. Hanson is deeply immersed in the Burgundy wine trade and shares his immense knowledge of the subject. It includes considerable detail on the practices and growers of the region.
- *Burgundy* (Kindle edition), by Robert M. Parker, Jr., 2010. Parker goes e-book where he rates the growers and reviews their wines. He provides an in-depth evaluation as well as comprehensive details on the region.
- *World Atlas of Wine*, by Hugh Johnson and Jancis Robinson, 2007. A complete explanation of the wine regions of the world, including grape growing and winemaking, and maps.
- *Hugh Johnson's Pocket Wine Book 2012*, by Hugh Johnson, 2011. This annually updated book provides country-by-country ratings of many vintages of over 6,000 wines. The book has maps, label guides, vintage charts, and more.
- *Parker's Wine Buyer's Guide (seventh edition)*, by Robert M. Parker, Jr., 2008. This comprehensive guide rates more than 8,000 wines. Parker rates the producers of every wine-growing region on a five-star system, but then he reviews specific wines using his 100-point system. Read the reviews, but don't take the precision of the ratings too seriously.

- *Sherry*, by Julian Jeffs, 2006. Includes the history of Sherry, from Chaucer's time to present, and the entire grape growing and winemaking process.
- *The New Connoisseur's Guidebook to California Wine and Wineries*, by Charles Olken and Joseph Furstenthal, 2010. Comprehensive and authoritative regional coverage of hundreds and hundreds of wineries with critical ratings of individual wines and vintages.
- *The Oxford Companion to Wine*, edited by Jancis Robinson, 2006, 3rd edition. This 1,000-plus-page tome includes just about every detail you want to know about wine. The book is written by experts in each field.
- *Vino Italiano: The Regional Wines of Italy*, by David Lynch and Joseph Bastianich, (second edition) 2005. An in-depth coverage of the wines of Italy, providing details of all the important regions.

CHAPTER 28

The Wine List, Monsieur!

In This Chapter

- Wine by the glass
- Evaluating the wine list
- Bringing your own bottle
- Sizing up the sommelier (wine steward)

Life offers no finer experience than a superb meal with a noble wine. The experience is particularly rich in the opulence of a three-star restaurant, with dining companions who share your appreciation of wine and cuisine.

Sadly, unless you have money to throw away, your aspirations quickly will dissipate as you discover that a $400 bottle of Le Montrachet is $1,200, a $30 bottle of Volnay $95, a $26 bottle of Champagne $65, and a mere $8 Beaujolais Village $20. A three- to five-times-retail markup is not unusual at better restaurants.

I will not pay such prices, and I recommend you don't either. But that's just me. Most wine-lovers feel that no fine dining experience is truly complete without wine. But trying to complement a restaurant menu can be a frustrating, and sometimes futile experience. Three things can go wrong here:

1. Exorbitant prices from outrageous markups;

2. A small wine list (or, worse, a large one!) that's limited to a choice of undistinguished wines, varied only in their degrees of mediocrity; and

3. The appearance of a key-jangling sommelier (wine steward), overtly condescending and, pretensions to the contrary, not necessarily familiar with the wines, their vintages, and availability.

Put these three all together, and we can make a great case for ordering a cold beer or a cup of coffee.

Okay, let's be fair: Some restaurants do offer a good selection of wines, meticulously matched to the cuisine—something, to my great relief, to which more and more eateries appear to be putting thought. A few even afford an opportunity to try wines unobtainable elsewhere. When the wines are fairly priced (the economy being what it is, many more restaurants have realized that affordable wines may encourage people to enjoy more than one bottle), dining with wine can live up to your greatest expectations. Or even surpass them.

Wine by the Glass

Ordering wine by the glass seems like a good idea. For one thing, it's easy. Your choices are limited to a few different reds or whites (sometimes rosés). Ordering wine is as trouble-free as choosing among tea or coffee, cola, or ginger ale. The problem is, if all the restaurant offers is the "house wine," you may wish you had chosen the cola!

Tasting Tip

What if you are the only person at your table who wants wine? Or the big California Cabernet chosen by your red meat-eating companions would easily overpower your delicate filet of sole? Wine-by-the-glass might be your best choice, even though the selection might be less exciting.

Depending on the restaurant, your single glass of mediocre wine can cost anywhere from $8 to $12. As the next section explains, you can order wine by the glass without being disappointed (or ripped off).

House Wine

House wines are sold by the glass or carafe. Rarely do you find a house wine that is a superb choice, although with the rise in popularity of wine and wine and food pairing, more eateries are upping the ante slightly on their choice of a house wine. And of course, if you happen to be dining in an area of the country known for its vineyards, your chances are even higher. Even then, you still need to be very sure of your restaurant.

House wines generally are your ordinary California, Italian, or, more often today, Australian or South American generic, mass-produced wines, purchased in large containers and then marked up—frequently to 10 times over cost. Think of it: You're paying more money per glass for your nondescript wine than the restaurateur paid for the whole bottle! The word for most house wines, unless the restaurant lets you know what it is and where it came from (even better if they know the vintage!) so you can make an informed decision, is "avoid."

Better Pours

Many more restaurants today include a selection of premium wines by the glass. Yes, this does mean a higher price, but it also means better quality. Premium wines by the glass usually range from $10 to $15 (sometimes more) per glass for wines that retail at around the same price per bottle.

What if premium wines are not available by the glass? One trick is to be a little enterprising. If you see no premium listing—or if only one or two wines are listed and they are not to your taste—don't be afraid to ask about other selections. Specify what type of wine you want. The worst your server can say is that something is not available, and a helpful and knowledgeable server may suggest something comparable.

Pricing Bottles of Wine

Determining a "fair" restaurant price for a bottle of wine is difficult. Here's one guideline I offer: For wines that require neither aging nor special handling, twice the retail price is probably more than fair. And for the more expensive wines full retail price, plus $10.

Generally, restaurants mark up wine to three times the retail, which is four to five times their cost. In other words, you can expect to pay $30 or so for a bottle of wine retailing for about $10 at your local wine shop. And when they think they can get away with it, some restaurateurs go six or seven times above cost!

For prestigious or scarce bottles, the markup can be even higher, with an expensive wine carrying a markup of several hundred dollars or more. All this for no greater effort than buying the wine by phone and pulling the cork at the table!

In my opinion, no wine, no matter how rare or expensive, should be marked up more than $50 over retail. After all, the restaurant only needs to store the wine, but the retailer must store the wine and provide costly display space. If the retailer can make a profit selling the wine at retail, the restaurant can do so, too.

For a restaurant, profits from wine sales (and other beverages) go directly to the bottom line. Overhead, advertising, and staff expenses are calculated in setting the food prices. When a restaurant charges from $12 to $20 for $2 worth of chicken, it should not gouge the customer who wants to enjoy a bottle of fine wine with his dinner. I refuse to pay these prices and instead seek out restaurants that permit us to bring our own wines, either for free or for a modest corkage charge ranging from $10 to $20 a bottle.

Heard it Through the Grapevine

To the unwary consumer, older wines can present a real risk. Cashing in on the vintage mystique, many restaurants assume any older wine is better and worthy of exorbitant prices. Old is not necessarily better. Nor is it always good.

I have seen poor or past-their-prime vintages of prestigious labels, like Château Lafite-Rothschild or La Romanée-Conti, offered at astronomical prices. Years ago, I found a 1965 Lafite-Rothschild—one of the worst vintages in many years and retailed for $4 a bottle when released—listed at $70. At this particular resort hotel, the wine was selling quite briskly, though it was nothing short of dead!

Rating the Wine List

There is an old joke among wine-lovers. There's a restaurant that has a wine list that looks like this:

1. Chablis
2. Burgundy
3. Rosé

Please Order Wine by Number

That joke is not so funny when you're trying to select a wine that will complement your meal and enhance your dining experience. Variations on this theme are all too common. My motto for ordering wine in a restaurant is the Scouts' "Be prepared!"

I feel fair treatment on the wine price list contributes to a restaurant's mood, no less than a well-matched wine to enhance the dining experience. The first step, of course, is the wine selection. If the list offers nothing worthy of the meal you order, you're stuck.

Whenever I decide to order no wine, I make my objections clear to the owner, manager, or maitre d'. I feel they ought to know my reasons. Then again, many restaurants with a poor wine policy attract me frequently, anyway. The ambiance is excellent, the cuisine superior, or both.

The Sommelier Says

Prices outrageous? Try to bargain by ordering two bottles at a lower price. A small profit on each of two bottles is better than none at all, and the restaurateur may get a loyal customer out of it.

It's worth a try. Just call in advance to negotiate a deal to avoid an embarrassing confrontation in front of your guests.

The Short List

The list of one white, one red, and one rosé may be a joke, but in all humor there is truth. Abbreviated wine lists with maybe two wines per color, one or two wines from an "exotic" location (anything other than France, Italy, or California), and perhaps some sparkling variety are still common. A restaurant with this type of list is one that goes through the motions of serving wine without any sensitivity to its customers or desire to attract wine-lovers.

The Familiar List

Does that wine list give you a feeling of déjà vu? Hmmm. That red leatherette cover is strikingly familiar! You know what wines are there even before you open it. And you don't check for vintages because you know, somehow, they aren't there at all.

That wine list was not compiled by the restaurant at all, but by a wholesaler or distributor whose primary motive was self-interest. I mean, why not supply the binder and printing for a list stocked with the distributor's most profitable wines!

You may see such a list in an Italian restaurant one weekend, in a small French restaurant the next. The restaurateur using this list opts for economy, convenience, and minimal personal effort. (I wonder how much attention the food gets!)

The Brand List

This is a variation on the familiar list. Suspect any wine list with a preponderance of major, nationally distributed brands: B&G, Mouton Cadet, Bolla, and Paul Masson, for example. These wines are not necessarily bad, but a list dominated by one or two popular brands is much too restrictive.

Offering wines that are commonly available and all too familiar suggests the restaurateur prefers to allow a sales representative to prepare the wine list, making no effort to match the wine with the cuisine. The wine cellar has neither imagination nor creativity. (Chances are both are missing in the kitchen as well.) Check to see if most California wines come from one producer or if most imported wines are from one shipper/importer. If so, you have a brand-dictated list.

The Fat Wine List

Although an extensive wine list is always nice, one that reads like a doctoral thesis or a Henry James novel can bog you down when you're trying to make a simple selection to go with dinner. The best managed restaurants provide an extended list for patrons willing to lose themselves in wine land, and an abridged version for those who simply are trying to match their meal.

The Good Wine List

I love wine lists that offer variety and global appeal—that is, a wide selection of wines from the major wine regions of the world. Of course, I also like an indication that the owner exercised a modicum of care in the wine selection. Here are examples of a good wine selection:

- Bordeaux from different châteaux
- Different vintages of the same wine
- Wines spanning a wide price range
- Wines from a local producer
- Wines chosen to complement the restaurant's menu

These wines are the beginning of a good wine list. This type of list shows that the owner or beverage manager is quite knowledgeable about wines. Generally, this person will be enthusiastic in suggesting wines within your price range.

The Reserve Wine List

No, a reserve wine list does not mean that all the wines on the list are "reserve" wines. A few upscale restaurants offer a special list of rare wines in addition to the regular wine list. If the occasion really is special, and cost is no object… Well, why not? On the other hand, if you have any doubts, stick with the regular list. Should you choose the reserve list, ask for assistance from the sommelier. You do not want to be stuck with a very expensive mistake.

Tasting Tip

The key to finding a good value on a restaurant wine list is a general familiarity with prices, vintages, châteaux and producers, not to mention importers and shippers.

If the wine list neglects such important details, don't hesitate to ask your server or wine steward.

Bringing Your Own Bottle

We all know about BYOB (bringing your own bottle) where the restaurant has no liquor license. Small ethnic restaurants often fall into this category, along with restaurants that have just opened and whose license still is pending.

Heard it Through the Grapevine

A reasonable corkage fee is anywhere from $10 to $20. Some restaurants try to discourage the practice by charging an exorbitant fee. If this is the case, visit a different restaurant that knows a reasonable fee makes for a loyal customer.

What most people don't realize is that BYOB is also a time-honored tradition at restaurants with a weak wine list, or even a restaurant with an adequate list, when you want to enjoy a special wine of your own. First check your local regulations to be sure you're allowed to bring a bottle of wine to a licensed restaurant. Some places say no; others, yes. Second, be sure you follow a sensible protocol and are prepared to pay a corkage fee. You are not out to alienate the proprietor. BYOB is appropriate under the following conditions:

- The wine you want to bring is something special, not on the list.
- You consider ordering another bottle from the list to maintain goodwill.
- You call ahead to ask for approval and to find out the corkage fee.
- You are a fairly regular client.
- You include a reasonable value for the wine when you are calculating your tip.

Go Ahead! Send it Back!

The question is a big concern for many restaurant patrons: Under what conditions can you refuse and return a bottle of wine? (This option seems to be exercised quite often by an elite few and not at all by the vast majority.)

Don't break out in hives. The decision simply comes down to this: Don't accept defective or flawed wines. The confusion for some people lies in deciding whether a wine's taste and smell are defective or just unfamiliar and unusual. (But isn't this one supposed to smell like skunk?)

The Sommelier Says

If a white wine is dark yellow or brown in color and smells like Sherry (and isn't from Jura or an orange wine purposely made in this style!), it is over-the-hill and likely maderized (see Chapter 22, Legendary Madeira). Red wines past their prime are somewhat brown in color, often orange around the rim. A dull flavor—like the smell of dead leaves—and a sharp, short finish are sure indicators to send the wine back.

Of course, if you see, smell, or taste any of the defects mentioned in this book (Chapter 8, How to Spot a Bad Wine), do not hesitate. Send it back. However, experience is the best teacher for helping you detect the most common off-aromas.

When in doubt, ask your server to sample the wine. If the server is confused about its merits and acceptability, then you are off the hook and another bottle should be forthcoming. But never return a wine you ordered out of curiosity but then did not like!

In my experience, a well-run restaurant will not quibble or get into a battle of wills with its customers. Customer service is the hallmark of the hospitality trade. "The customer is always right," has always been the policy with food and is used more often these days with wine. Just remember: Don't abuse the restaurant's good will.

Evaluating Your Sommelier

In many higher-priced restaurants, the wine list and your order are handled by a sommelier. A sommelier, or wine steward, should be knowledgeable and familiar with the wines listed.

Better yet, the sommelier may have bought, stored, and cared for the beloved wines and even trained the rest of the staff in wine protocol. France, Italy, and a few other countries have professional schools to train sommeliers, and the U.S. is gaining in comparable programs.

Therefore, you must learn to distinguish between the well-informed, full-fledged sommeliers and the impostors who strut around with pomp, ceremony, and haughtiness (and whose sole purpose is to intimidate and ultimately coerce people into buying wines with high markups or wines purchased in some big-quantity deal—actually, an attitude like that is usually a dead give-away. The best, most knowledgeable somms tend to be enthusiastic and generous with their information because they are secure in their knowledge). Worst of all, these characters survive because customers, unsure in their own knowledge, are afraid to speak up.

Tasting Tip

A good sommelier is supposed to taste the wine to determine its quality before serving it to you. (You could check by asking a few of the questions you used to evaluate your wine shop.) When a sommelier is present, the practice of tasting wine at your table is an acceptable ritual and not a charade.

Taking Home the Rest of the Bottle

You have half a bottle of wine left, and you're sure that one more glass will be imprudent. Wine is an awfully expensive commodity to leave sitting on the table! How do you ask for a doggie bag for your wine?

Wine etiquette has no protocol that forbids requesting to take your unfinished bottle home with you. In some states, however, the practice is restricted by law; so your request for the bottle may be turned down. Don't blame the owner or manager for being difficult or haughty. Of course, you might ask the restaurateur to keep the corked bottle refrigerated until your next visit.

Ensuring Good Service

As a paying customer—especially at the price restaurateurs charge for wine—you are entitled to fair service. These few suggestions can help you get a fair deal:

- Make sure you see the bottle you order. Check producer, type, vintage, etc.
- See that the wine arrives with cork and foil capsule intact. The possibility exists that a bottle may have been refilled with inferior wine or returned by another diner.
- Take some time away from your friends and guests to study the bottle. Slow the sommelier or server down to your pace—it's your money.
- Hold the bottle and check its temperature. A red wine, unless it is Beaujolais Nouveau, should be slightly below room temperature. A bottle that's too warm can indicate poor storage. White wines should be chilled, not frigid.

The Sommelier Says

If your white wine arrives at your table iced like a beer bottle, beware. Wines kept too cold for too long lose their verve. You don't want an overpriced flat wine. (You are better off to have white wine delivered to your table at room temperature, then placed in an ice bucket for 15 minutes.)

- Do not let the sommelier open the wine bottle until you have given your official approval. Do not let the sommelier pour the wine into other glasses until you have tasted and accepted it. Most important rule: Don't rush.
- Check the wine glasses for size and type (and cleanliness!). If you are not satisfied, ask for others. Champagnes and sparkling wines are best served in glasses without hollow stems. Flutes are preferred, but an all-purpose wine glass may be your only alternative.
- Make certain the capsule is cut neatly and the cork is removed cleanly. The cork should be offered to you, and it certainly should not crumble under your touch. Of course, Champagnes and sparkling wines should be uncorked with a minimal pop, if any. That movieland pop will land half your expensive bubbles on the carpet.

The wine should not just smell clean and free of defects. Its bouquet should be consistent with its type. These characteristics assume some knowledge on your part, which you are developing if you've read this far. (Of course, if you select an unfamiliar wine at random and discover it's not to your taste, that's your problem. Live and learn.)

Tasting Tip

Smell the empty glass. I know. This sounds silly. But the slightest smell of soap or detergent ruins Champagne and impairs most table wines. If you detect a detergent smell, ask the waiter to scrub the glasses carefully. When he returns, don't be afraid to recheck. A once-over light rinse won't always do the trick.

If you followed the sommelier or server's recommendation and description, but the wine does not resemble what was described, the problem is the restaurant's. You can refuse the wine. Be polite but persistent.

Heard it Through the Grapevine

A word about timing. Far too often, about the time your food arrives, you are informed that the wine you ordered is not available. Because some of us plan the meal around the wine selected, this is bad news! You can avoid this dilemma by requesting that the wine or wines be presented and brought to the table well ahead of the food.

Vintage wines deserve special mention. If you intend to bring an old vintage with you or contemplate ordering a really old wine from the list, check ahead for several reasons. Old wines mean old bottles, and they are subject to enormous variations in storage. Find out if the management stands by the quality of the vintage bottles in its cellar. If you're bringing your own dowager wine, inquire if the restaurant has the necessary decanter, glasses, and a person experienced in decanting old wines.

An old wine is like a special entrée: It should be ordered ahead of time, allowing the staff to make proper preparations that include standing the bottle upright for several hours or more, preferably the day before. The wines should be ready to decant when you arrive.

f you have not finished it during your meal.

CHAPTER 29

Wines for Everyday

In This Chapter

- Everyday wine quality
- Savings in packaging
- How everyday wines differ

Throughout this book, we've looked at the very finest wines you can buy anywhere in the world. And we've looked at some of the most expensive (not necessarily the same wines). I've noted excellent wines from many countries that I think are pretty good values—and some pretty good wines that are excellent values. So why should we even bother with the sorts of everyday wines that anybody can buy any time any place? (And without any special wine knowledge, either.)

Because everyday wine has its place. Sometimes it's perfect in a punch bowl recipe, or as an ingredient in a summer "cooler." Ordinary wine may be good any time you might feel like enjoying a sip.

Everyday wines lack the complexity of better wines. (We'll not mention breeding and finesse!) But still these wines are the product of fermentation of grapes, a process that yields unique flavors, found nowhere else in nature. If your everyday wine hasn't been doctored with non-wine ingredients, it still can offer you at least a few of wine's many pleasures—and for surprisingly little money.

Cheap Doesn't Mean Bad

Do you remember how much personal computers used to cost? And color TVs? (And how much less capability you got for your money, too!) Many everyday things have become much cheaper over the years, not even counting inflation. (Movie tickets and popcorn are another matter.)

The reason is technology: new tools, new materials, new manufacturing methods, and new distribution systems. They all work together to deliver more value at less cost.

To some degree, this has worked in wine production, too, but mostly at the cheap end of the price spectrum. When it comes to superior and noble wines, there's no substitute for the intensive skilled and semiskilled labor that goes into their making. Technology—say, temperature-controlled stainless steel fermentation tanks—may help make quality more reliable. But it does little to reduce labor costs.

As we move down a few price and quality grades, though, there are more opportunities for automation, replacing expensive labor with machinery. And at the very lowest level, winemaking has more in common with mass-production manufacturing than with any art or craft.

Heard it Through the Grapevine

Comparing wine prices over time is a little tricky. You have to correct for consumer price inflation. Years ago, when I noticed that it was possible to buy some California white wines for only $1.35 a bottle (equivalent), I was curious. So I checked:

In terms of consumer price inflation, that $1.35 is equivalent to 22 cents a bottle in 1960, 30 cents in 1970, 66 cents in 1980, and a dollar in 1990. We never before saw wine at those prices!

This isn't a bad thing, actually. Good wines are still good—and still expensive. What we call jug wines, however, have become better, because of the quality control that automation allows. And they have become cheaper.

For Less Than Ten Bucks

There's a lot that goes into the price tag on that bottle of imported wine from France, Australia, or Argentina. There's shipping (the glass bottle as well as its contents). There are import duties. And profits for winery, broker, importer, and retailer. Oh, and federal, state and local taxes. Still, we can buy a bottle of imported wine for less than 10 dollars.

Tasting Tip

Here's where you can forget all about that knowledgeable wine seller at your favorite store, the one who stocks fine wines and great vintages. Such a store cannot afford to give space to these cheapest wines. If you're looking for a bottle of wine for less than five dollars, you're best off in one of those large chain discount stores (if they allow these in your state).

Some of the larger wine outlets—the ones with the big price display signs in their windows—offer a surprising selection of inexpensive wines from France, Italy, Spain, Australia, New Zealand, Chile, and Argentina. And let's not forget California.

For this little money, you can afford to experiment now and then. I mean, select a bottle—a red Bordeaux or something white from Italy. Take it home, and serve it. You might like it. Or bring one home and save it for your next brown-bag wine tasting. See how it scores. (You might risk embarrassing a few friends, though.)

Before I continue, let me remind you what you're giving up when you choose something for less than 10 dollars—namely, finish, texture, and complexity.

The experience isn't without value. You'll still get basic aromas and flavors. You'll sense the alcohol. But mostly, you'll enjoy the economy.

Miserly Magnums

A magnum is two bottles. Once upon a time, this was the giant economy size for wines. One bottle, one label, and one cork (or screw cap) all mean a better price. Also, a magnum takes less room in your refrigerator than two bottles, if it's something you need to chill for a party.

I have seen magnums of lesser French wines, honest vin du pays, selling for 10 dollars or so, Italian wines for 10 to 15 dollars, and unpretentious wines from California for 6 to 10 dollars, including some at the lower end from Gallo, in interesting pinch-waist bottles.

Bargains in a Bag

Wine in a bag. Bag in a box. This is a triumph of packaging technology, sometimes referred to by its brand name, Tetra Pak. Wine in a rectangular box, inside a polyethylene bag, solves three problems: cost, space-efficiency, and storage.

First, these bag-in-box setups hold 6.67 standard bottles! And the cardboard and plastic components cost less than a single glass bottle. It costs less, per bottle, to warehouse and ship, too, and are often recyclable.

Next, as the folks at UPS will tell you: A box is more efficient than a cylinder. Large, rectangular bottles are hard to make, and they're more fragile than their rounded cousins. (Can you imagine a chicken laying rectangular eggs?) But a plastic bag inside a cardboard box makes for a rectangular package that's both cheap and strong.

Heard it Through the Grapevine

Some people call the package "wine in a box." But of course, you don't pour wine directly into cardboard boxes. The wine's in a polyethylene bag, which is equipped with its own spigot. The bag protects the wine. And the box gives it its shape.

The bag-in-box concept has been used for fruit juices and other liquid foods, but it's wine that seems to have taken most strongly to this packaging.

These boxes fit easily on a deep shelf in your refrigerator, taking less than four inches of horizontal space. Imagine, if you will, three of these boxes, side-by-side. Now imagine the 20 standard wine bottles they replace. Space efficiency? No contest!

Finally, the bag-in-box can protect your wine from its worst enemy: oxygen. At no time is the wine exposed to air, even when the bag-in-box is nearly empty.

You've seen packaged plastic bags, perfectly flattened. That's how the polyethylene bags look before they are filled with wine. When the wine is pumped into them, there's no air to pump out. In other words, there's no ullage (the air space between the wine and the top of the bottle or jug).

And when you fill your glass from the built-in spigot, you'll hear no glug-glug sound, which would have been air entering to replace the liquid that's lost. The bag simply collapses as it's emptied. No air gets in at all.

When you're storing five liters of inexpensive wine, you may be keeping it your refrigerator for weeks. Forget about its losing flavor. The simple flavors of this inexpensive wine aren't the sort time can destroy. What's important is that this wine won't oxidize. A half-filled gallon jug, on the other hand, won't keep very well. (Nor would you like a spare jug taking up so much space in your refrigerator.)

Vino Vocab

The English call it plonk—cheap, undrinkable wine. The word may be a corruption of the French vin blanc (white wine). Mass-produced inexpensive wines of today, while cheap, are hardly are plonk.

The Australians are big on this bag-in-box concept. And I must admit, it's a great way to ship these inexpensive, mass-produced wines. Today, you'll probably see mostly California wines in these packages on your shelves, but other producers—notably, the importer Jenny & Francois southern France "From the Tank" boxed wines—are offering decent quality that can be more easily found.

The price? Fifteen to 35 dollars for a 3-liter box. This works out to be about four bottles of wine for, at most, $8 and change per bottle! This is a high-tech manufactured product in a high-tech packaging. These wines are not bad, though they offer only a few of those things we treasure in better wines. Compared with the cheapest products of 20 years ago, these wines are much better and more consistent in quality. And they're cheaper. Not a bad deal.

And for a Little More

Cheap is a relative term. We've looked here at wines that sell for less than 10 dollars a bottle—sometimes a lot less. But it's remarkable what a few dollars more can buy.

The countries are the same. But the packaging is different. Here's where we leave behind the bag-in-box, the jug and even the magnum. (To be sure, some very fine wines sometimes are bottled in magnums, but not in this chapter.) These will be individual glass bottles of standard 750 ml size. And they'll all have corks.

Instead of less than 10 dollars a bottle, we're moving up to 11 to 12 dollars. For these few dollars more, you will get a little more body. You actually will detect some texture and finish. And you will note the beginning of wine complexity. Some of these wines can provide enough of the wine experience to make them genuine everyday partners—even if you own a connoisseur's cellar (see Chapter 31).

And for a few dollars more? As we move up to 12 to 15 dollars, we get, generally, a little more of everything. I say generally, because in this price category, as in all wine price ranges, cost is not a sure indicator of quality.

I remember once I needed a wine with little or no character. I had wanted to demonstrate the differences between cheap wines and those of moderate price. So I spent four bucks on a bottle of Dao (a wine region of Portugal). We pulled the cork, and you know what? It wasn't bad! It should have been very ordinary, but it wasn't. You, too, can be so lucky.

A Little Reverse Snobbery

In the broadest terms, there are two kinds of wine drinkers: Those who take most of their pleasure from the prestige of label, scarcity and price. And those who take it from the wine itself, through the experience of sipping.

I think an occasional excursion into everyday wines helps us maintain our appreciation of the basic product of grape fermentation. (And if we happen to find something less expensive that seems a good value, we shouldn't hesitate to enjoy it and to share it.)

Heard it Through the Grapevine

To many people, the dividing line between good wine and the rest is the use of a cork instead of a screw cap. The fact is, corks do not guarantee quality. And screw caps are not an inferior bottle closure.

The modern screw cap is an interesting bit of technology. It's actually formed from aluminum in-place right on the threads of the bottle neck. A bit of plastic underneath ensures an airtight seal, at least until it's opened.

I really think wine snobbism works two ways: If we adopt snooty attitudes around others, we make ourselves vulnerable to the dictates of other snobs. And then we will have forsaken our wine pleasures to pursue others of a less substantial kind.

Never, never forget: The appreciation of wine is a personal experience. That experience can range from the mildly pleasant to the ecstatically sublime. But all that enjoyment, in whatever degree, is legitimate.

Where Does It Come From?

Everyday wines are produced everywhere wine is produced. Wine is an important beverage in many cultures, and its importance continues to grow in North America.

Only a very few vineyards can produce a noble wine, no matter how hard others might try. But viticulture is a big and important industry in France, Italy, Spain, Portugal, Germany, Australia, New Zealand, Argentina, and Chile. And let's not forget California, a country in its own right. Add to that New York and the many other burgeoning wine areas in the United States. The quantities of grapes and of finished wines are enormous, and these find their ways onto world markets, sometimes at remarkably low prices.

CHAPTER 30

Attending a Winetasting

In This Chapter

- Different kinds of winetastings
- Winetasting etiquette
- How to find a winetasting
- The value of winetastings

You've heard of winetastings, haven't you? Men and women in evening dress, social-register all, tasting and talking in discrete tones at some toney house in the Hamptons. Right? Not quite.

You can't throw a grape without finding a winetasting these days, such a growing phenomenon that they've become in the U.S. (as is the enjoyment of wines). There are no class boundaries, or even limitations (beyond legal ones) to the surroundings in which you sample. You don't even need to be on someone's invitation list. They're everywhere, and usually, the price is right (if not free!).

What's a Winetasting?

A winetasting is a gathering of people for the purpose of tasting and comparing wines. This can be serious, or it can be laid-back fun. There are all kinds.

Professional winetastings exist for people in the wine trade. But there are plenty of consumer winetastings meant for your amusement, entertainment, and education. If you're interested in learning more about and enjoying more wine, you really ought to try one (or several). I don't know a quicker or more economical way to advance your wine knowledge and experience.

But don't you have to be something of an expert first? Nope! People attend winetastings who never had experienced anything beyond a glass of chilled rosé from a Tetra Pak at someone's summer get together. And among the kinds of people who attend most winetastings, there's very little snobbery.

If I went to one, what wines would a winetasting taste? And how many? The answer lies at the furthest reaches of your host's imagination. But here are some samples:

- A tasting of Chardonnays
- A tasting of Bordeaux
- A tasting of different wines from the same vintage
- A tasting of wines selected within a specified price range

Or how about this idea? A certain number of red (or white) wines from different regions or countries to explore geographic differences. Or maybe a focus on wines from some emerging wine country or region. Or maybe the theme merely is variety, with wines of all colors, prices, and origins.

Tasting Tip

A little economics: Let's say you want to sample twelve wines, Premier Cru White Burgundies. At $50 a bottle, that's about $600, if you did it alone. But let's say you're one of 12 people bringing just one bottle to a winetasting. Those 12 bottles are enough for all of you, with everyone getting about two ounces, which is enough to do the job. (See Chapter 3.)

Now let's look at a few types of winetastings.

Stand-Up Tastings

Expect a table. Or maybe several tables. There's no need to worry about seating. There isn't any—not at the tables, anyway. So there'll be no name cards, none of that boy-girl-boy-girl business. Just a table, or several, with lots (you hope) of bottles of wine.

The tablecloth will be white, of course, the better to assess the color of your wines. It might be linen. Or it might be paper. It depends on who's hosting, and how much you paid (if you had to pay at all).

Of course, there will be glasses! Possibly two per person. Real wineglasses, you hope, with lots of room for your nose. And you'll see something else, most likely. Spittoons. Not the sort found in old-time barbershops. Perhaps only a few little buckets at table-height. More on spitting later. (You can't wait, I'll bet!)

You can expect good lighting, preferably bright incandescent. Flourescents, even the "daylight" sort, cannot give you a reliable color reading.

There may be chairs or sofas in the room. But around the wine tables, just free floor space. This is the setup for the standup winetasting.

Now's your chance to learn about a lot of wines—at your own pace. You'll visit each bottle, pour (or, more than likely, be poured) an ounce-and-a-half or two ounces into your wineglass. And you'll taste at your own leisure. But you need not swallow. In fact, if you arrived by car, you shouldn't swallow. That's the reason for the spittoons. But more on that later.

Sit-Down Tastings

You've been invited to (or invited yourself to) a sit-down winetasting. Yes, it's a bit more formal, a bit more structured. But there's no need for panic.

The seating may be fixed by your host, or it may be seat-yourself. Either way, you will be seated.

In front of you, there will be several clean glasses, perhaps three or four; maybe more. And somewhere beside you, somewhere to discard the contents of your glass or mouth, and possibly a basket of plain crackers or bread to neutralize your palate after a few tastes.

Instead of your going to the wines, the wines come to you—three or more at a time. These are called flights. The wines in each flight will have something in common. And they will have features that distinguish them. It's easier to understand, perhaps, if I give you a few examples:

Let's say you are attending a sit-down Bordeaux tasting:

- First flight: Three (or whatever number) from the Cru Bourgeous Petit Château.
- Second flight: Third and fourth growths, Cru Classé from the Médoc.
- Third flight: Second growth Cru Classé from the Médoc.
- Fourth flight: First growth Cru Classé from the Médoc.

Pretty neat, huh! And it's very scientific. You get to compare wines within a quality tier. And you get to compare wines of differing qualities. Are the differences greater within a tier? Or from tier-to-tier? These are important questions. And I know no other way to answer them apart from a full-blown winetasting (short of springing for 12 or 16 bottles of Bordeaux).

Heard it Through the Grapevine

Wine tastings can be vertical or horizontal. Please! No jokes about "being on the floor"!

A vertical tasting is one that features several vintages of the same wine (for example, Château Palmer in each vintage from 1979 to 1991). A horizontal tasting would feature wines of a single vintage from several different properties, usually of a similar type, such as 1993 California Chardonnay.

How about another example? Let's say your host has decided to compare Chardonnays from California, France, and Australia. This time, we'll use six glasses per person:

- First flight: Two wines from each country, under $12 each.
- Second flight: Same, but priced at about $20–$25
- Third flight: Same, but $30 to $50. For instance, you might compare a Premier Cru Meursault with a Premier Cru Chassagne Montrachet, along with the two wines each from California and Australia.

In engineering testing labs, this is called balanced-block experimental design. In a winetasting room, you can call it fun, as you engage in what amounts to a real scientific investigation.

Brown Bag

Now we really get scientific—with blind tasting. That is, you will sample wines from bottles that have their labels hidden. Better still, from unmarked decanters. Regardless of one's experience and professed impartiality, we all know that seeing a label can influence judgment.

It's our human nature. All our lives, we've learned to discern and remember patterns, and to use them to develop expectations. That protects us when we want to cross a busy street. But prior knowledge inevitably will color our taste perceptions of wine.

Let's say you know the wine you are going to taste is very expensive, or very highly regarded. Or maybe it's an old friend, a wine you have served yourself many times. Do you really believe you could be impartial?

The Sommelier Says

The worst possible thing to happen at a blind tasting is for the host to lose track of which wine went into which decanters. I've known this to happen at more than one private tasting.

You'll probably know it's a blind tasting before you go. But if not, you'll know when you see your host has covered all the labels. I use those slender paper bags from the wine or liquor stores. Aluminum foil works well, too, but it reveals the bottle's shape, and you want to eliminate all clues. Decanters are best. Apart from color, aroma, bouquet, and taste, no clues.

After a time, your interest in wine tasting may develop to a point where you'll want to discover more than which wines appeal to you. You can make the tastings more interesting and concentrate on fine-tuning your abilities through blind tastings. This learning process proceeds on its own. No need for a teacher or a syllabus.

Heard it Through the Grapevine

You can tune up your palette with these blind tasting tests:

- A triangulation test is easy. All you need are two wines and three glasses, tagged with some sort of identifier. Have someone pour one of the wines into two glasses and the other wine into a single glass, recording which went where. Your task is to pick the two glasses filled from the same bottle. Piece of cake, right? It's harder than it sounds, even for experienced tasters.
- Another test is working with pairs. Have your friend pour two wines with some dissimilarity into four glasses. You have to match pairs.

In time, you'll find yourself guessing a wine's origin, vintage, region, winemaking style, and even brand. Wine tasting is like listening to music. Can you tell Beethoven from Bebop? How about Brahms from Bartok? Maybe even Bach from Buxtehude? You may not realize

Tasting Tip

In the beginning, testing is easier if you taste wines that are substantially different. As your palate develops, choose wines that are increasingly similar.

it at first, but your unconscious mind is filing and processing information: composer, period, style, and so on. You'll get there!

Blind wine tastings are a great way for you to test your developing expertise and as a safeguard against developing prejudices or a smug sense of certainty. A blind wine tasting may be a chance for you to show off But as happens more often than not, it can also be a humbling experience. The blind test is the Test of Truth..

The important thing is not to make tasting a chore. Think of the test as a game of knowledge and sensory skill. But don't take tasting so seriously that you wind up ruining your enjoyment.

To Eat or Not to Eat

Standup or sit-down, there's going to be food. Your host will have been very careful in its selection. And if you're serious about getting the most out of your winetasting experience, you'll be careful about your eating, too.

Maybe the invitation or advertisement reads "Wine and Cheese." That's reasonable. Everybody knows wine and cheese go together. But in this instance, your host will have selected rather bland, neutral cheeses. Cheese with big flavors or aromas can interfere seriously with your tasting. You won't find any blue-veined Roquefort or runny Camembert. (Or you shouldn't.)

Heard it Through the Grapevine

The best way to clean your mouth between tastings? Water. I prefer a neutral or mineral water because it cleans the palate without adding any taste. Some city water is over-treated with chemicals, and that can affect your ability to taste. Likewise, some of the alkaline hard water common in parts of the Midwest and Southwest will interfere with your sense of taste.

Also, your host will make sure there aren't any distinct cooking odors from food being prepared in the kitchen next door. Yes, food and wine do go together. But not at a winetasting! The ideal time to serve food is after the tasting is complete. For eating during the tasting, I recommend nothing fancier than some plain bread or unsalted crackers. But I don't recommend eating, at all. A glass of plain water is best.

Themes

Every winetasting will have a theme, even if it's "Let's use up all this leftover wine from that wedding I catered!" Most themes, of course, are a lot more structured.

The theme could be the wines of the Southern Hemisphere. Or Gewerztraminers from around the world. Or vintage comparisons. Or maybe different treatments of the Merlot grape. Themes add fun and intrigue. They also help guide us in our continuing wine education.

Etiquette Tips

As I've tried to point out here, you don't have to know much about wines to attend a winetasting. These are an effective and economical way to expand on your wine education, no matter how far you have come. But it does help to know just a few points of winetasting etiquette.

It might seem obvious, but I feel I must mention it: Don't be a hog. Your host probably has allocated a bottle of each wine for each 10 to 15 people. If you go through the line three times at a standup winetasting, there's a chance someone else will miss out altogether.

You don't need a large amount of wine to assess its properties. Two ounces would be plenty. It's inconsiderate to pour too much. And it's unnecessary.

To Spit or Not

Okay. I've put this one off as long as I could. But we need to talk. Spitting is okay. At least, it's okay at a winetasting, if not absolutely necessary.

Tasting Tip

At the very least, your host will have provided some sort of container into which you can dump the remaining contents of your glass. Most will provide buckets, generally tabletop height, for spitting the contents of your mouth. If not, it's okay to spit into a cup, and to dump from that.

Outside the winetasting room, spitting would be bad manners. Inside, it's perfectly okay. Taking up too much alcohol to make good tasting evaluations is not okay. Taking too much alcohol if you intend to drive is worse than not okay.

Dress for Tasting Success

There's no special uniform for winetasting. As with any social occasion, there will be appropriate dress.

Sometimes the invitation or announcement will stipulate dress. If not, use common sense. If it's a hotel meeting room at eight P.M., wear business attire. If it's in the basement of the fire hall on Saturday afternoon, jeans and a T-shirt might be fine.

Come as You Smell

Arrive clean, of course! But whatever you do, do not apply cologne when you are attending a tasting. In fact, avoid anything strong smelling—from pungent deodorant to overly perfumed lotion. Use products with neutral or no smell. You want to be able to get the full aroma of the wine in your glass, not the impact of Chanel from your wrists!

The Sommelier Says

Of course, when you do your winetasting at a winery, everything you sample will come from that winery. You won't have the variety of experience that many other tastings afford. But you will have an opportunity to sample the winery's line of goods. And to learn a bit about that winery's vinification process.

Who Gives Winetastings?

Winetastings no longer are the provenance of the rich and the famous. Many people, old and young, well off and not so, attend winetastings. If no one's invited you to one yet, maybe it's time for you to look around. Believe me, you won't have to look far. Check your local newspaper for announcements, check the web page of your favorite wine shops, or even call the paper's food editor (or wine editor if they have one) for information.

Wineries Woo You

Visit a winery! Tastings there are generally low-cost ($5 to $15 for a group of three to six wines, generally). And if you find something you like (that's what they hope), you can buy it right there. (In some states, you can save some money, too.)

Plan your next summer vacation, home or abroad, around winery visits. Imagine a winetasting a day! Two, maybe!

Restaurants Reach Out

There's money in winetastings. For the cost of an average bottle of wine and a meal, a restaurant can hold a tasting (or a monthly tasting night), charge you fifty or a hundred bucks, and make a profit. And maybe, make a new customer, too. And if you get to taste eight or 10 wines and eat a meal, too, that's not a bad deal!

How good are these? It depends a lot on that restaurant's own wine knowledge. This is something you can ascertain when you attend their tastings (or by accessing their wine list online, if they list it). It's good to know in advance who's good with wine and who isn't.

Everyone Benefits

If there's profit in winetastings for restaurants, there's profit for charities, too. For a fee, service clubs, nonprofit groups, and special fund-raisers can engage a professional wine expert who will set up and run a winetasting to help raise money.

What about some organizations you are involved in? Does that give you any ideas?

Don't Forget Your Friends

You want to taste wine? All you need are two things: Wine. And people. How many friends and business colleagues do you have? How many would like to learn more about wine? Maybe you'd like to host a winetasting in your own home? (See Chapter 31, Your Own WineTasting.)

Tasting Notes

What did you eat for lunch the Thursday before last? What was the headline at the top of last Saturday's newspaper? Let me ask you one more question: Do you really think you'll be able to recall all your winetasting experiences?

It's never too early to begin keeping tasting notes. It's never too late, either. Your impressions never will be keener than when they are fresh. While you wouldn't take out a notebook at a formal banquet or in fancy restaurant, it wouldn't make much sense to attend a winetasting without something to record your impressions. (See Chapter 31, Keeping Notes.)

Join a Wine Club!

Most large cities and many smaller ones have wine clubs. Most of these, actually, are organized specifically to hold winetastings. There's no profit motive here, so these provide terrific value to their members (and lucky guests).

Ask about local wine clubs at your wine dealer. If yours is the right kind of shop (see Chapter 26, Finding a Good Wine Merchant), the local club might buy its wines from that very store.

Or check at your local library. The reference desk can help you track down most local organizations. (Maybe they even meet at your library.)

PART FIVE

Wine at Home

CHAPTER 31

From the Cellar to the Centerpiece

In This Chapter

- Storing your wine
- Stocking your own wine cellar
- Entertaining with wine
- Keeping records

It started simply the day you bought two bottles, drank one and kept the second for another day. And then the day came when you noticed you had accumulated five bottles. Then 10. Then….

Is it time to give up this new wine hobby, the one that threatens perpetual clutter? Not at all! You deserve to keep wine at home, as much as you like. Your wine deserves good treatment. And your hobby deserves good records.

That's what this chapter is all about.

Storing Wine at Home

You might want to look back into Chapter 4. That's where we discussed choosing the perfect wine rack or climate-controlled home storage unit. Numerous models are available, and new models seem to come out every week.

Your taste in decor may be traditional, contemporary, or eclectic. Your budget may be tight or limitless. No problem. With a little looking, you're sure to find a storage unit to suit your needs and taste. (And if you're handy with tools, you might be able to combine two hobbies and build your own.)

Forget the real-estate section of your paper. You won't find too many castles for sale, or even for rent. But you can dream, huh! Imagine: Great hillside location; spacious, airy, with deep, dark cellar for storing wine. Okay. Dream over!

Lacking a natural storage cellar, most of us need to be resourceful or clever. Let's review and expand a bit on some of the things we discussed in Chapter 4.

Keep It Dark

Your wine is maturing. It's not hibernating. Those bottles don't need to be kept in total darkness, but they do need a place away from direct sunlight.

Sunlight is rich in ultraviolet. That's the part of the light spectrum that does the damage, by changing molecules from one form into another and by hastening certain destructive processes, like oxidation. A moderate amount of artificial light won't harm your wine. Neither will indirect daylight, if not too strong.

But when in doubt, darker is better.

Keep It Cool

Prolonged storage in very warm or hot conditions will damage your wine. Seriously damage it. Extreme heat causes wine to mature precociously. It goes from adolescence to senility without even passing through a golden middle-age.

The best temperature? I recommend 55 degrees Fahrenheit. But anything between 50 and 60 degrees F is excellent. (For you metric folks, that's between 10 and 15.6 degrees C.)

The Sommelier Says

When it comes to wine storage, vibration is bad news. Excess vibration can cause uneven maturation. Keep your wine rack away from nearby foot traffic. A rack mounted to the back of a closet door is a poor idea.

Keep It Humid

Wines like humidity even if you don't. Too dry, and your corks may lose their grip, allowing more air to enter into the bottle and oxidize your wine before you even get to enjoy it.

That would be a disaster for those bottles of vintage Bordeaux you had laid up for your grandchildren.

Try to keep your wine cellar between 75 and 90 percent relative humidity. Humidity above 95 percent encourages mold.

If the air is dry, your wine can seep into and through a too-dry cork. This is a very slow process. But so is maturation of some fine wines. The resulting condition is called ullage, a word we use also to denote the empty space between the wine and the cork.

When you lose wine through ullage, it's replaced by air. And air contains oxygen, which is poison to wines. Oxidation is the last thing you want for your valuable collection.

Vino Vocab

A hygrometer measures relative humidity. The amount of moisture air can hold increases with temperature. But drying-out depends only on moisture relative to the maximum air can hold. That's why wine cellars need hygrometers.

You should buy a hygrometer, an inexpensive instrument used to measure relative humidity. You can find several specially designed for wine storage areas.

Some hygrometers are single units. Others are mounted with a thermometer (a great idea). You can find these quality-control instruments in wine accessories catalogs and at some better retailers.

How Important is Temperature?

The ideal of a constant 55-degree temperature is a good goal when you select your storage space. But remember, we live in a less-than-ideal world. Unless you have a very deep basement, it's unlikely you have such a spot in your house.

Don't despair. Uniformity of temperature is more important than absolute temperature. Avoid any area with sudden temperature fluctuations over a short period of time. Slow, gradual changes, free of extremes, offer no threat. Let's say you have a typical basement (not all of us do, of course), and its temperature varies from about 50 degrees in winter to about

70 degrees in summer. No problem. If you can keep it steady and less than 70 degrees, don't worry at all.

Your Own Wine Cellar

The idea either excites you or it terrifies you: Keeping your own wine cellar, just like Dom Pérignon (See Chapter 21). Let's face it: Some people are not comfortable with that kind of responsibility, providing a controlled environment over the course of years. Decades, maybe. How you feel about this aspect of wine collecting is a big consideration when comes to choosing how, where… or how many.

Tasting Tip

Do you want to make a decorating statement with your wine rack? You can, of course. There are some beautiful wine racks out there, even of very modest size.

But think: The best place for your wine might be in a closet, or in the corner of your basement. It's better to purchase wine for its drinking potential than for its decorating promise.

How Much Should I Keep?

Perhaps your needs are modest: a ready bottle for casual drinking or an emergency stash for unexpected visitors or a quick grab for a gift you need to bring to a dinner or party. You'll be happiest with a small rack (many hold 10 to 15 bottles) or even with the case in which your wine arrived (see Chapter 4, Wine Racks; Wine Walls).

If you're starting to feel the collector's urge, especially if you're thinking of buying long-aging wines as an investment, just remember you do need to put some effort into upkeep. A bit of honest introspection should give you the answer to how much wine you ultimately will need to store.

Basic Cellar for Everyday Drinking

A basic cellar should include a diverse collection for everyday drinking as well as wine for special events. For your everyday collection, select the styles you prefer in your usual price range for everyday wines. Then supplement this group with a few bottles of better-quality wines for when the occasion demands something extra. Non-vintage Champagnes and good-quality sparkling wines also fall into the special-occasion category.

Then for those momentous occasions, keep a bottle or two of tête de cuvée (best of the lot) Champagne on hand. For occasions when bubbly may not be appropriate, some excellent choices are a Premier or Grand Cru Burgundy, or a Cru Classé Bordeaux from vintages that are ready-to-drink.

The Fifteen-Hundred-Dollar Cellar

You can create a serious collection from a $1,500 investment. This cellar includes the basic selections, above, with a few additions. Here's where you add to the ready-to-drink Premier and Grand Crus Burgundies and Cru Classés Bordeaux a few of their less mature cousins. These should be a few years away from drinking—not decades.

Include some white Bordeaux, a selection of German wines, and Burgundies, red and white. And do a little shopping from the U.S., with some California Cabernet, Chardonnay, and Zinfandel.

And for Three Grand?

Now we're getting into some long-term commitment on your part. You will graft this cellar onto the $1,000 cellar. You will add a case of Cru Classé Bordeaux, some red and white Burgundies, and some of the California reds that need five to 10 years of aging.

Heard it Through the Grapevine

Isn't $3,000 too much to spend for wine? If you haven't taken the time to develop your palate and to learn about and experience the world's better wines, any investment might be excessive. But once you have decided an appreciation of wine in all its nuanced variety is a part of your life, it's not so much.

A collection of 1,000 downloaded songs on your MP3 player isn't extraordinary. Neither is owning eight place-settings of fine china. Yes, you actually consume your wine collection. But you were going to drink wine anyway, collection or not. Right? So you simply replace what you drink, and enjoy the knowledge that your maturing vintages are a living asset.

Now, include several bottles of mature, ready-to-drink vintage Port; mature, ready-to-drink Sauternes; and a few bottles of German Late-Harvest wines. This collection becomes the core of the Connoisseur's Cellar.

The Connoisseur's Cellar

The connoisseur's cellar is what you wish every restaurant or hotel maintained. (Many of them wish they could, too.) This collection includes a good selection of wines for everyday drinking, while it houses noble and rare wines of the utmost breed and finesse. Lay down your Bordeaux, Burgundies, California agers, and vintage Ports for joyous future consumption.

Tasting Tip

If you enjoy the world's more distinguished sweet wines, by all means bring in several of the sweet Sauternes and the German Beerenauslese and Trockenbeerenauslese Rieslings. If yours is a connoisseur's cellar, these may belong there, as they age beautifully and can offer very special surprises in complexity and development as the years wane on. This is your cellar, remember, which must reflect your taste and preferences.

The Connoisseur's Cellar also should include some esoteric wines, like vintage Madeiras, high-quality Sherries, and perhaps a curiosity or two. Try Hungarian Tokay. Follow your fancy!

Should I Insure My Wine?

Home insurance policies generally insure the furnishings and other contents of your house for up to half the value of the policy. Policies for renters, also cover furnishings and such things as a television or two, audio equipment, camera gear, and personal computer system. However, insurance underwriters don't expect wine cellars.

Very few regular homeowners' policies cover wine in case of fire, theft, breakage, or other damage. (Actually, some policies will cover up to a few thousand dollars.) To be certain your collection is covered, you need to purchase a "rider" on your home- or rental-insurance policy. I recommend the all-risk rider. It won't cost much more. Then you're covered even if your home air-conditioning or your wine refrigeration unit fails, and your wine cooks.

Figure the cost of wine insurance to be about 40 to 50 cents per $100, per year. For instance, if your wine inventory is worth $75,000, your annual premium might be about $350.

Heard it Through the Grapevine

You can appraise your own collection. It's tedious, but not hard. For your younger wines, check current catalog prices. For your older wines, you need to research recent auction sales.

If your appraisal is for insurance purposes, however, you'd better get a professional appraisal. That way you avoid contention with the insurer in case of loss. I recommend Roger Livdahl (323-460-6999, www.wineappraisals.com), a well-respected certified appraiser, or William Edgerton (203-857-0240, www.edgertonwineappraisals.com).

Two major insurers with experience in wine coverage are the Chubb Group of Insurance Companies (www.chubb.com).

One thing you need to make clear on your policy is that your wine will be insured for its replacement cost, not for what you paid for it. Consider that vintage bottle you purchased for $50 20 years ago. Today it's worth $500. How much will you recover if you lose it? You need to know.

Another thing you'll need to do is keep good records—of your purchases and of current prices. Insurance claim adjusters are paid to save their companies' money. They're fair, but tough.

Entertainment with Wine

Every wine enthusiast looks forward to social opportunities to serve wine. Wine lovers like to share their appreciation of fine wines. I feel it enhances the wine experience to know that others are sharing in the colors, aromas, mouthfeel, taste, and aftertaste. The following few guidelines can help you plan events with confidence—verve, even, not apprehension.

Which Wines Should I Serve?

Different occasions and different folks in different numbers suggest different selections of wines. The people and the occasion will determine the overall atmosphere much more than the wines you select. For example, you can't create an upscale impression serving vintage

Bordeaux or Burgundy to a clubbing crowd. (Besides, they'll beg for Gatorade to replace all that sweat from dancing.) And despite its association with gaiety and festivity, Champagne is not always the right choice. For a less-formal party, I suggest understatement.

Tasting Tip

For a party where food is incidental (traditional snack foods: a plate of crudités here, a pot sticker there), it's best to stick with wines that may be drunk easily without culinary accompaniment. I recommend an inexpensive, unoaked California Chardonnay. This wine is fruity, refreshing, and very popular. For a red wine, choose a Beaujolais, which is medium to medium-light bodied, fruity without being overpowering, and easy-going with lots of foods. If it's holiday season, Beaujolais Nouveau is perfect.

At a formal dinner party, it's traditional to serve a wine with each course. (Some more elegant dinners serve two wines with each course.) If you own different glasses for different wines, make sure to wash them carefully (no trace of detergent!) and bring them out. If not, you don't need to go buy them. The basic styles are fine (see Chapter 2, A Glass Act).

The rules for choosing your sequence of wines are:

- Light wine before heavy wine
- White wine before red wine
- Dry wine before sweet wine
- Simple wine before complex wine

Of course, there always are conditions where one rule says one thing and another, something else. For instance, if you are serving a light red wine and a rich, full-bodied white, you need to be colorblind and use the "light before heavy" rule. Or, if you're serving a super spicy appetizer that is better offset by an off-dry or sweet wine, it's okay to start off the meal in this way. When in doubt, follow your instincts. Once you know your wines, these generally will be sound.

As your guests arrive, you'll want to offer them an aperitif. A white wine, sparkling wine, or Champagne—usually inexpensive to moderately priced—is the ideal icebreaker. If the party is especially elegant, add a few extra dollars to your bottle. Just don't get carried away. The aperitif is the opening act, not the headliner.

Now your guests are sitting at the table. This is your chance to show how skillfully you marry wine with cuisine. But don't worry about this! Choosing wines is not an esoteric practice like yogi breathing. (For a full discussion of matching wine with food, see Chapter 32.)

Heard it Through the Grapevine

Each guest should have a fresh glass for each wine. This enables them to savor fully the flavors of each and to drink at their own pace. The glasses don't need to be of different or "correct" styles. An ample supply of the basic wine glass will do the job nicely.

On the subject of glasses, don't forget the water! We drink wine because it's a noble sensory experience, not because it contains water. Healthy dining requires ample libation. Make sure there is plenty of chilled water on hand and that your guests can refill their water glasses easily.

How Much Wine Do I Need?

There are no hard-and-fast rules regarding quantity. The amount of wine you serve depends on the type of party, the preferences of your guests, the number of wines served, the pace of service, and the number of hours you expect the party to last. Here are a few suggestions that might make your decisions easier:

- For an informal party, figure two-thirds of a bottle of wine per guest, which I find is an average by party's end.
- For a formal dinner party, the simplest rule is a full bottle of wine per guest. If you think this amount will leave your guests weaving their way home, don't worry. You are gearing your service to a leisurely pace, integrating wine consumption with several courses of food.

Popping the Cork

Serving Champagne (or any sparkling wine) for too long has been surrounded by silly ritual and needless pomp. The occasion may be special, but opening the bottle should be no more ceremonious than opening any other type of wine. Be cautious, however. The contents are under tremendous pressure. Forget the rituals and misconceptions, and keep it safe.

The Sommelier Says

Glass is a very strong material. Without glass bottles, Champagne never would have survived its discovery. But glass with scratches is very vulnerable to fracture. (Engineers tell us scratches concentrate stresses.) Always handle your Champagne purchases with great care.

Treat an unopened Champagne bottle with the same respect as a loaded gun. Never point the bottle in anyone's direction, including your own. Hold the bottle at a 45-degree angle away from everyone. Because a sudden temperature change possibly could cause a bottle to fracture, take special care when handling iced or over-chilled Champagne. (I know. Some people like it that way.) Use these simple guidelines:

- Always inspect a Champagne bottle for deep scratches or nicks. A badly scratched bottle has the potential to explode.
- Never chill Champagne below 45 degrees. Colder temperatures increase the risk of a bursting bottle if it has deep scratches.
- When removing the wire cage around the cork, always place your palm over the cork to prevent its shooting out of the bottle.
- Always point the neck of the bottle away from yourself and others (and light fixtures, too!). A flying Champagne cork works only in the movies. In real life, you run the risk of hurting someone or breaking something.
- Remove the cork with a gentle, twisting motion with your palm over the cork. When the edge of the cork clears the neck, you will hear barely a poof and maybe a wisp of "smoke." Loud pops and gushing foam are vulgar—and an awful waste of good wine.
- If the cork is difficult, push gently on alternate sides with your thumbs. When the cork begins to move, cover it immediately with your palm.

Your Own Winetasting

You may have the impression that winetastings are undertaken only by those who are deemed (or who deem themselves) wine experts. This is nonsense. You're learning more about wine each day, and your collection is growing. There's no reason why you shouldn't consider a winetasting party on your own. Your guests never will forget the experience. (See Chapter 30.)

Keeping Notes

Whether you're a novice oenophile (wine-lover) or you can boast of notches on your taste buds, recalling from memory the details and nuances of a particular wine can be challenging. It's impossible, actually.

Tasting Tip

There are no hard-and-fast rules for describing a wine. Ultimately, your own perception is what counts; so the terminology you use should be your own, not that of some expert.

Many wine enthusiasts keep notes, not only from organized tastings, but from social occasions that feature wines worth noting. (Do not, however, sit at a formal dinner party with a notepad—not if you want to be invited back.) You can write your notes in detail or abbreviate them with terse symbols. Tasting notes are an invaluable aid, both to help you remember your impression of a wine and as a record of your winetasting education.

You should describe your wine experiences in your own words, but there are certain things you should not neglect:

- Olfactory and taste perceptions. Aroma, bouquet, fruitiness, savoriness, etc.
- Structure. Balance of alcohol/sweetness/tannins/acidity
- Texture. The feel of the wine in your mouth

You'll also want to chronicle the development of your tasting experience from the first impression to the lingering aftertaste. (See Chapter 3, More than a Beverage.)

Your Wine Journal

There is no single or best way to organize your tasting notes. Some people love blank notebooks that they can label and file. Still others prefer special wine journals created for this purpose. Others love using new smart phone applications that allow you to even snap a photo of the wine bottle in question and save that as a visual cue alongside your saved tasting notes in the app. If you're a fan of this kind of electronic organizing (which certainly saves space on shelves and tables!), you can find software (check wine accessories catalogs), or even create your own, using a simple Excel spreadsheet or other database package software.

If you have a large, established cellar or even if you are a beginning collector, a cellar log is a useful tool. This log enables you to chart the development of your wines from their date of purchase (don't forget price) through the first sampling (with a note of when to sample next). Even record a lingering, distant impression or two long after you have consumed the very last. As with your wine journal, you can set up your own cellar log or purchase a formatted journal or software.

Scoring Systems

Once you become really serious about wines (it happens), you will want to develop a scoring system for your tastings. This is a good way to catalog particular favorites. Professionals and advanced wine buffs use several systems, but these tend to be unnecessarily complicated. My advice: Keep it simple.

You can use the traditional star system, giving a wine five stars (or three, or one-half). You can use a letter system (A, B, C, D, F), though that may seem too much like a report card. Choose your own symbols: smiley-frowny faces, little bottles, say. An accumulation of stars like your third grade teacher gave out for good work. Just don't get too cutesy. A page covered with pictures of grapevines or corkscrews over time may discourage you from reviewing your own ratings.

Heard it Through the Grapevine

Never downplay the importance of your personal preferences when you rate your wine. After all, wine evaluation is a personal matter. There is no right or wrong way to respond. Our impressions boil down to two things: what we perceive and what we like.

We may perceive easily a wine's high acidity or residual sugar, or its light or heavy body. But these are separate from what we like. One doesn't matter without the other.

Comparing your own evaluations with those of others is the best way to learn about wine and also about how your perceptions and preferences differ. Understanding why another taster's preference is different from yours is more important in terms of learning about wine than knowing which wine is the better one. The best wine for you is the one you prefer. Knowing why you prefer one wine over another is the essential point.

As you develop more experience, your preferences will change. This is common when you share your tasting experience with someone whose palate and expertise are more sophisticated than yours. Your "wine mentor" can help you to isolate subtle sensations you may have missed. Or your mentor may help you articulate those nuances that you know, but can't pin down. A word of caution: Not every experienced wine taster is a good wine teacher. Above all, never feel that you must adjust your preferences because one wine buff prefers a wine you don't. Follow your own instinct—and palate!

CHAPTER 32

Matching Wine with Food

In This Chapter

- The basic rules for matching food with wine
- Going beyond the basic rules
- Becoming your own food and wine matching expert
- Some food and wine matches

Let's start with a premise: Certain wines and foods go very well together, while certain wines and foods clash. Okay?

I'd bet you've already had some success matching wine with food. Maybe you've said to yourself, "I'm having filet of flounder; so I'll have a light white wine to go with it." Or perhaps something spontaneous, like, "Serving this Beaujolais at brunch with eggs Florentine was a brilliant idea! Who would ever have thought it would work!"

On the other hand, you've probably experienced a little failure, too. Perhaps you chose a Salade Nicoise with vinaigrette, only to have a friend arrive with a bottle of full-bodied red wine. Or maybe you've absent-mindedly munched smoked almonds as you've sipped a light, young wine. What harm could they possibly do? Read on…

Wine and Food Basics

Some wines and foods simply are not compatible. For example, a very dry wine with a sweet dessert. Try that, and you can chalk up another faux-pas learning experience.

Matching a wine with the wrong food (or vice-versa) can make both taste bad. Bone-dry wine and the pastry torte? As we say in New York: Fuhgeddaboudit! The wine destroys the dessert's essential sweetness. Sometimes food can neutralize your wine's flavor. Let's say you expect subtle complexities, a symphony of finesse. You intend to show off your noble wine at its peak. But with the wrong food, what did you taste? A very, very expensive jug wine!

Tasting Tip

All wine-lovers agree that wine is the natural accompaniment to a meal. A meal without wine is a meal without salt and pepper. But would you put salt on a wedge of Camembert or pepper on chocolate ice cream? Matching wine with food is like adding condiments to a dish. Your aim is to bring out the product's full potential, not to alter or mask its distinction.

Heard it Through the Grapevine

To hone your wine-matching skills, you need to develop a taste memory, or sense-memory, for wine. You already have a taste memory for food. Think of a pear... Now a banana... Rib roast... Your favorite flavor of ice cream... Good. Chances are you can recall coffee, cola, or orange juice in a flash, right? Of course you can; and it seems pretty easy to do, doesn't it?

Now try this test with wine: Imagine Beaujolais... Cabernet Sauvignon... Chardonnay... Any other wine... What? Not so good? Here's a tip: Visualizing the wine first may help. Here's another: Associate wine with some particular occasion, particularly one where it went well with the food. Better, huh!

Perfect wine and food matching is rare. Success requires knowledge of food and a lot of good luck. Even the greatest chefs don't make a dish exactly the same on each occasion. (Maybe that's what makes them great chefs.) Just a smidgen extra of this or a dollop of that is enough to mar—or if luck is smiling, enhance—the intended combination. Wine can be quirky too, as you've gathered, already. It may not be quite as full or as fruity as you had thought, or those tannins may not have settled.

A Few General Rules

To understand the rules of this game, firsthand experience definitely is required. You may study art history, diligently, but your experience of reading about van Gogh's brush strokes will differ greatly from that of seeing the master's "Sunflowers" up-close. Despite all the great things you've read, you may or may not like the painting, depending on (guess what?) your personal preferences. Just as in art, it's your taste preference, and ultimately your own judgment, that counts in wine-matching.

The trick is to trigger your wine and food memory, and play a matching game. Whenever you taste a wine, think of what flavors go with it to build in your taste memory. This may seem strange at first. I mean, what type of food goes with a wine that evokes tar? But the idea's not really that strange when you think of the terms we use to describe wines—fruity, herbaceous, creamy, tart.

Immediately, certain foods come to mind that have these same qualities. These similarities do not mean that wine and food need to have the same traits! You can work two rather different ways: You can match wine with foods that have similar characteristics. Or you can decide that opposites attract. (It's similar to decorating color schemes, isn't it?)

Use these three basic categories as your guide:

- Components. Sugar, acid, bitterness, sourness, and so on.
- Flavors. Peachy, berrylike, herbal, buttery, minty, vanilla, and so on.
- Texture. Medium-bodied, thin, velvety, viscous, and so on.

The first category is the trickiest. These elements directly affect our taste buds. The components of both food and wine stir the sensory buds in these areas:

- Sweetness. This one is easy. Sweetness is residual sugar in wine, natural or added sugar in food.
- Saltiness. Some foods are naturally salty (briny oysters or mussels), but most have some added salt. Saltiness rarely is associated with wine. (However, Manzanilla Sherry is said to have the tang of the salty air, and wines from Jura, France, also have an unusual, briny characteristic.)
- Sourness. Sourness in food is related to high levels of acidity, which can be natural (lemons, limes) or added (salad dressings). In wine, sourness or tartness is directly related to acidity.
- Bitterness. Bitterness is a component you want to taste only sparingly in food or wine. Strong coffee and tea are pleasantly bitter. In wine, a bitter taste or finish can mean a winemaking flaw, such as too much tannin or oak influence. But the right amount of tannins can afford an interesting bitterness—as with fine espresso.

Keep in mind a few essentials when you are matching, either by contrast or similarity:

- Acidic foods are a good combination with acidic wines.
- Acidic wines go well with salty foods.
- Acidic wines go well with cream-based foods.
- Acidic foods can overpower low-acid wines.
- Salty food and high-alcohol wine taste bitter in combination.
- Salty food and sweet wine are a good match.
- Sweet wine and sweet food go well together (the preferable way is a sweeter wine and a less sweet dessert).
- Sweet wine and spicy foods complement each other's flavors and sensations well.
- Bitter food with bitter wine is just plain bitter.

Heard it Through the Grapevine

You need to remain alert to the possible similarities and contrasts in wines and foods. After a while you'll develop an instinct for what wines go with what foods. Generally, your decision will be based on a flavor, texture, or some other attribute of the food. Singling out some dominant element is an important aspect of choosing wines for a dish.

After you have your components in mind (and palate), pay attention to similarities and contrasts. Ultimately, the judgment is yours, but you might appreciate a few suggestions:

- When thinking of flavor similarity, use your taste memory to evoke each specific flavor. For example, Gewürztraminer is usually characterized as a spicy wine, but not in the hot-spicy way. Spicy foods, however, can be anything from Asian curries to Mexican chilies. When it comes to flavors, we can't generalize.
- Food and wine that trigger similar flavor sensations probably will go well together—like almonds and Fino Sherry.
- Some foods have no real similarities. After all, no wine tastes like fish, garlic, or pork. Adding condiments, fruits, cream sauce, or tomato sauce to such foods, however, may give you matching cues.

White or Red—Any Rules?

As with all conventions, the white-with-fish-red-with-meat rule originated from the best intent. Meat is heavier than fish, after all; so a meat dish needs a robust wine that can stand up to it. And light, acidic white wine is similar to the lemon juice we squeeze on fish. Also, tannins can mingle unpleasantly with fish and leave a metallic finish.

So this old concept is not just blind tradition. It has some sense of logic. However, these rules go back to the last century, and our wines and eating habits have changed. (And how! Have you ever seen a Victorian-era cookbook? Twenty ways to eat yourself into a heart attack!)

A century ago, the only whites that could hold their own with red meat were the big white Burgundies—an expensive addition to any meal. For most people then, white wine meant light wine. Moreover, reds were robust, full-bodied, and rich. Always. Rhônes were as much in fashion as Bordeaux, and Bordeaux was heavier then than it is today. People also drank Port with dinner. And red Burgundy of last century was beefed up with heavier southern reds (a practice that no longer is legal).

Now that we have a selection of New World wines, we have relatively inexpensive alternatives to white Burgundy, such as Chardonnay from California or Australia, Falanghina from southern Italy, or Assyrtiko from Santorini, Greece. And the reds have gotten lighter, too. Connoisseurs have discovered a range of light, red wines like Chinon (Cabernet Franc from the Loire Valley), Barbera from Piedmont, Italy, and Rioja (Tempranillo from northern Spain). Just as many other rules of late have changed, so have the rules of wine matching.

The rule of "white wine with fish and red wine with meat" is a good general rule—as far as general rules go. But as we all know, following rules all the time is no fun.

Consider the rule of serving white wine with white meat. Here is one variation that works well and is not too radical:

- White meat; white sauce; white wine
- White meat; brown sauce; red wine

Some people don't follow color-coding (or rules) at all. Certain red wines are excellent with fish, and some whites are great with meat. You might consider these pairings and their variants:

- Serve red meats rare (broil, grill, sauté) with red wine.
- Cook red meats rare but with unusual spices or methods (like deep-frying) and serve with white wine.
- Red meats cooked for a long time can work with either red or white wine.

White Before Red?

The traditional order of serving white wine before red is subject to modification, too. Again, this theory goes back to the light-and-heavy distinctions appropriate to older wines.

White wine usually is lighter. However, a light-bodied red certainly should precede a full-bodied white. Rosés generally are the lightest of all; so if a rosé is on your table, open it first.

Heard it Through the Grapevine

The rule of dry wine before sweet wine has had great staying power. And it is hard to challenge. Occasionally you may find an iconoclastic chef who serves a sweet Sauternes with an Thai or Indian-inspired appetizer, followed by a medium-dry, full-bodied, low-acid wine. This actually can work. But in general, dry before sweet is one rule your taste buds will not readily forego.

Another traditional rule is to serve young wines before old. This rule may be based more on the vintage mystique than on real sensory experience. The fact is, you may be able to appreciate better the subtle nuances and complexity of an older wine early in the dinner, before your palate has been assaulted by those fruity and tannic youngsters.

On the other hand, if your vintage item is a Port or Madeira, absolutely nothing can follow those acts! (Not even another Port or Madeira.) I'd say the same for a rich, intense, aged Bordeaux. Serve the younger, lighter wines first.

From the Deep

Just as there are light, delicate wines and robust, full-bodied wines, so there are light, delicate fish and robust, full-bodied fish. There are quite a few viscous fish too (though oily is a more suitable word). Then there are shellfish: lobster, shrimp, clams, oysters, and mussels. In each group, certain wine pairings work, while certain others do not.

Here are a few suggestions to help you match wine with fish:

- If you serve red wine with fish, choose one that is young and fruity.
- Choose a high-acid wine, either white or red.

- Stay away from oaky whites and tannic reds.
- Simple fish dishes work with light whites and light reds.
- Use only very light reds with shellfish. (Better yet, follow the rules, and serve white.)
- Avoid red wines with fishy or oily fish.

Light and Delicate Fish

Fish like sole and flounder are delicate in taste and texture. These most definitely are white-wine fish! The only red that should come anywhere near these fish is a light Beaujolais. Rosés usually are light and may be enjoyable, especially with a summer meal.

Salmon and Other Big Guys

It's no coincidence that the menu often reads "Salmon Steak." Or sometimes, "Tuna steak." They have similar qualities. Both are robust, oily, and substantial in body. These fish easily can overpower many whites. White Burgundy or full-bodied California Chardonnay are your best white matches. Fish in this category even can stand up to red Burgundy or similar wines.

Tasting Tip

Bluefish, mackerel, anchovies, sardines, or herring—oily, all—are best kept with acidic white wines like a French Muscadet or Chablis.

Lobster, Shrimp, and Crabs

These tender shellfish deserve something special—and it's generally white. The succulent and delicate meal of lobster calls for a big white Burgundy or a California Chardonnay. Fine Champagne works well too. Lobster Newburg goes well with a French Chablis, a white Burgundy, a white Rhône wine, or a California Chardonnay.

Grilled prawns or scampi go well with Californian or Australian Chardonnays or with big white Burgundies, like Meursault. Curried shrimp calls for a spicy wine, say an Alsatian Gewürztraminer.

Soft-shell crabs go nicely with a French white Bordeaux or a California Sauvignon Blanc. For crab cakes, try a California Sauvignon Blanc, Chenin Blanc, or Italian Pinot Grigio. For steamed crabs, like the Dungeness, try a German Riesling Kabinett from the Mosel, a Washington Dry White Riesling, or a California French Vouvray.

The rich and delicate meat of the Alaskan king crab calls for a white wine with considerable finesse, such as a French Puligny-Montrachet from Burgundy or a Premier Cru Chablis.

Clams, Oysters, and Other Delights

Oysters and Chablis are a traditional combination. The flinty acidic flavor of a young, simple Chablis perfectly offsets the briny mineral taste of the oyster. So does a light and crisp Muscadet, particularly one that is sur lie.

The Sommelier Says

Any restaurateur who serves one of the more expensive caviars will suggest a fine Champagne as accompaniment. Just a gimmick to get you to max out on your credit card? Unfortunately, no. The two go together. Perfectly. This is what I would call expensive good taste, not snobbism.

Speaking of delights from the sea, what better match for caviar than Champagne? If you opt for the real caviar (which includes beluga, the most expensive, or sevruga or osetra), go for real Champagne. The perfect match for caviar is a crisp, bone-dry French Champagne. (At the risk of being called a wine traitor, I consider another perfect match for caviar to be chilled vodka.)

Fowl, Domestic and Wild

With fowl you get white wine. Usually. Most reds overpower broiled or grilled dishes. However, this is another instance where the sauce or spices can help you get it just right—if you're not afraid to experiment.

With roast or broiled chicken, you might try a California dry Chenin Blanc (white) or a simple Spanish Rioja (red). With fried chicken, a red Italian Chianti or simple Spanish Rioja is a good choice. Coq au vin goes well with a Cote du Rhône or a Gigondas, both red. For chicken pot pie, consider an Italian Orvieto (white) or a French Beaujolais-Villages (red).

Chicken Kiev, with its rich buttery interior, calls for a good French white Burgundy or California Chardonnay. Roast game hens go well with an Italian Chianti or a simple French Burgundy. What you drink with roast turkey depends on the stuffing, but a California Chardonnay or French white Burgundy usually is a safe bet. For an apple or prune stuffing, you may want to consider a California dry Chenin Blanc, Riesling, or a French Vouvray.

Tasting Tip

Do you prefer poultry stuffings that are a little out of the ordinary? Then complement them with the right wine selection.

A Sauvignon Blanc from California goes well with an oyster stuffing. For a chestnut or walnut stuffing, try an Alsatian Riesling, a California Pinot Noir, or a French Beaujolais-Villages. A California Zinfandel is a nice match for a sausage stuffing.

Pasta and Casseroles

For pasta dishes, "going ethnic" with wine always is tempting. Pasta is Italian; so the wine should be Italian too. Right? Maybe.

If you're trying to create an atmosphere where your guests can imagine they see Mount Vesuvius over the horizon, by all means bring out the Chianti or Orvieto. But like everything else, pasta dishes have changed. Today we eat cold pasta with cherries. We mix all shapes of pasta with our favorite vegetables, some of which are more typical of California than of Calabria. What to do? I'd match California veggies with a California wine. (Next question: California red or white?)

For pasta casserole (or any other), break it down into components. Does the dish contain beef, lamb, chicken, fish, or pork? Is it vegetarian or encased in thick cheese? What type of sauce? What types of herbs and spices?

With lasagna, you may want to go with the Italian Chianti. With ravioli, select a white Italian Pinot Grigio or an Italian Dolcetto d'Alba or similar light red wine. With a meat sauce, try an Italian Montepulciano d'Abruzzo or an Italian Chianti. With a rich alfredo sauce, an Italian Pinot Bianco or Vernaccia is a worthy choice. Italian Orvieto (white) or an Italian Chianti (red) goes well with carbonara sauce. For clam sauce, try an Italian Gavi or Soave. Finally (and important to know), Italian Verdicchio goes well with a pesto sauce.

Picnics and Other Diversions

Some people think of rosés as picnic wines. They're light and outdoorsy and perfect for summer refreshment. Paté goes well with a simple Bourgogne Blanc or Rouge or a sweet wine like a Sauternes. But then, you may have some bold, full-flavored dishes on your picnic table. If a barbecue grill is in the picture, the complexion changes entirely. Try a California Zinfandel or an Australian Shiraz.

Heard it Through the Grapevine

Salads are great picnic foods. Traditional wisdom says never serve wine with a salad. The dressing will ruin any good wine. Contemporary thinking suggests that's not always so. You can match wine and salad and enjoy both. Just observe a few basics:

- Always serve an acidic wine.
- Stick with light-bodied wines.
- If the salad has something sweet, try a wine with mild sweetness.
- Avoid complex or subtle wines.

They tell us we never should serve eggs with wine. (Of course, honoring this rule would ruin the pricey Sunday brunches at many trendy restaurants.) Frankly, I don't like Mimosas with my omelet. But I can suggest a few options:

- Low-alcohol wines, like a Riesling from Germany, go best with eggs.
- Use the ingredients with which you prepare the eggs (cheese, meats, spices) as your flavor guide.
- Beaujolais can be a very good complement to egg dishes.

Finally, we have cheese—a great picnic food. And a course favored by wine-lovers as an essential part of any complete meal. Red wine with your cheese is the maxim, and among the red wines, Burgundy is my favorite with cheese. But be careful:

- Firm, dry cheeses go very well with red wine.
- Smelly cheeses overwhelm red wine.
- Salty cheeses, particularly blue-veined types, can overpower red wines. These are best served with a Port or similar wine.
- Soft or double- and triple-cream cheeses can go well with a red wine like a Burgundy or a white wine like a Chardonnay or Pinot Grigio.

CHAPTER 33

Cooking with Wine

In This Chapter

- Concentrating wine's flavors
- Marinating with wine
- Favorite recipes

Let's look through your kitchen. Yes, you have salt and pepper. Likely you have onions and garlic, too. Then, perhaps, celery and carrots, maybe some caraway seeds, oregano, and chili powder, cinnamon, clove, and nutmeg. And let's not forget parsley, sage, rosemary and thyme! We use all these (and many more) to season our foods.

So why not season your sauces and broths with wine? After all, wine is the source of the most wonderful flavors found in nature. Why not, indeed! First rule of thumb: If you wouldn't drink it, don't cook with it (more on this later). Start with this very easy, very basic rule of thumb, and you're already ahead of the game!

This chapter contains some wine-cooking basics and a few basic recipes. These will get you started with using wine in your kitchen.

Making it Thick

Wine flavors can run from simple to complex, delicate to authoritative. Wine, as I've said many times, offers flavors found nowhere else in nature. But wine is more than flavor and bouquet. It's liquid. Sometimes you need the flavor, but not all the liquid. After all, you don't want to dilute your sauce or gravy too much.

It's easy to concentrate the flavors of any wine. You reduce it. There are two ways to reduce wine. You can do it directly, by boiling away some of the liquid. Or you can do it indirectly, by adding unboiled wine to your gravy or sauce that you have made thicker than you want.

Tasting Tip

What about serving wine cooking to those who cannot take alcohol—for reasons of health, religion, or choice? With most wine recipes, that's no problem. Just bring your wine sauce or any other wine component to a boil. Because of its lower boiling point, the alcohol will evaporate long before any liquid bubbles. This guarantees an alcohol-free dish.

Usually, you will use the direct method, simply boiling off some of the water. All you need is a small saucepan and a range top. Reducing the volume by half is common. But I don't think of this so much as a reduction in volume as a concentration in flavor.

That flavor won't survive cooking unchanged, of course. Some of wine's subtleties come from lighter, more volatile compounds. But the essential flavor and bouquet will remain, even after reduction. Don't rush this process! Low to moderate on your burner is best.

Of course, the alcohol won't survive reduction in any wine recipe. That's because alcohol boils at 172 degrees F, 40 degrees cooler than water's 212 degrees F. (These are sea-level temperatures. Both become lower at high altitudes.)

You can store your reduced wine in your refrigerator for use as needed over a few days' time.

The indirect method is somewhat easier. Instead of reducing the wine, you just reduce the sauce you're using it in, and then you add the wine at the end, bringing it back to the right consistency. But let it cook a little to boil off the alcohol.

Marinade Aid

There are two good reasons to marinate your meat, poultry, or fish: Flavoring and tenderizing.

A wine-based marinade will add to the flavor of anything that once was hoofed, feathered, or finned. Here the white-with-white-red-with-red rule has a very practical basis. Red wine will darken the color of anything you marinate with it. The appearance of food influences our taste perceptions. Pink perch or blushing chicken breast may not do well, however good they might taste. (Of course, in a thick sauce, that's less important.)

The acids in wine will tenderize your dish. That's why vinegar is the basis of most marinades. The virtue of a wine marinade is that it won't leave behind any sourness. So wine's not right for Sauerbraten, but for many other dishes, I cannot think of anything better.

How long should you marinate? Four or five hours is good for most meat and poultry. Two hours does the job for fish. Longer times add little, if anything. A word of caution, though: You don't want to leave poultry or fish at room temperature any longer than necessary. Let your marinade do its work inside your refrigerator.

Here's a recipe for a simple, all-purpose marinade, one that you can modify to reflect your own preferences. I leave the choice of wine up to you.

(Of course, I'm always happy to make suggestions. If your main interest is tenderizing, choose a white wine, perhaps a Sauvignon Blanc. If you're looking to enhance the flavor of a red-meat dish, start out with a Cabernet Sauvignon.)

Basic Wine Marinade

The character changes with choice of wine.

1 carrot, sliced thinly
1 large onion, sliced
2 garlic cloves, crushed
1 sprig of parsley, snipped
1 bay leaf
Pinch of thyme for red meat, marjoram for white.
8 peppercorns
1 whole clove
2½ cups of wine, your choice

Mix the ingredients thoroughly, as you would a salad dressing. Place whatever you want to marinate into a dish deep enough to allow you to cover it, preferably one in which things can be a little crowded. Add enough marinade to cover, just barely. Then place it into your refrigerator for the desired time. Use paper towels to blot what you've marinated before you cook.

Here's an alternate to that deep dish: Marinate inside a plastic freezer bag. You can cover more food with less marinade, and it's a bit neater.

There's no need to discard your marinade after using. Just strain it, and keep it in your refrigerator in a closed jar. You can thicken it for use as a sauce. Or you can add a little butter and use it for basting.

Vino Vocab

How do people say "Enjoy your meal!" in some of the countries that make fine wines?

French: Bon appétit!
German: Gesegnete Mahlzeit!
Italian: Buon appetito!
Spanish: Bueno apetito!

Recipes! Yum!

Remember when you were little and got your first box of eight wax crayons? Good. Now think back to how you felt the first time you saw one of those boxes of sixty-four! You got it. That's how I feel about wine as a cooking ingredient. Wine offers us a variety of flavors and bouquets that's endless in its possibilities.

In this section, I'll share a few wine recipes. There's no shortage of such dishes in the vast literature of cooking. It's likely several lurk in your own favorite cookbooks, clipped magazine recipes, or food-centric websites, awaiting your knowledgeable wine touch.

Beef Bourguignon

Call it what you like: Beef Bourguignon, or go all the way with Boeuf Bourguignon. It's still Beef Burgundy, a very popular (and easy) dish.

Beef Bourguignon

Serve with French bread and greens.

3 lb. lean stewing beef, in 2-inch cubes
½ cup flour
½ tsp. salt
⅛ tsp. black pepper
2 TB. olive oil
3 TB. butter
¼ cup brandy, warmed
2 cups onion, diced
¾ cup sliced carrots
2 TB. minced parsley
1 bay leaf
½ tsp. thyme
3 cups California Pinot Noir (real Burgundy is too expensive for this dish)
12 pearl onions
2 TB. butter
1 tsp. sugar
24 firm white mushroom caps
1 TB. butter

Season the flour with the salt and pepper, and roll the beef cubes in it. In a skillet, brown the beef on all sides using the olive oil and 3 TB. of butter. Place in a casserole dish. Pour the brandy over the beef.

In a skillet, sauté the onions, garlic and carrots, until limp. Add these to the casserole, along with the parsley, bay leaf, thyme, and the wine. Cover and place into the oven at 325 degrees.

When 30 minutes remain, sauté the pearl onions with 2 TB. of butter and the sugar, until just a little browned. Then add them to the casserole.

With 5 minutes remaining, sauté the mushrooms in 1 TB. butter and add just before serving.

Serves 6 to 8.

Coq au Vin

If someone knows only one dish prepared with wine, this is it! Even if your French education ended with oui-oui and merci, you know that "au vin" means "with wine."

This is French cooking at its most basic. Variations of this well-known dish are served in country houses throughout France.

Coq au Vin

Serve with rice.

1 3-lb chicken, cut up
1 TB. butter
3 TB. brandy, lukewarm
1 kitchen match
1 Vidalia onion
1 TB. flour
2 TB. tomato paste
3 cups French Bordeaux or California Cabernet Sauvignon
2 garlic cloves
1 bay leaf
2 TB. minced parsley
¼ tsp. thyme
salt and pepper, to taste
½ lb. mushrooms
1 TB. butter

Sauté the chicken in 1 TB. butter until it's well browned. Add the warmed brandy and ignite it immediately. Shake the skillet until the flame goes out. Remove the chicken, but keep it warm.

Use the same pan to sauté the onion until it's translucent. Stir in the flour and cook for one minute before adding the tomato paste, the wine, the garlic and the herbs. Season to taste with salt and pepper. When the mixture boils, add the chicken and reduce the heat. Allow it to simmer for 1 hour, turning the pieces several times.

Remove the chicken to a warming platter. Turn up the heat a little, and reduce the sauce to about 3 cups. In another skillet, sauté the mushrooms in 1 TB. butter. Return the chicken to the sauce, and add the mushrooms. Serve from the skillet.

Serves 4.

Veal Marsala

This Old World dish takes its name and flavor from one of the world's oldest wines.

Veal Marsala

Serve over a bed of linguini.

1 lb. boneless veal leg top round steak.
3 TB. butter
1 cup sliced fresh mushrooms
½ cup chicken stock
¼ cup Marsala (ambro, if you can find it)
1 TB. snipped parsley

Cut the veal into four pieces. Use your meat mallet to pound each piece to ⅛-inch thickness. Season to taste with salt and pepper.

Melt 1 TB. butter in a large skillet. Cook half the veal over medium-high heat for 1 to 2 minutes on each side, until done. Remove from the skillet, but keep it warm. Repeat with the remaining veal and TB. of butter.

Cook the mushrooms in 1 TB. butter until tender. Stir in the chicken stock and the Marsala. Boil rapidly for 3 to 4 minutes. (This should reduce to about ⅓ cup.) Stir in the parsley, and pour the sauce over the veal.

Serves 4.

The Sommelier Says

Cooking with Sherry? Well, don't use "cooking sherry"!

To render Sherry legal for sale as a food, it's heavily salted to make it unpalatable as a beverage. That takes too much of the seasoning control out of your hands—not a good idea. Also, these special "cooking" wines are more expensive than the real thing and are far and beyond inferior in quality. Like I said in the very beginning: If you wouldn't drink it, don't cook with it. As you've seen throughout our discussions, there is an abundance of inexpensive, perfectly palatable wines (and sherries) on the market. Don't be fooled by supermarket alternatives!

Turkey au Chardonnay

This is my personal favorite. And I don't mind telling you, I developed this one myself. The Chardonnay in the stuffing suffuses the meat from the inside with compatible wine flavors. I hope you enjoy it as much as I do.

Turkey au Chardonnay

Serve with normal turkey dinner accompaniments.

The turkey:

1 young turkey, 14 to 16 lb.
3 TB. butter, softened

The stuffing:

2½ lb. fresh, whole chestnuts
1 bottle full-body, richly oaked, vintage California Chardonnay ($20 to $30), less 12 oz. (Have a second bottle handy.)
4 TB. unsalted butter
1 TB. salt

The sauce:

12 oz. Chardonnay
2 cups turkey drippings
½ lb. unsalted butter

Remove the neck and giblets; discard or save them for other use. Dry the body cavity. From inside, pierce between the ribs several places using a sharp knife, being careful not to break the skin.

For the stuffing, cut an X into the flat sides of each chestnut and simmer in boiling water until tender, about 15 to 20 minutes. Shell and skin the chestnuts. Mash them, but make sure there still is texture.

Melt 4 TB. butter, add the Chardonnay, and heat through. Work this mixture into the chestnuts, adding additional Chardonnay as needed—up to 2 cups—until you get the consistency of porridge. Allow it to cool. (You can do everything up to this point ahead of time.)

Pre-heat your oven to 450 degrees. Stuff the turkey, and lace the openings tightly to hold its moisture. Place additional stuffing (if any) into a separate casserole, covered with foil, and roast it along with the turkey during the last 40 minutes of cooking.

Brush the turkey with the 3 TB. of softened butter, and place the turkey directly on the bottom of a large roasting pan. Roast at 450 degrees for 15 minutes. Reduce temperature to 325 degrees; and cover your turkey with a foil tent.

Roast at 325 degrees for about 4 hours, without basting, until a meat thermometer inserted into the thickest part of the thigh reads 170 degrees F. At intervals during roasting, add warm water, up to 2 cups, to the pan to keep the drippings from burning.

Remove the foil from the turkey and continue roasting an additional 30 to 45 minutes, basting frequently with the drippings, until the meat thermometer reads 180 degrees F. Remove the turkey from the oven and allow it to stand 20 minutes before carving.

To make the sauce, reduce 12 oz. of Chardonnay by half over medium high heat, until the wine has the consistency of light syrup. Pour the pan drippings into a bowl, skimming and removing the clear fat. Measure two cups of the drippings. Add them to the reduced wine, cooking over medium-high heat, until the mixture thickens. Remove from the heat.

Then whisk in the unsalted butter, a few TB. at a time, allowing it to emulsify completely after each addition. The sauce should be very glossy and light in color and texture when done. Serve with the turkey. (You can hold this sauce up to an hour, covered in the top of a double boiler.)

Serves 8 to 10.

The Best Fondue

This is a dish that evokes the romance of an Alpine chalet, a log fire caressing the room in its warm glow, and someone you love. "Fondu" is the French word for "melted." Sometimes, it's hearts that melt, no less than the cheeses.

The Best Fondue

Serve with French bread chunks (and love).

½ lb. aged Emmenthaler cheese, shredded.
½ lb. Gruyère cheese, shredded
1 TB. cornstarch
1 clove garlic, cut in halves
1 cup German Riesling, Kabinett (either Rhine or Mosel)
3 TB. kirsch (colorless cherry brandy)
¼ tsp. dry mustard

Toss the cheeses with the cornstarch until they are coated. Rub the inside of a heavy saucepan (or double boiler pan) thoroughly with the garlic. Add the wine, and bring it almost to a boil. (Those first bubbles you see are the alcohol boiling off.) If you aren't using a double boiler, keep the heat low.

Add the cheese in small amounts, stirring each time until the sauce has no lumps. When all the cheese is in the mixture, add the kirsch and the mustard, stirring well. Then transfer to your earthenware fondue dish, which you'll keep warm.

Your fondue should seem a little thin so it will penetrate the bread. If it gets too thick, add a little wine.

Serve with day-old French bread, torn into chunks, each containing a bit of crust. Stick fondue forks through the crusts and swirl in the cheese mixture with a figure-eight pattern.

Serves 2.

Wine Desserts

Until the 1970s, Americans drank more dessert wines than table wines. And I wouldn't argue with anyone over wine's suitability as a dessert. A rich Sauternes, a vintage Port, a well-aged Sherry. But I promised you recipes, and here's one I selected because it combines a bit of the new and the old—fresh fruit with a sweet, rich zabaglione.

Nectarines with Zabaglione

Don't tell your doctor!

4 egg yolks
⅔ cup sugar
⅔ cup fino Sherry
1 cup heavy cream, whipped
12 nectarines, pitted and sliced

In a double boiler top, whisk the egg yolks until they're thick. Add the sugar gradually, while whipping. Stir in the Sherry. Place the pan over hot, but not boiling water. Cook until thickened, stirring constantly—about 15 to 20 minutes. Remove from the heat. Cool slightly. Stir in the whipped cream.

Spoon the fruit into dessert glasses and top with the zabaglione.

Serves 4.

CHAPTER 34

Wine and Health

In This Chapter

- Health benefits of a daily glass
- Wine and heart disease
- Consuming in moderation
- Considering temperance warnings

They call it the French Paradox. According to much of what we may know about heart disease, France should be one big coronary ward. Look at the French diet (it has its good points): the fat-equivalent of a Big Mac. And cigarette use: five times that of the U.S., per-capita (those foul-smelling Galois, at that). However, France did follow in the steps of the United and many other countries, banning smoking in public areas in 2007, although many of the Gallic persuasion have been a bit c'est la vie about the ruling. And the rate of heart attacks? About 40 percent lower than that of the U.S., with a life span two and a half years greater!

Why? Could it be the consequence of French friendliness toward foreigners? Au contraire. Many researchers say it's due to the traditional French practice of enjoying red wine at mealtime.

Wine? Good for us? But wine is an alcoholic beverage, right? Yes, these health claims are as controversial as they are surprising. Even potential supporters want to see more evidence. But that evidence continues to come in, from Mediterranean France, Italy, Spain, and Greece, and also from Scandinavia, the Netherlands, the U.K.—and from the home of the skeptics, the good old United States.

Daily Wine and the MD

If you grew up in the U.S. you must be aware that our culture regards alcohol as a dangerous drug. And indeed, it can be. But for the first time, doctors and others are speaking and writing about some of alcohol's benefits. For example, the latest 2010 version of the federal government's Dietary Guidelines for Americans gives thumbs up to light-to-moderate consumption.

This must play alongside those many messages—from governments and from private organizations—about the dangers of alcohol abuse. I feel we need some of each, the good news and the bad, to ensure we all make informed choices. But I do have some trouble with those messages that suggest an all-or-nothing approach. What's wrong with moderation?

Heard it Through the Grapevine

According to the French National Institute of Health and Medical Research, a moderate intake of alcohol cuts the risk of coronary heart disease by as much as 50 percent. This study has another angle. In addition to the French having far fewer deaths from heart attacks, their death rate from atherosclerotic cardiovascular disease (hardening of the arteries) is roughly half that of the U.S.

What it the reason for this amazing phenomenon? Many experts believe it's the presence of the chemical compound, resveratrol, which has been shown in study after study to reduce cholesterol in the blood, the big baddie ingredient in a perfect recipe for a heart attack. Moderate consumption of alcohol, specifically red wine in which amounts of resveratrol are found in the seeds and skins which are commonly left in contact with the juice during fermentation, appears to offset heart disease.

Cultural messages seem to imply that we are incapable of moderation. Slogans like "Just Say No," the youth-oriented message that lumps alcohol in with hard drugs, makes it seem as though there's only one reason to drink: to get drunk. Unfortunately, the slogan works well as a self-fulfilling prophecy and disregards the fact that few wine-drinkers drink to drunkenness.

In the countries of Mediterranean Europe—France, Italy, Greece, Spain, and Portugal, wine is an integral part of the family meal. Children who grow up consuming wine with their parents hardly regard it as some kind of forbidden fruit. Where's the thrill in sipping from a glass poured by your mother? With their parents and other adults as models, young people learn that a glass or two of wine is as natural as oil and vinegar on salad.

Tasting Tip

The tradition of wine with food says a lot about the personality of wine-drinkers. This is noted by Dr. Arthur Klatsky, writing in the American Journal of Cardiology. He found that people who prefer their alcohol in the form of wine tend to be the most moderate and responsible drinkers.

These European children learn another important health lesson, the value of leisurely dining. Can you imagine a Spaniard or a Greek standing at the table, briefcase in hand, shoveling in a few bites and then saying, "Gotta run. I'm outa here!"?

Combined with vino, the relaxed atmosphere of the Mediterranean dinner table has a dual effect:

- It acts as a stress-reducer, which not only makes you feel good but has a positive effect on digestion and the cardiovascular system. Stress can raise your blood pressure by constricting your arteries. Also, it can make blood more likely to clot and raise levels of LDL ("bad") cholesterol.
- The longer mealtime may affect the absorption and metabolism of fats. (Remember, the French diet is no lower in fats than our own.) It can mitigate the effects of fat on blood clotting, stabilize insulin levels, and moderate the absorption of alcohol, itself.

Provided that you enjoy the company, a slow-paced meal is more than nutrition. It's one of life's greater pleasures. Add a bottle of your favorite wine, and you and your bloodstream will both be happier.

Drinking wine with a meal may provide you with alcohol at just the right time: when you need wine's beneficial properties to counteract the effect of the fats you take in. Drinking with dinner ensures the protective effects of alcohol are strongest in the evening, when fatty foods are making their way through your bloodstream. This protective effect lingers into the next morning, the time when most heart attacks take place.

Heard it Through the Grapevine

We all know alcohol soothes feelings of stress. Alcohol acts as a vasodilator, enhancing blood flow by relaxing the muscle tissue of arteries. Alcohol decreases the potential for blood clotting in coronary arteries and increases the level of HDL ("good") cholesterol.

Good food and wine, consumed slowly and leisurely and in the presence of good company, are a powerful (and very pleasant) stress-reducing trio. You don't have to consult your doctor for that. Just refer to your own experience.

Wine and Heart Disease

Certain positive effects on the heart and cardiovascular system are associated with all alcoholic consumption, wine or otherwise. Moderate drinking may be good for you because it tends to:

- decrease levels of bad cholesterol and raise the level of good cholesterol.
- reduce the tendency of blood to clot in arteries and increase the ability to dissolve clots after they have formed.
- moderate the tendency of arteries to constrict during stress.
- lower blood pressure.
- increase coronary artery diameter and blood flow.

In Vino Longevity?

I've already discussed the complexity, the multi-dimensionality, the breed, the bouquet, and all those other factors that distinguish wine from other beverages. Now wine can take credit for something else. Some of the components in wine are part of a group chemists call phenols, which have antioxidant properties. Phenolic compounds exist in grape skins and seeds, and they contribute to wine's subtle nuances of flavor, aroma, texture, and color.

Fermentation makes these nifty phenolic compounds far more prevalent in wine than in fruits or fruit juices. For example, red wines have about five times higher phenolic levels than fresh grapes. The compounds tend to concentrate in the plant seeds, skins, and stems, parts that are discarded in the making of most juices.

In winemaking, however, these parts are fermented along with the juice, especially in making red wine. This helps explain why red wines tend to be more beneficial than white.

But don't despair if you prefer white wine: Both red- and white-wine drinkers reap the cardiovascular benefits of the vinified grape.

I saw one study that identified specific phenolic compounds as the ingredients that inhibit the oxidation of the harmful LDL cholesterol. One of these antioxidants is quercetin. This one may be anti-carcinogenic, also. Quercitin is in onions, garlic, and tea, as well as in wine, and it may inhibit the action of a cancer gene.

The Sommelier Says

Few public health officials seem to endorse wine for its likely cancer-fighting benefits. Instead, they remain quick to indict alcohol—if not as a major player, then at least as a conspirator—in various cancer risks. The government neglects to inform us, however, that these particular risks are associated only with heavy drinking.

As I understand it, quercetin is inactive in food, but it's stimulated into cancer-fighting action by fermentation or by certain bacteria in the intestinal tract. Studies show that high consumption of quercetin-containing foods lowers the incidence of digestive (stomach, intestinal) and other cancers.

Even where alcohol in the form of beer and spirits is implicated, wine still appears to come out the good guy. Indeed, wine may have a protective effect on health and longevity, in addition to flavor and fragrance, balance and breed, and just plain old-fashioned enjoyment.

Good Things in Moderation

Moderate consumption usually is defined as 25 grams (about an ounce) of alcohol per day. That's the vinous equivalent of two to two-and-a-half 4-ounce glasses of wine. Some sources will accept a higher level as moderate. A consensus seems to lie between 1.5 and 2 glasses a day. Fifty grams (five glasses) on a daily basis, however, generally is considered heavy drinking. Thus, one to two regular servings of wine a day is fine for most people.

The rate of alcohol metabolism varies from one person to another and affects the daily level of consumption that's moderate for you. Body weight is important, too. More weight means more blood, which means lower blood alcohol levels.

Heard it Through the Grapevine

Before you start thinking that maybe those extra pounds you had planned to shed now have a useful purpose, forget it! Body composition also is a factor. Lean body weight is what assists in the metabolism of alcohol. Body fluids exist in inverse proportion to body fat.

The more lean body mass you have, the higher the percentage of fluids. The more fat you have, the less fluid. Alcohol seeks out bodily fluids. So concentrations of alcohol will be weaker (more diluted) in a person with less fat. (Got that?)

In general, women weigh less than men, with a greater proportion as fat. (Of course, exceptions exist, especially in the fashion industry.) If you're not sure of your body composition or weight, you can get on a scale, take a pinch test, or look in the mirror.

My best advice is simply to recognize that the ability to metabolize alcohol varies a great deal among individuals. So "know thyself." The lower your weight, the lower your consumption should be. Table 34.1 shows how long it takes people of varying weights (with average lean body mass) to metabolize different quantities of alcohol.

Table 34.1—How long your body takes to metabolize alcohol.

Body Wt. (lbs.)	1 drink	2 drinks	3 drinks	4 drinks	5 drinks	6 drinks
100-119	0 hours	3 hours	3 hours	6 hours	13 hours	16 hours
120-139	0 hours	2 hours	2 hours	5 hours	10 hours	12 hours
140-159	0 hours	2 hours	2 hours	4 hours	8 hours	10 hours
160-179	0 hours	1 hour	1 hour	3 hours	7 hours	9 hours
180-199	0 hours	0 hours	0 hours	2 hours	6 hours	7 hours
200-219	0 hours	0 hours	0 hours	2 hours	5 hours	6 hours
More than 220	0 hours	0 hours	0 hours	1 hour	4 hours	6 hours

Benefits of Moderate Consumption

Evidence continues to come in—and most of it passes favorably on wine drinking. Studies continue to show that regular moderate alcohol consumption reduces the risk of heart disease in some people by 25 to 45 percent, and overall mortality rates by 10 percent. What's more, the benefits are greater for wine drinkers.

If you're worried about liver cirrhosis, the scourge of alcoholics, remember that the people who experience liver damage are very heavy drinkers. Regions of France with the highest wine consumption happen to have the lowest rates of cirrhosis, lower than figures from the U.S.

I have more for you: Wine drinkers have even been found to age more gracefully than nondrinkers. Perhaps you've heard that old joke about how giving up alcohol doesn't really make you live longer… it just feels that way. Well, it's not a joke. Keep up the wine-drinking and you may live longer—and happier.

Heeding the Cautions

With all the warnings proclaimed by the anti-alcohol crowd, and the sometimes confusing information from the medical community, it's difficult to tell which requires more caution: these voices of temperance or the wine itself.

Essentially, warnings about alcohol are based on the effects of heavy consumption—of wine or any other alcoholic beverage. One notable example is the label warning for pregnant women:

Fetal Alcohol Syndrome (FAS) is an unfortunate and avoidable condition that can result in profound mental and growth retardation resulting from a pregnant mother's alcohol consumption.

Guess what! We're not talking about the effects of a glass of wine or two daily, but about heavy drinking and the entire alcoholic lifestyle: low socioeconomic status, poor prenatal care, cigarette smoking, drugs, and poor overall health, all significant cofactors with alcohol.

Does this situation really merit such drastic warnings and scare tactics? Many women say no, and so do a growing number of physicians. Let's go back to those Mediterraneans for a moment. French and Italian women read no such warnings on their wine bottles. They continue drinking mealtime wine with no ill effect.

The Sommelier Says

Don't get the idea I am recommending daily wine to pregnant women. I'm just a wine expert. I'm not competent to make health decisions for anyone. All I care about is that we all make our own decisions, and that those decisions grounded in fact.

We wine-drinkers aren't the irresponsible revelers the voices of temperance may suggest. American wine drinkers are a moderate lot. Statistics reveal the average wine drinker consumes three to five glasses of wine per week, and usually no more than 1.5 glasses on any given occasion. Additionally, we tend to lead healthy lives. Very few wine drinkers smoke, for instance. (Cigarette smoke ruins the taste and aroma of wine.) And many wine drinkers exercise regularly and consume a produce-rich diet—habits we have in common with those robust Mediterraneans.

Wine drinkers may like to jog or hike, but we also drive cars. So let me close on a note of caution. Wine has been implicated in two percent of all arrests for drunken driving. I'd like to do my part to bring that figure down to zero.

Regardless of what beverage you enjoy, accidents caused by drunk driving are tragic and avoidable. Legal intoxication is usually set at 0.08 or 0.10 blood alcohol level. However, coordination and judgment are impaired well before that. Use your judgment before you lose it.

Wine affords many pleasures, but they are not free of all care. I advise you to consider the following, what I call The Wine Drinker's Commandments:

- Don't operate a vehicle just after drinking: cars, bicycles, motorcycles, boats, airplanes… anything that moves. (In England, which has a very tough drunk driving law, some people visit pubs on horseback.)
- Don't swim, surf, or water-ski when drinking.
- Don't participate in athletic activities that require balance and perception, land or water, while drinking. These include rollerblading, skateboarding, skiing, gymnastics, and others.
- Don't use firearms or other weapons if you've been drinking.
- Don't use power tools, particularly saws, mowers, drills, or the like, after drinking.
- Don't drink wine with antihistamines or similar medication. Drowsiness may result. For any other medicines, prescription or over-the-counter, check the label for guidelines. Or seek advice from your doctor or pharmacist.
- Don't drink under a physician's care except with explicit permission.
- Finally, don't ever let your guests drive home even a little bit tipsy. A responsible host will phone a cab or make other safer arrangements.

APPENDIX A

Recommended Wines

Wine Recommendations

One of the difficulties of recommending wines in a wine book is that wines come and go in the marketplace and a listing of wines in a book are quickly outdated. In addition, to do a proper job, an Appendix of wine recommendations takes up a lot of pages as does this appendix – 56 pages. Our solution is to offer this appendix on our website where it can be updated literally daily if necessary.

To view this appendix of recommended wines, simply visit the www.smartguidepublications.com website, click on the Appendices tab, and select The Smart Guide To Wine, where you will find the Wine Recommendation appendix. You may find other appendices there as well, depending on our development schedule.

APPENDIX B

Wine Words

acidic A description of wine whose total acidity is so high that it imparts a sharp feel or sour taste in the mouth.

acidity The nonvolatile acids in a wine, principally tartaric, malic, and citric. These acids provide a sense of freshness and an impression of balance to a wine. Excessive acidity provides a sharp or sour taste; too little results in a flat or flabby character.

aftertaste The impression of a wine after it is swallowed. It is usually described as the "finish" of a wine. It ranges from short to lingering. A lingering aftertaste is a characteristic indicative of quality.

aged Describes a wine that has been cellared either in cask or bottle long enough to have developed or improved. As a tasting term, it describes the characteristic scent and taste of a wine that has so developed while in its bottle.

American Viticultural Area (AVA) Official place-name designation for American vintners.

Amontillado (aw-MOHN-tee-YAW-doh) A dry sherry of the fino type, but darker, fuller, with nutty flavor.

année (aw-NAY) Vintage.

apéritif (aw-PEH-ri-TEEF) A dry before-dinner beverage.

Appellation d'Origine Côntrolée or AOC or AC (aw-peh-law-see-OHN daw-ree-ZHEEN caw-troh-LAY) The top category in the official French system of quality assurance. It means Appellation of Controlled Origin.

astringent A puckering, tactile sensation imparted to the wine by its tannins. A puckering quality adds to the total sense of the wine, giving it a sense of structure, style, and vitality. Tannins are an essential component in red wines, which are made to improve with age while in bottle. Red wines lacking in tannins are generally dull and uninteresting. Wines vinified for prolonged aging are harshly tannic when young, but mellow when the wines age and the tannins precipitate to form a sediment in the bottle.

aroma The basic olfactory elements present in a wine, generally the fruity smell characteristic of the varietal.

Asti Town in the Piedmont region of Italy, famed for sweet, sparkling Spumante.

Auslese (OWSS-lay-zeh) Literally, "picked out" (i.e., selected). Under the new German wine law, Auslese wine is subject to all regulations included in Qualitätswein mit Prädikat (quality wine with special attributes). Auslese wine is made entirely from selected, fully ripe grapes, with all unripe and diseased grapes removed. No sugar may be added. The wine is especially full, rich, and somewhat sweet.

balance The proportion of the various elements of a wine; acid against sweetness, fruit flavors against wood, and tannins and alcohol against acid and flavor.

Balthazar Large bottle, equal to 16 standard bottles, or 12 liters.

barrel-fermented The fermentation of a wine in a small oak cask as opposed to a large tank or vat.

Barbera (bar-BARE-aw) Red wine grape grown in northern Italy and parts of California.

Beaujolais (BOW-zhoh-lay) An early maturing red wine from the southern Burgundy district in France.

Beaune (bohn) Small medieval city in Côte d'Or, headquarters of French Burgundy wine trade.

Beerenauslese (BEAR-en-OWSS-lay-zeh) "Berry-selected," i.e., individual grape berries picked out (by order of ripeness) at harvest for their sugar content, quality, and their amount of Edelfaule (noble rot).

Bereich (beh-RYSH) A geographic region for German wine classification.

blanc (blawk) French for white.

Blanco (BLAWN-koh) Italian for white.

Blanc de Blancs (blawk-duh-BLAWK) Describes a white wine made from white grapes. The term refers to both still table and sparkling wines. The words "Blanc de Blancs" do not signify a quality better than other white wines.

Blanc de Noir (blawk-duh-NWAWR) White wine made from black (red) grapes. Champagne made 100 percent from Pinot Noir grape.

Blauburgunder (BLOU-BOOR-goon-dehr) German for Pinot Noir grape.

bodega In the Spanish wine trade, a wine house, wine company, wine cellar, or even wine shop.

body The tactile impression of fullness on the palate caused by the alcohol, glycerin, and residual sugar in a wine. The extremes of "body" are full and thin.

Bordeaux (bor-DOH) Important seaport city in southwestern France, where Garonne River empties into the Gironde estuary. The heart of the Bordeaux winegrowing region. Many wine dealers are located there.

Botrytis cinerea A species of mold that attacks grapes grown in moist conditions. It is undesirable for most grape varieties, or when it infects a vineyard prior to the grapes reaching full maturity. Vineyards are treated to prevent its occurrence. When it attacks fully mature grapes, it causes them to shrivel and lose their water content, concentrating both the acidity and the sugar, and resulting in an intensified flavor and a desired sweetness balanced by acidity. This is beneficial and highly desirable for white varieties such as the Johannisberg Riesling, Sauvignon Blanc, Semillon, and Chenin Blanc, from which unctuous, luscious, and complex white wines are made in various wine regions of the world.

bouquet The scent of a mature wine, the complex mix of smells developed through fermentation and aging.

Bourgogne (boor-GOH-nyeh) French for Burgundy, the region or its wine.

breed A term used to describe the loveliest, most harmonious and refined wines that achieve what is called "classical proportions." The term is elusive to definition, but wines that deserve such acclaim are unmistakable when encountered.

brix Specific-gravity method used in U.S. to ascertain sugar content of grape must. Named for German chemist Adolf Brix.

brut (broot) French for raw, unrefined. Applied to driest Champagnes.

Bureau of Alcohol, Tobacco and Firearms (BATF) Part of the U.S. Treasury Department responsible for setting and licensing and enforcing labeling standards for alcoholic beverages, including wine.

Burgundy Region in eastern France. Several wine districts growing red and white wines, some renowned and expensive. Applies to any wine from that region or, generically, to many red wines.

Cabernet Franc (KAB-air-nay FRAWK) Fine red grape varietal, grown widely in the Bordeaux region of France.

Cabernet Sauvignon (KAB-air-nay SOH-vinn-yawn) Premium red grape grown widely in finest wine regions of Bordeaux.

cask Cylindrical vessel of wood or stainless steel in which wine is fermented or aged. Ranges in size from 135 to 2475 liters, depending on country and locale.

centrifuge Modern machine that uses forces generated by rotation to separate wine from its solid impurities.

Chablis (shaw-BLEE) Small town in north of Burgundy region, source of fine, rare white wine. Used generically to describe lesser white wines.

chai (shay) Above-ground winemaking and storage facility at French wine estates.

Champagne Sparkling wine from a small, controlled region in eastern France, south of Reims. In the U.S. some sparkling wines are called "champagne."

chaptalization (shawp-TAW-lee-ZHAW-see-ohn) The addition of sugar to the must to increase alcohol formation through fermentation.

Chardonnay (SHAR-doh-nay) White wine grape used in finest white wines from Burgundy and elsewhere throughout the world.

charmat process Also called "bulk process." Hastens second fermentation process for creating sparkling wines in large, pressurized tanks.

château French for castle. A French wine estate or the wine, itself. Plural: châteaux.

Chianti (kee-YAWN-tee) Famous red wine of the Tuscany region of Italy.

claret Generic term used by the English to denote light red wines in the Bordeaux style.

classico (KLAW-see-koh) Italian for classic. Smaller defined areas within a designated wine region of Italy.

Cliquot (klee-KOH) Madame Cliquot was a wine merchant's widow in early nineteenth century France, who developed and promoted the local Champagnes. Her cellar master developed the modern Champagne cork.

clone A grape variety developed through cutting or grafting to create new characteristics.

cooperage The wooden barrels and tanks used for aging wines.

corked Wine fault caused by a naturally occurring chemical compound called TCA that attaches itself to organic materials, such as cork. The resulting odor suggests putrefaction.

Côte de Beaune (koht-deh-BOHN) Southern half of Burgundy's Côte d'Or, home to noble red wines.

Côte de Nuits (koht-deh-NWEE) Northern half of Burgundy's Côte d'Or, source of superb red wines based on Pinot Noir.

cotto (KOT-toh) Italian for cooked. The process of adding caramelized must to some Marsala wines.

cru (kroo) French for growth. Applied to a vineyard and the wine it produces.

Cru Bourgeois Refers to red Bordeaux wines from the Haut-Médoc that rank just below the Grande Cru Classé wines of the 1855 Bordeaux classification.

Cru Classé "Classified growth." Refers to those wines originally classified as Grand Cru Classé in the 1855 Bordeaux classification.

crush Commonly used to refer to the grape harvest or vintage. Most specifically the breaking of the grape stems, which begins a fermentation process.

crust Sediment deposited on insides of bottles as wines age. Generally applied to old Ports.

cuve A large vat, usually made of wood, used for the fermentation of grape juice into wine.

cuvée The contents of a wine vat. More loosely used to refer to all the wine made at one time or under similar conditions. Sometimes a specific pressing, or batch of wine. Sometimes used as part of a brand name or trademark, or as wine label nomenclature to refer to a batch of wine.

decant To transfer wine from one container to another.

dégorgement Process of removing sediment from second bottle-fermentation of Champagne.

Denominació de Origen, DOC (day-noh-mee-nawth-YOHN deh oh-REE-hen) Controlled denomination of origin, the Spanish law for specifying place names for wines.

Denominación de Origen Calificada, DOC (day-noh-mee-nawth-YOHN deh oh-REE-hen kaw-lee-fee-KAW-daw) Highest designation used in labeling Spanish wines.

Denominazione di Origine Controllata, DOC (deh-NOH-mee-naw-tsee-OH-neh dee oh-REE-jee-nee kon-troh-LAW-taw) Controlled denomination of origin, the Italian law for specifying place names for wines.

Denominazione di Origine Controllata e Garantita, DOCG (deh-NOH-mee-naw-tsee-OH-neh dee oh-REE-jee-nee kon-troh-LAW-taw eh gaw-ren-TEE-taw) Italian quality designation above DOC.

Dom Pérignon Monk at Reims who developed controlled process for making Champagne in the early eighteenth century.

domaine The French term applied to wine estates in Burgundy.

doux (doo) French for sweet. Applied to the sweetest Champagnes.

dosage (doh-SAWZH) A small amount of sugar, Champagne, and brandy that is added to Champagne right after dégorgement. The final sweetness of the wine is determined by this step.

Einzellage (EYN-tsel-law-geh) Under German wine law, an individual vineyard or estate.

Eiswein (EYSS-veyn) Intensely sweet and rich German wine made from the frozen juice in the fruit of a Beerenauslese harvest, where freezing concentrates the must. Rarely made.

éleveur (eh-leh-VEHR) A wine firm that cares for wines in their barrels and bottles them, frequently blending to provide better structure and balance. Often, this firm is also a négociant or shipper.

estate-bottled A wine that has been bottled at the vineyard or winery in which it was made. Has legal significance in several countries, particularly France, Germany, and Italy, but is not controlled in others. Basically it connotes wine that was under the control of the winemaker from vineyard to bottle. It does not ensure the excellence of a wine, although it once did, as a general rule, many years ago.

Fass (fuss) German for oaken barrel or cask.

fermentation The process of converting sugar into alcohol, usually by the action of yeast on the juice of fruit, such as grapes. It is a complex process in which the yeast produces enzymes that convert the sugar into alcohol, carbon dioxide, and heat.

fiasco (FYAH-skoh) Old, bulbous style of Italian wine bottle covered with woven straw.

finesse A quality of elegance that separates a fine wine from a wine that is simply good. It is a harmony of flavors and components rarely found in wine. The term is hard to define, but a wine with finesse is unmistakable when encountered.

fining A clarifying technique that introduces an electrolytic agent, such as egg white, powdered milk, blood, diatomaceous earth (bentonite), or gelatin, to attract the solids and settle them to the bottom of a cask. Beaten egg whites or bentonite are the most frequently used agents.

finish The aftertaste of a wine when it has been swallowed. Usually consists of both flavor and tactile sensations from the acidity, alcohol, and tannins of the wine.

fino (FEE-noh) Spanish for fine. The palest and driest Sherry.

flor A film of yeast or bacteria, usually in the cask on top of a wine, but also found in unhygienically bottled wines. In Spain it is a specific yeast that grows in Jerez and imparts a delicate, nutty quality to its wines. When Sherry is affected by this yeast, called Saccharomyces fermentati, it is called fino.

fortified A wine to which alcohol has been added to raise its alcoholic strength. These wines usually range from 15 to 21 percent alcohol.

free-run juice The juice that is released from the grape as it is being crushed, before the pulp and skins are pressed. This juice, generally less harsh than press wine because of a lack of skin contact, is used for the finest wines. Free-run accounts for about 60 percent of the juice available from the grape for fine wine. This juice is separated immediately from the skins for white wine but is combined with the skins and pulp for reds. It is drained off the solids prior to the pressing of the remaining grape material.

French oak The wood from the great oak forests of France, particularly from Nevers and Limousin, which impart a distinctive and mellow character to wine aged in barrels made from them. Also used as a term to describe the flavor imparted to wine by barrels made from this oak.

fuder (FOO-d'r) Large German barrel, usually 1,000 liters.

Gamay (GAH-may) Red wine grape grown extensively in Beaujolais district of France.

generic wine A broadly used wine term signifying a wine type, as opposed to a more specific name, such as a grape variety or the actual region of production. Such names have frequently been employed on American wines using famous European place-names such as Chablis, Burgundy, Rhine, Champagne, or European wine types such as Claret or Sherry.

Gewerztraminer (guh-VERTS-trah-mee-ner) White wine grape grown in Germany and Alsace, France, and elsewhere. The name means spicy Traminer.

Gironde (zhee-ROHND) Large estuary emptying into the Atlantic. The finest wine districts of Bordeaux lie along its western bank.

Goût de Terroir (GOO deh ter-WAH) The specific taste characteristic imparted from the soil of a particular wine district.

Goût de Vieux (GOO deh VYOO) The distinctive taste of an old wine.

Grand Cru (graw KROO) Great growth. A classification of French wines considered to be superior in quality. Used in Bordeaux, Burgundy, and Alsace.

gravelly Term that describes wine with a clean, earthy taste.

Graves (grawv) District in France's Bordeaux region, a source of superb red wines. The name means gravel, after the soil type.

Grenache (greh-NAWSH) A sweet red grape used as a blend in France, Spain, and California.

Grosslage (GROHSS-law-geh) Under German wine law, a region intermediate between the large Bereich and the vineyard-sized Einzellage.

halbtrocken (hawlp-TRAWK-en) German for half-dry. Semi-sweet.

Haut-Mèdoc (OH may-DAWK) Wine region of Bordeaux responsible for its best wines.

hock Older generic English word denoting German white wines.

hybrids New grape varieties genetically produced from two or more different varieties—usually defined as varieties from different species, although the term is loosely used to include vines "crossed" within the same species.

hydrogen sulfide A chemical compound that is a natural byproduct of fermentation and imparts the smell of rotten eggs. With proper handling, it dissipates prior to the finishing of a wine, but remains in poorly handled wines.

Jerez (hayr-ETH) Spanish city, the wines of which have been called Sherry for hundreds of years.

Jéroboam A large wine bottle. In Champagne, four standard bottles (3 liters). In Bordeaux, six standard bottles (4.5 liters).

jug wines Refers to inexpensive, everyday drinking wines, usually bottled in large bottles known as jug bottles. Most wines in this category are generics, but occasionally varietals also appear in jug bottles.

Kabinett (kaw-bee-NET) A legally defined quality level of German wines that is governed by the German government. Kabinett wines are the lowest rank of Qualitätswein mit Prädikat wines, stringently defined as to geographical region of origin, natural sugar content, and other attributes.

Keller German for wine cellar.

kosher wine Any wine made under strict rabbinical supervision, suitable for Jewish observance.

labrusca Grape species, Vitis lambrusca, native to North America. Generally not suitable for making fine wines.

Landwein (LAWNT-veyn) German for regional wine.

Late-Harvest A type of wine made from overripe grapes with a high sugar content. Generally, Late-Harvest wines have been made from grapes deliberately left on the vine to achieve high sugars and concentrated flavors. White wine grapes are frequently affected by Botrytis cinerea, the noble mold, which further concentrates the grape and imparts its own unique, honeyed character. Most Late-Harvest wines are unctuously sweet, luscious in flavor, and are meant to be drunk with dessert or by themselves rather than with a meal.

lees The sediment that results post-fermentation from dead yeast cells. Wines are left on their lees to gain character and complexity.

legs The "tears," or streams of wine, that cling to the glass after a wine is swirled. Legs are usually a sign of a wine with body and quality and are caused by the differences in evaporation rates of alcohol and other liquids in the wine.

Liebfraumilch (LEEP-frouw-meelsh) Literally, milk of the Blessed Virgin. A trade name for a blend of white wines, widely exported.

Limousin (lee-moo-ZAN) oak The great white oak of the Limoges Forest in France, which is considered to be among the finest oak for aging wines and brandies. It imparts a mellow, complex vanilla character, with subtle nuances particular to its species, which adds complexity and elegance to a wine aged in casks made from it.

Loire (lwawr) Major river in France. Wines, red and white, of all qualities are grown along this large wine region.

maceration carbonique The whole-berry, intercellular fermentation by bacterial, rather than yeast action on the grapes in an airtight container. Imparts a fresh, fruity, jam-like quality to wines so treated, which are light in body and meant to be consumed when young.

Madeira Portuguese island in the Atlantic, off the coast of Morocco, long-time origin of famous fortified wines.

maderized A wine that has lost its freshness or has spoiled due to oxidation in the bottle, either from storage in an excessively warm area, or simply because of overage. Maderized wines tend to smell like the wines from Madeira, hence the term. They have a sharp, yet sweet, caramelized character that is not attractive. Maderized white wines darken in color to amber or brown.

magnum A large wine bottle, equivalent of two standard bottles.

Malbec (MAL-bek) Red wine grape grown extensively in Bordeaux.

Maître de Chai (MAY-truh duh SHAY) In France, a winery's cellarmaster, who is charged with tending the maturing casks of wine. Frequently he is also the winemaker. This position is the most important in a winery.

malolactic fermentation The secondary fermentation that occurs in some wines due to the action of certain bacteria on the wine, which transform the hard malic acid to softer lactic acid. It also imparts new subtle flavors which, depending on the wine type, may or may not be wanted. It is usually undesirable in white wines, which require malic acid for freshness.

Margaux (mar-GOH) Bordeaux district along Gironde that produces superb wines.

Marsala Famous fortified wine of Italy, from Island of Sicily.

Médoc (meh-DAWK) The heart of France's world-famous Bordeaux wine region.

mercaptans (mer-KAP-tens) Odorous compounds resulting from hydrogen sulfide, indicating faulty winemaking or storage.

Merlot (mehr-LOH) Famous red grape variety grown in many parts of France's Bordeaux region, and elsewhere through the world.

Méthode Champenoise The traditional method of making sparkling wine, and the only method permitted in the French district of Champagne where it was invented. It is the most labor-intensive and costly way to produce sparkling wine but also imparts a character and refinement not obtainable with other methods, particularly with regard to the quality of the bubbles produced. A shortcut to the Méthode Champenoise is called the transfer process, which eliminates the riddling and dègorgement steps which are the most costly and time-consuming and produces wines that are sometimes indistinguishable from the more complicated method.

Meursault (mehr-SOH) Region of France famous for its white wines.

Mevushal (MEH-voo-shawl) A term applied to wine that's kosher by reason of having been pasteurized.

middle body The part of the taste sensation that is experienced after the initial taste impact on the palate. It provides the core of the taste on which assessments are usually based. The first, or entry, taste and finish should both be in harmony with the middle body. A wine with a weak middle body generally gives the impression of being incomplete.

Mis en Bouteilles Sur Lie (MEEZ ahn boo-TEH-yah soor LEE) "Put in bottles on its lees," the practice of bottling a wine directly from the barrel, immediately after fermentation without racking. The wine (almost always white) retains a fresh, lively quality, often with a slight petillance due to carbon dioxide absorbed during fermentation that had not completely dissipated when bottled. "Sur lie" wines often experience a malolactic fermentation in the bottle, which also contributes to the petillance or "coming alive" in the bottle in the year after bottling.

Mosel-Saar-Ruwer (MOH-zl zawr ROO-vehr) German wine-growing region just west of the Rhine regions.

mousseux (moo-SUHR) French term that means foamy, applied to sparkling wines that aren't Champagne.

mouthfeel Wine textures, apart from taste, detected in the mouth.

Meuller-Thurgau (MUH-lerr TOOR-gouw) A Riesling-Silvaner hybrid that is most widely grown grape in Germany. It's planted elsewhere through the world.

Muscadet (mis-kaw-DEY) A popular, light, dry wine from France's Loire Valley.

Muscatel Any wine made from the Muscat grape. In California, the term is applied to certain fortified wines of low quality.

must The unfermented grape juice produced by crushing the grapes. It is a loosely defined word and equally defines grape juice, crushed grapes, or the juice after pressing.

must weight The number of grams above 1000 of a liter of grape juice, a reliable indicator of sugar content, because sugar is denser than water.

Nebuchadnezzar The largest Champagne bottle, rarely used, containing 20 standard bottles (15 liters).

nègociant (nay-goh-SYAWN) The person who sells or ships wine as a wholesaler.

nero (NAY-roh) Italian for black. Any red grape variety.

noble rot Common term for the fungi of genus Botrytis that infect grape skins, sometimes contributing to the complexity of a finished wine.

nutty A wine flavor attribute, generally associated with Sherry or Tawny Port.

Organic Grapes into Wine Alliance (OGWA) An association of U.S. organic growers and vintners.

oaky A wine flavor attribute that is toasty and reminiscent of vanilla.

Oechsle (ERKS-leh) A scale used in Germany and Switzerland for ascertaining sugar from must weight.

oenology The study of wine. (Sometimes spelled enology.)

oenophile A wine-lover. (Also, enophile.)

Oporto Portuguese city famed for shipping Porto (formerly Port) wines.

overripe Wines with more sugar, less acidity, because of extended ripening. If out of balance, may be a wine fault.

oxidation The process of oxygen from the air combining with some wine compounds to form new compounds, which usually detract from the wine's quality. Oxidized wine is said to be maderized.

Pauillac (Poh-YAK) Bordeaux district along Gironde that produces superb wines.

phenolic compounds Chemical compounds occurring naturally in skins, seeds and oak barrels, which contribute astringency, flavor and color to wine.

Pinot Blanc (PEE-noh Blawk) A white wine grape that is part of the Pinot family, distinct from the Chardonnay.

Pinot Gris (PEE-noh GREE) Grey-colored member of the Pinot family of wine grapes.

Pinot Noir (PEE-noh NWAH) The most important red grape of France's Burgundy region.

plonk Any wine so lacking in character and quality as to render it unsuitable for any reader of this book.

Pouilly-Fuissé (poo-YEE fwee-SAY) Distinguished white wine from southern Burgundy region.

Prüfungsnummer (PREE-foongz-noo-mer) Registration number appearing on German wine labels, indicating the wine has been inspected and certified.

Qualitätswein (kwaw-li-TAYTS-veyn) Literally "quality wine," which, under the German wine law, is one grade above Tafelwein ("table wine") and one grade below Qualitätswein mit Prädikat (quality wine with special attributes). Quality wine must come from a single district, and among other qualifications, must be of a minimum alcoholic strength.

racking The traditional way of clarifying a wine by transferring it from one cask to another and leaving the precipitated solids behind.

raisiny A wine flavor attribute suggesting raisins, characteristic of late-harvest wines.

Rehoboam A Champagne bottle containing six standard bottles (4.5 liters).

residual sugar The unfermented sugar remaining in a wine. It is usually described in terms of the percentage by weight, and is detectable when it exceeds three quarters of one percent. Above two percent it tastes quite sweet.

reserva (ray-ZEHR-vah) Spanish quality designation for good wines that have met aging requirements.

Retsina (ray-TSEE-nah) Greek wine made in ancient manner, with added pine-tree resins

Rheingau (REYN-gouw) One of Germany's finest wine regions, planted widely in the Riesling grape.

Rheinhessen (REYNN-hess-en) Germany's largest wine region.

Riesling (REEZ-ling) Germany's most distinguished grape, producing that country's greatest white wines. Grown widely elsewhere.

Rioja (ree-OH-hah) Red wine from a designated region in the north of Spain.

Riserva (ree-ZEHR-vah) Italian for reserve, applied to DOC and DOCa wines that have been aged.

rosé (roh-ZEY) French for pink. Applied to wines lightly colored.

rosso (RAWS-soh) Italian for red, applied to red wines made from approved varietals.

Rotwein (ROHT-veyn) German for red wine.

robe The color of a wine in general, and, more specifically, to the wine's color when the glass is tipped at an angle.

Saint-Estèphe Bordeaux district along Gironde that produces superb wines.

Saint-Julien Bordeaux district along Gironde that produces superb wines.

Salmanazar Large Champagne bottle, 12 standard bottles (9 liters).

Sauternes (soh-TEHRN) A Bordeaux appellation from which come some of the world's greatest sweet white wines.

Sauvignon Blanc (SOH-veen-yawn Blawn). White wine grape widely cultivated in France and California.

Schloss (shlohss) German for castle. A wine estate.

sec Literally means "dry," and a dry wine. Its use is not legally defined, and it frequently appears on wine labels of wines that are off-dry or even somewhat sweet.

sec (sehk) French for dry

seco (SEH-koh) Spanish for dry.

sediment The deposit precipitated by a wine that has aged in the bottle.

Sekt (Zekt) German sparkling wine.

Sèmillon (seh-mee-YOHN) White wine grape planted around the world.

Sherry A fortified wine made in the Jerez DO of Spain.

Shiraz Australian name for the Syrah grape.

Silvaner White wine grape once the most prevalent in Germany. (Also spelled Sylvaner.)

Solera (soh-LEH-rah) The traditional Spanish blending system used in making Sherry. The Solera, itself, is a series of Sherry casks containing wines of various ages which are fractionally blended by transferring part of the contents of a younger cask into an older one.

sommelier (soh-meh-lee-EH) Wine steward.

sparkling A wine that, under pressure, has absorbed sufficient carbon dioxide to bubble, or "sparkle" when poured into a glass.

Spatburgunder (SHPAYT-boor-GOON-der) German name for Pinot Noir

Spätlese In German nomenclature, a wine made from fully ripe grapes.

Spumante Refers to Italian sparkling wines.

still wine Any wine that has no bubbles.

sulfites A class of compounds created from sulfurous acid, the result of contact with sulfur dioxide gas, which is used widely in winegrowing and winemaking. Some individuals may be sensitive to these compounds.

sur lie (soor LEE) French term applied to wines aged "on the lees." Believed to add complexity and texture.

süss (Zeess) German for sweet.

Syrah The red grape favored in France's Rhône region. In Australia, called Shiraz.

Tafelwein (TAH-fel-veyn) German for table wine.

tannin An astringent acid, derived from the skins, seeds, and wooden casks, which causes a puckering sensation in the mouth. Tannin is an essential preservative for quality wines. A moderate puckering sensation caused by the tannins adds to the pleasurable character of a red wine.

tawny The dark, oxidized color characteristic of aged Port wine.

Tonneau A Bordeaux measure of wine, equivalent to four barrels, or one hundred cases of wine.

terroir (tehr-WAHR) French term referring to the unique combination of soils and micro-climate that distinguish one fine wine from another.

tinto (TEEN-toh) Spanish word meaning red when applied to wine.

Tokay (toh-KAY) The great, sweet white wine from Hungary.

transfer process A shortcut method of making bottle-fermented Champagne. In this process, the wine is filtered rather than riddled and disgorged.

trocken German word for dry.

Trockenbeerenauslese The highest Prädikat a German wine can carry. It signifies that the wine is made entirely from late-picked, individually selected grape berries that have been allowed to shrivel on the vine, usually after being attacked by the Botrytis cinerea, the noble rot, which imparts a special quality to the finished wine.

ullage (oo-LEEZH) The empty space at the tops of bottles and casks, sometimes applied to loss of liquid through faulty storage or container.

unfiltered A wine that has been bottled without being clarified or stabilized by filtration. When bottled without any cellar treatment, such a wine is labeled as "Unfiltered and Unfined."

unfined A wine that has not been fined as part of its cellar treatment. Also infers that the wine has not been filtered and has received a minimum of treatment.

Vin Délimité de Qualité Supérieure, VDQS (VAN dee-lee-mee-TAY deh kaw-lee-TAY soo-pehr-YOOR) Delimited wine of superior quality, the French quality classification just below AOC.

varietal Refers either to a wine named after a grape variety, or one that is made entirely from a single grape variety. As legally defined, such a wine need be made only from 75 percent of the named grape.

varietal character The recognizable flavor and structure of a wine made from a particular variety of grape.

vin (van) French for wine.

vinho (VEE-nyoo) Portuguese for wine

Vitis vinifera The species of grape varieties known as "the wine bearers," which are responsible for all the finer wines of the world.

vinify To turn grapes into wine.

vino (VEE-noh) Italian for wine.

vinosity The characteristic flavor of a wine as a result of fermented grape juice. It is distinct from any other flavors such as those of the unfermented grape, oak cask, or other flavor components.

viticulture Grape-growing, particularly for wine.

viticultural area A delimited region in which common geographic or climatic attributes contribute to the definable characteristic of a wine. Although it is called by different names in various countries, it is usually referred to as an Appellation of Origin. In the United States, such an appellation is called a viticultural area, and is defined by geography alone, as opposed to requirements regulating the varieties of grapes grown, yield, or nature of wine produced.

Vitis vinifera The species of grape that accounts for all the world's best wines. Indigenous to central Asia and Europe.

volatile acid The acid component of a wine that can be detected in the aroma. In wine this is acetic acid, the acid of vinegar. It is always present in wine, usually undetectable or at low levels that add to the complexity and appeal of a wine. When excessive, it is an undesirable defect.

Wein (veyn) German for wine.

Weisswein (VEYSS-veyn) German for white wine. (In the German alphabet, this is written Weißwein.)

yeast The single-celled microorganism, reproducing by budding, responsible for fermentation of grapes and other liquids containing sugars.

APPENDIX C

Recommended Books for Further Reading

1855: A History of the Bordeaux Classification. Dewey Markham, Jr. 1998. 535 pp. Hard. $69.95

A Companion to California Wine: An Encyclopedia of Wine and Winemaking from the Mission Period to the Present. Charles L. Sullivan. 1998. 368 pp. Hard. $39.95

A Passion for Piedmont: Italy's Most Glorious Regional Table. Matt Kramer. 1997. 336 pp. Hard. $28

American Vintage: The Rise of American Wine. Paul Lukacs. 2005 386 pp. Soft. $16.95

American Winescapes: The Cultural Landscapes of America's Wine Country. Gary L. Peters. 1997. 176 pp. Soft. $18

An Ideal Wine: One Generation's Pursuit of Perfection and Profit in California. David Darlington. 2011. 368 pp. Hard. $26.99.

Austria: New Wines from the Old World. Giles MacDonough. 1998. Hard. $35

Back Lane Wineries of Napa. Tilar Mazzeo and Paul Hawley. 2010. 272 pp. Soft. $19.95.

Bordeaux Chateaux: A History of the Grands Crus Classes since 1855. Hugh Johnson and Dewey Markham. 2009. 324 pp. Hard. $34.95

Bordeaux: A Consumer's Guide to the World's Finest Wines. Robert M. Parker Jr. 2007. 1264 pp. Hard. $60

Bordeaux: A Legendary Wine. Michel Dovaz. 1998. 268 pp. Hard. $75

Burgundy. Anthony Hanson. 2006. 688 pp. Soft. $33.95

Burgundy and Its Wines. Nicholas Faith. 2008. 144 pp. Soft. $19.95.

Champagne: A Global History. Becky Sue Epstein. 2011. 136 pp. Soft. $17

Christie's World Encyclopedia of Champagne & Sparking Wine. Tom Stevenson. 2003. 352 pp. Hard. $50

To Cork or Not to Cork: Tradition, Romance, Science, and the Battle for the Wine Bottle. George Taber. 2007. Hard. 277 pp. $26.

Discovering Wine. Joanna Simon. 2003. 160 pp. Soft. $21

Essential Wines and Wineries of the Pacific Northwest: A Guide to the Wine Countries of Washington, Oregon, British Columbia, and Idaho. Cole Danehower. 2010. 309 pp. Soft. $24.95.

Food & Wine Magazine's Official Wine Guide 2011. Anthony Giglio. 2010. 320 pp. Soft. $12.95

Harvests of Joy: My Life, My Way. Robert Mondavi. 1998. 368 pp. Hard. $27

Hugh Johnson's How to Enjoy Wine. Hugh Johnson. 2006. 120 pp. Soft. $11

Hugh Johnson's Pocket Wine Book, 2012. 320 pp. Soft. $15.

Hugh Johnson's The Story of Wine, 1999. 480 pp. Hard. $25.

Italian Wines 2012. Gambero Rosso. 978 pp. Soft. $35

Judgment of Paris: California vs. France and the Historic 1976 Paris Tasting That Revolutionized Wine. George M. Taber. 2006. Soft. $16

Keys to the Cellar: Strategies and Secrets of Wine Collecting. Peter D. Meltzer. 2006. 258 pp. Hard. $29.95.

Making Sense of Wine Tasting: Your Essential Guide to Enjoying Wine, Fifth Edition. Alan Young. 2010. 196 pp. Soft. $29.95

Making Sense of Wine. Matt Kramer. 2004. 208 pp. Soft. $15

Napa Valley: The Ultimate Winery Guide, revised. Antonio Allegra. 2004. 120 pp. Soft. $19.95

New Wine Lover's Companion. Ron Herbst. 2010. 720 pp. Soft. $16.99.

Oz Clarke's Australian Wine Companion: An Essential Guide for All Lovers of Australian wine. Oz Clarke. 2005. 176 pp. Soft. $19.95.

Oz Clarke's Pocket Wine Guide 2011. Oz Clarke. 2010. 352 pp. Hard. $14.95

Oz Clarke's Wine Atlas: Wines and Wine Regions of the World. Oz Clarke. 2007. 336 pp. Hard. $60

Parker's Wine Buyer's Guide, 7th Edition: The Complete, Easy-to-Use Reference on Recent Vintages, Prices, and Ratings for More than 8,000 Wines from All the Major Wine Regions. Robert M. Parker, Jr. 2008. Soft. $35

Passions: The Wines and Travels of Travels of Thomas Jefferson. James M. Gabler. 1995. Hard.

$29.95

Pauillac: The Wines and Estates of a Renowned Bordeaux Commune. Stephen Brook. 2005. 192 pp. Hard. $45

Port and the Douro. Richard Mayson. 2006. 416 pp. Hard. $34.95

Romancing the Vine: Life, Love, and Transformation in the Vineyards of Barolo. Alan Tardi. 2006. Hard. 348 pp. $25.95.

Sauternes and Other Sweet Wines of Bordeaux. Stephen Brook. 1995. 192 pp. Hard. $24.95; Soft, $15.95

Sauternes: A Study of the Great Sweet Wines of Bordeaux. Jeffrey Benson and Allistair MacKenzie. 1990. 184 pp. Hard. $39.95

Seasons of the Vineyard. Robert Mondavi, Margrit Biever Mondavi and Carolyn Dille. 1996. 224 pp. Hard. $40

Secrets of the Sommeliers: How to Think and Drink Like the World's Top Wine Professionals. Rajat Parr. 2010. 240 pp. Hard. $34.50

Sherry, fifth edition. Julian Jeffs. 2006. 318 pp. Hard, $29.95; Soft, $14.95

Slow Wine 2012: A Year in the Life of Italy's Vineyards and Wines. Slow Food Editore. 350 pp. Soft. $25.

Sonoma: The Ultimate Winery Guide, Second Edition. Heidi Haughy Cusick. 2005. 120 pp. Soft. $18.95

Sparkling Harvest. Jamie Davies and Jack Davies. 1997. 140 pp. Hard. $45

Story of Champagne: The History and Pleasures of the Most Celebrated of Wines. Nicholas Faith. 1989. 246 pp. Hard. $21.95

The Battle for Wine and Love or How I Saved the World from Parkerization. Alice Feiring. 2008. 271 pp. Hard. $23.

The Billionaire's Vinegar: The Mystery of the World's Most Expensive Bottle of Wine. Benjamin Wallace. 2009. 336 pp. Soft. $14.95.

The Bordeaux Atlas. Michael Broadbent and Hubrecht Duijker. 1997. 400 pp. Hard. $50

The Commonsense Book of Wine. Leon D. Adams. 1991. 168 pp. Soft. $8.95

The Connoisseurs' Handbook of the Wines of California and the Pacific Northwest, fourth edition. Norman S. Roby and Charles E. Olken. 1998. 448 pp. Soft. $1995

The Essential Guide to South African Wines. Elamari Swart. 2008. 201 pp. Soft. $29.95.

The Great Domaines of Burgundy: A Guide to the Finest Wine Producers of the Côte d'Or, third edition. Remington Norman. 2010. 288 pp. Hard. $45

The Food Lover's Guide to Wine. Karen Page and Andrew Dornenburg. 2011. 352 pp. Hard. $35.

The Great Domaines of Burgundy, third edition. Remington Norman. 2010. 288 pp. Hard. $35.

The Great Wines of France: France's Top Domains and Their Wines. Clive Coates. 2006. 192 pp. Hard. $50.

The Instant Wine Connoisseur: A Practical Guide to Tasting, Buying and Cooking with Wine, second edition. Mervyn L. Hecht. 2002. 240 pp. Soft. $9.95

The New Spain: The First Complete Guide to Contemporary Spanish Wine. John Radford. 2006. 224 pp. Hard. $40

The Origins and Ancient History of Wine. Patrick McGovern, Stuart Fleming and Solomon Katz, eds. 1995. 528 pp. Hard, $85; Soft, $45

The Oxford Companion to Wine. Jancis Robinson, Third ed. 2006 Hard. $65

The Port Companion: A Connoiseur's Guide. Godfrey Spence. 2002. 224 pp. Soft. $23.95

The Renaissance Guide to Wine and Food Pairing. Tony DiDio and Amy Zavatto. 2003. 366 pp. Soft. $18.95.

The Taste of Wine, second edition: The Art and Science of Wine Appreciation. Emil Paynaud. 1996. 346 pp. Hard. $60.50

The University Wine Course, second edition. Marian W. Baldy, Ph.D. 1994. Soft. $35

The Widow Clicquot: The Story of a Champagne Empire and the Woman Who Ruled It. Tilar J. Mazzeo. 2009. 304 pp. Soft. $15.99.

The Wild Bunch: Great Wines from Small Producers. Patrick Matthews. 1997. 288 pp. Soft. $13.95

The Wine Atlas of France. Hubrecht Duijker. 1997. 264 pp. Hard. $45

The Wine Project: Washington State's Winemaking History. Ronald Irvine. 1997. 456 pp. Soft. $29.95

The Wine Routes of Argentina. Alan Young. 1997. 176 pp. Hard. $29.95

The Wines of Alsace. Tom Stevenson. 1994. Soft. $24.95

The Wines of Bordeaux and Western France. John J. Baxevanis. 1987. 288 p. Hard. $45

The Wines of Burgundy. Clive Coates. 2008. 896 pp. Hard. $65

The Wines of Chablis. Rosemary George. 216 pp. Hard. $29.95

The Wines of Chile. Peter Richards. 384 pp. Hard. $29.95.

The Wines of France, New Revised Edition. Clive Coates. 2000. 436 pp. Hard. $50

The Wines of Germany. Stephen Brook. 2006. 464 pp. Soft. $10

The Wines of Italy. Burton Anderson. 2004. 224 pp. Soft. $19

The Wines of New Zealand. Rosemary George. 1996. 330 pp. Hard, $33.95; Soft, $16.95

The Wines of the Northern Rhône. John Livingstone-Learmonth. 2005. 720 pp. Hard. $65.

The Wines of the Rioja. John Radford. 2006. 304 pp. Hard. $29.95.

The Wines of Spain. Julian Jeffs. 2006. 300 pp. Hard. $29.95.

Temecula Wineries: The Ultimate Temecula Winery and Temecula Wine-Tasting Guidebook. Jeff Johnson. 2008. 116 pp. Soft. $20

Vines, Grapes & Wine: The Wine Drinker's Guide to Grape Varieties. Jancis Robinson. 2006. 272 pp. Soft. $27.95

Vino Argentino: An Insider's Guide to the Wines and Wine Country of Argentina. Laura Catena. 2010. 239 pp. Hard. $27.50.

Vino Italiano: The Regional Wines of Italy. Joseph Bastianich and David Lynch. 2005. 544 pp. Soft. $21.95

Vintage Feasting: A Vintner's Year of Fine Wines, Good Times, and Gifts from Nature's Garden. Joy Sterling. 1996. 240 pp. Hard. $22

White Burgundy. Christopher Fielden. 2010. 184. pp. Hard. $20.

Windows on the World Complete Wine Course. Kevin Zraly. 2009. 338 pp. Hard. $27.95.

Wine Appreciation, second edition. Richard P. Vine. 1997. 480 pp. Hard. $65.95

Wine with Food. Joanna Simon. 1999. 160 pp. Hard. $25

Winequest: The Wine Dictionary. Ted Grudzinski. 19985. 469 pp. Hard. $28

Wines of the Graves. Pamela V. Price. 2010. 388 pp. Hard. $45

Wines of the Loire: Earthly Delights from the Garden of France. Jacqueline Friedrich. 2011. 272 pp. Soft. $34.50.

World Atlas of Wine, sixth edition. Hugh Johnson. 2007. Hard. $50

APPENDIX D

Wine Toasts

Among friends:

Friends and colleagues, here we meet.
First a toast, before we eat!

May the quiet opulence of this rare wine bring us, also, peace and plenty.

The wine is dear; our fellowship, priceless.

Let us praise sparkling wine and sparkling wit!

To food, to fellowship and wine
And all those others things as fine!

May our hearts remain as true as this wine is red!

Age before beauty, they say. Okay. To old wine! Now to new friendship!

Let us experience the warmth of our camaraderie in the warmth of our wine.

Wine-lovers

May the sunshine of Bordeaux infuse our spirits!

To sun, to rain, to grape, to all
That brought this wine into our hall!

And here's to Bacchus, but for whom this toast would not be possible!

A glass of Rhine let's lift on high,
As we the bonds of friendship tie!

Business and politics:

With wine of noble appellation,
Let us honor our great nation!

May our blue-chip friendship forever pay dividends!

A glass of wine to tinge our cheeks:
Now we toast him; then he speaks.

Champagne now we all must tally,
As we to our party rally!

The soup is hot; the wine is cold:
Let us begin our venture bold!

Lift high your glasses, as high as your hopes.

Humor

A fine white wine, and not too chilled,
Now let's all drink it, 'fore it's spilled.

Doctor, dentist, lawyer, thirst:
Which do you think we'll pay first?

Champagne for my real friends! (Real pain for my sham friends.)

In wine there is truth. May the truth ever be in us!

T'ain't Champagne; I've got to warn ya:
This here wine's from California!

Special events:

With this wine of flavors supple,
Let us toast the happy couple!

A toast, a cheer! To couple's love, to families united!

A vintage year, this glass of wine,
To toast our guest before we dine!

Old wine in new glasses. To old love and new dreams!

Wine to lips around this room
As we toast our bride and groom!

Toast him now! Let's toast him doubly!
Elevate your flutes of bubbly!

Sparkling wine to toast the product of that spark of love!

APPENDIX E

Wine Accessories

Wine Tags. Write the name of your wine on these nifty reusable plastic tags and hang them from the neck of the bottle. You will no longer have to pull your wine out of the rack to determine what it is. About $15 for 100 tags. www.wineenthusiast.com

Grapevine Coffee Table. Glass top coffee table with a base made out of the trunks of very old grapevines. Quite attractive. About $1,200. www.etsy.com/listing/66330875/old-vine-grapevine-coffee-table-100

Wine Rack Coffee Table. Glass top coffee table with solid wood frame and dual shelving that holds 38 bottles, plus a small drawer for wine accessories. About $220. www.wineracksstore.com/Wine-Coffee-Table/

Wrought Iron Wine Racks. These attractive wine racks come with a curved or flat top. Sizes range from 12 bottles to 144 bottles. $40-$500. www.wineenthusiast.com

LCD Wine Thermometer. Via a probe, this digital read-out unit gives you the actual and ideal temperature for your bottle so you can compare and make sure you're on target. $14.95. www.windandweather.com

Riedel Wine Glasses. Crystal wine glasses from this German manufacturer are considered the very best. They come in many shapes and sizes—and, lately, price points, too, as they have started a few new affordable lines for the broadening wine market in the U.S. The middle-of-the-road Vinum line starts at about $50 for a set of two. www.wineenthusiast.com, or most major department stores. The Vivant line is lead-free Tyrol crystal and runs about $40 for four glasses. www.target.com.

Wine Punts. Fun, everyday table wine glasses made from the bottom portion of recycled wine bottles. $30 for a set of four. www.winepunts.com

Bonsai Grapevine. A real miniature grapevine that goes through all the natural seasonal changes of branching, budding, fruit bearing and dormancy. Produces real grapes. About $60. www.bonsaiboy.com.

VinoCellier wine cabinet. Sleep temperature controlled wine storage unit with a 267-bottle capacity, adjustable temperature control, hygrometer, and five adjustable shelves that can be positioned to hold your bottles in three different ways Start at $400. www.vinotemp.com.

Wine Credenza. Decorative furniture meets function with this elegant hand-crafted piece that holds 28 bottles on one side, and stemware and accessories on the other. $1,495. www.wineenthusiast.com.

Stemware Washing Brush. A dishwashing brush designed especially for wine glasses. Super delicate material that will clean without nicking or scratching. $6.95. www.highgravitybrew.com.

Wine Decanters. A beautiful way to serve your wine. Essential for older wines. Many styles and sizes are out there, but for a good selection at discounted prices, try a clearing house like Overstock.com. Start at $25.

Champagne Key. A special device to grip the cork and make removal a breeze. Stainless steel. About $5. www.houseandwine.com

Perlage Champagne Preservation System. A little on the gizmo-ish side with its accoutrements and CO2 canisters, the Perlage System comes as close to perfectly preserving the remaining contents of an open bottle of Champagne as you will find. $295. www.winehardware.com

Marble Wine Cooler. Suspend your wine's temperature a little longer with the natural cool-holding properties of marble. This unique, gun-metal gray cooler will maintain your wine's temperature for hours. About $26.95. www.crateandbarrel.com.

Monopoly – Napa Valley Edition. America's best loved board game in the winelover's edition. Own vineyards and wineries. Become a wine baron. $35. www.amazon.com.

Wine Luggage. Protect your wine while traveling. Carry up to a case on the plane home. $95. www.winevine-imports.com.

Cork Retriever. Cork pushed into the bottle? Retrieve it with this nifty device. About $12. www.eckraus.com.

APPENDIX F

Wines for All Occasions

Weddings

French Champagne

California sparkling wine.

Moderately priced red wine such as a French Beaujolais.

Moderately priced white wine such as a California Sauvignon Blanc or unoaked Chardannay.

Bar-Mitzvah / Bat-Mitzvah

Old style Concord grape kosher wine.

Modern style kosher wines from California, France, or Italy such as a Merlot, Cabernet Sauvignon, or Chardonnay.

Anniversary

A fine Bordeaux or Burgundy from the year of your marriage.

A high-quality French Champagne.

First date

Good qualiity Bordeaux or Burgundy.

A reserve California Cabernet Sauvignon or Pinot Noir.

A high-quality California sparkling wine.

Marriage proposal

The best French Champagne you can afford.

Birthday

A wine from year of birth.

A good California sparkling wine.

French Champagne.

APPENDIX G

Wine Faux Pas

Wine Faux Pas

Don't store wine in hot places.
Don't keep wine in the trunk of your car.
Don't shake an old bottle of wine.
Don't store your wine standing up.
Don't keep a wine past its prime.
Don't store wine in the sunlight.
Don't store wine around strong odors.
Don't store a wine around vibration.
Don't order expensive wine storage equipment from someone you don't know.
Don't let your guests drive home inebriated.
Don't let your Champagne bottles get scratched.
Don't push the cork into the wine bottle.
Don't serve wine in unwashed glasses.
Don't serve wine in musty glasses.
Don't fill a wine glass more than halfway.
Don't pop the champagne cork.
Don't aim the champagne bottle at anyone.
Don't use saucer or hollow-stemmed champagne glasses.
Don't use wine glasses with hollow stems.
Don't serve maderized wine.
Don't serve a white wine too cold.
Don't put ice cubes in a glass of wine.
Don't use stemware that's too fragile.
Don't buy wine from the store window.
Don't patronize a wine store with a bad attitude.
Don't patronize a wine store with unknowledgeable clerks.
Don't give too much attention to wine snobs.
Don't assume a cork in a bottle is a sign of quality.
Don't assume a vintage date means good quality.

Don't fail to ask when you don't understand wine terminology.
Don't take 100-point rating systems too seriously.
Don't confuse the Silvaner or Grey Riesling with the noble Johannesburg Riesling.
Don't confuse wines made from the Muscat grape with "Muscatel" or with Muscadet, for that matter.
Don't confuse the Bordeaux Grand Cru Classé with Burgundy's Grand cru.
Don't assume "Estate bottled" or "Grown, produced and bottled by" are indicators of quality in California wines.
Don't assume all Napa Valley wines are superior.
Don't assume Australian "Rieslings" are made from the Riesling grape.
Don't assume all champagne is Champagne.
Don't confuse "fermented in the bottle" with "fermented in this bottle."
Don't pour bottle-aged wines in haste.
Don't assume all wine labeled "Port" is real Porto wine.
Don't assume all wine labeled "Sherry" is real Sherry.
Don't assume the words "reserve" or "classic" on a U.S. wine label have any significance.
Don't assume all bottle-aged wines in a single case will be of the same quality.
Don't neglect to note mouthfeel when you drink wine.
Don't use "cooking wines" sold in supermarkets.
Don't let the sommelier intimidate you.
Don't accept a faulty wine in a restaurant.
Don't accept a bottle in a restaurant that hasn't been opened at your table.

APPENDIX H

Wine on the Internet

Resource Sites

AUCTIONVINE
www.auctionvine.com

This site conducts wine auctions for several auction houses and well-known wine retailers. It is worth visiting if you buy wine at auction. All wines purchased carry a money-back guarantee.

ROBIN GARR'S WINE LOVERS' PAGE
www.wine-lovers-page.com

Great educational resource, lots of tasting notes, a weekly newsletter, and a very active discussion forum. Continually updated.

TOM CANNAVAN'S WINE PAGES
www.wine-pages.com

Originating in the United Kingdom, Wine Pages offers personal tasting notes, regional guides to wine producing regions, an online wine course and more. Updated continually.

NEW WINES OF GREECE
www.newwinesofgreece.com/en/home/index.html

A site focusing at once on education for consumers not familiar with Greek wine varietals, as well as on how the industry has leapt into the 21st century (well, in some cases anyway). Here you can explore different appellations, modern winemaking techniques being applied in them, vintage information, as well as wine travel and food. Another good grape-centric Greek site: Wines From Santorini. www.winesfromsantorini.com.

WINES FROM SPAIN
www.winesfromspain.com

A great resource for all-things Spain in the world of wine, from grape varietals to regions, both old and emerging, producers, events, foods that pair well them different Spanish wines and styles, news, travel information, and more.

INTO WINE
www.intowine.com

Good information about wine in general. Plus features are the vintage charts for a number of regions, serving temperature guide for wines, wine storage, and a few other wine-related sections.

WASHINGTON STATE WINE
www.washingtonwine.org

A good resource site for discovering the wineries of Washington State and myriad varietals grown there. Maps of the state's eight regions as well as winery descriptions, and upcoming events.

WINES OF PORTUGAL
www.winesofportugal.info

A great source for learning about not just Port Wines, but Portugal's unfortified wines, too, as well as history, regions, and news.

TASTINGS.com
www.tastings.com

This site is operated by the Beverage Testing Institute in Chicago, Illinois, which founded the World Wine Championships. They review thousands of wines each year and maintain a searchable database where you can view tasting notes and scores of over 30,000 wines, along with a list of producers they recommend.

DRINK THINK ENGLISH
www.englishwineproducers.com

Yes, there are wineries in the British Isles and if you want to know more about the history of winemaking there, grape varietals, and the wine-producing regions of England and Wales, this is the place to start.

WINES OF CANADA
www.winesofcanada.com

For a personal website, an incredibly in-depth, well-maintained one-stop spot for information on the wines of Canada, both historically and modern-day information. Also maintains a handy source of links to myriad Canadian wine-region associations and wineries.

MATCHING FOOD AND WINE WITH FIONA BECKET
www.matchingfoodandwine.com

Becket is the British wine columnist for The Globe and offers thoughtful, well-thought-out pairing suggestions, as well as a handy plug-in, food-and-wine search engine.

RIEDEL CRYSTAL
www.riedelcrystal.com

Bilingual (German and English) Information at this site includes competitions, tastings, news, and a wine search facility to identify the most suitable glass for any wine.

WINE OF THE WEEK
www.nettivuori.com/weeklywine

Personal tasting notes organized by date and region with some very appealing and interesting photographs accompanying the prose.

LOIRE VALLEY WINES
www.loirevalleywines.com

Blow-by-blow information on each appellation of the Loire Valley, starting with Muscadet in Nantes near near the Atlantic Ocean and traveling east to Sancerre. Weekly winemaker interviews, YouTube videos, history, and visitor information.

A+ AUSTRALIAN WINE
www.apluswines.com

Information resource for Australian wines, wineries, individual producer stories, regions, a glossary of terms, and travel information.

WINES OF BRITISH COLUMBIA
www.winebc.org

Information about the BC wine industry, the wineries, and the VQA (Vintners Quality Alliance) program.

BUREAU INTERPROFESSIONNAL DES VINS DE BOURGOGNE
www.bivb.com

French and English versions. Information about the Burgundy region of France, the appellations, news, events, etc.

CHAMPAGNE FRANCE
www.champagnes.com

Presented by the Champagne Wine Information Bureau. History. Regional information, winemaking, food pairing, etc.

NEW ZEALAND WINES ONLINE
www.nzwine.com

A virtual tour of New Zealand and its wines. Includes winery information, food and wine, maps of wine regions and in-depth information on them, statistics on the wine industry, event information, and more.

OREGON WINE
www.oregonwine.org

A good starting point to learn about Oregon wines, the appellations, history, wineries, events, etc.

NEW YORK CORK REPORT
http://lennthompson.typepad.com

What started as a small, personal site has grown into an award-winning blog with tons of in-depth information on the New York wine (and some spirits) industry. Reviews, winemaker interviews, events, news, etc.

SOUTH AFRICAN WINE
www.wine.co.za

South African wine directory, news, wine industry, brief information is given for a lot of wineries and their wine lists, etc.

VINEYARDS OF THE RHONE VALLEY
www.rhone-wines.com

Multi-lingual. Regional information, winery information, wine notes, news, history, tourism information, and more.

AUSTRIAN WINE
www.austrian.wine.com

Multi-lingual site with information about wineries, wines, vintages, history, events, etc.

ITALIAN MADE
www.italianmade.com

The Italian Trade Commission's official website on Italian food and wine with information on history, wine-label laws, and more.

WINES OF GERMANY
www.germanwineusa.com

A bilingual language site with wine information, food pairings, grape varieties, and news.

TERROIRS BOURGUIGNONS
www.terroirs-b.com

A multi-language site. Information about the Burgundy region in France including news, events, selected wineries, gastronomy, tourism in the region, etc.

Magazine Websites and Blogs

TASTING ROOM, FOOD & WINE MAGAZINE
www.foodandwine.com/blogs/tasting-room

Blog written by the F&W's wine editor, Ray Isle.

THE WINE SPECTATOR
www.winespectator.com

Online edition of the popular printed magazine. Reviews, articles, food and wine, reviews, tasting notes, etc.

WINE ENTHUSIAST
www.winemag.com

Daily articles, vintage charts, wine and cigar buying information, etc.

WINE & DINE
www.winedine.co.uk

Wine reviews, news, etc.

IMBIBE MAGAZINE
www.imbibemagazine.com

In-depth wine coverage on interesting topics from biodynamics and climate change to seasonal wine and food pairing and trendy topics like orange wine.

JANCIS ROBINSON'S PURPLE PAGES
www.purplepages.com

British Master of Wine Jancis Robinson's wine ratings, vintage reviews, and general observations on the wine world at large.

PALATE PRESS
www.palatepress.com

News, reviews, and global wine info.

DR. VINO
www.drvino.com

Wine, politics, and business.

JAMIE GOODE
www.wineanorack.com

Wine reviews.

THE TERROIRIST
www.terroirist.com

Daily-updated wine recommendations and tasting notes.

Winery Sites

Schlumberger – Austria
www.domaines-schlumberger.com

Fortant de France – France
www.fortant.com

Moet & Chandon – France
www.moet.com

Couly-Duthei – France
www.coulydutheil-chinon.com

Bouchard Pere et Fils – France
www.bouchard-pereetfils.com

Joseph Drouhin – France
www.drouhin.com

Louis Latour – France
www.LouisLatour.com

Chateau d'Yquem – France
www.chateau-yquem.fr

Chateau Figeac – France
www.chateau-figeac.com

Chateau Haut-Brion – France
www.haut-brion.com

Chateau Lafite Rothschild – France
www.lafite.com

Chateau Margaux – France
www.chateau-margaux.com

Lingenfelder Estate – Germany
www.lingenfelder.com

Bava – Italy
www.bava.com

Bolla – Italy
www.bolla.com

Castello di Monterinaldi – Italy
www.monterinaldi.it

Castello Banfi – Italy
www.castellobanfi.com

Gruppo Italiano Vini – Italy
www.giv.it

Marchesi Antinori – Italy
www.antinori.it

Croft Port – Portugal
www.croftport.com

Real Companhia Velha – Portugal
www.realcompanhiavelha.pt

Bodegas Torres – Spain
www.torres.es

El Coto de Rioja – Spain
www.elcoto.com

La Rioja Alta – Spain
www.riojalta.com

Domaine E. de Montmollin Fils – Switzerland
www.montmollinwine.ch

Beringer Vineyards – USA
www.beringer.com

Clos Du Val Winery – USA
www.closduval.com

Domaine Carneros by Taittinger – USA
www.domaine.com

Joseph Phelps Vineyards – USA
www.jpvwines.com

Robert Mondavi – USA
www.robertmondavi.com

David Coffaro Vineyard & Winery – USA
www.coffaro.com

Kendall Jackson Winery – USA
www.kj.com

Quivira Vineyards – USA
www.quivirawine.com

Schug Carneros Estate Winery – USA
www.schugwinery.com

Husch Vineyards – USA
www.huschvineyards.com

Ridge Vineyards – USA
www.ridgewine.com

Chateau St. Michelle Vineyards & Winery – USA
www.ste-michelle.com

King Estate – USA
www.kingestate.com

L'Ecole No 41 – USA
www.lecole.com

Blue Mountain Vineyards – USA
www.bluemountainwine.com

Pellegrini Winery & Vineyard – USA
pellegrinivineyards.com

Channing Daughters Winery – USA
www.channingdaughters.com

Chateau des Charmes Wines – Canada
www.chateaudescharmes.com

Hainle Vineyards – Canada
www.hainle.com

Le Comte (Hawthorne Mountain) – Canada
www.hmvineyard.com

Sumac Ridge Estate Winery – Canada
www.sumacridge.com

Vina Santa Carolina – South America
www.santacarolina.cl

Vina Santa Rita – South America
www.santarita.com

Viña Viu Manent – South America
www.viumanent.cl

Coldstream Hill Winery – Australia
www.coldstreamhills.com.au

McWilliam's Wines – Australia
www.mcwilliams.com.au

Mildara Blass Wines – Australia
www.worldwidewines.com

Wynns Coonawarra Estate – Australia
www.wynns.com.au

Corbans – New Zealand
www.corbans.co.nz

KWV – South Africa
www.kwv.co.za

Morgenhof Wines – South Africa
www.morgenhof.com

Simonsig – South Africa
www.simonsig.co.za

Carmel Mizrachi – Israel
www.carmelwines.co.il

Chateau Musar – Lebanon
www.chateaumusar.com.lb

Marsovin Group – Malta
www.marsovin.com.mt

APPENDIX I

Wine Magazines, Newsletters and Catalogs

Wine Magazines

Decanter. Published in London, monthly, $80 a year. Telephone (USA): 800-875-2997

Wine Spectator. 15 issues, $49.95 a year. Telephone: 800-752-7799.

The Wine Enthusiast. 12 issues a year, $29.95 a year, 800-648-6058

Wine & Spirits. 8 issues a year, $29.95 a year. 888-695-4660

Newsletters

Stephen Tanzer's International Wine Cellar. Bimonthly, $48 a year. Telephone: 800-946-3505.

The Wine Advocate (Robert Parker). Bimonthly, $75 a year. Telephone: 410-329-6477

Connoisseur's Guide to California Wine. Monthly, $90 a year. Telephone: 510-865-3150.

Catalogs

The Wine Enthusiast (800-356-8466)

International Wine Accessories (800-527-4072)

INDEX

C

D

E

F

G

H

I

J

K

L

M

N

O

P

Q

R

S

U

V

Y

Z

ABOUT THE AUTHOR

Philip Seldon has lived his life with wine. He had his first taste of wine at age five at the traditional Passover Seder. The wine was sweet kosher wine (not the kind of wine that's subject of this book although we cover kosher wine) and watered down, but nevertheless delicious. From this first introduction came a lifelong fascination with wine that made him a leading figure on the international wine scene. In the mid'60s, he drank his way through the classified growths of Bordeaux and the Premier and Grand Cru of Burgundy with abandon, as great wines were extremely inexpensive in that decade, and thus honed his wine tasting skills on the world's finest wines. After graduation from college, he devoted two years to world travel in quest of knowledge of gourmet food and fine wines. The great restaurants of the world as well as the elegant dining tables of gastronomes he befriended in his travels served as the classrooms in his wine education.

In 1971, he founded the wine-magazine publishing industry in America with his launch of *Vintage Magazine*, America's first wine magazine which he published and edited for 17 years after which he moved on to other business endeavors.

Philip Seldon is a member of numerous prestigious gourmet and wine societies including the *Commanderie de Bordeaux* and *Chaine de Rotisseurs* and was founding chairman of the Wine Writers Circle in New York. He is author of the best selling *Vintage Magazine Consumer Guide to Wine* and *The Complete Idiot's Guide To Wine.* He is the designer and patent holder of the *Le Cellier* modular polymer wine rack. He lives in New York City in an apartment overlooking the East River. He is presently the Wine and Food editor of the Smart Guide series.